TABLE OF CONTENTS

This book is dedicated to the ones I love. Or who made my skin crawl and my blood run cold, who made me stop and think, who helped me grow, who made me laugh. **Appearing in the order of their appearance:** GOD Mom Dad Grandfather Lila Santa Claus The Tooth Fairy the author of <u>The Seven Sneezes</u> The boy who punched me in the stomach in Sunday School My Brother Jim (until he got his platinum curls cut) Nancy (pinpoint bric-a-brac bomber) Holmes Sister Lydia (Twitch) Miss Benkert Mrs. Wooley Mrs. Findlay Miss Leidy Sally Starr Howdy Doody Kukla Fran & Olie Lambchop Hop Along Cassidy Margerite de Angeli Miss Edwards & Freddy Aunt Mable, BJ and David My Sister Lisa Nan Rochester Betsy Robertson Linda Carol Cherken Betty Huber Marilynn Rex Debbie Goodwin Miss Hawkins Joe (first kiss) Evans Bette Davis Katharine Hepburn Errol Flynn Clark Gable John Wayne Yuha Moisla Cynthia Saunders Kathy Lewis Mr. James Lurch Grubby & Ted Reid Carroll Sterling Freddie Kipnes The Freshman English teacher who said I couldn't write The Freshman history teacher who flunked me (when I had a B average) because of my attitude Henry James D.H. Lawrence Aldous Huxley Lady Ottoline Morrell Dorothy Parker Georgia O'Keeffe Suzanne Cartwright Gunther Cartwright Max Harry Kulkowitz Herb (before the Dump) Denenberg Barbara Noska Elizabeth Kilraine Gary (before Odeon) Bachman Steve (after the Frog) Poses George Pechin Jay and Gil Guben Bud & Yvonne Agazarian Alexis, Becky and Stanley Branche's gun-toting, bodyguard asleep with a hole in his sock Hillel Levinson Mary Smith FRANK RIZZO frannie rizzo Ken Klein Dr. & Mrs. Henry Klein Ronnie Klein Norman Esibill Kathy Hilaman Ted (before the vice-presidency) Rosen Elaine Tait Julia Child Richard Olney Simone Beck Elizabeth David MFK Fisher Marcella Hazan Alice Waters Dear Abby **Erica (I always wanted one just like that) (Berman) Romitelli and Marvin (my hero) Berman** Bawa Carl Eden Ski & Anexora & Lola Jerry 'Seagull' Seelig Werner (EST) Erhard Marjorie & John, Jesse and Morgan's 4 heart sisters Phyllis Holst & David Goltra Betty Friedan Simone de Beauvoir Germaine Greer Virginia Woolf Isadora Duncan Studs Terkel Erma Bombeck Phil Donohue Oprah Winfrey Shirley Maclaine Stephen Hawking Loren Eisely Black Elk Robert M. Persig Joseph Campbell Bill Zeil & Carl Schaeffer Neil Stein and Lenny Amoroso Celeste Neil Stein and Gabe Marabella Ronald Reagan Larry & Karen & Molly John & Janet & Gabe The witch in Connecticut John & Joyce Isis **Morgan (my darling girl) Berman** Miss Kitty (Waters) Marion Cohen Shopper Lady Tom Michael (and his calculator) Marion Zimmer Bradey Sweetpea Ronna (Nutz) Schultz Jane Flory Nina Betsi Higgins Matthew (Sufi caretaker) Salata Rascal Murphy Brown Roseanne Gino Romitelli (and baby makes 3) Emma Amy Dacyczyn Sheila (Koen) Kowalsky Jacqueline Everly Dorothy Carroll Jody (Godiva) Campfield June (The Jewel) Park Beverly (Phone Fairy) Tscheschlog Justin (Cartoman Trailblazer) Ackerman Nibs...

# MANIAC WITH A MISSION

QUESTION: WHY ON EARTH AM I DOING THIS?

ANSWER: SO YOU WON'T HAVE TO (and so I can make some money).

❤ THE AMATEUR MANIAC'S STRUGGLE

- Try driving down Main Street USA, craning your neck looking for the next shop. You can wind up a tree.
- Try eavesdropping among the racks on fellow maniac thrifters in order to learn the name of a new store and how to get there.
- Then get lost trying to find the place.
- Finally find it, only to realize it's cash only and you're tapped out and there's no money machine.
- Or the shop is closed for the day or for the summer.
- Finally get inside and discover the shop's too expensive for the quality.
- Or you're shopping for 'whatever' and they don't carry 'whatever'.
- Now you're hungry and there's no place to eat.
- Now your back teeth are floating and there's no place to go; the rest room is employees only.
- This was supposed to be fun, but it's not.
- This was supposed to be saving money. Instead you're wasting time.
- Hasty conclusion: Thrift shopping is not for me.

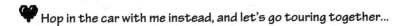 Hop in the car with me instead, and let's go touring together...

🏰 An Entrepreneurial Fairy Tale

🌹 *Long, long ago,* in another place and time, Nancy Berman was Nancy Lee Turner. Before meeting my Prince (King Marvin the first, last and always), I was a self-taught, fast track, Center City chef, who went from dishwasher to head chef in short order. 🌹 *Once upon a time,* my husband and I, casting our own spell of enchantment, decreed I would stay home to begin our dynasty. Twelve-hour work days, 6 days a week, would have made for a lousy mother/child relationship. However, this also meant a drastic reduction in our coffers. The King was off crusading in graduate school. You can imagine what that paid! Behold, I became pregnant, magically transformed from fire-breathing, burned-out chef into serene domestic goddess in ever-tighter duds. 🌹 *Nine months passed.* Princess Morgan was born. A miracle of copper-colored hair, amber eyes, peaches and cream complexion, bee-stung lips that all too soon will receive a wake-up call from her own Prince. Internal babysitting drastically altered my body. Nothing fit. I had a new babe to clothe. Royal duds waiting to be gurgled upon and outgrown. A colossal waste of money, and we had none to waste. 🌹 *Four years passed.* We became first-time castleowners in classic 'dungeon to turret' school of home design. So there we were: no furniture, no clothes, no money, regal tastebuds and trashpicker's purse. What to do? The solution: thrift and consignment shopping. My Queen Mother Muffy always said, "Put Nancy in an empty room and she'll come up with something." And I did. Fiscal necessity and an innate sense of fashion pushed and guided me into becoming the self-styled Thrift Shop Maniac. 🌹 *In a twinkling the babe,* Princess Morgan, was 7 years old and a third grader. Somewhere between being home all alone that first day of full-time kindergarten, and sitting here at the keyboard writing my third edition, I asked myself the burning question, "What's next?" 'Twas right about then I remembered one of my Prince's favorite self quotes, "Bliss is earning a living doing what you would have done for free." Gradually, I transformed this freewheeling fun I'd been having into my next career. 🌹 *My magical transformation* came to pass while traveling from one shop to the next. I found my chef-trained brain automatically composing restaurant-type reviews. Collecting, researching and teaching for free, as I "turned out" friends and taught them the tricks of the trade was magically transformed into teaching classes and leading tours. 🌹 *Now the Berman dynasty* has a high-fashion profile and a renovated, fully furnished castle, ready and waiting for photographers from Martha Stewart and Traditional Home. Hey, guys, where are you? Queenie earned her King's undying appreciation, doing it all for about 30% of retail.

🌹 *Now the Thrift Shop Maniac* is going public, for your profit--and loving it! Would-be maniacs read on, lace up your sneakers, rev up your steeds and get thrifting. They all lived happily ever after, and so can you.

🌹 The Beginning 🌹

(This was the original introduction to our first, 1992 Edition.)

THE REAL DISH : A SOAP OPERA IN THREE ACTS

SETTING THE STAGE

I loved writing the Fairy Tale, I really did, and many of you wrote to tell me how much you liked reading it. But it only captured part of me, part of my message and part of my journey. Even though I am an avowed chocaholic (dark only, please), tart has always been easier for me to savor than sweet. Clever over cloy any day, I say. (I also hate fake woolly lawn sheep and paper-towel geese wearing beribboned sunbonnets waddling all over the kitchen.)

Much has happened since first we met. Many of you wrote and called, asking me to address issues and problems, come up with suggested solutions and expand on particular ideas I had only touched upon in the first two editions. I puzzled over what to say and how to say it. Walking the dog, washing my hair (some people sing in the shower, I write), wandering around, my brain wondering what changes and additions to make, I prayed, wrung my hands, and waited.

Eventually my guardian angel, Shopper Lady, sitting up high on my right shoulder, whispered into my ear the now obvious: " Hey turkey, listen up. Use what you know, just like I'm always telling you. Expand on the fairy-tale idea, dummy." Then she bellowed in my ear, "THINK! What else is there?" So I did (as if I hadn't been).

First I thought of the Bible. Too controversial. What's more nitty gritty? Soap Operas! Which inspired resumes, which led to The Diary etc. (Next year a Lonely Hearts column and Personal Ads?) So, let's continue the journey we began, while shifting to another of my many voices and moods.

P.S. Thank you, Shopper Lady. (But what took you so long?)

ACT I

Scene 1 (Fade in from commercial) Setting: Morgan has just walked out our front door and left my outstretched arms and the warm fuzzy of home for full-time kindergarten. Marvin has been hassling me again, "Find something to do with your time." "As if I don't already have enough to do with my time. As if I'm not scared to death to reenter the job market," I fuss and mutter. Older and wiser, the roller-coaster ride of restaurant work has lost its lure. What next? After all that power and glory I can't begin to imagine some slow-but-steady, low-pay, part-time grind. I can imagine, like so many other moms, creating an at-home business. But what? My bright ideas always wind up one day behind someone else's.

Scene 2 Setting: Driving around doing my thing: ruminating, while thrift shopping. A new form of meditation? Writing imaginary Elaine Tait type "thrift shop reviews". (Always wanted her job, but she got it first. You get to be a foodie without the hassle.) Time to pick up Morgan before she turns into an after-school pumpkin. Frantically short-cutting my way from Paoli to Abington, praying to the thrift shop gods that the Turnpike won't be backed up, that the lights stay a lovely shade of synchronized green. Beat the clock again, just. "Why are you always late, Mom? Why am I always one of the last ones to be picked up?" she whines, her big honey-brown eyes imploring. How to explain to a five year old that I'm a maniac, addicted to thrifting? What am I doing?

Scene 3 On location: Standing at the counter of the Trading Post. I am surrounded by white light. I have goosebumps all over me. What caused this Shirley Maclaine adrenal and spiritual overdrive? I hold in my trembling hands a copy of a small, amateurish booklet, listing thrift stores in the Delaware Valley. A much-abbreviated Yellow Pages of sorts. It has no info on all the intricate details: erratic hours, what they specialize in, etc. Just some hokey ads for dry cleaners and auto body shops. But I suddenly know with all the certainty of a prophet, that I have the answer I've been looking for. This will stop Marvin's hassling, Big Time. (Commercial break)

☺ °°○○○°°°°° ACT II ○ °°○○°°°°°

Scene 1 (Fade in from commercial) Setting: Out of the blue, Ruth Brown, in her best assistant director's voice, is on the phone, pitching me to teach a class at Temple University's Adult School of Continuing Education. "You are always doing something interesting, Nancy," she entices. I have been sitting on this thrift shop idea for almost a year now, still scared out of my bejeezus to leave the safe cocoon of hearth and home. Scared that someone else will do a thrift shop guide first. Marvin: "I am tired of being the only one making money around here. We agreed that when Morgan went to school full-time you'd get a job." "You're right, of course. I'm not playing fair," I grudgingly admit. I've been in this place before, this place of fear. I know to let it compost, but the process is taking too long, even for me. And now opportunity knocks in the form of Ruth Brown. I answer the door.

Scene 2 Setting: At the dining room table, hunkered down and designing a course outline, Thrift Shop Mania comes to Temple. Will it be good enough? Will anyone sign up? The germinating idea for a thrift shop guide, a compendium of restaurant-like reviews, still tucked away in cerebral cold storage. The answer comes. The class is sold out. Harriet Goodheart of Temple's PR Department sends out a regular release over the newswire service. My class is deemed attention-getting enough to be included. Next thing I know, Karen Heller, a reporter from the Inquirer is interviewing me over the phone. The article hits, splashed all over the front page of the Magazine Section. Producers from Maury Povich and Radio Times are on the phone, honey sweet, grilling me to see if I can walk and talk (or sit and talk) at the same time. Every last white light, goosebump, hand-trembling prediction is happening. Batten down the hatches. We have a launch.

Scene 3 On location: Sweating my titties on a New York sound stage, overdressed in a beaded pink chiffon number, sandwiched between Amy Dacyczyn, author of the Tightwad Gazette, and some wise ass macho yahoo from Florida, also author of a money-saving moneymaker of a newsletter. We are waiting under the obligatory hot lights, wired for sound in front of a live-wired New York audience, waiting for Maury to do his thing. Mental musings: "What am I doing here? (Too late to wonder about that one.) Will it also be too late to get my book out before someone else steals my thunder? Coast to coast, big time, and all I have to sell is my little itsy bitsy adult night school class." She who hesitates...(fade to commercial)

ACT III

Scene 1 (fade in from commercial) Setting: One o'clock, two o'clock, three o'clock, rock. Marvin and I are at it again, AM and PM, fighting and writing, writing and fighting. He, playing the technical equivalent of court stenographer, computer nerd and self-righteous know-it-all: "I told you long ago you should have learned to use the computer. You make too many changes, just write the damn thing," all the while refusing to follow my lead. MEN! She, dictating and dictatorial, playing the highly vocal, long-suffering role of high priestess to the muse of high-strung creative genius, imperiously commands, "Shut up! I'm trying to write! Stop going off on your technical tangents and stay with me. Don't interrupt! You and your only-child, male ego. You can't stand playing second fiddle to anyone." WOMEN! And so it goes. The book has begun.

Scene 2 Director's Note: Beware the glassy-eyed stare of the true believer. I should have known. I came in contact with enough of those during my salad days. (You know the type: 'I looove to cook. I wanna open a restaurant!') I had become one of them, a wide-eyed fool, lost in the big-time world of publishing. It's not enough to have a good idea. It's not enough to write a book. You have to get the idea and the book on the bookshelves and get the word out that it's there. Minor problem. Folding laundry, I could be overheard asking myself: "Distributor, what's a distributor?" Eating dinner, mid-chew, I blurt out along with my lettuce: "ISBN number? What's an ISBN number?" Took me months to realize I had become a publishing house, a microscopic Random House, an ant precariously clinging to the elephant-sized rump of the world of publishing. Lose your grip and fall off? Guess what happens? Road kill. And then there was the day, not long after we had plunked down thousands and thousands of Marvin's hard-earned dollars, when the truck pulled up and they delivered 18 boxes of books to our front door. Kind of like the magic moment when my water broke--no getting out of this one. Border's original order was for five big ones, yes folks, 5 books. When Pedro at Borders' Center City store saw my opus, he upped the order to fifteen, leaving only 5,485 to go. If this doesn't work, maybe I can go into the wallpaper business, or perhaps call Scott Paper's Recycling Department.

Scene 3 Stage Direction: Pile the boxes in the back of the van and do the thrift shop maniac hustle, a new dance step to the song titled, "The Distribution Solution". The solution to getting the word out? Eternal thanks to: **Ruth Brown** for dropping the dime, **Harriet Goodheart** for her good heart and the good judgment to include my course in her Temple University press release. To **Karen Heller** at the **Inquirer**, for her "Three Cheers for Cheap" article, which was picked up by the wire services, and in turn spotted by **Donna Benner**, producer of the **Maury Povich Show**; fellow maniac **Susan Bray** (WWDB); **Marty Moss-Coane** and **Barbara Bogaev** (WHYY-FM); **Elizabeth Starr** and **Wally Kennedy** (AM Philadelphia); **Orien Reid, Channel 10,** for her series on thrift shops and her now-famous quote "Buy this book" while holding the guide up to the camera on the evening news; **Channel 6 Action News** for 5 o'clock coverage with **Lisa Thomas-Laury**; three **Discovery Channel** segments where I teach the host, **Susan Powell**, a former Miss America, (Yes America Miss America thrift shops!) "How to Thrift" on the new coast-to-coast show, **Home Matters**; **Paul** (take it ALL off) **Moriarty of Channel 3** for our under-$50 week's-wardrobe shopping excursion; **Ken Dilanian** of the Neighbors section of the **Inquirer** (Yes, I'm wearing my slippers in the photograph. I didn't think my feet would show.); **Roy Campbell** for a mention in his fashion column in the Sunday **Inquirer**; **Glenn Burkins** and **Sandra Salman** of the **Inquirer's** Financial Section; The **Times Chronicle's** who's-doing-what-to-whom section, written by **James F. Duffy, Marie Jones**, editor and mother confessor of the **Chestnut Hill Local; Barnes & Noble** and **Borders PR personnel** for innumerable book signings and fashion shows. Thanks to all this unsolicited publicity, the first edition (5,000 copies) sold out in months, the second (10,000 copies) in a year. Who, other than my guardian angel (and maybe Marvin in his wildest dreams), would have thought? Oops, A **Lifetime Channel** producer is on the phone... Gotta go.

(Wild applause, fade to commercial)

 (HARDLY) THE END

(This was the Volumn II, 1994 update in the continuing saga.)

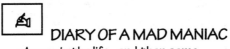

DIARY OF A MAD MANIAC
A year in the life...and then some.

Dear rambunctious reader: Here's my version of those mass-produced catch-up letters we all get once a year, stuffed in Christmas cards and envelopes with far away postage marks, written by more than acquaintances, but less than friends (A real friend would never send one. They'd know better.) Instead of only innocuous events, carefully manicured to remove any trace of unpleasantness, I have elected to tell the tale--warts, frogs, princes and all. Here's the next chapter of my life on the installment plan.

SATURDAY, JULY 31: Back in the saddle. Rippling waves of heat rise from the melting blacktop, almost knocking me over every time I open the door. (Don't open the door, dummy!) Tired and sweaty in an hour with hours left to go, even with air conditioner going full blast (designed with Alaskan summers in mind, no doubt). Marvin traveling with to provide life support and to make sure I actually get "there" and back. (Wherever "there" is.) I think he's having flashbacks to Corfu, summer of '83. Anglican midday swoon (no mad dogs in sight) on the back seat of our unairconditioned Greek rental. Eleven years later, another continent, another heat wave. Thoroughly lost scouting new Jersey shops. Most closed for vacation. I'll have to come back again (and again). Can't figure how the road system works. Or the towns connect. Or if they even exist.

THURSDAY, AUGUST 26: Two days after Morgan's birthday. Posh, outdoor lunch on a wide-angle, restaurant verandah, surprise jet ski ride on the river, followed by VERY chocolate cake. During digestive stroll around town, we stumble upon an upscale resale. Squeezed in what began as an undercover shopping trip. Marvin elects to blow our cover. MISTAKE! Engaged in heated debate with shopkeeper's friend? clerk? never did find out who or what she was to the owner, who sat by, silently. At issue? Wild-eyed and wildly opinionated, she doesn't want the veddy veddy upscale resale shop included in a book about "thrift" shops. Reminding us of her unconstitutional right to suppress our opinion, she is threatening, bordering on abusive. Outwardly, standing my ground as calmly as possible, I inwardly wonder if she has skipped her meds that day, and why the shopkeeper keeps mum. Her only response? Inclusively rolling her eyes heavenward. Afraid we'll scare away their upscale consignors with the catchall use of the word "thrift" in the title? Bet you she won't be such a snob if hordes of new, paying customers start coming to the shop because of a good review. I'd happily hand over $10 for a secondhand Ralph Lauren something in less tony circumstances, rather than $75 for the same garment in posh surroundings run by snotty stiffs, any day. Quality (in people and things) is where you find it.

WEDNESDAY, SEPTEMBER 1: Third-rate beach and board-walk motel. Matthew, full-time Tyler art student and part-time (gotta keep the wolf from the door) first class housekeeper, caregiver, gardener and unofficial adopted son/guru extra-ordinaire, is minding Morgan. They come and go: movies, water slide, miniature golf, whatever, whenever. We are stuck. Stuck in a rather nasty little room writing, editing away the day and our birthdays. Marvin's consulting work scheduled him in Vineland, so the camp followers tagged along in an attempt at a mini-vacation. Book nearing final paragraph, final period, final edit. We are nearing the end of our mutual ropes.

Computer keeps crashing. Waves crash even louder and more often. Hurricane due to come ashore any hour. We decamp, only after discovering Marvin's wallet is lost or stolen, and the motel insists on charging us for a day we will never spend here. They insist we can ride out the storm. I insist they are greedy and nuts. Later we appeal to the folks at the credit card company. We win. They remove the charge. One for the Maniac. Does this mean we will appear in a credit card commercial sometime soon? I doubt it.

SATURDAY, SEPTEMBER 4: Erica, Marvin's eldest daughter gets married today. More Betsy's Wedding than Father of the Bride. We have a blast. Only a second ago she was 10, standing in our living room watching us get married. More Frankie and Johnnie Get Married than Four Weddings and a Funeral. Or was it the other way around?

TUESDAY, OCTOBER 19: Interviewing potential printers. Meeting held at D's house. She's agreed to be my marketing maven. Sales reps file in on the hour, make their pitch, show samples, leave. Which one to pick? Never done this before. Attempt to look and sound like I know what I'm doing. I don't. We go for the woman. She looks like she knows what she's doing, and we like her. Uh Oh.

THURSDAY, OCTOBER 21: Favorite shopkeeper, silent and unbidden, hands over $3 keep-'em-coming-back-for-more rebate (kickback?). As a regular customer I'd grown used to discounts, debited from shopkeeper's 50% side of the ledger. As the Maniac, I must return it. New policy: never pay one penny more or one penny less than ticket price. Don't want it to come back and haunt later. The rumor mill is alive and well. Can a good review be bought? Is the Maniac on the take? Squeaky clean is the only way to go.

TUESDAY, OCTOBER 26 and WEDNESDAY, OCTOBER 27: We both forget our anniversaries. This is a first. (We were married, twice, within two days. But that's another story for another time. Or another edition.) Book is 160 pages. 30 too many. Too expensive to print. Two days of slash and burn to save our butts. Computer, enjoying a late night snack, nibbles on edits overnight, swallowing whole another two days' worth of work. (Real life friend and editor, Nancy, never does red pencil (edit) the book. No time, hence typos.) Matthew too sick to work. Also sick for weeks, I write reviews, do final undercover shopping trips, laundry, homework with Morgan, dinner, walk the dog, you know, life. Get "The Thing" to printer Halloween Day. Figures. The goose-free (see Soap Opera) roll of paper towel in the kitchen says: "Every day provides new gifts."

PR person from Barnes & Noble calls. Just spoke with D. Sorry to learn D is no longer handling my bookings and marketing. News to me. What's this about? A better deal somewhere else? Raging hormonal shifts from early stages of pregnancy? Mid-therapy, unconscious latent wish to kill her mom? Acting out well-deserved, but misplaced revenge against former employers who recently fired her? Enough psycho gobbledy gook. I'm gonna kill her. Consciously.

WEDNESDAY, OCTOBER 27: Marty Moss Coane's Radio Times. Yippee!! I love doing her show. She is sooo nice and sooo intelligent, and she even thrift shops. Interview made in talk show radio heaven. I'm here to plug the about-to-be-but-as-yet-unpublished-but-soon-to-be-I-hope opus, providing an update to last year's interview. WHYY presells 90 copies over the air during the Fall fundraiser at $60 a pop. My God, what if this thing (the book) never gets off the disk? (Assuming a lifeforce of its own, I've begun calling the book, The Thing.) I no longer seem to have creative, editorial or any other kind of control over it.

FRIDAY, OCTOBER 29: Annual school Halloween parade. Morgan tired of being a pretty-in-pink princess or luminous, powder blue, wings-and-all fairy. She wants to take over costume design. Victorious ninja warrior, or immortal but gruesome vampire are more like it. Asking more and more questions about injustice, death, sex, all the easy ones. What will she become when she's all grown up? When we go out and "do shops", as it's referred to around here, she wants to have a say in how many hangers a shop gets or to write part of the review, especially if it's a thrift junker (in reach of her allowance buying power) or a kid's shop (after all, she's a kid). Mini-maniac-in-training?

THURSDAY, NOVEMBER 4: Crawl (prostrate) to our banker to get a second mortgage. Distributor will only accept costly perfect binding (a spine) on the book. No distributor, no distribution. No distribution, no sales. Sold too many copies first edition for the bookstores to take us through the front door anymore. Backdoor deliveries only. Big time only. This is gonna cost big bucks. So you wanna be a writer......

MONDAY, NOVEMBER 8: Blue Monday. Marvin just got notification he's being audited by the IRS. Keep reminding myself he's just about the only person on the face of the earth who got a refund the first time this happened. Our accountant still marvels.

SATURDAY, NOVEMBER 13: Cheltenham adult class. Good news? Beyond sold out. Given the small auditorium to use. Bad news? Still no book. Here we go again. Hand out chits the students can later present to thrift shops that will sell the guide. Students can claim their should-have-been-included-with-the-class copy, when The @#^* Thing is finally ready. Hand out Volume I freebies to calm the natives. This is getting dense.

FRIDAY, NOVEMBER 19: The blankety blank disk has been at the blankety blank printers for almost three weeks. Computer "specialist" can't make our disk print out on their printer. His space-age equipment doesn't match our Neolithic word- processing software. No disk print out, no book. I hate computers. History just keeps repeating itself. Computers are a 20th century reenactment of the tower of Babel. In typical manly fashion, the printer's computer nerd struggled on, alone and unaided, in silence. (Just like when Marvin insists on driving around in circles, lost and late, and won't stop to ask for directions, making us even later.)

Adding to this fiasco? Printer saleslady (remember her?) doesn't know computerese. Unintentionally adds to confusion by mixing up words and meanings. Since it's her account, and since it's company policy (daddy used to own the company), we are forced to talk to computer nerd through her. Marvin assumed she knew what she was talking about. Not so. We have a translator who cannot translate. Wonderful. When we finally catch on, we confront her with this little discrepancy. She giggles. We don't. We are behind the proverbial ticking time bomb eight ball. We have lost weeks of production time, weeks worth of potential sales, or so the theory goes. No book, no sales. No sales, no house. (Second mortgage, remember? I do.)

SATURDAY, NOVEMBER 20: Walked Emma. Did five loads of wash. Shopped the farmer's market. Bought too much food. Cooked too much dinner. Ate too much dinner. Bit off more than I can chew?

SUNDAY, NOVEMBER 21: Calendar entry: Fashion Show and Book Signing, Barnes & Noble Bookstore, Bryn Mawr. Slight hitch: Printer can't have The @#^* Thing ready in time. $200 and endless hours later, mock up books Xeroxed at some rinky-dink printer in New Jersey, enough to cover potential book signing sales. (Rare collector's edition?) Can't believe this is happening. Copies are so expensive to make ($8 each), whatever is sold during the event must be sold at cost. No room for profit. They'd have to charge $20 retail. Then there's the not-so-subtle aesthetic difference between the mock up, hereafter known as Son of Thing, and The Thing.

Call PR person at B&N and told my sad tale. Grovel at her feet. If she wants to cancel, under the circumstances, I'll understand (As They Grow, The Junior League and Village Boutique, presenters at the fashion show, will not understand. They will kill me.) If B&N wants to go on with the show, so be it. Whatever they want, I want. (I want the @#^* copies of The @#^*

Thing to be ready.) Manager opts to go on. No one seems to notice anything wrong. As I hold Son of Thing in my hands, the large floppy format gives me the beginning of an idea for a national How To/Why Thrift book. Perhaps Marvin (The King) and Shiva (Hindu God) are right. Chaos is the seed of creation.

THURSDAY, NOVEMBER 25: Thanksgiving Day. Erica and Gino's new New Jersey cottage in the woods. Gathered round the dining room table, the picnic table, the card table: Gino's first-, second-, and third-generation Italian Catholic family. Also in attendance: Marvin and I and Morgan, with our inter-religious, multi-ethnic cross currents and let us not forget Marvin's first wife, Marjorie, her second husband, John, and their four children, three of whom are close to Morgan in age. We refer to them as her 'heart sisters'. No relation by blood, closely related by circumstance, they play together happily all day. Aren't we an evolved bunch? There was a time...but that is gratefully in the past. We have all grown up, together. Erica, the tie that binds, time the great healer. What a miracle. Please pass the turkey.

TUESDAY, DECEMBER 7: BOOKS! The Thing is ready. Do you have any idea what 10,000 books translates into in boxes? It looks like the Great Wall of China down there in the basement, and that's only 25%. The rest are stored back in the printers warehouse. God, what have we done? Even worse? My roots still aren't done.

DECEMBER 7,8,9,10,11: A week in the life. Dr. and Mrs. Maniac recovering from a 6-week-long, belatedly diagnosed bout of pneumonia. No wonder our butts were dragging. Drugged with $75 atomic-bomb antibiotics, I cough through a phone interview, radio interview, and a day with a reporter. Photographer comes early, I'm not ready. Two telephones break. The hard drive crashes. Backup disc is defective. The lawn mower breaks. My hairdresser, Anna, and I take turns being too sick to do my roots. A dining room chair breaks. The sewer lines back up. We use the bathroom at Tyler for 4 days. Phyllis and David, house guests, flee. Chicken wings with 5 days left to go on the supermarket label are rotten. I swap them. Second batch? Also rotten. The restaurant where I am to meet Marvin and guests? Gone out of business. Never do eat together. Forget to return the rental car. Drive to Willow Grove. Rental office open till noon; it's 1pm. Instead of one day, we pay for three. Oh yeah, we didn't need the car after all. Cooktop burner won't work. Custom-made frame crashes to the floor and shatters. Morgan gets another cold. I'll probably get it too, I always do. Marvin? Never.

WEDNESDAY, DECEMBER 22: Drive van load of books to distributor. Get my hair cut and my roots done. Everything will be OK now.

TUESDAY, JANUARY 18: Bookstores actually order, deliver, stock, shelve, and display The @#^* Thing. Customers actually buying it. Another miracle.

WEDNESDAY, JANUARY 19: First hate mail. Irate shopkeeper reminding me of my rights (why is it that cranks always remind us of our rights and then try to take them away?). Threatening to sue if I publish a review about her shop ever again. She even got a good review. What does she want? Treacle? Of course, why didn't I think of that. What do READERS want? The truth, the whole truth and nothing but the tongue-in-cheek truth. (What is truth? What is beauty? Does God exist?) I believe that beauty, like truth, is in the mind's eye of the beholder (and God and the Devil are in the details).

The rest of JANUARY, most of FEBRUARY and some of MARCH: Midst snow and ice and wind and more snow. SUSAN BRAY, WWDB, ORIEN REID, HOME MATTERS, AM PHILADELPHIA, ORIEN again. And again. (Channel 10 gets 10,000 calls from the first of three segments. Unprecedented.) Newspaper interviews, photographers, fashion shows and book signings, workshops, classes, all the hoopla of marketing. This is the fun part. This is what all the hand wringing and late night writing were about.

workshops, classes, all the hoopla of marketing. This is the fun part. This is what all the hand wringing and late night writing were about.

MONDAY, APRIL 18: Marvin and I seated on the Metroliner, headed for NYC and interview with J.E. Months earlier Marvin met her by accident, also on the metroliner. Strikes up a conversation with lady seated across from him, and describes our little cottage industry. She listens, intently, asks a lot of questions, answers his. Punch line? She's J.E., editor and big cheese, Senior Vice-President of Marketing & Sales at D_____. Tells him who and what she was and did, and offers a follow up meeting. (Shopper Lady, again? See Soap Opera.) They are interested in publishing our Guide. Nationally. After much discussion and even more hand wringing, we decide to keep it in the family. Like the local publisher we turned down for Volume I, they can only offer us 7% advance against royalties. On our own we've generated a 45% profit margin against the wolf at the door. Many authors go for the glory of being associated with a great publishing house. We go for the gold. Let us now pray.

THURSDAY, MAY 5 through TUESDAY MAY, 10: Mother's Day, Palm Beach, Florida "Thrift" shopping thrives in downtown Palm Beach, no less. Upscale ladies-who-lunch resale shop: each garment protected with see through plastic shoulder shields. Tres Classy. Also: glass-enclosed secondhand Chanel (as in #5) boutique. Next door: $3,000 Brioni men's suits, now $225. Marvin bites and buys one. We eat, no, make that dine, at Bice. ("Bee-chay"?) (Bitchy?) Marvin, mood matching ambiance, places a cellular, table-side phone call to The Coast. Describes The Scene to Jerry, a.k.a. Seagull, the one-friend-above-all-others-most-likely-to-appreciate. One day bottomfeeders, the next day uppercrust. Pardon my mixed metaphysics.

MONDAY, JUNE 27: Oh God. Summer again. I feel as if I've been run over by an out of control tractor. Author in me: "I think I'll compost awhile." Publisher in me: "Get to work." Author wins. Publisher stews.

SATURDAY, JULY 16: Still composting. But doing it on Block Island. Not a bad view for a vegetable. Still can't bring myself to write. Hotter here than I ever remember. Don't care if I ever thrift shop again. (Probably not a good career move.)

THURSDAY, SEPTEMBER 8: School starts. The heat breaks. The maniac lives to shop (and write) again.

P.S. Third edition? Released (7 months later) to bookstores on April Fool's Day. No foolin'!

 RESUME OF A MANIAC

In answer to all those **JUST WHO DO I THINK I AM?** questions

Nancy L. Maniac, Ph.D. T.*
P.O. Box 27540 Philadelphia, PA 19118 215-635-4207

EMPLOYMENT OBJECTIVE: World-class publisher, celebrated author.

WORK HISTORY: (Dates are best guess only in no particular order. See Tour #17 for additional information.)

(1980) For one sweet, all too short summer, single-handedly, seven days a week, three meals a day, I ran the kitchen for a privately owned club on a privately owned island off the coast of Maine. No phone. No TV. Mail delivered to a nearby island by boat. Alone, but not lonely, I learned to meditate at low tide on a big black rock surrounded by Casco Bay. The island was called Hope.

(1982) Sold Bec Fin-quality groceries in Society Hill out of the back of a 1965 hearse with candy cane-stripped curtains and bows in the windows. It got too hot. The greens wilted. So did I. But I learned to hustle.

(1983) I went back to being a chef. I endured 110° plus temperatures standing over the deep fryer, the ovens set to 500°, the grill turned to High, the salamander a glowing red broil, my feet in a bucket of ice water, 12 hours a day, six days a week. I learned endurance and stamina and working as a team. I learned to be a boss. I saw my bosses drink, womanize, use drugs, get knifed, get arrested, and generally act like Type-A overachieving jerks. And oh yes, I learned a little about cooking.

(1972) I did research for Herb Denenberg at the University of Pennsylvania, Wharton School of Business, for almost three years, watching him transform himself from a sweet nebbish of a professor to well on the road to becoming Denenberg's (of the ascerbic) Dump of Channel 10 fame. Doing a little research of my own, I learned how to self promote. I also picketed the President's office, demanding better working conditions for women and joined a women's group. I'm back to wearing a bra (gravity), I always wore makeup (vanity).

(1975) I worked as legal secretary and administrative assistant to Managing Director Hillel Levinson and during his first campaign, and was one of three secretaries to soon-to-be Mayor Frank Rizzo. I relearned what I didn't like about kowtowing and about politics. (Yes, it's all true.) **(1969)** I was a travel agent. I quit to travel. I camped across the country, from one end to the other. I learned to cook over an open fire. I learned to wash my hair in icy cold water. I hiked, climbed and backpacked, slept on the ground. I surprised myself by learning to like it very much. **(1967)** I sold cosmetics. I learned about glamour. I sold clothing at Lord and Taylor's **(1962)**, and furniture at Bloomingdales **(1982)**. I learned how to dress and what goes into making good furniture. **(1968)** I sold nosebleed-expensive original works of art at the defunct Kenmore Art Gallery. I learned about color, shape, and perspective but not bookkeeping. I job-hopped a lot during this time. I learned flexibility. Somewhere in here I

RESUME Page 13

worked as a cocktail waitress in a nightclub (The Erlanger) for one month. It was a looong month. Great money, too much smoke, too many hands. I learned I was a morning person.

EDUCATIONAL EXPERIENCE:

I attended a private girl's school of 200 students, kindergarten through 12th grade. I learned embroidery and took long nature walks with a Russian émigré, the only one of her family to escape the revolution. I learned to love history and English. I sang soprano in the choir, loved art, hated the food, played right wing on the hockey team and beat out everyone at high jumping, even Connie Morris. A Lutheran school run by celibate Protestant nuns wearing blue and gray and white habits, crosses swinging across their bosoms like pendulums. We had chapel every day and Bible Class twice a week. I learned to talk to God on a regular basis, like it or not. I went to a backwater liberal arts college near the Chesapeake. I studied political science and philosophy and men (finally!). I was lying to myself about wanting to study back then. I'd had enough of that in High School. I was raised to be a cheerleader, marry a doctor and have children. (Eventually, I did three out of three, but not exactly the way Mom and Dad had in mind.). I got mono. I fell far behind. I dropped out of college. Overprotected and under prepared for life, I wanted to learn how the world worked. I learned the hard way, but the best way I know--on the job. Postgraduate work has come with the territory. I've picked up more than I knew watching and listening to Marvin whenever he wore his business consultant's hat or assumed his shrink's stance, expounded on his theory of life in groups, or sat in his director's chair creating interactive videos.

LIFE EXPERIENCE:

I've regularly camped across America and eaten my way through Europe. I was almost raped twice, scared off or ran off my attackers. (I chased one with my car and would have run him over. I drove the wrong way down J.F. Kennedy Boulevard for one block trying to nail him, until my frontal lobe kicked back in.) The house has been robbed, our van stolen and the driver's side window smashed. It cost us $140 to replace the window. The thief got a handful of coins and some ratty old tapes. I love music, have a growing appreciation for Opera, but still experience physical discomfort with way-far-out-there-jazz and heavy metal. I love horseback riding, cooking, gardening and decorating. I am a graduate of EST, one of the single most important, liberating things I ever did for myself, other than marrying Marvin. (Yeah, we did get to go to the bathroom.) I've been to Europe five times now and look forward to going again soon. I have one child, Morgan, two cats, Nibs and Sweetpea, one dog, Emma, have been married only once and intend to keep it that way. Marriage has taught me about love and stick-to-it-iveness, and mostly about myself. Motherhood has taught me the frailties and the glories of being human and of loving someone more than yourself. I've always loved to read. I've devoured several libraries worth of books, always studying how the good writers did it. I find it more than coincidental that the woman who owned our house before us was also a writer. I've kept a journal, but only fitfully. The desire to write was always there, I just never believed I would or could, until now.

MEDICAL AND EMOTIONAL HISTORY:

Hanging around Marvin lo these 15 years, I've earned an amateur black belt in shrinking and massage, as applied to self and upon others, had regular preventative acupuncture and chiropractic care. I've endured postpartum depression so bad, I thought I'd permanently misplaced myself somewhere. I had no idea how much I would like being married or having kids. I still wish I'd had one more child. But God doesn't give us more than we can handle. I've regularly attended Alanon (no, not AA) meetings. I drink wine, socially and with meals. I am a pacifist with a temper. I would like to be a vegetarian, but I love the occasional lamb chop or flank steak, medium rare, please. I use only olive oil and real butter. I have never used artificial sweeteners or margarine. They can't be good for you. I hate diet soda. I avoid doctors and prescription medicine, but I'm no stoic and I'm no Christian Scientist. Our medicine cabinet contains aspirin, Tylenol, homeopathic cough medicine and Vicks, ONLY. I get the lack-of-sunshine blues every time the winter solstice rolls around, but discovered the joys of long winter underwear. The only surgery I've ever had was to remove my tonsils and four impacted wisdom teeth. Principal forms of exercise are housework, gardening, walking the dog, dancing, typing and talking too much. My roots are naturally brown, my hair is unnaturally blonde. I am overweight, but not too much. (TV really does pack on the pounds.)They say you either keep your figure or your face. I never had much of either, so I've got nothing to lose.

PERSONAL CHARACTERISTICS:

I'm a first-born Virgo. I was a tomboy. We used to play fort and I had my own cowgirl hat and belt and gun. I was the leader. Or at least I thought so. Nancy Holmes, my best friend since we were three, tells me I was always getting us both in trouble. Taking charge, being critical, taking risks came naturally. I like to do personal appearances and TV and radio work. I avoid parties where I don't know anyone. I like giving them. I'm an introverted ham. As a family we don't go to church or synagogue, but we observe each others holidays. I light the Chanukah candles, he schleps the tree. I think God would find all these denominations and separations silly and unfortunate, but completely necessary and human. We pray as a family almost every day. I pray for good stuff for others, not myself. I always ask to be shown what to do, and for the good grace to do it. We compost. We recycle. We donate. (What goes around always comes around.)

**For further information please call me at
215-635-4207. I look forward to hearing from you.**

Sincerely yours,

NLB, Ph.D.T. (*Doctor of Thrift)
P.S. If you think I told you EVERYTHING, you're nuts.
P.P.S. Short but sweet version? I thought of It. I wrote It. I did It. I dared. You bought It. That makes me qualified!

 HOW THE RATING GAME WORKS

♥ **SCENARIO:** Thrift shops are the gypsies of retail, everything from private, secondhand department stores to 50-year old charitable pillars of the community. Some are hidden and out of the way, well-kept neighborhood secrets. Others occupy prominent locations with the marketing skills, technology and merchandise of a Bloomingdale's or a Fifth Avenue boutique. Some will take anything: the good, the bad and the ugly. Some are picky, picky, picky. Some buy outright. Some are donations-only. Some are consignments-only. Some are a combo, to go.

♥ **QUESTION: How to review and rate this retail stew?**

♥ **SOLUTION:** After a lot of hand-wringing and floor-pacing the idea of using hangers (à la Michelin's) came to mind. That solved what symbols to use. Now, how to figure out which stores get how many hangers? Some worthy shops obligingly slipped right into my imaginings. Others elusively crisscrossed all over the place. What to do?

The following six categories begin to describe the possible range of quality:

TOP DRAWER Everything about it--looks, goods, service--are the best, only the best.

CLASS ACT Reaching for the Top Drawer. Shop may have most of the service and/or some of the look and goods of a Top Drawer, above average with a sprinkling of the very best.

STATUS QUO Good quality, serviceable merchandise, some dreck, a few treasures. Little or no pretense at interior design or display. Clean and organized with good to indifferent service. Most thrift and consignment shops fall into this category.

BOTTOMFEEDER Neither a good nor bad designation. Just like Popeye, it am what it am. Sales volume measured in tons. Large store, often a chain, located in low-rent district. You'll spend lots of time for low to high yield for your efforts, depending on taste and the toss of the dice. It's the next to last stop for goods on the recycling express. Last stop? Mattress felt or Tanzania.

HO HUM Mostly uninspired to dreck merchandise, display and/or service, with the rare fabulous find. Few redeeming social or esthetic graces. Shop here if you happen to be in the neighborhood, passing by.

DOWN & OUT Characterized by low turnover, many damaged items, erratic pricing, poor organization, lousy attitude. Dreary shop and neighborhood.

OVERALL EVALUATION
(0-4 hangers 4=BEST).

YUCK. CAVEAT EMPTOR.

POOR. DON'T SAY I DIDN'T TELL YOU.

SO-SO. DON'T GET YOUR HOPES UP.

WORTH A LOOK. DON'T GO OUT OF YOUR WAY.

GOOD. CHECK IT OUT. YOUR TIME WILL TELL.

BETTER. GO OUT OF YOUR WAY. THEY DO.

BEST. GO NO MATTER WHAT OR WHERE.

THE BEST OF THE BEST 4-hanger shops with that extra special something.

 SHOPPER ALERT: Bestowed upon shop in recognition of excellence in a **particular** category of merchandise or service.

 STANDARDS:

- I look for merchandise that's **CLASS ACT** and **TOP DRAWER** at **BOTTOMFEEDER** prices, the best for the least. Ambiance, courtesy and organization count for a lot, but you can't take them home.
- Old-timers with **HO HUM** decor and **CLASS ACT** merchandise get more hangers than newcomers with spic-and-span stores and **STATUS QUO** merchandise.
- **HO HUM** decor and erratic quality or prices get about the same number of hangers as boring shops with boring merchandise but cheap prices.
- Newly opened stores get a six-month grace period. I might write a review but I won't assign hangers.
- The Maniac promises to shop each store at least twice before evaluating. Follow-up phone calls, gossip-gathering interviews with salespeople and fellow maniacs, a third or fourth visit until I'm absolutely certain.

As with restaurants, the reviewer must take clear standards, apply them, then add that personal dash of experience and taste to decide just how good 'good' is. This is where my two-cents makes the half-hanger, plus or minus difference. **Sometimes a shop will get a WOW review, but few hangers. Sometimes it's a 4 hanger shop with a so-so review. It's my way to achieve balance.** It's also where debate may rage, but hey, I'm the Maniac and this is my Guide. I've done my best to be fair. I hope you'll agree.

INTRODUCTION TO THE MANIAC'S CRAWLING, WALKING, RUNNING, DRIVING GET THERE ANY WAY YOU CAN, BUT GET THERE GUIDED TOURS

FILL 'ER UP

Anticipation is not one of my fortes, especially traveling somewhere new. What if I get lost? Is the tank filled with gas? What if the car breaks down? What if I have to pee? Where can I eat? Did I remember the umbrella? Maps? Parking quarters? What if I get lost? (Oh yea, we did that one.) When my cerebral springboard is wound as tight as it can possibly get, I rev engines and let 'er rip. Journey begun, the crazies depart, and I begin to wonder what all the fuss was about. Thrift shopping mania eventually grows more powerful than my fear of the topographically unexplored. Reciting my mantra over and over again--"The shop's not going anywhere, the shop's not going anywhere" (usually true.)--I come to realize, that sooner or later, I'll find it (usually true.). Armed with a canvas bag stuffed with zip code maps, maps by county, statewide maps, regional maps, I set off into the great uncharted world of resale.

MAPS, MAPS, MAPS

What must it be like for you? Well, you wrote and told me, and you called and told me. Some of you even told me off. You wanted the book organized into areas or zones. You wanted maps. You wanted bigger print. You're going to get two out of three. Can't afford the larger print. I have too much to say, there are too many shops, and the book would have cost too much for you to want to buy or me to make any money. We did change the font (the actual shape of the letters), to one that is fuller and rounder, like moi, and easier to read, also like moi. While I love thrifting, I also love paying the mortgage. One of my little quirks.

TOURS, TOURS, TOURS

At great trouble and little expense, Marvin, bless his sore little fingers, hunched shoulders, numb tushie, red eyes and kvetching soul (did I lay it on thick enough?) electronically scrambled our A-Z Volume II and my new reviews, cut and pasting them into the heart and soul of a regionally organized Volume III, hence the title change: Guided Tours. Subtle, but profound. We sweated over the maps. I grant you they are not up to Rand McNally's standards; that's not my calling. **They are not drawn to scale. Not even close.** But they will get you aimed in the right direction. You want more than that? Go buy your own. I added a little intro to each tour to tell you about favorite, cheapo eating spots, emergency bathrooms, local history, gossip and alternative shopping. You're almost right here with me in the van. Shops are clustered the way I think about them and travel to them. Where possible, I've included a shop smorgasbord: resale boutique, furniture, kid's, bottomfeeders, charity, etc.

You may wonder (as I often do) how I get the job done? There's method to my maniac madness. Always wear: big patch pockets, the better to conceal tape recorder in one, portable phone in the other. Stowed in the van: laptop, 3-ring binder, holding review forms, a tattered copy of Volumn II, updates inked in all over the old review. There's also a blue canvas bag holding maps, stapler, three hole punch, snacks and spring water, and a printout Marvin made of every shop address and phone number in our data base. Next year, a fax and Xerox?

LOTS OF ISSUES & SOME OF THE ANSWERS

Most of you have adjusted (rather well, thank you) to my spouting off, mid-review, giving my read on the manners and mores of our times. Well, I've gone off the deep end AGAIN. Woven into many of the reviews and most of the tours, I go on at length about **THE BIGGIES** of our times as well. I've schlepped this growing info-baggage around with me for a while now. Grown so large, it was time to share. I've just enlarged the scope a tad. Now it's not only lawn sheep, Elvis and polyester, but also unemployment, illiteracy, computers, cancer, crime, child abuse, nuclear waste, homelessness, drug addiction. You know, THOSE... When the BIGGIES first started appearing on these pages, even I was startled. It took me awhile to make sense of what I was doing. An instant replay, I suppose, of "Who Does She Think She Is, Anyway?" I wondered (and still wonder) if it's O.K. to include all this stuff. Whether I'm working at cross purposes? But holding back on part of what I've seen going on out there wouldn't be telling you the story, the whole story and nothing but the story.

Driving around our region, day in and day out, I've been given the opportunity to see for myself, firsthand, the issues that bring us together as Maniacs and too often keep us apart as a country. I can't help but take the previous night's dose of ever-so-neutral terror called the 11 o'clock news, and each morning's banner screaming headlines along with me in the van. I find myself 'replaying and rereading' them in the streets of every town I visit. Just as I once carried around in my head the factual cacophony of shop consignment policies, hours, and inventory that eventually became The Guide, this Issue I found myself holding mini 'Talk of The Nation'-type 'programs' all alone on my way to the next shop in the next town. It was getting a little crowded in here. I know, I know. Some of you thought you were only buying a light-hearted Guide on thrift and resale shops. But whether it's American Family Services on North Broad Street or The Trading Post in Paoli or Sophisticated Seconds on Rittenhouse Square, whether it's someone climbing out of their Jag to make a donation, or a homeless person changing clothes in the aisles, or a working Mom looking for a snappy suit, we all swim in the same pond.

AND THE WINNER IS...

Back of the last edition in very fine print, I promised to award a freebie to the reader or readers who came up with any outstanding ideas I actually wound up using. **To LOUISE SPERBER, a retired teacher of Cheltenham, Pa.,** go the spoils. Louise wrote, requesting zones, maps, etc. in her letter postmarked January 6, 1994, getting the jump on Kathy Fearnside and Ann Purcell, March 11, and Carol Love, March 22. **A free copy of the Third Edition is yours Louise,** wending its way to you care of the US Postal Service. Let us all pray it has a safe and speedy journey. Thanks to all of you for writing, especially those who shared favorite and not-so-favorite shops. Some cooks never share a recipe, some share, but leave out an ingredient, some give out the entire recipe and a tip or two thrown in for good measure. Whether the glass is half full or half empty depends on your perspective, doesn't it?

P.S. Same offer is good for Volume IV, if I survive to do this again.

P.P.S. Be brave. I know it can be scary to go to new, unexplored places. Believe me, I've been really scared at times, too. But go anyway. Take the chance, and go. Good things will happen.

P.P.P.S. Yes, yes, I know, I know the print is too small! **Go buy secondhand glasses!**

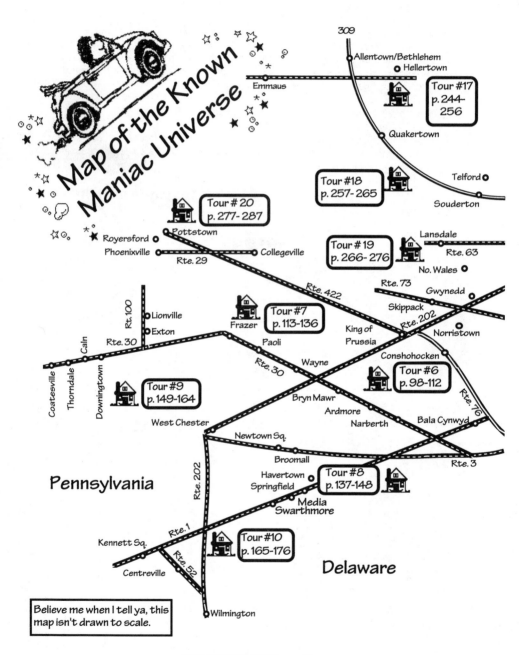

Map of the Known Maniac Universe

309

Allentown/Bethlehem
Hellertown

Emmaus

Tour #17
p. 244-256

Quakertown

Telford

Tour #18
p. 257-265

Souderton

Tour #20
p. 277-287

Royersford   Pottstown
Phoenixville   Collegeville
Rte. 29

Lansdale

Tour #19
p. 266-276   Rte. 63

No. Wales

Rte. 73

Rte. 422   Skippack   Gwynedd

Rt. 100   Lionville   Rte. 202
Exton   Frazer   Tour #7   King of   Norristown
Caln   Rte. 30   p. 113-136   Prussia
Coatesville   Thorndale   Downingtown   Paoli   Conshohocken
Rte. 30   Wayne   Tour #6
Tour #9   p. 98-112
p. 149-164   Rte. 76
Bryn Mawr
West Chester   Ardmore   Bala Cynwyd
Narberth
Newtown Sq.
Broomall   Rte. 3

Pennsylvania   Rte. 202   Havertown   Tour #8
Springfield   p. 137-148
Media
Swarthmore

Kennett Sq.   Rte. 1   Tour #10
p. 165-176   Delaware
Rte. 52
Centreville

Believe me when I tell ya, this
map isn't drawn to scale.

Wilmington

UNIVERSE MAP Page 21

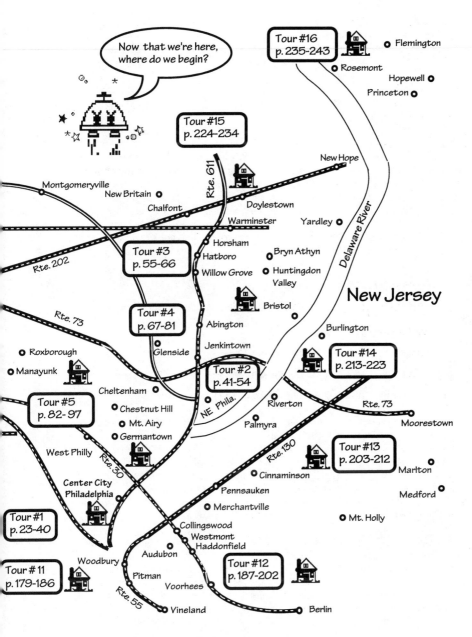

TOUR #1
UPTOWN, DOWNTOWN, ALL AROUND THE TOWN

I've lived at 24th & Locust, 4th & Monroe, 20th & Spruce, 7th & Bainbridge, and finally 10th & Chancellor Streets. I got around a lot, then and now. I willingly walked from one end of Center City to the other, thinking nothing of going from 7th & Bainbridge to the Italian Market to the Reading Terminal and back, all on foot, pushing Morgan's stroller bulging with bundles and bambina. I promised myself I'd never live in the suburbs. But with a kid and a dog and two cats, two home offices and a third office outside the home...you get the picture. "And another one bites the dust."

Seven years later and Center City still beckons. I get down here as much as I can. When I looked at the very long and potentially confusing list of thrift and resale shops in town, trying to figure out how to get it to make sense for you, I realized that I sorted it all out long ago when I was a Center City resident, shopping what I considered to be zones or mini-communities. Organized this way, everything is within a short walking distance, just as if I were still living here, tooting around, doing my errands and visiting friends. Only now, the car is home base. Park it centrally in one of these 6 areas, and let the Guide and your feet take you here, there and everywhere.

I)   Pish-posh Rittenhouse Square

II) Stylistically funky (or just plain funky) South Street Corridor

III) Historically correct Society Hill

IV) Hangin' on the corner in South Philly

V)   West Philly secondhand urbane outfitters

VI) North Philly (always) lean and (sometimes) mean streets

Each has its own flavor, its own sense of neighborhood and its own cluster of shops and places to eat. Park the car and forget it, train in, or map out one area and stick to it for the day if you are on foot, unless you are used to taking buses. With buses you can crisscross town all day long. Call Septa ahead and get schedules. They even have maps. But without the car you have to haul stuff yourself or leave the big booty behind, paying to have it delivered. I use the car as a storage locker, timing mini-excursions in 2-hour intervals, to match the meters. With all this in mind, pick a zone and do the town.

Here are a few helpful hints on pit stops and cheap eats. If you get into town before 10am, it's a good time to grab a parking spot or a cheaper all- day rate in a lot, but a lousy time to shop. Most Center City thrift and resale shops don't open till 10:30am, some as late as 11am, and even a few late-night types on South Street prefer noon. So I go to the Reading Terminal to do the day's food shopping, grab a late breakfast and/or a take-out lunch, and gratefully use the

TOUR #1 Page 23

restrooms all the way in the back near the Arch Street side. When will City Council get us those European style kiosk commodes? A chicken (and a finger) in every pot we've got, thanks to Mr. Clinton and the Tyson Chicken scandal. Now how about a toilet on every corner? Are you listening Mr. Rendell?

I like thrift-shopping-day dining to be fast and cheap. I like to invest my time and money in the things, not the food. Even so (old chefs never die, they just become food critics), I still like it to be GOOD. Sooo, here's a brief list of places where I like to eat on the run. And yes, **numbers in front of the restaurants match the area zones listed above and on the shop list.**

I) The **Cantina** at the Reading Terminal Market, The **Marathon Grill** at the corner of 15th & Sansom, or the **Sansom Street Oyster House** on Sansom near 16th, but only if you're feeling flush, and only afterward for dinner. Nip into **Borders** at 17th & Walnut (for a copy of The Guide) and second-floor cappuccino-induced recharge and snack.

II) **Randazzo's**, near Seconds on South, is just as good if not better than Boston Chicken, and far more intimate. Or try **Towne Pizza** 1900 Pine Street.

III) Near 4th & Bainbridge? Tea and pastry? **Pink Rose Cafe**. Roast turkey on rye, fries, and a black and white soda? (David, the calories!) **Famous Deli**. Greek? **South Street Souvlaki** near Thrift for AIDS. Lebanese? **Cedars** at 616 So. 2nd Street. Mexican? **Copabanana** 4th & So. Seafood? **Walt's Crabhouse**, 806 S. 2nd.

IV) The **Melrose Diner** on Broad St. Walk, shop and eat up and down **9th Street's Italian Market**. **Mara's** on Passyunk Avenue for pizza.

V) The **Tandoor Indian Restaurant** at 106 So. 40th, the **Palladium** on Locust Walk (U. of P. campus) if you're feeling flush or **The American Diner**, corner 42nd & Chestnut, if you're not.

VI) Bring a sandwich.

TOUR #1

 I) Pish-posh **Rittenhouse Square**
2 BARGAIN ANTIQUE AND THRIFT SHOP
3 FIGHT FOR SIGHT
5 HANGERS ★
8 IMMORTAL ★
4 NEW TO NEARLY NEW (& MAN TO MAN)
7 ORT VALUE CENTER
1 SALVATION ARMY
6 SOPHISTICATED SECONDS

 II) Stylistically funky (or just plain funky) **South Street** corridor
13 ASHLEY'S
9 GOOD, BETTER, BEST
14 JELLYBEANS
10 SECONDS ON SOUTH
11 THRIFT FOR AIDS ★
12 TIME ZONE

III) Historically correct **Society Hill**
19 THE BRIDAL EXCHANGE
15 FEDERATION THRIFT SHOP
18 PENNSYLVANIA HOSPITAL BARGAIN SHOP
17 SECOND CHANCE
16 VENUS IN FURS

 IV) Hangin' on the corner in **South Philly**
22 AMERICAN THRIFT STORES
21 FABULOUS FINDS BOUTIQUE
20 SEASON TO SEASON

 V) West Philly secondhand urbane outfitters
23 THE SECOND MILE
24 TOVIAH THRIFT SHOP

VI) North Philly (always) lean and (sometimes) mean streets
25 AMERICAN FAMILY SERVICES
26 BEV'S DOUBLE TAKE
27 THE ENCORE
28 VILLAGE THRIFT

*Note: This list has a shop's entire name. Names in review boxes may have been shortened a tad to fit. Numbers before each shop name correspond to their numbered location on each map. **Shops with a star sold Volume II. Volume III? ASK!**

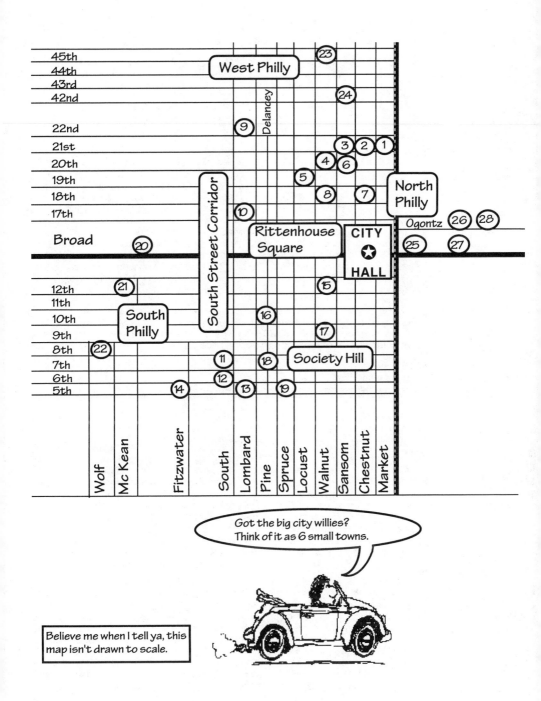

American Family Services, Inc.	
910 N. Broad St. Phila., PA 19122 **765-2900** **Look:** BOTTOM FEEDER **Goods:** DOWN & OUT–TOP DRAWER **Prices:** CAN'T GET ANY LOWER **HOURS:** Mon–Sat 9-5	Supermarket size. Super-duper stuff. Not for nervous nellies. **SUBURBANITE ALERT:** Dress very down, don't wear real jewelry, place money on your person in several places, wear shoes you can run in, and only go in if you can park right out in front. The drug capital of center city, a.k.a., The Badlands is blocks away, but hey, so are Temple University, traffic court and City Hall. Inside, **the store is quite safe.** Trolling the endless rack-miles of bleach-stained polyester and torn cottons turned up: Valentino unworn apricot linen blouse, $2.95, Ann Taylor black velvet dress, $14.95, raw silk sport coat, original Boyd's tag intact, now $3.95. St. Laurent silk ties, $1. Limited Editions and Mousefeathers dresses for Morgan, originally $90-$120 each, now $7.95. Fringed red plaid wool stadium blanket, $2.95, unworn leather, sheepskin-lined slippers, $45 in Land's End, here, $4.95. Copper bowl set: $9.95. Spend $40-$60 and walk out with trash bags filled with glad rags. Check carefully for damage. They're serious members of the 'You Bought It, You-Own It' school of marketing. Wear earplugs unless you like the Sesame Street/Billy Graham mutant blend that blasts unrelentingly center stage from the two TV screens blaring down at you from the ceiling.Some days I can tune it out.Some days it gets on my nerves so bad my emotional circuits overload. The intention may be captive audience conversion, the result is acoustical abuse. Toss finds over the racks to work a section. Keep a protective eye peeled on your pile. Buy as you go. Too heavy? Check your new purchases with the guard. Go back to the racks for more. **WATCH OUT** for holes left in garments by those darn staples they use to affix prices and missing price tags. One's come off? The item is returned to processing and can't be purchased until the next day. Don't even bother to ask.
CLOSED: Holidays	**CONSIGNOR ALERT:** Donations only.
American Thrift Stores	
8th & Wolf St. Phila., PA 19148 **336-6626**  **Look:** BOTTOMFEEDER **Goods:** DOWN & OUT–STATUS QUO **Prices:** LOW–HIGH **HOURS:** Mon–Sat 8:30-5	All thrift stores have a personality profile, a feel to them, an energy level. This one is no exception. Depression and despair are indigenous, slipping in with customers and employees, or delivered through the back door in boxes and bags. This is the Ellis Island of thrift shops, but without Our Lady of the Lamp to guide the poor and weary. Recent waves of immigrants have pushed and shoved past the edge of one of the last century's long-established ethnic strongholds. Newly arrived strangers struggle daily for the right to live in a part of South Philly where front steps certainly aren't scrubbed every day, and the wide-ranging assortment of curb-side litter can hold its own with any inner city anywhere. These "strangers" shop alongside "natives" who didn't realize their own American dream and never made it out of "The Neighborhood" or are too set in their ways to ever dream of leaving. When this place gets their collective hands on what the powers-to-be consider a quality piece of merchandise, the price goes through the roof. Just like some poor slob who gets hold of an authentic reproduction of gold-rimmed collectors' plates depicting, in gen-u-ine hand-painted, living color, Elvis Presley's six favorite last meals, American Thrift thinks it's really got something. And when it does, it tries to up the ante. The rusting, peeling white paint over cast iron garden bench that probably cost $400 new, was $250. Someone had begun restoration, then given up and abandoned a tissue paper-thin wood and veneer music stand with bubbled and peeling varnish. Fork over $89 and you could take it home and finish the job. **Over the door a sign proclaims:** "Where a quarter goes a long way." Sometimes.
CLOSED: Holidays	**CONSIGNOR ALERT:** Donations only. They buy in volume from other sources.

Ashley's	
508 S. 5th St. Phila, PA 19147 **413-1022**  **Look:** STATUS QUO **Goods:** HO HUM – STATUS QUO **Prices:** LOW–MODERATE **HOURS:** Tue–Fri 12-6, Sat 12-5	Turn the corner. Leave behind the surging, fair-weather Saturday-afternoon promenade of South Street show-off shoppers and gangs of gawkers. (Are-we-having-fun-yet?) Walk a few doors down Fifth Street, past long-gone-to-seed Wildflowers' replacement restaurant. Keep going till you spot the makeshift sign announcing Ashley's Recycling Center and perhaps the two little pigtailed girls playing timeless sidewalk games under mom's just-inside-the-door watchful eye.

South Street is the only shopping locus in Philly that manages to turn on itself until it turns inside out. Ashley's is an outtie, not an innie. Meaning? South Street is market-ing. It's about seeing and being seen. It's about critical mass. It's about what's hot. What's in. Who's out. Ashley's is in some sort of marketing warp zone. Here is a mom, managing a shop, managing two little girls, playing it straight, running a business, making a living. No hype. **A classic, small town, side-street thrift shop in neo-chaotic na na land.** She's so straight, she just might be the next wave of cool. Is she a registered Republican? Items that caught my eye: A Nan Duskin-label, white mohair coat, for $30. Now a springboard for the imaginative wardrobe. A weird outer layer à la St. Laurent? Or snip off the bottom, add frog fasteners, and it's a bed jacket? Or add lace or sequins or splice and re-sell it for big bucks? Also spotted: two Spa label pink or purple cotton dresses, $7.50 each (catalog price $58). Two pair of Cotton Express pants, forest green or purple, never worn, $8 each. Some fair to middlin' men's and children's. Tedious chachkas. Motherhood can be tedious, too, but look at the rewards you can reap if you stick with it. |
| **CLOSED:** Holidays | **CONSIGNOR ALERT:** Buys outright. Donates (??%) to American Cancer Society. |

Bargain Thrift Shop	
2043 Chestnut St. Phila., PA 19103 **751-0492**  **Look:** STATUS QUO **Goods:** HO HUM - CLASS ACT **Prices:** MODERATE – HIGH **HOURS:** Mon–Thu 10-5:30, Fri 10-6	**Antiques & Thrift Shop,** to be precise. Is this a funky, moderately priced antique store, or a funky, high priced thrift shop with the usual rotating inventory of junk and the occasional real find? Both, I suppose. The manager, **recently featured in an article in the Inquirer Magazine,** is experienced enough to know what is in and what is hot, and therefore what to charge for what.

There's been everything from a matching set of four orange vinyl and black metal bar stools, circa 1954, to low-grade veneer, low-grade Deco bedroom sets at high grade prices ($750), circa 1924, to a gorgeous, $642 bird's-eye maple, drop-leaf table, circa 1854. When I asked if her price was firm, she reluctantly but pleasantly dropped her voice and the price to $600, then contradicting her decision by stating "on Pine Street (antique row) such a table could easily bring $1000." Ruefully: "I guess that's why neither of us is on Pine Street," I quipped. Plastic and china salt and pepper sets from the 20's through the 50's. A lorgnette worn by a proud Victorian lady, early Depression depressing "home sweet home" prints and the odd piece of office furniture, all mixed together to create a bargain hunter's tossed salad.

LAYAWAY ALERT: You lose your deposit after **only 7 days!** |
| **CLOSED:** Holidays | **CONSIGNOR ALERT:** Buys everything outright. Will deliver large furniture pieces to the Main Line, West Philadelphia and Center City only. |

Bev's Double Take	
5934 Ogontz Ave. Phila., PA 19141 **424-2940**	Yet another shopkeeper's request to "please include my shop in your next edition" dropped into my mailbox and crossed my desk. Carefully formed, evenly spaced words on composition paper (cut rather than torn), crowded the left-hand margin, leaving the right-hand open. Half the words were without the preliminary stroke. The bottom was deep and generous. Otherwise, the height above the thin blue line was consistent. They conveyed thoughts which were carefully chosen and businesslike. As an off and on dabbler in handwriting analysis (as well as numerology, astrology and all things Shirley Maclaine), I divined a number of 'new age' insights about this person and her shop. They were born out. Bev's handwriting and shop are neat,
Look: STATUS QUO **Goods:** STATUS QUO **Prices:** LOW– MODERATE	well-organized, with a good comfort zone between all the words and the racks. Some of the clothing is 'hot', as evidenced by the deeper bottom stroke. The majority, as represented by the more cautious upper stroke, is good solid-citizen stuff.
HOURS: Tue–Thu, 11-6, Fri 10-5, Sat 12-5	The shop is located in the midst of a neighborhood struggling to keep its slim edge in America's middle-class dream. Bev's use of a child's school book paper rather than good-quality personal stationery or professional letterhead speaks to that struggle. Yet her entrepreneurship got her **featured in the Daily News and by Orien Reid on Channel 10.** Her marketing sense isn't bad either. A local woman provides the shop with samples of her brightly-colored, cellophane wrapped, baby shower gift baskets.
CLOSED: Holidays	**CONSIGNOR ALERT:** 50-50% split. $5 fee. 30 days. By appointment.

The Bridal Exchange	
Society Hill, PA 19106 **923-8515**	Brides-to-be and their maids (no grooms, no best men, no men of any kind) can **gain entree only by appointment**. Not wanting to carry this undercover shopping thing too far, and certainly no bride, I decided to call and do a phone interview, asking all the relevant questions. Word out on the grapevine is this is **THE place for secondhand bridal shopping in the Delaware Valley.**
	Here's the dish: 70% are new samples. They just got in 33 salon and manufacturer samples and consignments with labels like **Marisa, Yumi Katsura, Vera Wang, Richard Glasgow, Cristos, Diamond Collection, St. Pucci and Scaasi.** Local designers included too, especially **Janice MacBride** who was recently featured in Philadelphia Brides's Magazine. Your $350 can purchase a gown originally worth $700. $2200 to spend? Figure a $5000 creation can now become your dream dress. Consigned or custom made headpieces go for $60-$400. You can also order many brides' and bridesmaids' gowns. There are 3 experts available to do alterations.
	Call and make an appointment, available six days a week, Tuesday through Sunday. They will gladly make appointments on weekdays up till 7pm, with the last one on Saturdays and Sundays no later than 4pm. Payment in full must be made at the time of purchase.
	CONSIGNOR ALERT: 50%-50%, 12 mos. exclusive contract. No fee. Gown must be cleaned before they will accept it ($40-$60).

The Encore

7607 Ogontz Ave.
Phila., PA 19150
927-4110

Look: HO HUM

Goods: HO HUM -
CLASS ACT

Prices: LOW –
MODERATE

HOURS:
Mon–Sat 11-5

CLOSED: July 4 –
Labor Day

Cars drive by too fast, playing music too loud, on streets that are littered and bubbling with heat. What am I doing here? Can't find the store. I have the address. It should be right here. It isn't. Try again. Oops, small trees hide the sign. After leapfrogging a van backed up on the sidewalk, I'm greeted by a dead-ringer for Leona Helmsley. What on earth is 'she' doing here? Must have left her white gloves at the hotel. The van is here because the store's being emptied. Everything is headed to a charity thrift store in another part of town to make room for fall consignments. Overcoming the incongruous sight of the regal Leona amid such surroundings, I am further shocked to discover Rittenhouse Square-caliber labels awaiting their final, less than limo, ride. How does she get Rittenhouse types to consign here?

Tripping over hangers and clothing scattered all over the filthy floor, struggling to make a look-see space on the rack, and losing the struggle, I have a second-by-second Maniac stack attack. Mixed in with the stained, torn, moth-nibbled and trampled are **more good labels in good condition for unbelievably lower prices** than some tony stores in litter-free neighborhoods. The "dressing room" is in a mirrored corner of the shop, completely hemmed in by racks of men's clothing. I have to push and shove my way in. Fortunately no man comes in during my dressing room duress. Emerging from a très intimate half hour spent with Anne Klein, Carol Horn, Vittadini, Sonya Rykiel, etc. etc. etc., I am exhausted. It's like changing clothes in a meditation tank, wearing a straitjacket while wrestling an alligator. But I emerged victorious. The Sonia Rykiel blue and black velour cardigan, $15, a purple Vittadini cotton shell, trimed in lace and ribbon, $7, and a pair of unworn Unisa black suede flats for Morgan, $12, are all mine. I'd hate to see this place made into yet another lace-hung yawn, but really darling...

CONSIGNOR ALERT: 50%-50% split. No fee. No appointment. Unlimited items.

Fabulous Finds

12th & McKean
Phila., PA 19148
336-5226

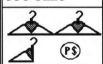

Look: STATUS QUO

Goods: STATUS QUO

Prices: LOW –
MODERATE

HOURS: Tue–Fri
10:30-5:30,
Sat 10-3

CLOSED: August,
except Fri & Sat
10:30-3:30

Requisite sneakers hung from telephone lines. Newly requisite burglar alarm signs prominently displayed in every lower, right hand corner of the front windows, competing with traditional statuary, plastic flowers and overblown lamps. Women called upon each other, climbing scrubbed granite gray steps, knocking on enormously overscaled front doors of the stucco and brick-facing row house city within a city, seeking fresh coffee and fresher gossip. Men hunched over steaming take-out cups and shifted from one leg to the other trying to keep warm, hanging out on the corner in a hardier, outdoor version of the same time-honored pursuit. Others scurried by, pushing wailing babies in carriages or dragging squeaky wheeled shopping carts on their way to market. So begins another day in South Philly.

So too, another day at Fabulous Finds. The owner fed and hushed her hunger-cranky baby behind the register. The shop assistant tidied up from the previous day's business. Early customers were already working the racks. The current generation of the big hair crowd and their now more conservative, but once beehived moms will find just what they need to keep up with the latest South Philly look. From the linoleum-lined, combination bargain basement and fully functional kitchen/ laundry area, up the stairs past kiddie's and mom's, outside to the display-strewn sidewalk, crowding the front steps with bowling balls, kids toys and exercise equipment, **it's a neighborhood corner store in the middle of The Neighborhood**

CONSIGNOR ALERT: 50%-50% split. $2.50 fee/25 items.60 days. By appointment only.

## Federation Thrift Shop 1213 Walnut St. Phila., PA 19107 **922-9526**  **Look:** BOTTOM FEEDER **Goods:** DOWN & OUT –TOP DRAWER **Prices:** LOW–HIGH **HOURS:** Mon–Fri 10-5 **CLOSED:** Jewish holidays, 4th week of July, 1st week of August	🖐 📠 CC L P$ The burning question haunted countless center-city and suburban foodies for years? Would the Reading Terminal become a soulless plaything of marketing mavens and transient conventioneers? We held our collective garlic breath as the drama unfolded. After much hand-wringing and political in-fighting, we have the answer. The Terminal, a venerable institution to generations of Philadelphians, including my own family, has miraculously survived renovation hell, unscathed. Federation has not been so lucky. I had favorably compared the Federation's busy lunchtime crowd to that of the Terminal. Not so anymore. What is going on here? I realize all too well that inevitable changes are afoot in charity resale. The burgeoning boutique resale and consignment industry has siphoned off countless would-be donations. Consumers want more bang for their buck. Is management here trying to compete? If so, this was a case of good idea, bad follow-through. Upstairs at the bins, shoppers were ferociously intent on grabbing up purposely torn and rent manufacturer samples. The original, famous backroom is boarded up, relocated to the the vast, dirty, mercifully dark basement, partially elbowing out what was once a fabulous secondhand furniture department. Snaking lines of competitive lunchtime crowds are gone, replaced by dazed and disgruntled shoppers. Downstairs the clothing is overpriced, tired, often stained and frequently punctuated by moth holes. One shopper, identifying herself as an AIDS hospice volunteer, thrust a garment at a bewildered Federation volunteer and insisted it be removed from the racks, pointing out that moths in the garment would spread. The ROI of these munching freeloaders beat out the two-legged variety, wings down . **CONSIGNOR ALERT:** 50%-50% split. No fee. By appointment only.
## Fight For Sight 2027 Sansom St. Phila., PA 19103 **561-0549** **Look:** DOWN & OUT **Goods:** DOWN & OUT–STATUS QUO **Prices:** LOW – HIGH **HOURS:** Mon–Fri 10-4, Sat 10-2 **CLOSED:** Last two weeks of July and first two weeks of August	 No sign, no street address, no prices ticketed or even posted, except for neckties, $1. Progress here is glacial. But in spite of the unnecessarily obscured location, obscure appearance, absence of price tags, I am happy to report a modest organizational kick in the secondhand polyester pants has occurred. The place is cleaner. Our Mayor must have been by with the mop and bucket brigade. Thank you, Ed. Inventory is another matter altogether. I am loathe to give a DOWN & OUT rating to any store, especially one which is charity driven, even more especially one that benefits children, but, there's no getting around it. With all due respect for intentions and charitable goodwill, no one would fight over most of the merchandise. It has the appeal of the tail end of a well picked-over tag sale that was slim pickings from the beginning. The people who manage this place should get out and about, check out the serious competition, hold brainstorming sessions, hire a new and proven manager, or Jimmy Carter to do some rehab, whatever it takes. They need their spiritual vision checked. Surely the children's clinic of Wills Eye Hospital will ultimately benefit if these observations and suggestions improve their (non)profit margin to contribute toward acutely needed research and surgery. While the **occasional furniture find** might induce a scuffle or two, the only fight worth fighting here is the one that would occur if and when Wills Eye volunteer powers-that-be take a stand and become ready, willing and able to get this place out of the bargain basement of Center City thrift shops. Where there's a will there's a way. **CONSIGNOR ALERT:** Donations only. Benefits Children's Clinic of Wills Eye Hospital.

Good, Better, Best	
511-517 S. 21 St. Phila., PA 19146 **545-2978** 	White oil cloth protected by a clear plastic sheet, carefully spread over the long table. Places set for lunch, food cooking on the stove. Women workers, all in white uniforms (from Coopers', no doubt) bustled around the kitchen, set off from the selling floor by an expanding accordion-style gate, usually used to keep small children from straying, but here corralling an agressive, barrel-chested chihuahua (honest). What have we got here? Father Divine's dwindling, geriatric empire, located in the basement of Unity Mission Church Annex under the huge slate steps, and where they answer the phone with "Peace."
Look: Basement HO HUM **Goods:** HO HUM– STATUS QUO **Prices:** LOW-HIGH	Jammed with **furniture on a scale, and of a quality and style to put me in mind of Rittenhouse Square** condominium and apartment buildings back in the 60s. A custom-made cherry-wood bookcase cum entertainment center cum bar, at least 16' long and 10' high, $1,000. (These ladies aren't shy about pricing.) A queen size poster bed waiting for Doris Day and The Rock, $250. Pink, marbelized formica, rectangular dining room table, $40, a glossy pink laminate, wedge-shapped end table, $30, a peach-color formica kitchen cabinet, $30. Lots and lots of worth-a-
HOURS: Mon–Fri 10-6, Sat 10-3	glance household items and **books and records**, an unpriced, early Polaroid camera, and mostly forgettable clothing, including large assortments of dated shoes and pocketbooks that will probably be here long enough to become vintage.
CLOSED: Holidays	I made my way to the door. A lyrical voice with a magical quality, belonging to one of the stooped-over ladies in white, wished me "a good day and many of God's blessing," while the taped voices of the discordant Rosebud choir (I asked) lurched toward their greater reward. **CONSIGNOR ALERT:** Donations only. Benefits the Unity Mission Church Annex.
Hangers	
1953 Locust St. Phila., PA 19103 **854-0100** **IN A CLASS BY ITSELF!** 	Stroll by and you'd never know... walk in and you'd never know... glance at the racks and still you'd never know....Architecture, decor and clientele are the height of **drop-dead Center City chic.** Names on the labels and prices on the tags are, too. Did you find Nan Duskin intimidating? Or was it home away from home? Would you like to have moved in , but couldn't afford it? Come on in, kick off your Ferragamos and join Duskin's "slumming" former clientele and their "castoffs." Floor-to-ceiling white, white walls and classic columns. Wall-to-wall banker's grey hush leading up steps to (gasp!) a communal dressing room. Hangers' softly selling owner and staff hover in the narrow entrance way. There is no door or curtain, while you're half-naked in a room full of mirrors, bulges and strangers. Wear undies. Silk only, please!
Look: TOP DRAWER **Goods:** TOP DRAWER **Prices:** HIGH–NOSEBLEED	If labels in these clothes could turn into the designers who fashioned them, and the consigning owners magically flesh out their own garments, you'd find yourself mingling in the midst of an international jet-setter's soiree. Champagne, anyone? In Waterford, of course. A most reassuring place to take immodest thrift shop virgins or those with full wallets, high fashion sense and no time or inclination for less. **Hangers is in a class by itself.** Including it would have thoroughly skewed these rat-
HOURS: Tue–Sat 10:30-6	ings in a manner that would have been unfair both to Hangers and their competition. **This is as good as it gets. It's also as expensive as it gets. (I hope.)**
CLOSED: Holidays	**P.S. Featured on Home Matters on the Discovery Channel.** I took the host, Susan Powell, a former Miss America "thrifting" here. She loooved it. **CONSIGNOR ALERT:** 50%-50% split. No fee. 11:30-4:30 Tuesday–Saturday. Call first.

Immortal

125
S. 18th St. 2nd Fl.
Phila., PA 19103
563-2344

**Undergoing a
transition.**
 (P$)

Look: TOP DRAWER

Goods: CLASS ACT
– TOP DRAWER

Prices: MODERATE
– HIGH

HOURS:
Mon–Sat 11-6

CLOSED: Holidays

They say you've gotta have a gimmick, and Designer Consignor had a good one. But gimmicks, by their very nature, come and go, quickly. Kiki Olsen, between flights to Rio and Paris and videotapings for the talk-show circuit in New York, was the gimmick, when she was in town, which wasn't often. Climb up the step-aerobic staircase to this elegant little Rittenhouse Square perch, and you just might have caught a glimpse of Ms. Olsen peering at you through a monacle and sporting a parrot-green feathered, 50's chapeau that bobbed and weaved, mimicking her every move. And she made a lot of moves. One of them was to buy out Designer Consignor's original owner and install herself, while keeping Susan, the store's original manager to day-in and day-out run the show. Well, Kiki has made another of her many (predictable) moves...out of the resale biz.

Susan, God bless her, has "outlived" 'em all. She and a business pal, the former owner of She's Gotta Have It in Manayunk, (bought out and renamed by Wear It Again Sam's owner Kelley, but that's another story on another page), just agreed to an over-time **buy out of Kiki's Designer Consignor.** New, but hardly green, they are bursting at their secondhand seams waiting until the January takeover. The Immortals want to try out their own concept "wings." Gotta-have-a-gimmicks like: live modeling in the enormous sun-drenched, second story bay window; private wine and cheese after hours; invitation only, secondhand shopping parties for small corporate and social group; selling local vintage retro designs and offering personalized shopping. Good luck, ladies. That's one hell of a name to live up to.
PS. Voted <u>Philadelphia Magazine's</u> Best Thrift Shop for 1993.
CONSIGNOR ALERT: 50%-50% split. No fee. No appointment. Call first.

Jellybeans

505 Fitzwater St.
Phila., PA 19147
440-0123

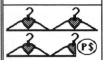

Look: STATUS QUO

Goods: HO HUM–
TOP DRAWER

Prices: LOW–
MODERATE

HOURS:
Thu–Sat 10:30-5:30
Till 3:30 from
January-March

CLOSED: Holidays

I just couldn't seem to get my sticky fingers into this candy jar. I can't tell you how many times I tried. Hours weren't posted. I called, no answer. Finally someone answered and explained they were only open three days a week. That explains it. I grabbed Morgan's hand and off we flew, burbs to berg in 20 flat. After a yummy turkey sandwich and best-ever French fries at Famous, we strolled down Fifth St. and - did Our Girl Thing. It was time for dessert.

We prowled, we poked, we pushed, we pulled, we hemmed, we hawed, we grabbed and we giggled our way through the colorful, rumpled place. We had a little competition. A blonde bambina with bouncy ringletts, excellent elocution and precise diction kept requiring Morgan's help. She poked through the 50% off rack of size 10 and 12 and 14 jeans (now $2.50), tops (now $1-2) and dresses ($4), playing a well-practiced version of pay-attention-to-me-NOW-peek-a-boo. If Morgan held something in her hands, that was The Thing worth seeing RIGHT NOW. I saw lots worth having RIGHT NOW too, especially **little kid's clothing, baby furniture** and **equipment**, especially since we just learned Marvin's 24 year old Erica is pregnant. She might like one of the many stacked and piled cribs, or have a hard time choosing from a lineup of thirteen car seats and swing seats, two sassy seats and two high chairs (the one still in the box was $45), a Cookie Monster back of Dad's or Mom's bike seat, a Little Tykes two-seater boat swing, and two pair of Micky and Minnie slippers, $4.50 each. A Drevi Paloma changing table, $115, was parked near a lineup of big kids two-wheelers. Only yesterday Erica was 10. Going from peek a boo to Look Ma, No hands, to Look Dad, I'm pregnant! Doesn't take long, does it.
CONSIGNOR ALERT: 40%-60% split. No fee. No appointment necessary, call ahead.

New To Nearly New (& Man to Man)	
2008 Walnut St. Phila. PA 19103 **496-9348** 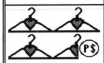	Moving day. Katie and crew rolled the metal clothing racks right down Walnut Street. Two shake, rattle, and roll blocks later, they had relocated from the commercial edge of town to just inside a Center City shopper's inner circle. What a difference two blocks can make! Foot traffic has picked up exponentially. And feet are shod in heels **and** wing tips. Husband and wife, co-workers, girlfriend and boyfriend, boyfriend and boyfriend, girlfriend and girlfriend, whatever your taste or inclination, now you can shop here together. Man To Man and New To Nearly New now share the same space.
Look: CLASS ACT **Goods:** STATUS QUO-TOP DRAWER **Prices:** MODERATE	Thrifty men have had it rough. Guys don't buy as much, and what they do buy they all too often wear out or hold onto so long, we're talking Nehru jackets, moth holes, elbow patches and Columbo raincoats. Guys, shop here, and your ROI will be bullish. They **have a stylish assortment of everything the well-dressed man could want.** I like this place. I go whenever I venture downtown with time to spare. A little dark, a little crowded, but overall very pleasing. It's got a **good range of women's** clothing, shown to advantage in the lace-draped front window. As a morning person, I sometimes get faked out when I forget they open at 11am, a half to full hour later than many surrounding shops. It's so good, I do other errands and return here before leaving for home.
HOURS: Mon–Sat 11-6	☞ **SHOPPER ALERT:** Women's evening and office wear .
CLOSED: Holidays	**CONSIGNOR ALERT:** Annual Fee of $5 with a 50-50% split. No appointment necessary

ORT Value Center	
29 S. 19th St. Phila., PA 19103 **563-2377** 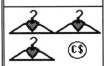	Here you'll find all the warmth and good attention you'd get going to Grandma's house for Shabbos dinner. You can almost smell the matzoh ball soup simmering on the back of some imaginary stove. A clutch of volunteers who appear to be longtime friends gather near the register and kibbitz. Over 20 years of mitzvot (that's Hebrew for good deeds) have kept this happy little place prospering.
Look: STATUS QUO **Goods:** HO HUM - CLASS ACT **Prices:** LOW - MODERATE	Nothing big or heavy sold here, as the staff wouldn't be able to move it around easily and space is limited. Silver, linens, lace and jewelry are all kept behind sliding glass doors, some locked and some not. Lots of chachas (that's Gentile for chachkas) up on the shelves. The overall quality of the shop is consistent yard sale/spring cleaning with **some real treasures** mixed in. Collectors of all things **Vintage** might check out the very small, but **occasionally designer level**, rack. One HOT pink shantung, sweeping-the-floor-length evening coat with all but the beribboned bodice cut away in the front, took my breath away. Jackie Kennedy and Audrey Hepburn came alive for an instant.
HOURS: Mon, Tue, Thu, Fri 10-4:45, Wed 9:30-5:15	**P.S.** They won't accept bills larger than $20. Color-coded tags indicate 50% off.
CLOSED: 2 weeks in August. Call first.	**CONSIGNOR ALERT:** Donations only.

PA Hospital Bargain Shop	
719 Delancey St. Phila., PA 19106 **829-3497**	Yes, it is clean and well organized. Yes, the sun was shining in. Yes, they had classical music on the radio. Yes, the **volunteers were friendly** and forthcoming. Yes, everything is **very inexpensive**. But no, there was nothing to buy. Nothing fashionable, that is. Well, there was a kelly green, cotton Laura Ashley in very good condition for $5, but it was for a young teen. That ain't me.
Look: STATUS QUO **Goods:** HO HUM – STATUS QUO **Prices:** LOW	t's just that I would feel fashionably depressed if this was where I HAD to come to shop. Everything was so clean, organized, inexpensive and forgettable. Lots of white nurse's uniforms....wonder where they came from?

I listened to a few more bars of music and walked back outside into the thin November sunshine. Falling autumn leaves floated by. |
| **HOURS:** Mon–Fri 10-4:30 | |
| **CLOSED:** Mid-July to late August | **CONSIGNOR ALERT:** Donations can be made beginning at 9:30am. Benefits Pennsylvania Hospital |

Salvation Army	
2140 Market St. Phila., PA **567-9734**	If you live or work in Center City, you've probably passed by this corner landmark almost every day. Big glass windows usually have stuff hung askew as an example of one of the earliest forms of marketing known to man (or woman). Managers probably went to business school back when the wall peg was invented, predating the invention of mannequins. Clumsy attempts at window dressing had been just one more pre-thrifting reason for me to avoid going inside. (Dirty windows were another.) It always looked sooo, well you know, so unappealing.
Look: BOTTOMFEEDER **Goods:** HO HUM – CLASS ACT **Prices:** LOW	But as my mania progressed, I finally began to wander in from time to time, often during the lunch hour, and roam through the two-floors-big shop, munching on some take-out treat or another. The basement here is a place to frequent if you're in the market for **furniture**, taking weekly, even daily excursions if you have the time. The more often you drop into a bottomfeeder, the better your ROI. They're so big. Daily they move so much in and move so much out, that the turnover (and the competition) is fast and furious. You never know what you might be missing (or who you'll bump into on their lunch hour.)
HOURS: Mon, Tue & Sat 9-5, Wed–Fri 9-6	
CLOSED: Holidays	**CONSIGNOR ALERT:** Donations only.

Season to Season	
1535 S. Broad St. Phila., PA 19147 **755-3794** 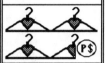 **Look:** CLASS ACT **Goods:** STATUS QUO **Prices:** LOW–MODERATE **HOURS:** Tue–Fri 12-5:30, Sat 12-4 **CLOSED:** Mid August–mid Sept.	**Ladies, size 10 and under, read this review.** Just as a pet's character and personality come to match the owner's, so too a secondhand store's. Lorraine, the dainty blondish owner of Season to Season, located deep in the heart of South Philly's double-parked Broad Street, has selected and designed an equally dainty shop to reflect her diminutive size, high fashion taste and neighborhood inflection. Distant soul sister to Merel's in the equally far Northeast, it offers garments and accessories ranged in quality all the way from DKNY and Carol Horn, etc. for the moms to brand new Bellini shoestore close-outs for tots down to a few mall-crawler gum-snapper/wrapper-tight duds for teens. Even though portions were skimpy, so to speak, there was significantly more food than fodder. It's a **very pretty little place** with a **pleasant owner**, fresh coat of paint, new carpet and new fixtures. There is no dressing room, but there is a mirror covered door. Children's sizes, mostly girls, mirror Mom's choices in quality and price, up to size 12. Petites, attracted by the **riveting front window** dressed with sixes to the nines, all in stunning black and white, will only be able to manage with a struggle merchandise provocatively suspended from second-tier racks mounted 8 feet off the floor. Unsolicited advice? Bag boy's and men's, which are almost nonexistent anyway, increase womens' size range, or focus, and become the region's first "petite only" resale store on purpose, rather than by default. Big time success is tantalizingly close, but just out of reach. **CONSIGNOR ALERT:** 50%-50% split. $3 annual fee. 60 days. By appointment.

Second Chance	
927 Walnut St. Phila., PA 19107 **627-4416** 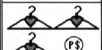 **Look:** STATUS QUO **Goods:** STATUS QUO - CLASS ACT **Prices:** RISING **HOURS:** Mon-Fri 10:30-5:30 Sat 12-5 **CLOSED:** Holidays	Stand outside the store and you can spend 10 minutes just figuring out what's in the **front window, which holds more worthwhile merchandise than some stores offer on their entire selling floor.** And indeed that's just what many weary SEPTA travelers stationed just outside do to pass the time. Whether or not you miss the bus, don't miss the shop. Drop in this place by parachute or use an enormous shoehorn to squeeze inside. Early rat-packers-died-and-gone-to-heaven motif CRAMMED WITH GOODIES. Only one person can fit between the racks. Shove and drag the squealing, screeching wire hangers across the metal racks to get at the stuff. This is strictly a no passing zone, but definitely STOP. Every clothing label ever issued winds up consigned here sooner or later. I saw my first Made in Finland garment label. I also saw the employees previewing the consignments with an eye to expanding their own wardrobes. He liked the furry mohair sweater. **P.S.** Ask to look at the **TOP DRAWER** goodies stashed behind the front counter. **CONSIGNOR ALERT:** 50%-50% split. No fee. 6 mos. By appointment.

The Second Mile	
210-16 S. 45th St. Phila., PA 19104 **662-1663** **Look:** BOTTOM FEEDER **Goods:** HO HUM – TOP DRAWER **Prices:** VERY LOW **HOURS:** Mon–Fri 10-6 Sat 9:30-5 **CLOSED:** Holidays	One of many bits of New Age trivia picked up from my dear ex-hippie, healer hubby is the notion of negative ions. They are in the air. They are good for you. They have a calming effect. The more moisture in the air, the more ions. Waterfalls are great places to experience the 'bennies' of increased ions. The Second Mile must have lots of ions in the air. I experienced a beneficial calming effect the moment I got in the door. Took a while for me to catch on. I was being affectionately brainwashed by soaring music, the kind that is music first, religious second. So pleasant I didn't mind, unlike similar attempted conversion by audio and visual overload. Listen up American Family Services. Can't remember the last time I experienced such **genuinely thoughtful service.** Staff were human beings in the way American Indians use the term, Christians the way Christ would've wanted. Too many of us have lost our humaness these days. Not these folks. They hum the tune and walk the walk. They helped with customer's children. Carried bags to the car. Calm and unfazed, they went out of their way to anticipate what we needed, then did it. **Three separate stores** here: **1)** Books and anything electronic, **2)** clothing and furniture, **3)** everything else. On my first visit, everything else was closed. I thought it was an antique shop, and gave it no mind. Imagine my pleasure on the second visit to find **so many useful, inexpensive, lovely things.** The 214 shop uses red, blue and green ink on the price tags to keep track of markdowns, which change every Saturday. **2)** Larger, more utilitarian looking shop, has color-coordinated clothing and lots of mostly scruffy furniture. A swell Calvin Klein charcoal grey dress, a Jessica McClintock nightgown, never worn satin and lace, a Nancy Heller linen peach coatdress with shell buttons. Each $7.50. Men's had labels like Gap, L.L. Bean and Polo. **1)** Not to be mistaken for #1, is good at books, poor at electronics. Too dated, unless you're a mad engineer and rob them for parts. Even then... **CONSIGNOR ALERT:** Donations only.

Seconds on South	
1745 South St. Phila., PA 19146 **546-0612** **Look:** STATUS QUO **Goods:** HO HUM– CLASS ACT **Prices:** LOW **HOURS:** Mon–Fri 11-6, Sat 10-3 **CLOSED:** May close Sat in summer	She was wondering outloud if she could get the local meter maid to fix a ticket. I began wondering to myself if I had put enough money in the meter. She was unpacking the latest grocery bag full of donations. From the back (my viewpoint) it looked like any other used white T. She dropped it in horror. "What would organ donors think?" Surprise! It had a three-dimensional, not-so-still-life, soft-molded plastic rendering of in-living-color internal organs quivering on the front. I suggested she place it in the window for Halloween. She dumped the offending shirt in the discard bag, lowering her eyes from mine, disgust curling around the edges of her mouth. I guess my sense of eyecatching window-display humor is not for everyone. It's all a matter of perspective. Jaeger, C. & A. Kleins, Talbot, Ungarro, Lauren, St. Laurent and Gap schlepped in by the bag and bundle by hospital staff members and their mates. **If they stick with it and play it smart, this could become a great thrift store.** So far, clothing inventory, quality and prices are as good as or better than Thrift for AIDS, but space is tight, their housewares are pitiful, and they're at the wrong end of South St. They lack sufficient and suitable racks and bins. Volunteers grumble about how we're messing up the place after they've just straightened it. Welcome to housekeeping, boys and girls. Other stores, dying for lack of a customer base, should be so lucky. Rumor has it they may be moving to bigger, better digs. Me, too. **CONSIGNOR ALERT:** Donations only. Benefits Graduate Hospital community clinic and ambulatory care program.

Sophisticated Seconds

110 S. 20th St.
Phila., PA 19103

561-6740

Look: TOP DRAWER
Goods: CLASS
ACT–TOP DRAWER
Prices:
MODERATE–HIGH

HOURS: Mon, Tue
Thu–Sat 10-6,
Wed 10-8

CLOSED: Holidays.
2 weeks in summer.
Call ahead.

Bursting with the enthusiasm of a beauty still in her 20's, but already a wary veteran of the Philly rag biz, Valorie has not prematurely lost her taste or inspiration for The Scene. She has held tight to her vision nurtured at Mom's knee, tested in the career-strewn "who-knows-whom, capped-teeth-shark-smile-to-the-face-and-silver-knife-in-the-back" fashion scene, and honed in her first year as resale shopkeeper. Her unique and powerful concept--to open and operate the first chic, resale only, department store on Rittenhouse Square, is reality. Valorie is well on her way. Dad is too. On his way out. All those chic print ads she's run all over town, announcing her fabulous duds, have been luring the secondhand shoppers in droves.

Daddy made room for his entrepreneurially expanding girl, by signing over the first floor (eventually all?) of his successful law-office building, so Valorie could expand her energetic empire. Now Daddy's business is being crowded out. Predictably, push will come to shove. Will Daddy be the one to go, or will Valorie take that next step, realizing her Boyd's and Duskin dream, secondhand? An elevator, à la Boyd's, slices through the heart of the shop. Customers shuttle fhrough four floors of fabulous resale. From the **intimately tasteful, overwhelmingly high style**, women's only first floor, to the winsome, helpful blonde sitting at the very top, meeting and greeting **male customers, who are obviously surprised and awed by the vast range and quality of international duds.** Back on the first floor, the enormous streetside window frames a peaceful salon oasis. Evening and bridal gown department are up on Two, please. Wine, anyone? Or creme de la creme in your coffee? **Watch out Hangers, she's a comer**
CONSIGNOR ALERT: 50%-50%. No Fee. No appointment. Will come to you.

Toviah Thrift Shop

4211 Chestnut St.
Phila., PA 19104

382-7251

Look: DOWN & OUT

Goods: DOWN & OUT–
STATUS QUO

Prices: LOW

HOURS:
Mon–Sat 10-5

CLOSED: Christmas
–New Years Day

The relentless sun, like some housekeeping inspector general, poured through the enormous, Windex-free window and fixed its relentless x-ray vision upon every spot and stain and smudge. Half-used **books**, half very used stuff, altogether a small, smelly, dirty shop on the verge of chaos. Book-half more organized than stuff-half. **Possibly worth a curious collector's look-see.** Stuff half could contain the occasional find. Stylishly shaded woman's vintage beaver coat, collar and shoulders of dark fur, opening to alternating, splayed fingers of light and dark fur pointing toward the hem. Ice skates and winter boots piled on kids' and women's shoes in a heap on the floor. Cockeyed wire hangers with musty, stained clothing, dangling half on, half off. Rare finds to real vintage to recent duds thrown together at the very bottom at the very end of the last stop on the retail chain. A flower-encrusted lid from some long lost Italian faience handpainted cachepot, its linger-ling quality shining through amidst the broken bits of household castoffs. A set of four matching chair pads, still shiney chintz floral, snatched up by a family on a shopping expedition.

A busy duo worked feverishly amidst the mountains of discombobulation piled over, behind and around the counter, busy hands keeping rythm with chattering mouths. No matter how hard and happily they worked, they didn't make a dent. The store benefits a religiously affiliated school. Let's hope classrooms are cleaner and better organized than the thrift shop. But learning, like bargains, can happen anywhere, under any condition. You just have to have an open mind. (Not, necessarily, a clean one.)
CONSIGNOR ALERT: Donations only.

Thrift for AIDS	
629--635 South St. Phila., PA 19147 **592-9014** (info) **592-4327** (store) **Look:** BOUTIIQUE BOTTOMFEEDER **Goods:** HO HUM – CLASS ACT **Prices:** VERY LOW **HOURS:** Mon–Thu 12-9, Fri & Sat 12-10, Sun 12-9 **CLOSED:** Holidays	Formerly housed in the protective shadow of The Book Trader, Thrift For AIDS has moved around the corner and up South Street to the old, but still glamorous Berkowitz building, once home to one of Philadelphia's more successful, now defunct, dress shops. Thrift For AIDS ultimately oozed their overdonated (can there be such a thing) overstock next-door, taking over 635 as well. In just two years they have grown from a side-street cubbyhole into **Center City's premiere, thrift department store** sharing an adjoining wall and high energy marketing force field. Grand dame Berkowitz's drop-dead grand entrance stairway and enormous expanse of open-book bay windows showcase whimsical to outrageous to superb household goods and furniture. I'm Too Sexy For My Cothes are all that's sold next door at 635, where the neon night scene has equally fantastic window displays. Great music and a great sound system throb through the floors, the walls and the customers. A phalanx of volunteers, some friendlier and more helpful than others, man and woman the counters and stalk the floors of intimate-vision-gone-big-business. Little burb girls with too-dark lip-liner pouts, snap gum and egg each other on to buy the next "Oh it's so cute" requisite ugly-duckling garment. Burb parents come to gape, then surprise themselves by actually finding something to buy. Center city types take it all in stride and just plain shop. **There is truly something for everyone here, and at fair market value.** An Ellen West cotton summer dress, $5, pedestrian-stopping, modern black armless chair and ottoman displayed in the window, big baggy refugee colored sweaters and worn torn jeans, classic wedding dresses, teapots, cookie jars, old records, new Polo trousers. Come, take in the scene and nose-ring around. **It's as good as a nightclub and a lot cheaper.** **CONSIGNOR ALERT:** Donations Only

Time Zone	
535 South St. Phila., PA 19147 **592-8266** **Look:** TOP DRAWER **Goods:** CLASS ACT **Prices:** HIGH **HOURS:** Mon–Fri 12-10, Sat 11-10, Sun 12-8 **CLOSED:** Holidays	Cool begat hip, which begat far out, which begat awesome, which begat 'way cool,' which begat Time Zone. **Very South Street, very expensive, young retro-rethinkers merchandising** clunky waif, bebop, hippie dippie retread threads. What's old is new, what's new is old hat. New is priced appropriately, old is overpriced, all of it is overrated. Kind of like a one stop how-to manual on being down or having your own urban ghetto persona-shopper. A colorful South Street tourist trap with, I predict, a predictably short life span, they are making their concept money while they can. I can already see them trying to figure when to grab the next marketing wave. Overheard among the racks, "In retail you can expect to have one sold, one stolen and one unsold." I say, "In resale, you can expect one to open, one to close and one to keep." **CONSIGNOR ALERT:** Buys, sells, trades.

Venus in Furs	
1004 Pine St. Phila., PA 19107 **922-8887** **Look:** TOP DRAWER **Goods:** STATUS QUO - TOP DRAWER **Prices:** MODERATE **HOURS:** Mon–Sat 12-6, Sun 1-5 **CLOSED:** Holidays	About 7 seconds before going to print last year, this shop changed its name from Something Blue (someting old, something new, something borrowed, something swapped?) to Venus in Furs, an absolutely outrageous name. Brings to mind extravagantly sensuous images does it not? No, this is not a secondhand fur store. While vivid, the name is a provocative misnomer, although they do carry a few vintage furs. **A really pretty store, really.** Tin ceiling and twinkle lights, faded 40's fabric, movie star pictures stapled all over the walls, a squishy-soft sofa with pillow overflow in the front bay window. Lime-green, gold and turquoise sheaths shimmer on the walls to the driving rhythm of cutting-edge music. Dance out the door wearing any pair of platform shoes in the place, $30. Would like to see the hours posted somewhere, anywhere! The business card, the window, the door. Came by a couple of times midday, nobody home. No note on the door saying when they would return. When I did get in, the salesperson answered my questions, nothing more, nothing less. Another visit, another mood-- two guys, very playful, very kind, bantered and bargained with Marvin the entire time we were there. **CONSIGNOR ALERT: This shop swaps and trades up.** They only buy outright once in a while. Bring your 40's, thru 70's overflow and strike a deal. Only God and her accountant know how they stay in business this way.

Village Thrift	
5741 N. Broad St. Phila., PA 19141 **No phone #** 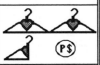 **Look:** BOTTOMFEEDER **Goods:** DOWN & OUT - CLASS ACT **Prices:** LOW **HOURS:** Mon–Fri 9-9, Sat 9-6, Sun 10-5 **CLOSED:** Never	Half again as small as the Germantown Village Thrift, which is half again as small as the Village Thrift in Pennsauken (read the Pennsauken review for the lowdown on all three), which is the mother of them all. All are worth a stop if you're in their neighborhood, but Pennsauken is worth the trip even if you're not, if only because it's gigantic, thereby greatly increasing your ROI. **Remember.** To keep bottomfeeding rewarding, you must play time against find. If you've spent hours and hours of your valuable time in one of these less than esthetic environments and you keep coming away empty handed, either the shop's pull of 'donations (?)' doesn't work for you or you're just not a bottomfeeder at heart. Solution? Give it up. Move up the food chain. Try church basement thrift shops or the huge, ever-growing pool of neighborhood three-hangers. Not everyone is built to bottomfeed. Some of us like the filtered sunlight midway, some of us like to skim plankton at the surface. Me? Never met a thrift shop I didn't like, going up or coming down. **Pssst!** Two additional unreviewed locations: 917 W. Lehigh Ave. and 2917 Kensington Ave. **CONSIGNOR ALERT:** Curiouser and curiouser.

TOUR #2
THE GREATER, AND IN SOME WAYS LESSER NORTHEAST.

I'm told by a dear friend, who lived in the area as a child, that as recently as 1949, cows grazed at what would eventually become Cottman and Bustleton. Now the only "silo" in sight hawks TVs and refrigerators. The postwar baby boom generation became fruitful and multiplied (only to subtract and divide decades later). They needed housing. They set to work, plowing under, one by one, the once vast, undeveloped land resource of dairies and farms, planting rows of developments and fields of blacktopped shopping centers instead. It was touted as the latest innovation in crop rotation to date. The automobile and the elevated extended everyone's range of work and play. Long-time residents said bye-bye **Kensington** and **Frankford** and hello **Burholme, Fox Chase** and **Mayfair**, if not to Rockledge just over the county line. They migrated north and west to the promised land, and the dream of a white-picket cottage in the burbs. So, O.K., it was really a row house just like every other, all in a row, and the fence was chain link. But there were trees and grass and, even for a while, fresh air.

The old neighborhood held on for a long time. Now it's holding on for dear life. The **Frankford** shopping district, locally referred to as Under the El, flourished, then floundered as the blight of Center City drug addiction and crime gradually migrated north. (Are we beginning to see a trend here?) Roaming the Avenue, warily casting a city survivor's glance about me as I go, I take in the boarded-up shops, the litter, the vile crack vials, the homeless vagrants, viable businesses huddled behind roll-up metal grates and window bars. Blown and scattered outside the newly opened Pearl Nail Salon, left over from Chinese Year of The Pig celebrations, Tiger Head firecracker wrappers are colorful, welcome litter by contrast to unmentionable flotsam and jetsam found at the curb and just inside boarded-up doorways.

Signs of life? Workmen paint a fresh mural of vegetables and fruit over the white plaster facade of a market. Second visit? Trash swept away. The new roving police station on wheels is parked at the curb at Oxford & Frankford. Standing in the shadow of the El, The Mayor's Action Committee office is a symbolic, if not active (depends on who you ask), commitment to a promise of better days to come. Perhaps as part of that promise, the El is getting a face-lift. Workmen scamper up and down a two-story yellow ladder on wheels, applying a happy new coat of robin's egg blue paint to the rusty, dusty old gal. Unfamiliar with the neighborhood sights and sounds, when a train actually rumbles by overhead, I automatically flinch from its flickering shadow, ducking for safety.

The chimera of safety appears exponentially assured the farther north you travel up Frankford Avenue or Roosevelt Boulevard. The **Mayfair Diner** promises and delivers hefty portions of comfort food. Crossing guards stand as timeless, reassuring sentinels, waving their white-gloved hands to pass on the next-generation flock of schoolchildren. Litter is all but banished. The pretzel man hustles his traditional wares in heavy traffic. School lets out. Big kids flood out the door and down the steps of Northeast High, heading home. Cars jam the lot at Roosevelt Mall.

Stop in at **Wanamaker's**. Did I really say that? Heresy you say. No, not at all. Even though it's hardly thrift, it can be very thrifty in the slightly manhandled, and thereby secondhand, furniture bargain basement. Check it out. There's clothing, too. Mostly buyers' nightmares, and a few finds. Remember, I'm a nondenominational shopper. Everything from trash to Saks. That's my motto. This is just one more stop on my shopper continuum express. So is **Franklin Mills**. I can't possibly leave that out. Resale boutique owners beware, neither should you. Boogie up 95. Take the Woodhaven Exit. Check out what Saks, Ann Taylor, and Neiman Marcus sell all day, every day (and evenings and Sundays), new. Armed with this information, you'll keep your pricing competitive enough to keep us coming back for more. Why would anyone want to buy a secondhand Scaasi for $125-$175 resale, when she can get a brand new one for $90 at Saks' outlet store? I see this pricing differential all the time. Buyer (and seller) beware.

Since the Northeast is so close to home, I usually don't eat lunch out around here. I can get back to the home range and fridge pronto (thereby saving money). **Fox Chase** has one of the few restaurants I can recommend. I've eaten several times at **Joseph's**, located practically next door to Jeanes Hospital Thrift Shop. They have sandwiches, salads, burgers, pasta and pizza. Dollie probably got her donut at **Butler's Bakery** across the street at 6906 Torresdale, on the same block as **New Station Pizza** (good crust, lots and lots of cheese, too little tomato sauce). I lunched at, but do not recommend **Athenia** at 6833 Torresdale, unless you smoke. I don't. They did. The designated No Smoking area, consisting of one narrow half of a 12-foot-wide room, was a joke. Four women, obligingly sitting in the smoking area, lit up all at once right under my nose. I gobbled my grilled cheese (it was good), and fled, still chewing. I can recommend **Ristorante Italiana,** in the strip mall on Roosevelt Boulevard (try their eggplant rolitini), and the 50's place called **Nifty Fifty's** at 2491 Grant Avenue (onion rings and real New York egg creams are divine).

TOUR #2

The following shops are located in the Greater Northeast:

18   A, A & C

11   Bob' S Olde Attic

2   Burholme Thrift

5   Collector's Corner

10   Dollie's Baby Attic

14   Frankford Hospital

15   Frankford Thrift

18   J&L

6&7 Jeanes Hospital

3   Little Bit Of Everything

8   Medical Mission Sisters

4   Merel's

16   Neighborhood Family Thrift

17   Rachel's Future

19   Ralph's Place

1   Salvation Army

13   Salvation Army

9   Uptown Consignment

12   White Elephant Boutique

*Note: This list has a shop's entire name. Names in review boxes may have been shortened a tad to fit. Numbers before each shop name correspond to their numbered location on each map. **Shops with a star sold Volume II. Volume III? ASK!**

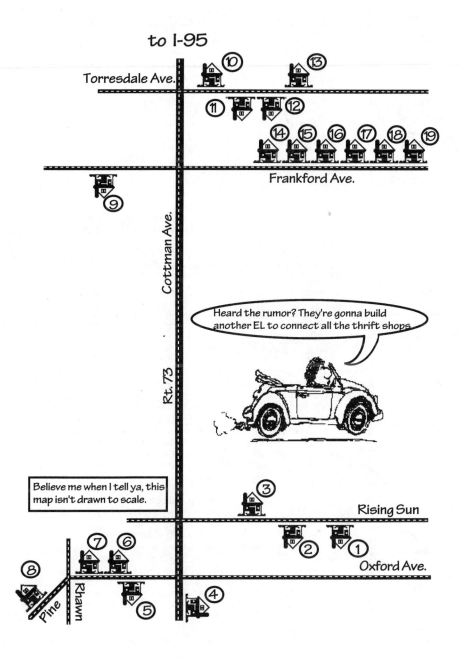

to I-95

Torresdale Ave.

Cottman Ave.

Rt. 73

Frankford Ave.

Heard the rumor? They're gonna build another EL to connect all the thrift shops.

Believe me when I tell ya, this map isn't drawn to scale.

Rising Sun

Oxford Ave.

Pine

Rhawn

TOUR#2 MAP Page 44

A, A & C

4435 Frankford Ave.
Phila., PA 19124

533-2836

Look: HO HUM

Goods: HO HUM

Prices: UNMARKED

HOURS:
Mon–Fri 11-4

CLOSED: Christmas
and New Year's Day

A Jetson-style sofa landed over in the corner and sat there, lost. A 50's anachronism, its chrome legs and tight-back, mirror shiny, black cushions reflect its even more curious surroundings. Over by the front door is a new white aluminum kitchen hutch with sliding glass doors on top and metal swing doors below. Barry Manilow's face, open-mouthed, beams down from a wall clock. Deep in the back and along the side of the shop are scattered three brown kitchen tables, a rectangle, a square and a circle, each one surrounded by a total of 14 identical tufted brown vinyl and aluminum chairs. Poked and prodded by time and use, they leak tufts of white stuffing from an assortment of holes. An old-fashioned, portable Singer sewing machine has $25 scrawled on the lid in black crayon. It, and a few small appliances, were the only things priced in the entire store. You could take home a **$6 Presto popcorn maker, a $12 Proctor Silex wide-slot toaster** still in the box (unused?), or pick and choose among a small assortment of waffle irons and such. The shop card invites you to "Check Out Our Prices." Go figure. Or should I say, go ask Anna Maria, Anthony or Connie, the owners.

You could also snap up the enlarged black and white-framed memorial photo of a pair of someone else's beloved pooches. They sit propped up against a chair back, surrounded by carefully glued pale green, real velvet trim in a pile of photographic, fallen leaves, captured forever in some long-ago moment in their long-ago lives. The reflected light of the camera caught them in a glassy eyed, unnerving, almost sullen stare. I knew how they felt.

P.S. They seem to be selling new furniture from a glossy three-ring binder.

CONSIGNOR ALERT: Buys outright.

Bob's Olde Attic

6916
Torresdale Ave.
Phila., PA 19135

624-6382

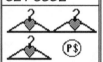

Look: STATUS QUO

Goods: HO HUM –
CLASS ACT

Prices: MODERATE

HOURS:
Mon–Sat 9-5

CLOSED: Holidays

Bob was bored. He was playing solitaire. I couldn't tell who was winning. He eagerly interrupted his game to discuss the merits of the crackled, mustard yellow handpainted oriental-motif, 1920's mahogany dresser with four drawers and unpolished brass pulls. It reminded me so much of some of the pieces we'd inherited from Marvin's grandmother, Millie. She had lived high on the hog in Hollywood back in the 20's: Chauffeured limo, heavy dark and brooding baronial-type furniture, the whole ball of wax. Here was a chance to learn more about our inheritance. She had been uncharacteristically tightlipped about this time in her life. Seems there was a big skeleton in the ancestral closet, big enough to write a book. Another story for another time...

Finished, Bob went back to his phone buddies and his solitaire. I roamed around. A pop singer was going on about California sunshine on the radio. This, while we were under a foot of snow outside. Yellow seemed to be the color theme here. A yellow French provincial bedroom set. A yellow Lady Kenmore washer. A blonde veneer, 5-drawer, single-door wardrobe, cedar lined. A $250 yellow dining room set. A graying bust, features looking more like a guy than a girl, but with a profusion of classically waved hair caught up in a bun, wearing a raised necklace and earrings set off by all too real, intact rhinestones, $14.95. An old khaki-colored army uniform hung on the wall. **Reproductions** of Aunt Jemima, with her sunny smile, were everywhere. Made me crave a stack of pancakes. Going out, I spied three horseshoes nailed to the doorway overhead. Good luck, Bob.

CONSIGNOR ALERT: Buys outright.

TOUR #2 Page 45

Burholme Thrift	

<table>
<tr><td>

7106 Rising Sun Ave.
Phila., PA 19111

742-8877

Look: STATUS QUO

Goods: HO HUM–TOP DRAWER

Prices: MODERATE –HIGH

HOURS: Mon, Wed, Fri, Sat 10-3

CLOSED: July & August

</td><td>

It was one of THOSE places. Four visits and still no go. Even when the place was open, it wasn't. I couldn't get my big toe in the door. The owner had rearranged EVERYTHING over the weekend, piling it in the foot-wide pathway wending through two small and smaller rooms. Peeking 'round corners, I could only guess the square footage. There were so many layers of objets d'art and racks of clothing and protruding shelves and stalactites and stalagmites of stuff, stuff and more stuff, there was no way of telling. She requested I return on the morrow. She would be finished rearranging EVERYTHING. I could shoehorn myself inside. I sputtered and fumed about how I had tried to get in. But I could see it was hopeless. She sweetly, patiently explained she had been sick for months. She had recovered. But only last week, someone she knew died. Sadly she had to close up again for another week.

Determined, I returned the next day. The key to the magic kingdom twisted in the lock, the doorknob turned... "Wait just a few minutes please, won't you?" A clerk emerged, carting suitcases, a plastic plant, a rusted wagon, a baby doll rocker, a Bissell sweeper and three bags of clothing outside in hopes of catching a flyby customer or two. It was also probably the only way they could get back in. I spent 15 minutes pacing in the winter sunshine, waiting. **Finally! More jewelry, bric-a-brac, paintings, lamps, dolls, doll furniture, accessories, people-size furniture, curiosities and antique linens than I have ever seen in one place at one time.** I was afraid to move. With every step I systematically prelocated myself in space, best guessing which way I should move to take the least risk of breaking EVERYTHING. Rather than going on and on about it, go see for yourself. If you can get in, that is. **CONSIGNOR ALERT:** More state of mind than written policy. She'll negotiate.

</td></tr>
</table>

Collector's Corner	

<table>
<tr><td>

7492 Oxford Ave.
Phila., PA 19111

745-7740

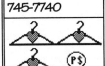

Look: STATUS QUO

Goods: STATUS QUO

Prices: LOW – MODERATE

HOURS: Tue–Fri 10-7 Sat 10-4

CLOSED: Holidays & 2 summer weeks

</td><td>

Collector's Corner is housed in the same tiny room as Mike & Kate's Sport Shoppe. Sport, as in hunting animals with guns. To my way of thinking, there is nothing 'shoppe' about a gun shop. What were they thinking of? Bambi? Some reviews write themselves, others I have to wrestle to the mat. Some I go in once and know exactly what I'm going to say, only to do a 180° on the second. First-visit-only review would have said: Ah isn't it cute. Shared life, shared space. Yin and yang of the sexes. She, **knickknacks**; he, shoot-'em-up bang-bang type. Guns turn faster than knickknacks. Zeroed in on the thrifty half of the scene, ignoring, denying the rows of guns lined up in the display case. Second visit? New perspective. Read on.

Two neighborhood boys, around nine and eleven, entered. School had just let out. Instead of going to the candy store or playing video games, another kiddie option is hanging out at the local gun shoppe. "Mister, you sell any BB guns?" Casting a very wary eye upon these gun-toter wannabes, much to my relief, the shopkeeper said no, he did not. One pint-sized, not-so innocent, went on to compare the .38 in the case with the one he claimed to already own. With professional calm, he did some prospective window shopping with an eye to upgrading. Entering the shop with these two, my instincts, my guardian angel, went on red alert. Leaving, I met the sad gaze of the Virgin Mary looking out from a picture, eyes upward, toward a row of old, now **collectible** and therefore valuable, school lunch boxes, playfully bumping one another, hugging the rafters, displayed above a wall of gun accessories, holsters, belts, bandoleers. It was all there. It always is.
CONSIGNOR ALERT: 60% You-40% Store. No fee. 60 days. No appointment. Trades.

</td></tr>
</table>

Dollie's Baby Attic

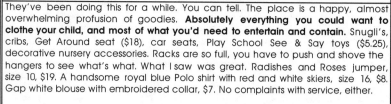

6905 Torresdale Ave. Phila., PA 19135 **332-0305**	They've been doing this for a while. You can tell. The place is a happy, almost overwhelming profusion of goodies. **Absolutely everything you could want to clothe your child, and most of what you'd need to entertain and contain.** Snugli's, cribs, Get Around seat ($18), car seats, Play School See & Say toys ($5.25), decorative nursery accessories. Racks are so full, you have to push and shove the hangers to see what's what. What I saw was great. Radishes and Roses jumper, size 10, $19. A handsome royal blue Polo shirt with red and white skiers, size 16, $8. Gap white blouse with embroidered collar, $7. No complaints with service, either.
 Look: CLASS ACT **Goods:** STATUS QUO–TOP DRAWER **Prices:** MODERATE	Snarfing down a donut, white powdered sugar on her chin, Dollie agreeably interrupted her late-morning snack long enough to tell me all I needed to know about the shop and her policies. I'd like to see pricing on ALL of the equipment, and even more a 50%-50% consignment/shop split. Those two factors were all that stood in the way of this being a four hanger (it already has lots of heart). I went back and forth, arguing both sides of the equation. After listening to the defense and DA's closing arguments, the ladies and gentlemen of my internal jury stood up and read their decision out loud to the judge. Judgment for the consignor, your honor. Hearing is adjourned until next year. (I've been watching too much O.J.)
HOURS: Tue–Fri 11-3, Sat 11-4	
CLOSED: Week after Christmas	**CONSIGNOR ALERT:** 40% You-60% Shop. No fee. 15 items/visit max. Call first.

Frankford Hospital

4711 Frankford Ave. Phila., PA. 19124 **831-6798**	They were having their semiannual bag sale. $4 could have gotten you a Hastings and Smith collarless blue cotton shirt with white pearl buttons, a recent and attractive LIZ all-season navy and floral dress with self belt, a 6'-long fringed royal blue scarf, a red wool vintage Boy Scouts of America jacket with double breasted
 Look: STATUS QUO **Goods:** HO HUM–STATUS QUO **Prices:** LOW	flap-top pockets, a woman's Russ charcoal colored blazer, an Italian all-wool men's charcoal and rust and navy sweater, a pair of beige bucks for your guy, a white Loyd Williams white-on-white striped blouse with attached ascot in polyester, size 8, a Virgo beige and white summer dress, several new waitress or nurse uniforms if you were in either biz, a metal baseball bat thrown in for good measure. If you're on a tight budget and want good solid-citizen stuff hanging in *your* closet, this was a good day to come strip *their* closet clean. Quite a number of women from the neighborhood were doing just that. They swooped in at dawn, grabbed goodies, stuffed bags, and then its so long Charlie, till the next sale
HOURS: Mon–Fri 10-3	Three volunteers were wearing the same salmon-colored smocks Mom used to wear when she went off to do good deeds at our neighborhood hospital. One cradled a customer's infant in her arms. The blonde, hazel eyed little girl was fighting sleep. Her forehead was hot, her feet felt like ice. Her mom had her hands full trying to manage the two other small ones with her. Sizing up the situation, the remaining volunteers distracted the older children with talk and toys. Free to work the racks, Mom gathered up bundles of clothing for her family. The volunteer patted the baby's bottom gently, rocking the red faced, wailing infant back and forth. Whispering softly as she must have so long ago with her own children, she reassured until the cranky little one finally fell asleep. Watching, I suddenly under-
CLOSED: June-August	stood what my mother had been up to every week. I tiptoed out, not wanting to disturb all the **good work** going on inside. **CONSIGNOR ALERT:** Donations only. Proceeds benefit Frankford Hospital.

Frankford Thrift	 $ P$
4601 Frankford Ave. Phila., PA 19124 No Phone (P$) **Look:** BOTTOMFEEDER **Goods:** DOWN & OUT–STATUS QUO **Prices:** EVERYTHING $1 **HOURS:** Mon–Sat 10-6 **CLOSED:** Holidays	Too bad the name Dollar Store is taken. This place may be on to something. EVERYTHING is a buck. Depending on your budget and your fashion destiny, you might or might not think there was a lot going on here. The place is **big and clean and full** of inventory. White walls, white drop ceiling, charcoal carpeting, florescent lighting, little or no heat, racks arranged just so. That's it. No aesthetic. But for a dollar, who cares? No other bottomfeeder beats this day-in and day-out pricing. I like this guy's concept and he's willing to hustle. Half jeans and sweats and T's, fewer suits and dresses, many slacks and skirts and blouses. **Kid's was good.** I saw quite a few Gap and Esprit labels. I bought two pair of cotton chintz Gap slacks, one for me and one for Morgan. I also got her an unworn puckered-cotton, V-neck, white-lace and pink-ribbon-trimmed, long-john-type top so cute it deserves to be seen. The owner sat up front, submerged in a show-all, tell-all, who-did-what-to-whom talk show. When I interrupted the verbal going-nowhere game of one-upmanship to make my purchases, he gladly turned down the volume. He works seven days a week, five for the phone company, here on his two days off. He claimed they process over a thousand pieces a day. He's constantly cycling new stuff in, unsold stuff out. As soon as I left the store, the TV sparring resumed. I wonder who, if anyone, won that one? I know I did. **CONSIGNOR ALERT:** Buys outright.

J & L	$ L P$
4423 Frankford Ave. Phila., PA 19124 No Phone (P$) **Look:** HO HUM **Goods:** HO HUM - TOP DRAWER **Prices:** UP & DOWN **HOURS:** Mon–Sat 9-5 "usually" **CLOSED:**	In a block dominated by secondhand furniture stores, in an area struggling to survive, this one's been here for a while. So, too, the owner. He has the wary, waiting look of someone who's been dealing with the public for a looong time. Way in the back, his sidekick (call him Roadrunner because of the cartoon character pinned to his cap) was picking, choosing, arranging, rearranging, repairing and generally sprucing up the wide-ranging assortment of curb-to-castle stuff, stuff, and more stuff. A cobalt blue eyewash glass, unpriced, caught Morgan's attention. Joking about it as being expensive, he never did name the price. Comic books and plastic encased old newspapers with banner headlines that all but screamed **2ND A-BOMB DROPPED...J.F.K. SHOT**, clothespinned to lines strung across the ceiling. A Zen-worn tin box labeled Crawford & Savoy, with a smiling, portly old gent from Scrooge's era portrayed on the lid, sipped Sherry and coyly nibbled on one of his own biscuits. The price on the bottom was $25. A small, clear plastic, snap box held slate blue, celadon, rose, peach and brown cameos, one an unbelievably tiny 1/4". $300 gets the discerning collector 6 new additions. I gotta tell ya, even after Roadrunner's efforts, its dirty and jumbled. The first time I came here it gave me the creeps. I didn't take the time to really look. I tried to get in on several other days to perform my obligatory second undercover visit. This shop and others like it disappear behind roll 'em up, roll 'em down protective metal shields. Many don't have addresses displayed. One day I was inside, prowling, the next I couldn't find them. Bad weather had probably convinced owners not to open. On what I had decided was to be my final attempt, I got in. Morgan's appreciation of the place helped me SEE it. **CONSIGNOR ALERT:** Buys outright.

Jeanes Hospital

CLOTHING:
7963 Oxford Ave.
Phila., PA 19111
342-8444

FURNITURE:
7977 Oxford Ave.
Phila., PA 19111
742-0698

Look: HO HUM–
STATUS QUO

Goods: HO HUM–
STATUS QUO

Prices: LOW

HOURS:
Mon–Fri 10-4,
Sat 10-3

CLOSED: Holidays

Active volunteerism is becoming difficult for most younger women, emotionally electing or financially forced to work outside the home. This trend threatens the very existence of charity thrift shops. With this graying volunteer work force comes a lopsided set of values. A vibrant place needs the energy and enthusiasm of the young, *and* the thoughtful restraint of the older and wiser. Too much youth and vitality--too many agendas, too many chances taken. Too much restraining wisdom--stagnation and clouded organizational vision. Unlike puff pieces you occasionally see in local newspapers extolling the virtues of yet another thrift store, or the local restaurant reviewer who never ate a meal she didn't like (the reviewer's meals are, after all, free, and the restaurants do, after all, pay for advertising in the newspaper), I am an unaffiliated critic. As such, and much as I would love to give a glowing review to the kindly ladies of this shop, I cannot. It's resting on faded laurels.

There is a particular and peculiar color green I have never seen used anywhere else by anyone else for any other purpose than to cover hospital walls. And why would they? it's such a yuckie shade. Guess where all the leftover hospital green paint went from the last face-lift at Jeanes Hospital? Here it is in living color, all over the walls and their business cards. Stylishly sedate seniors and soon-to-be-seniors, looking for the familiar comfort of the same old 'same old'("well that's what I've always worn") will feel they belong. So would a picker for a retro neo Manayunk or South Street shop. I 'did' the 60's and 70's. I've moved on. Like their loyal, but dwindling customers, many older volunteers running and managing charity shops are frozen in the fashionable do-good attitudes of 50 years ago, when **decent, usable, clean, warm, comfortable, organized, and helpful** were enough. Now shops, private or charity, have to retain all those traditional values *and* add on concepts like style, dressing rooms, credit cards, sachet, decor, advertising, if they want to stay in 'business'. Here? Start with the walls and keep going.
CONSIGNOR ALERT: Donations Only. Benefits hospital auxiliary.

Little Bit of Everything

7211 Rising Sun Ave.
Phila., PA 19111
745-6140

Look: HO HUM

Goods: HO HUM –
STATUS QUO

Prices: MODERATE

HOURS:
Tue–Fri 10-5,
Sat 10-4

CLOSED: Holidays

Rainbow, the clown, is gone. Another brave and adventurous female has bought the shop. Well, two brave and adventurous females, Linda & Tammy, a mother-and-daughter team. They have ventured far afield to attract and acquire new consignors with bigger bucks and better duds than the average man, woman and child on their home turf. This dynamic duo have scattered flyers as far away as Huntingdon Valley. It's working. The inventory is definitely improved.

There's only a passing nod to men. Shirts are $4, mixed in with a few suits and sweaters, that's all folks! **Women and kids get the green light**. Elizabeth slate-blue two-piece wool knit, never worn, only $20. Even so, the owner was willing to take off 10%. Plaid Gap blazer, $28. Solid blue Gap blazer, $18. Anne Klein black satin evening slippers with a triangle of rhinestones on the toe and heel that I'd seen at Dan's for $65, here $20 used, but still 'mint.' "Name The Dog" and "Bravo" in letters on a white background with black, Spot-the-dog-type spots on a two-piece tot romper set, $12.50. Purple Oshkosh overalls with horsies, $10. Jewelry and housewares (mostly gift shop closeouts and new mugs) get the yellow light.

CONSIGNOR ALERT: 40% You-60% Shop. $5 fee. 60 day. By appointment only.

Medical Mission Sisters	
8400 Pine Rd. Fox Chase, PA 19111 **745-7930** 	Less than ten minutes from Cottman and the Boulevard, people are raising vegetables on a small farm off a dusty country road. Drive past the oriental women hoeing zucchini, follow the sloping road toward the large barn-like structure to your left. You've arrived. Only you've also left. You've left the 20th century, trading it in for a taste of the 19th. **Huge and cheap** with a pack rat's passing nod to organization, it is one of those places where you get to root and rummage and squeeze past and peer under, and lift up and dig deep. And they don't mind. As long as you sort of put it back to where it sort of was. **A place like this you can always turn up something exceptional if you come back often enough.**
Look: HO HUM **Goods:** HO HUM – STATUS QUO **Prices:** UP & DOWN but usually DOWN	One woman lugged an old plastic laundry hamper around the store, filled to overflowing. Crazed laundress? No. She looked sane enough. Volunteer? No. She wore her coat. Donating? No. Wrong part of the store for that. Shopping? Big time. A resident of Vermont, she used to live right around the corner. Now, whenever she's in town visiting Mom, she stocks up. They don't have much of anything in Vermont, except mountains. "So it costs $100! I can't get stuff this good at home. I come here once or twice a year and load up. The bargains are great." Never once deterred from sorting, working men's, she racked up another score.
Hours: Mon–Sat 10-3	**I find this an especially good place to unearth vintage** or soon-to-be vintage. There was one $5.95 black polyester blouse with each charcoal, silver and black bead intact, outlining the pointy collar and seams running up the front and down the back, a precursor to the Western fab fad of today, it would have been perfect for some good ol' retro party gal. A raging purple, boxy, sleeveless sheath with a simple, bold line of rhinestones tracing the collarless neckline and dropped hip, then a per-
CLOSED: July–August	pendicular line of flashing glass ran front to back, forming a large cross for some modern-day fashion crusader to take up and bear. **CONSIGNOR ALERT:** Donations Only.

Merel's	
912 Cottman Ave. Phila., PA 19111 **745-1640** 	Merel's is an antidote to the malls. It speaks to the eternal need for community and the human love of gossip. Greater Northeast high fashion-types frolic here, in two small, clean, bright rooms. Seems to be just as high a concentration of sizes 4-8 as 14 and 16. The proprietor (I'd guess she's a size 8) talks to you, informs you. Custo-mers respond in kind and keep returning for more: more clothes, more savings, and more 'who did what to whom and why?'
Look: CLASS ACT **Goods:** STATUS QUO–CLASS ACT **Prices:** MODERATE	**Merel's also has the highest concentration of glitter, sequins, studs, fur, feathers, gold, glitz, fringe, lace, chains, appliqué, and look-at-me beadwork of almost any other place outside Hollywood or Miami.** Merel's secondhand inventory is a lot like Cache or Paul Harris. Another resale phenom? Lots and lots of good labels with black marks or scissor strokes through the names. Within easy reach of Franklin Mills, many consignments were originally bought at the outlets. Wisely, prices here are kept in line with the facts of retail-life markdowns. Merel doesn't get carried away with label mystique. After all, we all know how much the consignor paid when the garment was new, and are all wary enough to resist being overcharged
HOURS: Mon–Wed, Fri 11-6, Tue, Thu, Sat 10-5	**P.S.** Drive by **SLOWLY**. It's easily missed, but don't miss it. Parking lot is a bumper-car game in miniature; there's no on-street parking.
CLOSED: Holidays	**CONSIGNOR ALERT:** 50%-50% split.$5 fee. Garments kept till sold. By appointment.

Neighborhood Family Thrift 	
4509 Frankford Ave Phila., PA 19124 **289-8075** **Look:** DOWN & OUT **Goods:** HO HUM - STATUS QUO **Prices:** LOW	Some places, like some people, can be clean AND organized. Others manage to be either organized or clean, but never both. This place, willingly or not, chose dirty over clean, organized over messy. A lot of other choices got made along the way, too. It looked like the last stop on the train to nowhere, the end of the line. A good ol' country/ western singer gave out an occasional hoot 'n holler as he delivered the gotta-get-religion message playing in the background. Without the pounding beat and his warbling voice to keep me company, the paint-peeling pockmarked place would have been even more eerie. A valiantly overdressed, heavily made up woman worked the racks of overwashed clothes (at least they were clean), holding a wire-hangered blouse up for inspection, appraising it's worth with a small, sparrow of a friend wearing a drab brown winter coat. They seemed to be old shopping buddies with the familiarity of years of such moments behind, if not ahead, of them.
HOURS: Mon–Sat 10-5:30	Even with MAB just down the street, there was no attempt at decoration, let alone a basic paint job and repairs. There're **bargains to be found** in the increasingly busy shop. One guy gleefully turned to the manager saying "You're going to need skates today!" The 50%-off sale hadn't hurt. A sweet, flower strewn little Danskin outfit, $2.95, a LIZ or two, $5.95 each. A blue hospital gown, $2 on the ticket, $1 today, it was the perfect head-to-toe cover-up with its small bows turned to the front and tied. Morgan adorned it with splashes of paint within minutes of her next, weekly art class. I'm beginning to doubt that Morgan will choose either clean OR organized. But I am certain that whatever she chooses, she'll do it with verve, and to music.
	☞ **SHOPPER ALERT:** Clothing
CLOSED: Holidays	**CONSIGNOR ALERT:** Buys outright.

Rachel's Future	
4437 Frankford Ave. Phila., PA. 19124 **533-5613** **Look:** HO HUM **Goods:** HO HUM - STATUS QUO **Prices:** UNMARKED	And someone else's long-gone past. Everything this way and that, scattered, dusty, mostly unpriced. Upstairs, two unicorns, one large, one small, both with legs curled under them, horns missing. Does that mean they are horses now? Mounted on either side of an exposed-flame gas, wall heater were two large, gilt framed pictures of former elegance. A smug Blue Boy posed in one. In the other, merry courtiers from the prerevolutionary French court gathered around a gaming table, playing whist, wiling away their carefree lives till the ax fell.
HOURS: Tue–Sat 10-4	The stairway leading down to the depths was festooned with red, white and blue gas-station opening-day banners. I felt like I was undersea, diving in a small sub. My roaming beam of discovery focused on a set of plastic sliding doors, leaning up against the wall, and a big porch rocker, seat busted, revealed in the gloom. I spied a wooden porch swing. No, it was a slat futon, thrown up on a 'reef' of unrecognizable objects. Slowly, carefully rounding the bend, in the increasingly murky light, I made out the outline of bicycles, a metal frame medicine cabinet with paint peeling, metal bed frames, springs stored under the overhang created by the steps. Remains of a tin ceiling hung down like sides of a sunken ship. I came up for air. On the glass door going out, room settings of furniture--store pictorial equivalents of those oriental, take-out phony-food photos--hung to lure and tempt possible customers. Pick one dining room set from column A, a living room set from column B. Like Chinese restaurants, they had little or nothing to do with what's inside.
CLOSED: Holidays	**CONSIGNOR ALERT:** Buys outright.

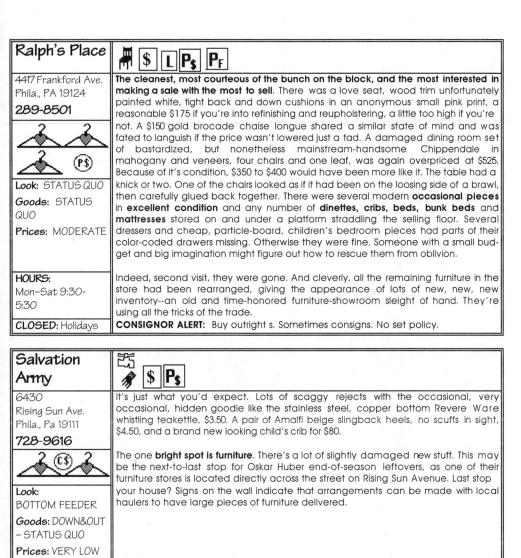

	Ralph's Place

Ralph's Place

4417 Frankford Ave.
Phila., PA 19124

289-8501

(P$)

Look: STATUS QUO

Goods: STATUS QUO

Prices: MODERATE

The cleanest, most courteous of the bunch on the block, and the most interested in making a sale with the most to sell. There was a love seat, wood trim unfortunately painted white, tight back and down cushions in an anonymous small pink print, a reasonable $175 if you're into refinishing and reupholstering, a little too high if you're not. A $150 gold brocade chaise longue shared a similar state of mind and was fated to languish if the price wasn't lowered just a tad. A damaged dining room set of bastardized, but nonetheless mainstream-handsome Chippendale in mahogany and veneers, four chairs and one leaf, was again overpriced at $525. Because of it's condition, $350 to $400 would have been more like it. The table had a knick or two. One of the chairs looked as if it had been on the loosing side of a brawl, then carefully glued back together. There were several modern **occasional pieces** in **excellent condition** and any number of **dinettes, cribs, beds, bunk beds** and **mattresses** stored on and under a platform straddling the selling floor. Several dressers and cheap, particle-board, children's bedroom pieces had parts of their color-coded drawers missing. Otherwise they were fine. Someone with a small budget and big imagination might figure out how to rescue them from oblivion.

HOURS:
Mon–Sat 9:30–5:30

Indeed, second visit, they were gone. And cleverly, all the remaining furniture in the store had been rearranged, giving the appearance of lots of new, new, new inventory--an old and time-honored furniture-showroom sleight of hand. They're using all the tricks of the trade.

CLOSED: Holidays

CONSIGNOR ALERT: Buy outright s. Sometimes consigns. No set policy.

Salvation Army

6430
Rising Sun Ave.
Phila., Pa 19111

728-9616

(C$)

Look:
BOTTOM FEEDER

Goods: DOWN&OUT – STATUS QUO

Prices: VERY LOW

It's just what you'd expect. Lots of scaggy rejects with the occasional, very occasional, hidden goodie like the stainless steel, copper bottom Revere Ware whistling teakettle, $3.50. A pair of Amalfi beige slingback heels, no scuffs in sight, $4.50, and a brand new looking child's crib for $80.

The one **bright spot is furniture.** There's a lot of slightly damaged new stuff. This may be the next-to-last stop for Oskar Huber end-of-season leftovers, as one of their furniture stores is located directly across the street on Rising Sun Avenue. Last stop your house? Signs on the wall indicate that arrangements can be made with local haulers to have large pieces of furniture delivered.

HOURS:
Mon–Sat 9-5

☞ **SHOPPER ALERT:** Furniture here is ⚖ ⚖ ⚖ ⚖

CLOSED:
Christmas

CONSIGNOR ALERT: Donations only. Make sure to bring them in before 4:30! **Please don't leave anything outside after hours, here or any charity. They will get fined.**

Salvation Army	$ P_F
6427 Torresdale Ave. Phila., PA 19135 **624-9487** (C$)	As is often the case, looking for one shop, I find two. Cruising down Torresdale, I unexpectedly came upon this Salvation Army. I know there are a lot of them out there, I know eventually I'll stumble upon them all. I don't go out of my way to find them. As a chain, they are predictably the same, and I don't want to bore you or myself being redundant. But the good works that go on here should be supported by our tired, sad world. A family who had recently been burned out of their home were here looking for replacement furniture. The manager and two clerks were gathered around to help. **Furniture is what they do best.** There were quite a few good sets--new, used and retro. Inquirer Magazine had just done a piece on a daughter's childhood recollection of her parents' 50's dining room set of life-resistant blonde furniture. I wonder if the author knows her parent's furniture is on sale here. Eight pieces: hutch, sideboard, table, leaf and chairs, $225. Sure enough, good as new! In the front window, employees had selected for display a new 'oak' table and four chairs, $175. By my second visit, every piece of furniture had been sold and replaced.
Look: BOTTOMFEEDER **Goods:** DOWN & OUT–CLASS ACT **Prices:** LOW	
HOURS: Mon–Sat 9-5	Best bet in clothing is the **enormous selection of jeans.** There were many rugged, warm looking sweaters in men's worth considering. Land's End, Woolrich, L.L. Bean, that sort of thing. Why is housewares in Salvation Army stores always so consistently, shall we say, uneventful? My only inspirational moment among the shelves came when I read an Air Force mug with the inscription 'Aim High.'
CLOSED: Holidays	
	CONSIGNOR ALERT: Donations only.

Uptown Consignment	$ ✍ L P_F P_$
7430 Frankford Ave. Phila., PA 19136 **332-0992** (P$)	On our way back from the wilds of New Jersey, we cross the Tacony Palmyra, and take a wrong turn to the gates of Holmesburg Prison. The trip becomes Social Studies 101. Yes, Morgan, that's what a prison looks like. She is deeply affected by the barbed and barren harshness. We turn around, quietly hunker down booking south, headed for hearth and home. Then it happens. Just as it always does. I am transformed into one of those trained French pigs or dogs. I have caught the scent. No ,not truffles... thrift shops. I know we are near one. I can sense it. I begin to visually root. Put my nose to the wind and bay. Voilà! Uptown Consignment reveals itself in the tangle of storefronts. Marvin makes an abrupt, efficient job of parallel parking in the middle of a downpour in the middle of Saturday afternoon traffic. He's had enough practice by now, and he's something of a frustrated NYC taxi driver.
Look: CLASS ACT **Goods:** STATUS QUO –TOP DRAWER **Prices:** MODERATE	I stumbled upon a Red Racer wooden wagon with drop-in slat sides, just like the one Nancy and I played with growing up. Boy, had I wanted one. Was I ever jealous. Now I could have it for $240. Am I having a flashback or hot flashes? A copper mold, $95. A charming small green pitcher with a bias relief avenue of shade trees disappearing down the line of sight, $18. A blue agate mold, $24. A handsome, carved, 1930's 11-piece dining room set, with matching small-scaled hutch, sideboard, table with leaves and chairs and pad, going for a very reasonable $850. And, I estimate, over 200 sets of keep-'em-laughing, salt and pepper sets merrily scattered about. This place is a little schizy. There's a slowly closing gap between quality and pricing, antiques and clothing. **Antiques win hands down.**
HOURS: Tue–Fri 12-7 Sat 10-5	
CLOSED: Holidays	☞ **SHOPPER ALERT:** Furniture and collectibles are  **CONSIGNOR ALERT: 60% You-40% Shop** . No fee. No appointment. No Tuesday consigning. Wednesday–Friday 1-6, Saturday drop-off only non-clothing items.

White Elephant Boutique	
6914 Torresdale Ave. Phila., PA 19135 **624-8072** 	Valentine's Day. The window was full of traditional red, pink and white, heart-shaped candy boxes and red red red clothing. So what's new? Everyone does that. But inside, **WOW. She really outdid herself creating a mood. Très boudoir. Très boutique. Very feminine.** Shoes lined up in rows, marching across the carpeting. Sachets and hearts adorned tabletops. Walls were hung with front-facing, eye-catching outfits, new and vintage. Hats and veils filled in the remaining spaces and poured out of beautiful old hatboxes mounted on top of shiny new, chrome circular, clothing racks. Sprayed on plaster had glitter shining between the zillions of bumps, giving a romantic glow to the high, dark ceiling. A fan circulated the warm-scented air. She's used every decorator's trick in the book to catch your interest and keep it. I wanted to move right in.
Look: CLASS ACT – TOP DRAWER **Goods:** STATUS QUO–CLASS ACT **Prices:** MODERATE	Clothing hung from the walls, hard to reach. The signature piece, the best the place had to offer, was an unworn, Evan Picone, two-piece black suit, gold braid scrolling down the lapel, $99. There was lots of everyday good stuff and a few vintage pieces scattered here and there, but also hard to reach. The large number of large circular racks were pushed against the walls to make room in the aisles. What was gained in floor space was lost in lack of back-of-the-rack access.
HOURS: Tue–Sat 11-5	
CLOSED: Holidays	**CONSIGNOR ALERT:** 50%–50%. $5 fee. 15 items/visit. 90 days. 20%/30 days, 50%/60 days.

TOUR #3
SMALL TOWN USA AND THE MALLING OF AMERICA

Demolished long ago, Willow Grove Park still echoes vividly in my dimming cache of childhood memories. Visions of serene white swan boats, floating on a small man-made lake, passing through the darkened Tunnel of Love, linger on in the scrapbook of my mind's eye. What's old and used and worn is always supposed to be replaced by better, but seldom is. All too often, better is what was, not what is. Memories are like that.

This tour encapsulates America's retail extremes: **Willow Grove**, home of one of the larger and more glamorous malls in Montgomery County; **Hatboro**, Small town USA; and finally the suburban strip-mall sprawl of **Warminster** and **Horsham**. These seemingly opposing magnetic poles have attracted more than their share of thrift, resale and consignment shops. Logically concluding shoppers are already conditioned to come to the mall in droves, four shopowners have found suitably lower rent, but not low-rent, properties within blocks of the very high-rent mall. The peripheral resale and thrift shops around Willow Grove Mall have to be reached by car, and there's plenty of free parking. After doing Big Bear, Pooh's Corner, Shikari, and Share & Care, shops all hovering in the vicinity, you could grab a piece of pizza or some fabulous Boardwalk Fries or ice cream or Chinese or...satisfy whatever fast-food craving you wish at the **Food Court** on the mall's third level. Use Sear's entrance, assuming you want to get in and out quickly. (There's also a bathroom up there!)

Hatboro's downtown shopping district is a friendly, 'hi, how are ya?' secondhand resource. You can comfortably walk one end of town to the other in fifteen minutes, reach all shops on foot and have lunch there as well. Shopping is another matter. That could take hours. While "doing" Hatboro, check out the **Sweater Mill** (several doors down from Second Impressions). It carries heavily discounted labels usually only found in Center City boutiques. If you're hungry by now, **On A Roll**, 119 South York Road, is a very clean and tasty sandwich shop sharing the same block as Second Impressions. Or try **Daddypops**, the smallest diner I've ever seen, situated at the far end of town heading toward Warminster. If hunger overtakes you while you are in **Warminster**, then stop at **Bertucci's** for all things fast, cheap and Italian.

Hatboro is a microcosm of another resale phenomenon. Two area shops went bust over the summer (Closet to Closet, Robyn's Nest) and Horsham Supply relocated to the Montgomeryville Mart. Two new shops, The Second Fiddle and The Insatiable Shopper opened over the summer. Busy, busy, busy. As the town goes, so goes the region. Of the 175 shops in Volume II, over 10% (20) went out of business, 6 relocated, I know of four others that are up for sale and God only knows how many new ones opened. During phone checks we discovered that 25% of shops in our Data Base had gone belly up. Please call or write and let me know, won't you, if your favorite isn't reviewed in The Guide or listed in the TSM

UnYellow Pages? The interest in becoming a thrift shop owner is growing almost as large as the inevitable fallout from inexperience and competition.

Rising up unexpectedly in a powerful burst of vision and masonry in an otherwise lyrical, typically American setting, **Bryn Athyn** is home to the world-famous, scaled to grandeur, gothic Swedenborgian Cathedral. A clutch of shops and houses seek and find sustenance (as you might in one of the many restaurants) in the long reach of its shadow, just as they would if we were in Europe sometime around the Middle Ages. Real estate values hereabouts are booming. Prospering parishioners = prospering thrift. The Cathedral-affiliated thrift shop is one of my favorite discoveries for the year. Since it's a little off the beaten path, here's a tip. Turn right at the former gas station/now car repair shop. Follow the signs to the elementary school, but look for the red, white and blue flag with OPEN emblazoned across the tricolored field--it's at the end of the driveway leading up to the barn.

TOUR #3

1	The Barn	Huntingdon Valley
3	Big Bear	Roslyn
2	Bryn Athyn Thrift	Bryn Athyn
14	Carrousel	Warminster
11	The Insatiable Shopper	Hatboro
13	Joys & Toys	Hatboro
12	Nearly New	Warminster
6	Pooh's Corner	Willow Grove
7	Second Debut	Horsham
9	The Second Fiddle	Hatboro
8	Second Impressions ★	Hatboro
4	Share and Care Boutique	Willow Grove
5	Shikari	Willow Grove
15	Stuff 'n' Such	Hatboro
10	YMCA	Hatboro

*Note: This list has a shop's entire name. Names in review boxes may have been shortened a tad to fit. Numbers before each shop name correspond to their numbered location on each map. **Shops with a star sold Volume II. Volume III? ASK!**

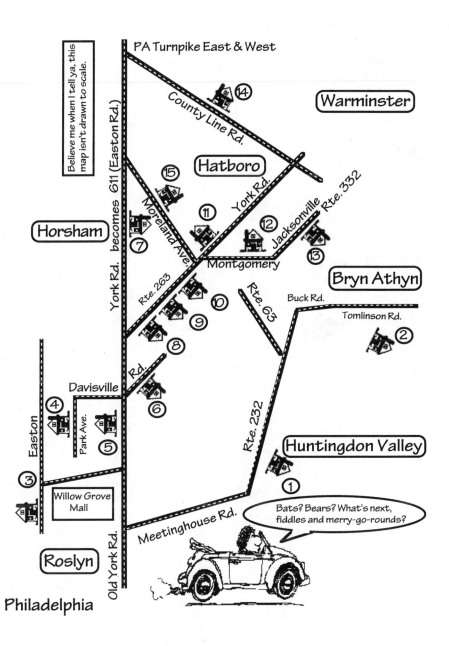

PA Turnpike East & West

Warminster

⑭

County Line Rd.

Believe me when I tell ya, this map isn't drawn to scale.

Hatboro

⑮

York Rd. becomes 611 (Easton Rd.)

Moreland Ave.

York Rd.

Rte. 332

Jacksonville

Horsham

⑪

⑫

⑦

Rte. 263

Montgomery

⑬

Bryn Athyn

Rte. 63

Buck Rd.

⑩

Tomlinson Rd.

⑨

② ⑧

Rd.

Davisville

⑥

Easton

④

Rte. 232

Huntingdon Valley

Park Ave.

⑤

③

①

Willow Grove Mall

Meetinghouse Rd.

Bats? Bears? What's next, fiddles and merry-go-rounds?

Roslyn

Old York Rd.

Philadelphia

TOUR #3 MAP Page 58

The Barn	$ P~F~
1648 Huntingdon Pike Huntingdon Valley, PA 19046 **947-8688**	The Barn is a barn is a barn. A traditional red barn with stone fireplace and walls, vaulting rafters, all set half into and half on top of a small man-made hill, like some sort of architectural maraschino cherry, surrounded not by cornfields, but by Holy Redeemer Hospital and retirement home. This is the end of the line not only for what was once fertile farm country, but also for possessions belonging to former residents. And as an undertaker's daughter, I can guess how most current residents get to be former residents.

Look: TOP DRAWER **Goods:** HO HUM– STATUS QUO **Prices:** LOW	**If I were giving out hangers for atmosphere, this one would be a "four."** The actual building deserves to be included in a cocktail table-quality photographic essay on the architectural history of barns. Or to be moved from its present site and put back to good use as a working barn or converted into a fabulous home. In its present incarnation as a thrift shop, it's rather like using a box from Tiffany's to offset costume jewelry. There is some stuff to buy and the ladies do their best. Resources and imagination just don't match the surroundings.
HOURS: Tue–Fri 11-4	
CLOSED: June–Sept	**CONSIGNOR ALERT:** Donations only. Benefits Holy Redeemer Hospital & Medical Center.

Big Bear	CC L P~F~
1342A Easton Rd. Roslyn, PA 19001 **659-3119**	The cub-size, stuffed brown bear, like some enormous house pet, loomed just inside. Worn and frayed by the exigencies of life, Big Bear kept mum. The owner, friendly and informative, did all the talking. Legend has it, Big Bear was found by a customer in a nearby quarry, an odd place for a stuffed bear, but just right for a real one. Big Bear kept silent watch for 5 years at an outdoor flea market in all kinds of weather, while his owner accumulated enough loot to be able to afford indoor accommodations. By now a dearly loved mascot, **Big Bear and his owner moved to this spot only a year ago, with Big Bear in the window so drive-by regulars would recognize their new digs.** Besides local real estate values, other basic factors contributing to a shop's quality are owner's life experience, personality and educ-
(P$)	
Look: STATUS QUO **Goods:** HO HUM– CLASS ACT **Prices:** More UP Than DOWN	ation. My best guess here? An innately intelligent and good-natured, roll-up-your sleeves life experience, some formal schooling, graduating from the school of hard knocks. My data? The things we surround ourselves with reflect our esthetic values and our journey through life. Here's what Big Bear's owner chose to sell, out of all the possibilities that must have come his way.
HOURS: Mon–Sat 9-6	Formica hutch and overpriced particle-board bookcase ($65), nearby neighbors to a reasonably priced, solid mahogany bedroom set ($650) and an especially attractive hand-carved floor lamp from the 20's –30's. Canary yellow vinyl love seat
CLOSED: Holidays	(Is that possible? Think about it.) from the 50's for $55, a fab fad bargain. Beveled glass, oak china cabinet, very nice, very expensive, over-restored, and then over-improved with new brass fittings. I prefer a patina. I don't like antiques mistaken for reproductions. On the other hand, while I admire the scratch, dent and chip look currently in vogue, I don't buy that either. Too messy for my taste, though in the right hands it looks spectacular. There, now you have *my* esthetic 'resume,' too.
	CONSIGNOR ALERT: Buys outright only.

Bryn Athyn Thrift Shop

520 Tomlinson Rd.
Bryn Athyn, PA
19009

947-7646

Look: BOTTOM OF THE FEED BAG

Goods: HO HUM–CLASS ACT

Prices: LOW–MODERATE

HOURS:
Tue–Thu, Sat 10-3,
Fri 10-12:30

CLOSED: Holidays

I didn't want to write this review. Not because it was hard to do or because the shop was awful, or something rude happened. Au contraire. I didn't want to write the review because I didn't and don't want to share my newest FIND. I want first dibs on all the good stuff. I don't want you guys to crowd the aisles, strip it bare, and stress out the charming volunteers till they're cranky. Bats, I am told, hung out upside down from the eaves of this gigantic old hill-hugging red barn. Sky peeked and snow drifted through wooden wall slats last winter. (You remember last winter.)

The dressing room was a horse stall, sans hay, etc. (Thank God there was no etc.) You'd have to be bats to work here last winter. But somehow volunteers survived. The shop prospered. Everything seems to prosper in Bryn Athyn, where real estate agents automatically add 20% to property values. Location, Location, Location. Which brings us to one of my favorite rules. Pickings are best where real estate values are highest. **Some pickin's!** Ship-captain's wheel mirror, smaller-than-child-size drafting table, mission-style oak chair, corner cupboard $50, whatnot shelf $40, antique brass or wood floor lamps, suitcases, cribs, antique harvest rake $50, four cane seat chairs (seat out) $10-$15 each, bath towel or quilt rack $30, two charming antique tins with someone's working horde of now antique buttons $18 each, a new portable dog run, 16 Christmas tree stands dating from the 40's to present.

The day of my second visit, renovations were underway. The electricity was out. Someone or something had cut an underground cable. Frivolities like insulation, heat and bathroom plumbing were being added. Some of the rugged charm will be gone soon. Hurry. **I'd shop forever if I had places like this to come to every day.**
P.S. Attention all B.A.T.S. volunteers. Don't over improve. I love you the way you are.

CONSIGNOR ALERT: Donations only. Benefits The Bryn Athyn Church School.

Carrousel

979A
W. County Line Rd.
Warminster, PA
19040

672-8840

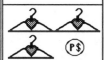

Look: STATUS QUO

Goods: STATUS QUO

Prices: UP & DOWN

HOURS:
Tue–Fri 10-5, Thu
10-7, Sat 10-3

CLOSED: Holidays

Ask any kid; they'll tell you. Merry-go-rounds are great. But some merry-go-rounds are better than others. My least favorite, most impressionable, merry-go-round memory? Falling off a single, stationary, brightly painted, antique wooden horse parked in the driveway of our family business. Why it was there I cannot recall. But I do have total recall of the bump it left on my forehead when I fell off. It's still there. My favorite merry-go-round ride? Ocean City summer evenings spent at the board-walk amusement center as a kid, grabbing and getting the brass ring. Marvin and I took Morgan there last year, carrying on this family tradition.

This merry-go-round is **good, clean, honest, and well organized**, but no brass ring. Fur coats, one of the few things in the shop made of natural 'fiber,' hung customer-and-shoplifter proof around the ceiling, just out of reach. And they were priced out of reach as well, by over a third to a half.

P.S. Recently added china, collectibles and the occasional 7-foot stuffed marlin.

CONSIGNOR ALERT: 50%-50% clothing, **60%You-40%Shop china & collectibles.** $6/season fee. Look for half-off-fee coupon.

The Insatiable Shopper

$ | L | P_F | P_$

221 N. York Rd.
Hatboro, PA 19040

675-2115

Look: CLASS ACT

Goods:
STATUS QUO

Prices: LOW –
MODERATE

HOURS:
Tue–Fri 10-6, Thu
10-7:30, Sat 11-4

CLOSED: Summer
Hours 10-3 on Sat

Here, the shoppers and consignors may well be insatiable; there was a time I was insatiable, too. Eventually, secondhand shopping only made the craving worse. I loaded up on everything I could find. It was all so cheap. Except when I stopped long enough to add it all up. Cumulatively, it wasn't so cheap. Finally, I hit the bottom of my closet and my budget. Those days are over (God willing). Downsizing by consigning and donating away the excess, now I only buy primo profundo secondhand. And primo is more selectively defined with every new shop I research and review.

Esthetically and functionally, the shop itself is everything I've come to expect and appreciate in a privately owned, boutique-style, middle-class shop in a middle-class neighborhood. Clean, well-organized and well-lit, with a border of gray-and-maroon-stenciled hangers and clothes, all askew, dancing across the top of the ceiling. Matching gray, industrial strength carpeting covers the floor. But mostly mall-grade acrylic and polyester knits and blends from Taiwan hang on the racks. Not nearly enough in-vogue, natural fiber, designer label quality (primo). **Men's had a more ample selection** than some and an unusual cache of size 44's on one visit.

Two out of three undercover visits, I browsed alone. The owner carried on a series of intense telephone conversations. Lone-wolf shopper that I am, I still couldn't help but think this was not the best way to build a business. "Are you: On our mailing list? Looking for something in particular? Do you know about our wish list? Have anything to consign?" Engaging topics of mutual benefit I would appreciate being asked.

CONSIGNOR ALERT: 50%-50% split. No fee. 60 days. 20% off/ 30 days.

Joys & Toys

   CC | L | | P_F

467 Jacksonville Rd.
Hatboro, PA. 19040

675-2880

Look: CLASS ACT

Goods: CLASS ACT

Prices: ON THE
MONEY

HOURS:
Mon–Sat 10:30–
5:30, Sun 11-3

CLOSED: Holidays

This is another one of those maybe-I-should-include-it, maybe-I-shouldn't, but-it's-so-good, how-could-I-possibly-leave-it-out tossups. If I were to put it in the same category as Fairygodmother in Downingtown, where they buy everything outright, it belongs in the Guide . If I take it as it appears, a toy and collectible shop, it's more a trip-down-memory-lane antique (I seem to like inventive hyphenation, don't I?). But the word antique can't be found in the name or on the card. Only "Collectibles From The Past." So, I'm gonna put it in. So there.

Every shelf, niche, tabletop and cupboard is full. Toys, salt and pepper shakers, old magazines, records, books, dolls, glassware and china fill every square inch. You can tell that every item is known and loved, that every item has its very own spot, carefully considered and intentionally chosen, that every item is immaculate, and that every item has just the right touch of playful, colorful humor. Like the orange-shaped and colored salt and pepper shakers with equally bright green alligators perched, lumbering and growling, on top. From Florida, of course. Aunt Jemima, Mickey Mouse, Ozzie & Harriet all the obvious, well-loved, once cheap, soon-to-be priceless, timeless icons of American mass marketing sharing in a good laugh. And the laugh is on us. We threw out, broke, gave away and lost all this stuff, one time or another. **Now it's all here. My childhood is all right here. And so, probably, is yours. For a price**.

CONSIGNOR ALERT: Buys outright.

Nearly New

223B York Road
Warminster, PA
18974

443-8010

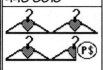

Look: CLASS ACT

Goods: STATUS
QUO–CLASS ACT

Prices: LOW –
MODERATE

HOURS: Mon–Fri 10-
5, Sat 12-5 Summer
hours: Closes at 4

CLOSED: Mon in
summer &
Christmas week

I must apologize. Nearly New should have been, was supposed to be, included in Volume II. The review was written and polished. And then the @#^* computer crashed. And then it crashed some more. In all this crashing and banging, the review was "lost," disappearing into bit and byte purgatory. Its absence went unnoticed until the final stage of preproduction known in publishing as the infamous blue line. Alas, too late. Reinserting this one review would have meant ripping the book apart, redoing entire sections and resequencing the entire @#^* book, already running weeks behind schedule, Nearly New never made it.

I can tell you now, what I'd have said last edition. **This is a very good kid's shop.** The bulletin board-like front door, with signs announcing hours, consignment wish list and all that stuff. One of the many signs inside--this one near the thoughtfully designed, secure play area--cautions parents: Children are your responsibility. A winged white- angel nightgown hung over one side of a blue picket fence, a pink and silver ballerina costume over the other. Rows and rows of shoes and boots, books and toys, line and top every display rack; lots of good play clothes peaking at size 8.

Sure enough of themselves and their future, their hours are printed on business cards, a rare sign of an established winner. Most shops hedge their hours because they can't be sure which customer traffic patterns work and which don't and just how many hours they can sustain. Hence, this vital information is often omitted.

P.S. Their neighbor is The Dollhouse, where all things miniature are sold.

CONSIGNOR ALERT: 50%-50% split. $8 annual fee. 20 items/consignment. Consigning hours: Monday & Wednesday 10-12:30.

Pooh's Corner

205 Davisville Rd.
Willow Grove, PA
19090

830-9920

Look: STATUS QUO
– CLASS ACT

Goods: STATUS
QUO–CLASS ACT

Prices: LOW–
MODERATE

HOURS: Mon-Sat
10-5, Thu 10-6:30

CLOSED: Holidays

A chain reaction of six closets held together by the owner's sheer force of organizational superego contain **the largest inventory I've ever seen, jammed into one of the smallest spaces I've ever shopped.** At one point my chin was forced to come to a rest in a nursery room clown's wicker balloon basket as I coaxed sliding doors back and forth, moving a wooden toddler chair, unused boxed nursing pillow and $30 Casco highchair out of my way to reach a prodigious amount of quality girl's size 12, 14 and 16. (Take away the doors?) If you're claustrophobic, don't come. I, however, was in an expansive mood.

The 8"x8" maternity "room," with chintz curtain strung across the doorway, doubles as a dressing room. Household back-of-the-door racks hold infants through pre-teen shoes. Narrow white chest is labeled gloves, mittens, hats. Floor-to-ceiling, closet-expanding, mind-boggling gizmos and widgets utilize every square inch. A rack of costumes by the register, just in time for Halloween, a mini, How To Pull Off Being A Parent-type lending library by the front desk, and **every crawling, carrying, bouncing, sleeping, feeding and strolling device known to Mom** complete the inventory explosion. There's even a mini play space by the front door, where Jason, the owner's son, with a patience born of personality and experience, played away the hours, helping out mom by occasionally answering the phone. Knee-high Entrepreneurial 101.

CONSIGNOR ALERT: 50-50% split. No fee. Reduced 50% beginning 3rd month. No appointment. No item limit. Call first in case they're too busy to fit you in.

Second Debut 	
356 Easton Rd. Horsham, PA 19044 **675-1288**	Just down the road from Dan's House of Darts and Memory Lane used music (don't you just love it?), the curve in Rte. 611 is so sharp, it looks like you could drive right in the front door. Which is probably what you might have done on opening day, blizzard of '93. What luck.
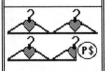	What we've got here is the pink-wall, white-lace-window, school of resale design. The sorority sisterhood of secondhand shopkeepers, in an attempt to keep the bogeyman of used, used, used at bay, consciously and unconsciously mimic one another. Cute, cute, cute. Could we have a little more imagination, please? Watch out or you will all start looking like a national chain with some kind of prechewed, easily recognizable identity.
Look: CLASS ACT **Goods:** HO HUM – CLASS ACT **Prices:** VERY LOW	Outside, colonial-period stone walls and turnpike-propelled kamikaze drivers. Inside, wide-plank wood floors, boarded up fireplace, drop ceiling, and blissful quiet. Any number of shopkeeper-suggested, potential outfits scattered about, hanging on the walls of both small rooms. Nice touch. **The owner has a genuine gift for coordinating the randomly consigned inventory into zingy contemporary outfits.**
HOURS: Tue, Thu, & Fri 11-4:30, Wed, 11-6, Sat 12-5	If you're confused as to how to put it all together, ask her for opinions. She's got them, and they're great.
	There's been a **consignments/inventory upgrade** since my last series of undercover shopping expeditions here. I am, therefore, delighted to be able to bestow an additional half hanger. I was touched to see a well-worn copy of my opus at the counter, no connection to the additional half hanger, but maybe a reason for their having earned it.
CLOSED: Mid-July thru Labor Day	**CONSIGNOR ALERT:** 50%-50% split. No fee. 45 days. 20% off/30 days. By appointment only.

The Second Fiddle 	
37 S. York Rd. Hatboro, PA 19040 **672-7724**	**A dense, helter-skelter sidewalk array** of snappy red, pink and blue bikes, swings with removable seats, high-chairs, strollers, and molded plastic toys in every inconceivable color and shape for **inconceivably low prices** beckon in disarray on good weather days. A parade of parents (well, Moms, anyway) file in, deposit their little ones in the huge, sunny Kids Corner and cheerfully compete for clothing, all the while catching up on local gossip, no matter what the weather.
	Roller skates and tiny, tiny shoes line the ledge inside the big picture window. Clothing inventory, heavily stocked in infants and toddler, tapers off at size 8, tops
Look: TOP DRAWER **Goods:** STATUS QUO–CLASS ACT **Prices:** LOW – MODERATE	out at 10 or 12. There were almost no party dresses or their male counterpart. Play clothes were the main event. Maternity rack space was minimal, but better minimal than nonexistent. Shopkeepers and assistants range from the tight and taciturn to the young and bubbly. In four visits, not one of them left the register area to engage customers. There is a printed consignment policy sheet, but they were considered too expensive to hand out. Penny-wise and pound-foolish?
HOURS: x Tue–Fri 10-5, Sat 10-4, Thu 10-8	**It's a big, bright, happy shop.** Every Small Town USA should have one (or two) like this. And indeed, these days most do.
CLOSED: Holidays	**CONSIGNOR ALERT:** 50%-50% split. $5 annual fee. By appointment only.

Second Impressions	
123 S. York Road Hatboro, PA 19040 **675-9920**	I hate cheap wood paneling. I can't tell how many thrift stores have used cheap wood paneling. This store has cheap wood paneling. However, this store also has class. They painted the paneling and stenciled it, so it resembles Laura Ashley wallpaper. Ta Da! Isn't that what thrift shopping is all about; trash to steam. Boutique-style store, owned by daughter, Susan and managed by her mom, Quinny, **it's a charming, intimate place, where the customer can feel comfortable from the first.** Ann Taylor, Talbot, and Calvin, lots of really good labels and looks are carefully culled from consignor's closets.
	Last Fall I found a salmon pink, Ralph Lauren cable stitched turtle-neck sweater for $15 here. This probably started out in life costing $225. This Fall I spent $50, here, and purchased the white and pastel twin of a black and primary color, hand knit sweater I had been overjoyed to get for $75 at a resale shop in Glenside last year. Originally around $250, it was an even better buy this second, second time around. I lived in the black version last Winter and hated the thought of eventually wearing it out, I love it that much. Now I've been able to "extend " it's life. Thank you Shopper Lady. **P.S. Men's and larger-sized women's** racks have been added since last edition. **P.P.S.** Year-round 50% sale rack.
Look: CLASS ACT **Goods:** STATUS QUO – CLASS ACT **Prices:** MODERATE	
HOURS: Mon–Sat 10-5, Fri 10-7	
CLOSED: First 3 weeks of August	**CONSIGNOR ALERT:** 50%-50% split. $5 annual fee. By appointment only.

Share and Care Boutique	
11 Park Avenue Willow Grove, PA 19090 **830-8677**	Tucked away, seemingly out of sight, yet within less than a block of the very busy Pathmark in Willow Grove in what is a white Victorian chapboard building that was once a country hotel. Front room is sunny and happy and full of good quality infants' and toddlers'. Back room is basement-bare and dark, exposed-pipe school of design, where maternity and older children's are hung. I was mystified to learn she had stopped taking consignments for the Fall and Winter season. It was only mid-October, and the larger kids' stuff was minimal and uninspiring. While Marvin waited in the car and caught up on data entries, I did find a seemingly brand-new pair of size-12 Guess overalls with floral appliqués for a very, very reasonable $10.
	The owner is yet another working mom with toddler in tow. Between the nap area in the very back of the shop and the play area in the very front, and mom at his side, the kid is handled. How handled mom can be under these circumstances, I'm not so sure. I know I can barely write and breathe at the same time. This arrangement probably works out most of the time, excluding those magic moments in resale when the shop is crowded, the kid is hungry and crying, someone is waiting to con-sign and then the phone rings. **My secondhand hat's off to you.**
Look: HO HUM – STATUS QUO **Goods:** HO HUM – STATUS QUO **Prices:** LOW	
HOURS: Tue–Sat 10-5 (call ahead)	
CLOSED: Holidays	**CONSIGNOR ALERT:** 50%-50% split. No fee, 90-days. 50%/60 days. No appointment.

Shikari

48 N. York Rd.
Willow Grove, PA
19090

657-5319

Look: HO HUM

Goods: HO HUM –
STATUS QUO

Prices: LOW

HOURS:
Mon-Fri 11-5:30,
Sat 11-5

CLOSED: Holidays

"Haggling $1 Extra," printed neatly and discreetly on the sign up front by the register. This in a place where one customer, well known to the owner, haggled the entire time I was there. The bill must have been jacked up 50% by the time they were done. The customer offered $3 for a men's camelhair sport jacket in excellent condition. It wasn't a gift. She planned to wear it herself, joining the ranks of young women with rolled up sleeves and the baggy body look many seem to prefer. Bored and already naturally baggy, I left before a deal had been struck.

The place is new, but dark and dreary. It looks like it has been here for years. Some things are ticketed, some are not. There is a vague attempt at organization, something I demand from would-be secondhand boutiques and don't mind going without in hodgepodge thrift shops, especially when there is a chance of finding a gem or two on the racks and on the shelves. Here, my chances were slimmer than a super model after a natural fiber laxative.

Perched on the edge of the Rte. 611 speedway, alias Old York Road, in what is left of pre-mall, downtown Willow Grove. Parking is hard to come by unless you try this hard-won tip. **Pull in the dirt road next door to First Fidelity Bank across the street.** This free lot has drive-through access to Pooh's Corner, located right around the corner on Davisville Rd. Voilà! One-stop shopping. Second visit? Camelhair jacket still there.

CONSIGNOR ALERT: Buys outright.

Stuff 'n' Such

102 W. Moreland Av.
Hatboro, PA 19040

674-9199

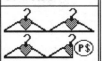

Look: STATUS QUO

Goods: STATUS
QUO–CLASS ACT

Prices: LOW–
MODERATE

HOURS:
Mon–Sat 10-5

CLOSED: July

We happened in on one of the rare days the owner was out. She was taking her first vacation in 4 years. And they think resale is easy. In the biz for 16 years, this location for 14, a survivor for good reason. **Quality is high, prices are low.** A three-piece wine-colored Vittadini with scattered florals, brand-new looking, $12. This would've easily commanded $28 in Center City or the Main Line. (Buy it, resell it and pocket the difference?) Mousefeathers navy-and-wine floral corduroy dress with charming navy ruffle at the throat $20, equally underpriced. Could have been as much as $36. Some would be glad to pay that in a snappy boutique. Mousefeathers retails around $120.

This is definitely not a boutique-style shop. It was begun before the gentrification process began and will probably outlast many newcomers. Make no mistake, no-nonsense big black block letters hang from the ceiling directing you to BOYS, GIRLS, etc. **The small shop** (across the street from Acme) **is packed to the rafters** with children's sizes up to 16, maternity and all the accessories and necessities; rollerblades, ice skates, toys, snow boots and shoes, books. ***Children's "Pre-loved" Everything*** it says on the top of the card. And it is.

CONSIGNOR ALERT: 50%-50% split. $5 fee. 60 days. Call for appointment.

YMCA	
8 York Road Hatboro, PA 19040 **672-7611**	Good news. High-ticketed polyester garments, formerly priced in the $20-$30 range, that wouldn't have been allowed in the door of a more discerning charity thrift, are now at least in the much more appropriate $8, $10 and $12 range. Last edition, I ranted on about the all-too-obvious disparity between price and style. Perhaps the rant did some good.

Look: HO HUM

Goods: HO HUM – STATUS QUO

Prices: LOW – MODERATE

HOURS: Mon–Fri 10-4, Sat 11-3

CLOSED: Several days in early Sept. and Feb. Call ahead.

Left to my own devices, **I'd keep coming back if I lived in the neighborhood** and happened to be passing by. As an inveterate thrifter, I know that if you live around the corner from a place like this and go in almost every day, you will find gems in the racks and on the shelves. Its just that the ratio here works against the occasional shopper with middle-to-upper-class taste buds. Stuff isn't bad, mind you, just not inspirational. The book section and housewares have more to offer than the clothing section.

Incredibly friendly, almost giddy, silver-haired, silver-tongued ladies of another era, who volunteer their time to make this place run, were kind and helpful. We talked, we laughed, we giggled. If they had been for sale, I would've bought my daughter a grandmother or two to go. After reading the newly published Volume II, one member of their ranks took the time to gently chide me in a sweetly reasoned letter of disagreement, offering herself up as spokesperson for the group.

She, as most time-and-heart-invested volunteers here, had a different perspective. She found it hard to believe I had even shopped there; perhaps I had confused it with another? I suggested that they might wish to get out and about more, check out what some of the 3- and 4-hanger charity thrifts were doing, reverse roles and rate themselves. I was raised to respect my elders. I was also taught to question authority. I hope Morgan will do the same.

CONSIGNOR ALERT: Donations only.

TOUR #4
IF IT'S TUESDAY, THIS MUST BE GLENSIDE (OR JENKINTOWN OR ABINGTON)

Glenside, dear Glenside, with it's 14 shops all beckoning at once, was my thrift shop home away from home. Was, only because my life's work (and play) now takes me hither and yon, farther and farther afield. It's harder to get here as often as I used to, as often as I'd like. But why don't you come for me and take up some slack? Just pull up to Virginia's Thrift Etc. freebie parking lot while you "do" Virginia's shop, and let the games begin.

Welcome to Glenside, thrift shop Small Town U.S.A. For our purposes, the town is divided into two sections. Unless you looove to walk and schlepp, you'll need a car to drive down (or up) Easton Road to connect the two halves, because they are spread too far apart for all but the most determined and dedicated of us to comfortably walk. Curiously, most of the ladies' clothing shops are in one half near Glenside Avenue, children's in the other. This isn't hard and fast, but it is a trend. The first cluster runs along Easton Road: head north, then hang a left on Glenside Avenue. There are six shops along this right-angle stretch. Nearby, **Rizzo's** is a great place for lunch. Stick to the pizza; it's won all sorts of awards. The second cluster? Time to get back in the car and drive up Easton Road to Keswick Avenue. There's a grocery (shop for dinner?), two good restaurants, the **Athena** for Greek goodies and **Joe Gabbi's** Italian family restaurant hugging the Keswick theatre (lunch?), the **Cafe Excellence** (espresso break?) and seven more shops (eight if you count Big Bear, which is on the edge of Tour #3, or the edge of this one, depending on your perspective).

Bring quarters. Most parking is metered. The lovely Rita meter maids of Glenside don't play around. This is one of the few places I've gotten ticketed, having such a good time making and overstaying my rounds. There are two mainstay thrifter services located in town: **Dip 'n' Strip** and my favorite **furniture repair and refinishing** man, **Mr. Owens**. Don't bother calling me, I won't give you his number. He's already swamped with work. Find your own. **Anthony** of Anthony's in **Jenkintown**, does **caning, furniture repair and refinishing**, too. When you trash pick and bottomfeed as I do, you can't get by without such skilled workers, unless you want or know how to do these jobs yourself. I definitely don't.

Jenkintown is prettier and smaller, with fewer shops (6) but a high restaurant-to-shop ratio. You can park and walk to all of them. **Mirna's**, my first choice if we've sold enough books that week, **La Pergola** for very good middle Eastern food, **Fiesta** for my old standby, pizza (crispy crust), **Tutte Fresco**, for the upscale pizza crowd, **Jenkintown Creamery**, the ice cream parlor, and **Stutz's** superb candy store (remember, dark chocolate only, please and thank you) give it a numerical culinary edge over Glenside. **Stazzi Milano** over by the train station, is too far on the outskirts of the resale action to count for our purposes, but it has a great post-thrifting, hangout bar. Good deli? Half way between Jenkintown and Abington, take a right at Barnes & Noble, go past all the car dealerships and go left into Baederwod Shopping Mall. Eat at **Murray's** (near the Acme). And of course **Barnes & Noble** for books 'n brew (and Guide).

Glenside and Jenkintown still struggle with the aftereffects of the invention of the automobile. Easton and Old York Roads zip right through the middle of town, bringing business but relinquishing some quality of life. Still, there is a sense of community, of people knowing each other. Pedestrians and locals from the surrounding residential areas actually walk from their homes to the stores to shop. Willow Grove Mall isn't the only game in town.

Abington lost the struggle. Even though it has a place-name and a dot on all the maps, it isn't a town as I understand the meaning. Surrounded by expensive, scattered, bedroom communities, it is a far-flung commercial collection of living-on-the-edge businesses in what were once private homes and hideous mini strip malls lining Old York Road. Most are boarded up and abandoned. It is an eyesore. Where was zoning? Foresight? Abington's "heart" is the Circuit City/Super Fresh mall. There have been conversations lately about trying to create a town center. How can you do that when a major highway cuts right through the middle of the body politic? Magic? Millions? Try higher taxes.

So when you "do" Abington, park in the lots behind Abbie's and Sandy's, do your thing, then skip town. There isn't one. As for dining, I'll take the discretionary high road and uncustomarily state, as my mother so often did, "If you don't have anything nice to say, don't say anything at all." Or as Andy, a friend and longtime resident of the township suggests, "Try the salad bar at **Shorday's** supermarket."

TOUR #4

1	Abbie's	Abington
9	Almost New	Cheltenham
7	Anthony's	Jenkintown
17	Betty's	Glenside
6	Breslin's Consignment Corner ★	Jenkintown
20	Glenside Kids Exchange	Glenside
3	Man to Man	Jenkintown
16	New to You ★	Glenside
19	Once Upon a Kid	Glenside
13	Ramblin' Rose Boutique	Glenside
21	St. Peter's	Glenside
2	Sandy's Second Act ★	Abington
15	Sports "n" Stuff	Glenside
14	Terry's Place	Glenside
12	Thrift Boutique ★	Glenside
11	Thrift Collectibles	Glenside
4	Twice is Nice-Plus ★	Jenkintown
10	Virginia's Thrift Etc. ★	Glenside
5	Women's Exchange & Next to New	Jenkintown
18	Yesterday & Today	Glenside
8	Your Mother's Closet	Jenkintown

*Note: This list has a shop's entire name. Names in review boxes may have been shortened a tad to fit. Numbers before each shop name correspond to their numbered location on each map. **Shops with a star sold Volume II. Volume III? ASK!**

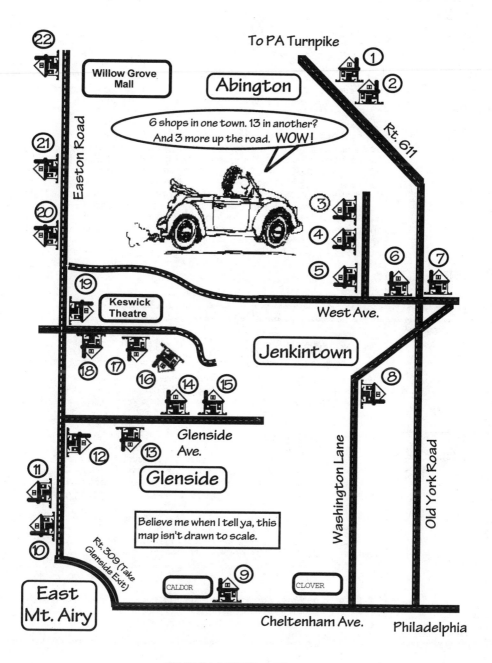

TOUR #4 MAP Page 70

Abbie's	
1157 Old York Rd. Abington, PA 19001 **884-7767**	**Friends swear by the place.** Run by kindly, tortoise-paced, senior citizen volunteers, whose time, energy and know how benefit Abington Hospital. Gathered round the register, warming themselves, they comparison-shop nursing homes, swap detailed medical war stories of the latest theater of operations, all the while covertly competing for winner of most exotic ailment du jour. All-too-real soap operas like these are commonplace, especially when volunteers are of a certain age.

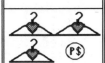

Look: CLASS ACT

Goods: HO HUM - CLASS ACT

Prices: UP & DOWN

Friends report prices inching up and spiking. I've noticed it, too. Preselected, charity shop, set-aside racks for so-called designer labels can be eyebrow raisers. Here is no exception. Some stuff is dated, some a real find. No matter. Being placed here always jacks up the price. The eyesight of some steadfast but dwindling volunteers ain't so good these days. A pure down, white and pink parka was worth the $25 price tag, till I spied the four random stains that might or might not wash out. Place your bets and take your chances. The woman that I spoke with explained prices do eventually average out; they use a price-off-color code system on the tickets. If it didn't sell right away, the price on the jacket would drop 25%, then 50%. I pointed out that a stranger or occasional visitor to the shop, but no stranger to thrifting, could only assume the pricing was erratic, possibly electing not to return. This system works best for regulars. Very catty corner from the hospital on very busy 611, the attractive, recently and modestly renovated shop is always busy.

HOURS:

Mon–Fri 10-5,
Sat 10-4

CLOSED: Holidays

SALE ALERT: End-of-season bag sales August and February

CONSIGNOR ALERT: Donations only. Benefits Abington Memorial Hospital.

Almost New	
2925 Cheltenham Ave. Phila., PA 19150 **572-0302**	Almost New describes itself well, as far as the name goes: **A good resource** for **way-too-new-to-be-antique** but **too-old-to-be-current** living room, dining room and bedroom furniture. One minute you're bumping up against cheapo-profundo formerly modern, sharing floor space with the occasional almost antique--usually, but not always, a plain-Jane piece. The next minute you'll be eyeballing lots of dinettes, ranging from '40's knotty- pine cottage, to Lucy and Desi 50's aluminum, to 70's Brady Bunch lime-green floral, to '80s brass and glass ('90s too new to be nailed down stylistically. See me in 10 years). A new, pickled-pine four-door cabinet ($499) and a similar but not matching, entertainment-center monolith $699 were very tempting. A girl's-room dresser and pop-up vanity combo, both for $149, had good "cheekbones," but needed a total face-lift. The hideous, cheap vinyl chair that is paired with the set only served to jack up the price. It didn't begin to match .

Look: STATUS QUO

Goods: HO HUM- STATUS QUO

Prices: MODERATE

Crowding out the almost new, which now represents the minority of their merchandise, are the new new new, unused flash-and-trash, lacquered and mirrored, particle-board dining and bedroom sets and relentlessly Scotchguarded polyester plaid, velvet and seriously depressed floral living rooms sets, refugees of the hard life on showroom floors or furniture store liquidations, so prevalent in recent years. I predict that soon they will only be carrying closeouts and scratch and dent.

HOURS: Mon, Wed, Fri 10-7, Tue & Thu 10-6, Sat 10-4

CLOSED: Christmas week

P.S. There's a **new merchandise catalogue.** Pick something out. If it's in the warehouse, they'll deliver within 24 hours.

CONSIGNOR ALERT: 60% You–40% Shop. If they come and get it, then its 50%-50%. Call for an appointment.

Anthony's

805
Greenwood Ave.
Jenkintown, PA
19046
885-2992

Look: STATUS QUO

Goods: STATUS QUO–TOP DRAWER

Prices: MODERATE –HIGH

HOURS: Mon, Tue, Thu, Fri & Sat 11-7, Sun 12-5.

CLOSED: Holidays

Anthony took a big risk. He moved from his original, very unchic, isolated and very successful location to high-speed, fly-by Old York Road to a section of Jenkintown where there's little or no foot traffic. It took Anthony quite some time to get a toehold on his new location, only to lose it to a rent increase and a bunch of rose wholesalers, who in turn bit the dust.

It was painful to watch his struggle, because **the man's got good stuff. He's relocated again.** This time across Old York Road and around the corner in smaller, less expensive digs, hard by the soft pretzel take-out window.

With lots of collectibles and some very nice furniture, ranging from almost new to actual antique, Anthony has added **recaning, re-rushing and furniture repair** to his services. With a year left on his latest lease, stay tuned.

CONSIGNOR ALERT: Mostly buys outright, except for items valued over $1,000. Individual pricing arrangements made. Call for an appointment.

Betty's

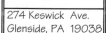

274 Keswick Ave.
Glenside, PA 19038
576-9881

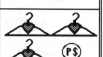

Look: STATUS QUO

Goods: STATUS QUO – CLASS ACT

Prices: MODERATE

HOURS:

Mon–Wed & Sat 10-4, Fri 10-5:30

CLOSED: July 30 thru Labor Day

Betty's is as old and comfortable and well broken in as your favorite easy chair. Indeed, the owners tend to sit by the front door in quiet moments, taking their ease. A regular wanders in from the neighborhood and takes up where they left off last visit. It's that kind of place: long on local history and neighborliness. Walk in, and the place beckons you to rummage about, linger, chat, try on a few garments, and come back again soon. On my first visit, it seemed familiar, as if I'd been there many times before.

If you're a thrift shop regular, accustomed to the usual gamut of goods, Betty's covers that gamut, and is **a fine place to shop.** Women's clothing is definitely their strong suit. Men's and especially children's are clearly an afterthought. There was quite a selection of women's sizes 14, 16 and 18 from which you could choose. The pricing was a trifle quirky. Garments I expected to cost more didn't, others seemed a trifle high for their original value or present condition. The price marked is the price. No sales. No markdowns. No bargaining. Of the three dressing rooms, an unusually large number for this size shop, two would (still) greatly benefit by some additional overhead lighting. Indeed, Betty's is so timeless, it has outsmarted and outlasted many a would-be competitor (bye bye Berkow's). So timeless, there was really nothing to add, change, or delete from last year's review.

👉 **SHOPPER ALERT:** Women's

CONSIGNOR ALERT: 50%-50% split. $8 fee. Consignign hours: Monday, Wednesday, Friday 10-1.

Breslin's Consignment Corner	
719 West Ave. Jenkintown, PA 19046 **884-5444**	Gerrie is the owner. Gerrie is a natural high. Her clear, vivid, turquoise-blue eyes, and optimistic entrepreneurial soul have carried her past the early naysayers and doubters' "Why would you want to open a thrift shop? Who would wear secondhand?" etc. to her present, well-deserved success as one of the longest lived, most successful shops in Jenkintown, new sale or resale.
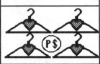	Staff demeanor reflects Jerry's sunny smile. Faithful consignors from the tonier sections of Jenkintown and Abington keep the shelves and the color-coordinated clothing racks stocked with **mid-range to high-fashion goodies**. Faithful customers, including those same consignors, come in droves, carting the stuff away as fast as it comes in. I almost never leave empty-handed. Neither does Dr. Maniac. On those rare occasions I can get him to come along, Marvin almost always finds something great in the cramped but **choice men's department** in the rear.
Look: TOP DRAWER **Goods:** STATUS QUO–TOP DRAWER **Prices:** MODERATE **HOURS:** Mon,Tue, Thu, & Sat 10-5, Wed & Fri 10-7	Resale owners are responding to the growing demand and profitability of larger sizes. Gerrie spotted the trend and the customer potential. Center stage is a circular rack full of **very attractive size 16 and up women's garments**.
CLOSED: First 3 weeks in August	**CONSIGNOR ALERT:** 50%-50% split. No fee. Tuesday-Friday 10-3. Drop and run.

Glenside Kid's Exchange	
466 N. Easton Rd. Glenside, PA 19038 **886-4442**	Tiny, tiny place packed with children's clothing, baby equipment and maternity. Run by two seriously coiffed and powdered ladies with the look and attitude of everyone's ideal grandma. When I say it's tiny in here, I may have understated the case. With the two owners, one customer with doll-clutching, screaming, just-learning-to-walk-but-managing-to-crawl-every-where baby and moi, the floor space was all but used up. So was the wall space. The ladies have efficiently used every possible square inch to sell, store or display what seems to be predominately infant-size 6x, but ranges all the way up to children's size 14.
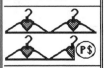	**Most of the garments and equipment are stylish and in excellent condition.** Some of the prices seem steep, perhaps because this place is run by its size. Smaller inventory could equal smaller profit margin. They've got to get the rent money from somewhere, or grandmas 1 and 2 would be out on the curb, and that is no place for such kindly, well organized get-up-and-go ladies.
Look: CLASS ACT **Goods:** STATUS QUO - CLASS ACT **Prices:** MODERATE -HIGH **HOURS:** Tue & Sat 10-2, Wed–Fri 11-4	Many would-be thrifters first get into the act by buying secondhand children's clothes, rightly rationalizing that it's money well saved. You can't buy children's garments then hold onto them and use them for years like you can with grown-up's. The little dears destroy, lose and outgrow it all eventually.
CLOSED: July	**CONSIGNOR ALERT:** 50%-50% split. Annual fee $5. Tuesday 10-2 .

Man to Man	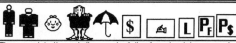

469 Johnson St. Jenkintown, PA 19046 **885-9230** 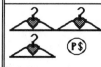 **Look:** CLASS ACT **Goods:** HO HUM – CLASS ACT **Prices:** MODERATE –HIGH **HOURS:** Mon 11-3, Tue & Thu 11-5, Wed & Fri 11-7, Sat 9-5 **CLOSED:** Holidays	The world, they tell me, is full of coincidence. Another hackneyed, but equally truthful notion is that there's nothing new under the sun. This could be a way to explain how the only two men's resale stores I've seen to date, could possibly have had the same name, even though they certainly didn't have the same owner. This isn't the first secondhand store to bear the name Man to Man, this is the synch- ronistic second. This is a prettier store, but downtown, the merchandise at newly merged Man To Man/New To Nearly New is prettier

To be fair, there may be more snappy dressers down in Center City than out here in the burbs (but my husband doesn't think so). I wish they would get rid of the retirement beige polyester pants and central Florida green jackets. The safe shetlands outnumber the sensational Alexander Julians, Polos and so on. Of course there's a market for conservative, there's just a tad too much of it here. Individually, the man and woman who run this place, are not into high fashion. Professionally it shows.

Don't get me wrong. **The inventory is mostly good to occasionally great.** It just lacks flare. They carry **boys all the way up to size 54 men's.** The shop is entirely new with **spit and polish-clean** carpet and walls and excellent lighting. It just lacks panache. Can flare and panache be learned?

CONSIGNOR ALERT: 50%-50% split. 60 days. $5 one-time fee. 20%/30 days. By appointment. No infant clothing please. Young boy clothes from 14 on up |

New To You	

244 Keswick Ave. Glenside, PA 19038 **884-8824**  **Look:** CLASS ACT **Goods:** STATUS QUO–TOP DRAWER **Prices:** LOW – MODERATE **HOURS:** Mon–Sat 10-5, Wed 10-7:30 **CLOSED:** Christmas	New carpet, newly painted kid pix on the newly painted white walls, a brand-new computerized inventory system and a perfectly seasoned owner, new to the business just 2 short years ago. Hers is now one of the places future second-hand- kid shop competitors go when they scope out the scene. Jodi told me, before my cover was blown, that she'd researched the business for 2 years as well, intending originally to open in New Jersey, until her husband was transferred to this side of the river.

Jodi's picked a great spot, sandwiched between an ice cream parlor and an orthodontist. That ought to bring the moms and their kiddies in droves. I was and continue to be **amazed at the low prices** on the tickets. Clothing racks are full to bursting with **good, better, best everyday clothes**, every day, and krispy kritter containment devices, i.e. cribs, playpens, etc.

Jodi has done everything right in my book. She's more than earned the big four.

I *would* like to see more party clothes. There's always next year. **P.S.** Congratulations on your " second little addition," Jodi.

CONSIGNOR ALERT: 50%-50% split. $5 one-time fee. 20% /30 days, 40% after 60. |

Once Upon a Kid	
355 N. Easton Rd. Glenside, PA 19038 **884-1143**	Hallelujah! P&J died and went to thrift shop heaven. Once Upon a Kid was born. Barely reaching the retail walking stage they pulled themselves up and used those wobbly, enterprising legs to carry them down the street and over to the other side. **Now they're the new kid on the block.** I guess they wanted to be part of the action, keeping company in this thrift shop playground with all the others playing nearby.
	Now there's a set of triplets. Glenside is home to the Glenside Kid's Exchange only a few blocks up Easton Rd. on the opposite side, and New to You just a hop, skip and a jump around the corner (down Keswick Avenue past Betty's). Sibling rivalry? Perhaps. Good for the resale rest of us? Definitely. Once Upon a Kid, just like real kids, outgrew its digs. Too many duds. Bigger 'kid.' **Bigger room. Nicer too.** I saw a
Look: STATUS QUO **Goods:** STATUS QUO **Prices:** LOW	very nice two-piece furniture set, marked sold, bumping up next to a Childcraft crib, $80.One grandmother scored 4 or 5 outfits, grandchildren in tow. I found a new $8.50 two-piece wrap skirt and tail-tying blouse in blue and white stripped cotton for Morgan. Very Gapesque. Just like what she had been going ga-ga over just last week when we walked past their Chestnut Hill window, hand in hand. I liked the feel of these prices much better. If you've just given birth, **this is a good place to come to**
HOURS: Tue–Sat 10-5	**soothe a new family's $$$ worries.**
CLOSED: Holidays	**CONSIGNORS ALERT:** 50%-50% split. No fee. No appointment. 20%/30 days. No consigning on Saturdays.

Ramblin' Rose Boutique	
20 E. Glenside Ave. Glenside, PA 19038 **887-8228**	The first time I ever came here, I was put off by the serious lineup of **brand new rock and roll and environmentally correct T-shirts and neon and pastel baseball hats.** Put off because I never was and never will be in that age group. But for those of you who choose to make this fashion statement, know that Ramblin' Rose has a steady pipeline to these goodies. Sometime during the last year, the owner rearranged the shop, bringing herself and her register to the front of the store. Past the T-shirt wall and venturing deeper, are my kind of clothes. **Carol Horn, Dominik Rompolo, St. Laurent, etc..**
Look: STATUS QUO **Goods:** STATUS QUO –CLASS ACT **Prices:** MODERATE	It's a small but pleasant place less than 3 years old and one of Glenside's newer resale stores. Melissa, the owner, was a Textile major with a fashion minor. She spent over a year as an employee researching 'Thrift Shop Management 101' at Pennsylvania Hospital's Bargain Shop on Delancey Street, before deciding to take the plunge and open her own place. She must have also taken marketing courses, because she periodically offers wine and cheese during the year as well as with her annual winter and summer sales. When I called to find out how the shop got its
HOURS: Tue–Fri 10-6, Sat 10-5 Call for summer evening hours.	name, turns out her high school nickname was Roses. Potential first-time customers pick her out of the <u>Yellow Pages</u> over others listed there because of her shop's unusual name. No mention of resale this or secondhand that, so this Rose stands out in the garden. Clever girl!
CLOSED: Holidays	**CONSIGNOR ALERT:** 50%-50% split. No fee. 60 days. By appointment only.

St. Peter's	
654 N. Easton Rd. Glenside, PA 19038 **576-9323**	Morgan and I were having another great mom-and-daughter, adventure-packed day. When we started out, her wallet was full. I had owed her for three week's worth of allowance and anted up right before we left. Mine, therefore was sides-sucking slim. She gets $9 per week, one for each year of her life. But before you get too excited about us spoiling her, know she does a huge list of chores every week. Skip one and we skip the entire allowance. And she only gets to spend 30% outright. Another 30% goes to long-range fun stuff for her or giving presents at birthdays and holidays. 35% goes to can't-touch-it-till-you're-18 savings and 5% goes to charity. This wasn't my idea. I copped it from a guest financial wiz on Oprah. I'm merely passing it along to thrifty, hardworking parents, everywhere. It works 100%.
	Volume I and I meant to include St. Peter's. Volumn II, I blew it again. Determined not to omit it from Volume III, here we are doing the final undercover shopping expedition. Morgan loaded for bear. Me loaded for chinchilla. The black velvet and chinchilla-collared 30's evening coat was in perfect condition and decadently stylish, but for an out-of-reach $200. According to the tag and the volunteers, I can return four weeks later in mid-December, when it will be marked down 25%, or again
Look: STATUS QUO **Goods:** HO HUM – STATUS QUO **Prices:** LOW	January, 16 when it will be half price. I must confess to surprise at finding anything so choice here. I have been in many times and it is a quietly classic church thrift shop straight out of the 50's format. The volunteer ladies are polite and sensible. So are
HOURS: Mon, Wed 10-4, Sat 10-1	the clothes. Morgan, however, perhaps because of all that loot burning a hole in her pocket, found a golden geode necklace (she loves rocks), and clip-on earrings shaped like little bells that really ring. **Housewares and women's clothes are strongest**. Men's is quaintly located round the corner and up the stairs on the curtained stage overlooking the community room. Accidently pull the curtain cord
CLOSED: Mid–June thru Labor Day	and you could have a sudden, impromptu, all-male burlesque review. **CONSIGNOR ALERT: 60% You-40% Shop**. $4 fiscal-year fee. Monday 10-2.

Sandy's Second Act	
1167 Old York Rd. Abington, PA 19001 **884-8342**	This store seemed to appear almost overnight; **making as strong an impresssion as many old timers**. Sandy was savvy enough to locate next to Abbie's (that must have shook 'em up) and have her consignment policies down on paper, ready for her first customer to walk through the lace-trimmed shop door. There's Waverly ivy chintz window valance and dressing room curtains with matching ivy wall stenciling, new carpeting to cushion soles, classical music to soothe souls.
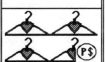	The front room is dedicated to the **serious pursuit of secondhand women's** fashion with two dressing rooms for trying on furs, leather, party clothes, and office duds.
Look: CLASS ACT **Goods:** HO HUM – CLASS ACT **Prices:** LOW-MODERATE	The kids and men's area are in the rear of the shop, which is also the front. How so? The eye-catching shop front window faces Old York Road, the actual entrance is in the rear, off the parking lot. Got you confused? Well there's nothing confusing about $18 for a men's light grey cashmere V-neck sweater-vest with a Sak's Fifth Avenue label, now is there?
HOURS: Mon–Sat 10:30-5:30	
CLOSED: Last 2 weeks in August	**CONSIGNOR ALERT:** 50%-50% split. 60 days. No fee. By appointment only

Sports "n" Stuff

268 Keswick Ave.
Glenside, PA 19038

885-8909

Look: STATUS QUO

Goods: YOU TELL ME

Prices: LOW

HOURS: Mon 11-5,
Tue & Wed 10-6,
Thu & Fri 10-7,
Sat 10-5, Sun 11-4

CLOSED: Holidays

Did you know that it can cost $500-$1000 to outfit an aspiring young ice hockey champ? A goalie's equipment can cost up to 2000 big ones. Keep in mind this is for a kids...kids keep growing...kids need larger sizes every year. New player's equipment costs $500-$1000. Same equipment here costs $125. Which would you choose?

Skates are hung on a line from the ceiling like so much laundry. Sunny days, they use the pavement, front and back, to increase the store's "selling floor" with a lineup of new scratch-and-dent and used bicycles and weight-lifting equipment. On the down side, the place is so small you'll have to rappel to tackle the mountains of skates and ski boots. Owners use networking and a 'wish book' to supplement limited floorspace. Lots of jocks out there have bought lots of equipment and now want to trade up. Baseball, football, basketball and soccer, archery, fencing, boxing, and scuba diving, everything from the everyday to the arcane. If you are an everyday sport, drop in. If you're arcane, call first. No pickup fee if it's big and heavy. Delivery handled on a case-by-case basis. **100% satisfaction guaranteed.**

P.S. They do bike and rollerblade repair on premises.

CONSIGNOR ALERT: 50%-50% split. No fee. No appointment. 60 days. Buys & trades.

Terry's Place

29 E. Glenside Ave.
Glenside, PA 19038

885-7149

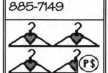

Look: HO HUM–
STATUS QUO

Goods: STATUS
QUO–CLASS ACT

Prices: MODERATE

HOURS: Tue & Thu
11-5, Wed 1-7,
Fri 11-7, Sat 11-5

CLOSED: August

Terry is Terry's. Terry owns one of the oldest shops in the biz. The basement's cramped exposed-pipe school of design has been brightened and renovated. Now, the shop decor begins to do her personality justice. Outgoing, with a sales approach that works, she's the **heart-of-gold type**, and that golden quality just lights up the place. Her expansive personality makes me feel there's enough room for everyone and everything. Even though it's an easily overlooked basement location, you can spot her shop from blocks away in good weather. Look for the eye-catching, brightly colored clothes set out on the sidewalk, fluttering in the wind like so many banners.

Terry prides herself on directing her inventory toward the "working gal," just as she directs her vast enthusiasm toward being the **best old-timer in the biz** with the best tales to spin. Front and center by the busy register are new arrivals that fly out as fast as they come in, Terry working feverishly trying to ticket before the stuff gets sold. Keep your sticky fingers off the layaway rack. I know, I know, everything looks so inviting, nevertheles, somebody else got their sticky fingers on it first.

CONSIGNOR ALERT: 50%-50% split. No fee. By appointment only.

Thrift Boutique	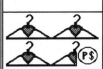

	It's tiny. The owner, also tiny, has a **big, vivacious personality**. She's an intense and intensely extroverted, savvy entrepreneur. "Glenside has been good to us," she's fond of saying. Indeed it has. And she's been good for Glenside, too. Son John, who helped out at the family business between semesters, recently completed law school and opened an office around the corner. Now Mom and son can do lunch.
107 S. Easton Rd. Glenside, PA 19038 **572-1707**	Vicki has an **enormous coterie of regular customers**, some so faithful they actually mail in their consignments from all over the U.S. Local consignors drop in over and over again to buy, chat and hang out.
Look:: STATUS QUO	The smaller, back room can have too many HO HUMs, yet **I almost always find something WOW** in the not-an-inch-goes-to-waste front room. Pour over the two jewelry cases filled with new and antique pieces. Check behind the register, casting your eyes heavenward. There's usually a special outfit or first-class handbag hanging there. **Knock-your-socks-off, strut-your-stuff front room goodies** this fall included a Sue Baseman (very expensive Jenkintown boutique gone bust) evening dress in body-clinging cream crepe, shot through with discreet, silver-encrusted dots of glitter ($75). Or how about a $250 (negotiable, Vicki told me). white and grey fur jacket that cost its soon-to-be-former owner $800 five years ago, but looks as if it had never been worn before by anyone but the fox and mink?
Goods: STATUS QUO–TOP DRAWER	
Prices: MODERATE-HIGH	
HOURS: Tue, Thu & Sat 10-5, Fri 10-7	
CLOSED: August	**CONSIGNOR ALERT:** 50%-50% split. No fee. No appointment necessary.

Thrift Collectibles	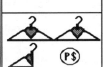

	Fabulous Finds by Peggy moved out and up the street, and then left town altogether. Inga, who owns the beauty parlor next-door (from whence commeth the permanenting solution that seeps in, insidiously scenting the shop) expanded into thrift shopping and moved in. So it goes in resale: opening, closing, enlarging, relocating, every week. A restless bunch.
126 Easton Rd. Glenside, PA 19038 **887-2273**	I did spot a custom set of bisque-colored pongee silk window poofs. Bored homeowner redecorating? Decorator's boo-boo? Originally hundreds of dollars each, except for the fact they were thrown on top of the pile like so much kindling, they looked brand-new.
Look: STATUS QUO	Densely packed, wildly divergent inventory, most of it **inexpensive**, dated, furniture and household items, encroaches upon more and more of the beauty shop. I'm someone who wants to subtly stand out in a crowd. If you're more low-key or the opposite, more flash-to-steam, this could be a good place for you. Owner Inga is a relative newcomer with a native language-to-English learning curve in its formative stages. I watched as she stood in front of a mirror rotating her hips, shoulders moving side to side, obviously considering the leather jacket's merits for herself. The international body language of bargain hunters, everywhere, came through loud and clear.
Goods: HO HUM – STATUS QUO	
Prices: LOW	
HOURS: Tue–Thu 9-6, Fri 9-7, Mon & Sat 9-5	
CLOSED: Holidays	**CONSIGNOR ALERT:** 50%-50% split. No fee. 20% off/ 6 weeks. No appointment.

Twice is Nice-Plus

469 Johnson St. Jenkintown, PA 19046 **885-9558**	All done up in pink and grey, with room-divider glass cubbies displaying classy accessories and jewelry. Twice is Nice-Plus fills a badly needed niche in the thrift shop scene: **Women's Plus Size Clothing For The Fuller Figure, size 14 and up.** I once tried to interest an old friend in just such a venture. Six months later I got a call from Molly Schatz, owner of Twice is Nice-Plus, asking to be included in TSMG. Well, my old friend went into the nut business (no kidding), but you larger women of fashion need look no further. (Now, how about a petite sizes only, and a few more men only?)

Look: TOP DRAWER **Goods:** STATUS QUO–CLASS ACT **Prices:** MODERATE	The ratio of stylish to sensible, silk to polyester is the same here as what's available for queenly sizes in department stores and specialty shops. Oprah Winfrey, in her (pre) salad days, did several fashion shows, hoping to instruct and cajole both designers and consumers in the real possibilitiy of being a fashionable larger size. Too often, it's been a matter of concealing 'flaws' rather than accentuating positive features, i.e., somber colors, serviceable fabrics and conservative styling.
HOURS: Tue–Sat 10:30-5, Fri 11-7	Let us hope designers and consumers get the message and there are even more goodies to choose from first-sale, filtering down to resale in the coming years. **Hard to find? It's exactly 1 block behind IHOP on Old York Rd.** Boy did I screw up last edition. Sorry Molly, I thought it was the *other* national brand-name chain of pancake houses. They all look the same to me. I make pancakes from scratch and refuse anything but pure maple syrup. None of that blueberry syrup that never saw a blueberry for moi, thank you very much. **P.S.** Ask about the charity cruise in August.
CLOSED: Holidays	**CONSIGNOR ALERT:** 50%-50% split. No fee. By appointment only.

Virginia's Thrift Etc.

136 S. Easton Rd. Glenside, PA 19038 **887-0967**	Virginia is a go-getter, a real entrepreneur. She has energy and ideas and is open to what's new. She's computerized. (Ya just don't wanna be around when all three crash at the same time). She's got those beige plastic security gizmos and video cameras instead of stenciled borders: Shoplifters beware! When the shop gets jumping, and jump it does, especially Saturdays, suddenly it doesn't have enough dressing rooms. (Who does?) If the humming intensity of a cheerful crowd is not your style, shop here some other day of the week. But no matter what, come.

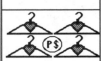

Look: STATUS QUO -CLASS ACT **Goods:** STATUS QUO-TOP DRAWER **Prices:** MODERATE	**Virginia has a great store, Glenside's biggest and for miles around.** She consigns merchandise in every category imaginable. Here the whole is greater than the sum of its parts. Some 4-hanger resale stores may be stronger in any one category at any given time, but there's nobody who manages so much, and so many, so well in one place. Goodies are mid-range in price and quality, with a growing stash of Gianfranco Ferre and upscale friends. The **huge furniture department** gets me all atingle. So good is Virginia at screening and training that this store has been the nucleus for several spinoffs, opened by former employees, including Breslin's in Jenkintown. The current, longtime **staff work together smoother than washable silk**
HOURS: Tue-Sat 10-5:30, Fri 10-7	. **P.S.** We shot the furniture segment for the Discovery Channel's <u>Home Matters</u> here.
CLOSED: August	**CONSIGNOR ALERT:** 50%-50% split. No fee. Consigning hours: Tuesday-Friday 10-3:30. No appointment.

Women's Exchange & Next To New

429 Johnson St.
Jenkintown, PA
19046

884-5642

Look: STATUS QUO

Goods: HO HUM–
CLASS ACT

Prices: MODERATE

HOURS: Tue–Fri
9:30-4, Sat 10-2

CLOSED: End of
June – Labor Day

Set back from the main shopping drag, this shop gets foot traffic that comes here on purpose, lured by the colored glass handsomely displayed on the many window ledges. This store's mood is appealingly anachronistic, the way they were way back when. Enter the sunny first floor with its somewhat sparse display of china, silver, knickknacks and jewelry, and you could be entering a 50's time warp. Good kitchen smells used to permeate the shop. There was a sweet (i.e., charming) bakery in the back, where Betty Crocker would have felt right at home. Alas, it is no more. Not as much call for sand tarts and bridge snacks as there used to be, I guess. Not many aproned at-home-moms to bake them, either.

I've been most successful at the **glass-enclosed jewelry cabinets** and poking into, around and through the crisply folded, ultra clean **stacks of antique linens**. Upstairs is another matter. The poor dears who draw guard duty on the second floor must get very bored. It's never, ever busy, at least not while I've been here. Frequently, the stuff is advanced ho hum, too recent to be romantic like downstairs, and too old to be exciting, like moi. Yet one day there was that tantalizing, French Creek, blonde suede and lambswool jacket for under $50.

CONSIGNOR ALERT: Clothing: $5 fee, **60% You-40% Shop** split. Consign Tue, Thu, Fri 9:30-11:30am. Household: $5 fee, **70% You-30% Shop**. Consign Mon 10-3.

Yesterday & Today

280 Keswick Ave.
Glenside, PA 19038

572-6926

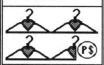

Look: STATUS QUO

Goods: STATUS
QUO–CLASS ACT

Prices: MODERATE

HOURS:
Tue–Thu 10-5,
Fri 10-8, Sat 10-5

CLOSED: Holidays

Strictly boudoir! All the faded finery of a movie star queen or a successful seductress can be acquired here, displayed on small pieces of furniture or tucked away in enormous glass cases. Linens and scattered lace, pairs of glass and porcelain vanity lamps, and a good collection of antique hats, pocketbooks, buttons and shoes. A cross-party-lines collection of political pins, perhaps left behind by a string of paramour pols?

Encapsulated amber distillation of perfume, discarded mauve satin slippers, white feather boa offhandedly tossed over a chair, the long-forgotten malachite watch marking hedonistic time on the mirror-topped dressing room table...all conspire to conjure the sinuously sculpted naked back of a finger-wave platinum blonde, exit stage left. (I had just seen Harlow's film bio. I couldn't help myself.)

I can help myself to apologize, though. After a Volume III return visit, I 've decided this **shop deserves a better rating than I gave it last year**. They've moved things around some, mostly for display and security reasons, but it really hasn't changed all that much. I underrated it by half a hanger, so here it is. Mea culpa.

CONSIGNOR ALERT: 50%-50% split. No fee. By appointment only.

Your Mother's Closet	
Washington La. & Rte. 73 Jenkintown, PA 19046 **885-0620**	So you think you know your mother well. Then one fateful day while she's away, you open her closet door, looking for something or other, and stumble upon the startling fact that mom is a cross-dresser. O.K., I'm being glib, but the thing is, the name of this place makes it sound like it only has things for women. And indeed the interior of Your Mother's Closet is a pretty shade of pink. So imagine my mild surprise when I came here the first time and found they also carried men's clothing.

Look: STATUS QUO –CLASS ACT

Goods: HO HUM– STATUS QUO

Prices: VERY LOW

HOURS: Mon, Tue, Thu, & Fri 10-3

CLOSED: Whenever women's center is closed.

Apparently I'm not the only one who was surprised. A meeting of all-female volunteers had just ended. Passing through the store to leave, they'd gather around the register. Rapid-fire comments like, "I thought they weren't going to take men's clothing" "They never said that" and "I like men" whizzed through the air. Wouldn't you know, the Maniac was lurking in the racks at just that very moment. What luck! What quotes! I loooove coming in here, you never know what they'll be talking about. Eat your heart out, Dorothy Parker.

They haven't begun to use the wall and floorspace potential. What's here so far is safe and dated. On the other hand, it's inexpensive, clean and tidy. The parking lot can be hard to maneuver and often close to or completely full. The thrift shop is on the **Washington Lane side of the Benson Manor in the basement** alongside the Women's Center of Montgomery County, the charity it helps to support. **There's wierd 'n wacky 'mom' energy here.** A volunteer let me in at the last minute, and she even smiled. The window box has half real, half plastic flowers. Nice touch. Even nicer? A play area please. This is a women's center, you know.

CONSIGNOR ALERT: Donations only. Benefits Mongomery County Women's Center.

TOUR #5
RISKY BUSINESS

Come to **Germantown's** frayed but bustling bazaar, where most things are well-worn, some broken. Some of the customers are, too. Come to **Germantown** if you're adventurous and it's high noon and there's a lot of people out and about. Not for the timid. Definitely for the bargain hunter. Germantown, where I used to shop Rowell's department store with my mom, and stop in at Dairy Maid on Saturday afternoons for an ice cream soda or hot fudge sundae with friend Nancy. We were 12. We went by ourselves; our overprotective parents never gave it a second thought.

Germantown 30 years later, where I and fellow shoppers utilize finely honed survival skills to brave the encroaching blight and the "department store" is Village or Bargain Thrift. Rowell's familiar shape still dominates the skyline, but the windows are darkened, the lights are out. Germantown, where the Avenue below the town square was once, not so very long ago, lined with antique shops rivaling Pine Street in Center City. Where **Cunningham Piano** maintains its niche, selling prime secondhand pianos, and **Asher's** candies flaunts a full line of mouth-watering chocolates through a buzz-you-in grated front door (there's a rumor they may relocate soon). Try the **vegetarian restaurant** in the **Maplewood Mall** for lunch. Their meatless burgers are great! The **rib place** next to Asher's got a Philly Mag award. I only use the lot next-door to Village Thrift to shop there or Whosoever across the street on Chelten Avenue. No spot, no stop. Perhaps I am overly cautious. I have never had a problem of any kind in Germantown, past or present. Or perhaps I am foolish, going there at all. But life is a risky business.

Change of venue, change of scene. Drive a few cobbled miles up Germantown Avenue to **Mt. Airy** with its perch on the edge of Lincoln Drive. Communities, like their individual and collective residents, have a life cycle and personality all their own. All those positive, intellectual, aging hippie, middle-class, integrated, Save The Earth vibes contribute to the overall aura. Since Mt. Airy, sandwiched between Germantown and Chestnut Hill, is more residential than commercial, there is only a handful of secondhand shops. So your time here will probably be brief. Don't pass up Past and Present if you are deep into vintage.

Chestnut Hill is an altogether different story. Chestnut Hill, for those who don't know, is an all-American small-town success story within a big city gone half-bust. Successful enough to have its own storefront Civic Association "welcome wagon" with a basketful of pamphlets announcing this upcoming event, that local endeavor and a mouth-watering description of every eatery in town. Everyone wants to shop here, live here and work here. So many everyones, in fact, that some old-timers want to get as far away from their who-woulda-thunk-it creation as fast and as far as possible. Too much of a good thing? There's that ol risk factor again...the upside and the downside. Either way it's all the same--pay as you play.

Civic visionary Lloyd Wells was his generation's William Penn equivalent, only on a slightly smaller scale. His leadership, and the work and determination of many like him, helped jump-start the Association's parking system and beautification program that make this generation's Chestnut Hill a booming, bloomin' success.

Still-life-inspired window boxes, strings of year-'round twinkling lights on the 'let's chop 'em all down' stinky ginkgo trees (just clean up after them, please, and stop all the fuss), open-air cafes, boutique-induced bumper-to-bumper traffic, and Madison Avenue-inspired colonial color schemes. This is what the dream realized looks like, so surface attractive it almost looks fake.

But peeking under the hard-won, pretty-as-a-picture surface, reading between the lines of The (Chestnut Hill) Local, or simply eavesdropping at **Caruso's Market** or the **Farmer's Market**, one hears seemingly discreet murmurings of political power plays and small-town gossip played out on an operatic scale. I know, I was once in the peripheral thick of things as a volunteer at Bird in Hand and as the controversial Maniac. (Who knew then? I certainly didn't.) All this to say, real estate values automatically add $25,000 to $50,000 to $100,000 big ones to the value of any house situated herein, thank you very much. All this to say, it's prime upscale resale hunting. So get going. And if the going gets tough, let 'em eat cake, or pie, or bread, or muffins, or biscuits, or scones, or popovers, or whatever, I say. And here's where:

Down the hidden alley from Monkey Business, there's **The French Bakery**, a tasty, cozy, Chestnut Hill lunch spot (with a bathroom). Morgan, Marvin and I are especially fond of the smoked turkey and melted cheese on croissant with honey mustard. If you're up by **Borders** and **Encore** (where they sell The Guide) and pooped, try Border's iced mocha cappuccino and cream cheese brownies (I bet they're from **Roller's**). Closer to the bus turnaround and ready to drop? There's Rollers best-ever takeout, or his catty-corner cafe, where you can sit outside in warm weather. Shopped till you've almost dropped? My absolute favorite for dinner is **Under The Blue Moon** (old buddies from my days at Morgan's Restaurant, when Gene and his wife Phyllis attended The Restaurant School). The appetizer sampler and the perennial favorite duck or sesame chicken entrees are my I'm-in-a-rut-but-who-cares-they're-fabulous favorites. Say Hi to Gene for me.

Finished beating the bushes looking for Bird In Hand? Tea time is at hand? Stop in down the hall at the **Women's Exchange** for fabulous, truly homemade baked goods and authentic tea sandwiches. To go, only. (Across the hall, the **Happy Butterfly** artisans' consignment shop is a must-see.) I also happen to be very fond of **Byrne Fabrics** directly across the street. Many of my Scarlett O'Hara, torn-green-velvet-tapestries-into-ball-gowns got their notions from here. They have a huge selection of buttons and bows. Tucked in the alleyway next to the **Cheese Shop** is a really great little **candy store**. Just thought you'd like to know. Sauntering down The Hill? Turn left past Jenks elementary school and stroll through **The Farmers' Market**, munch on lunch and do your marketing. You'll see the Maniac here every week, Thursday through Saturday, doing the same. Roll on down the Avenue just a teensy bit farther and you are within reach of the two new resale shops on the Hill and the **Night Kitchen** bakery, **Bredenbeck's** bakery and ice cream parlor, and **Baker Street** bakery. Hang a left on Willow Grove Avenue heading past Worth Repeating and you're in **Wyndmoor**. The hot dogs at the **7-11** are great! Or headed out of Chestnut Hill toward **Erdenheim**? **The Flourtown Farmers' Market** will take care of lunch and dinner.

Enough? Go home, pop a Tums, rest up, and live to shop and eat (burp) another day.

♥ ♥ ♥

TOUR# 5

15	Almost New	Germantown
22	Bargain Thrift Center	Germantown
23	Bargain Thrift Center	Germantown
5	Bird-In-Hand	Chestnut Hill
4	The Clothes Closet	Chestnut Hill
13	Cooper's Thrift	Germantown
14	Corrie's	Germantown
9	Dandelion ★	Mt. Airy
18	The Extra Hanger	Germantown
6	Ivy Hill Furniture	Wyndmoor
11	Just a Second	Germantown
21	McDaniel Furniture	Germantown
20	Mix & Match	Germantown
3	Monkey Business ★	Chestnut Hill
8	No Name Really	Mt. Airy
1	Opportunity Shop	Chestnut Hill
2	Pandora's Box	Erdenheim
12	Past & Present ★	Mt. Airy
17	St. Vincent's	Germantown
7	2nd Hand Rose	Wyndmoor
19	Village Thrift	Germantown
16	Whosoever Gospel Mission	Germantown
10	Worth Repeating	Chestnut Hill

*Note: This list has a shop's entire name. Names in review boxes may have been shortened a tad to fit. Numbers before each shop name correspond to their numbered location on each map. **Shops with a star sold Volume II. Volume III? ASK!**

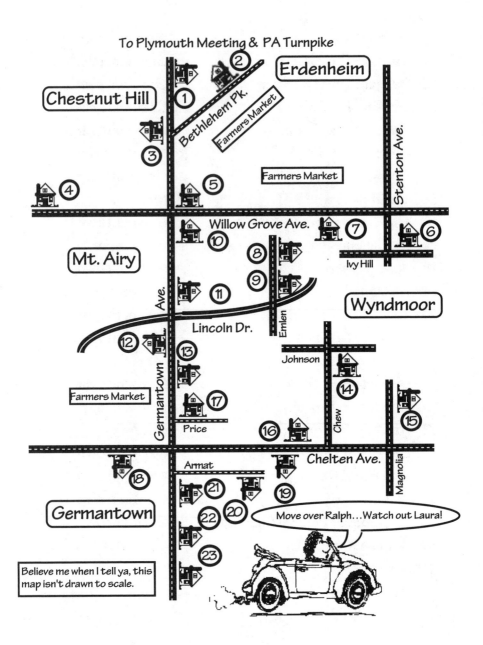

To Plymouth Meeting & PA Turnpike

Erdenheim

Chestnut Hill

Bethlehem Pk.

Farmers Market

Farmers Market

Stenton Ave.

Mt. Airy

Willow Grove Ave.

Ivy Hill

Wyndmoor

Ave.

Emlen

Lincoln Dr.

Johnson

Germantown

Chew

Farmers Market

Price

Armat

Chelten Ave.

Magnolia

Move over Ralph...Watch out Laura!

Germantown

Believe me when I tell ya, this map isn't drawn to scale.

TOUR #5 MAP Page 85

Almost New	
5701 Magnolia St. Phila., PA 19150 **572-0302**	Chelten & Chew, an intersection of crumbling, grafittied, boarded and abandoned homes and businesses, vulnerable to the person or event that will stir the remaining volatile ingredients of drugs and inner-city violence into a headline-grabbing moment on the evening news. It is also a neighborhood struggling to rise above its circumstances and become whole once more. Situated on the edge of this sadly oft-repeated urban landscape, Almost New is by comparison a thriving business, an example of what is possible. Cyclone fencing protects the lot, warehouse loading dock and entrance. **The interior space is huge, well lit and clean, the clerk friendly and helpful.**
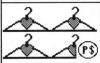	
Look: WAREHOUSE SHOWROOM **Goods:** STATUS QUO **Prices:** MODERATE **HOURS:** Mon, Wed, Fri 10-7, Tue & Thu 10-6, Sat 10-4	Many poorer families don't want secondhand reminders of what they're trying to leave behind. They want esthetic echoes of what they yearn to become, what they see on TV tonight, not yesterday's reruns. Mainstream "safe" secondhand, no retro-neo anything, sold here. Americanized French Provincial, homogenized colonial and overblown modern are the staples, mixed in with "new" slightly damaged and discontinued pieces and brand-new, priced-slightly-under-retail dining, living and bedroom sets. Yellow vinyl benches form an echoing circle under an artificial bamboo secondhand game table, $139. A slightly damaged, unused, distressed pine bedroom set by Florida Industries could be purchased for $1299. Catalogs by the register make it possible to order what you want from the factory if what you want has been sold out or is not displayed on the floor.
CLOSED: Holidays	**CONSIGNOR ALERT:** Buys outright. See second location reviewed in Tour #4.

Bargain Thrift Center	
5261 Germantown Ave. Phila., PA 19144 **849-3225**	Bargain Thrift is a vibrant, alternative, retail Mecca for residents of Germantown shopping for the maximum daily requirements of life at minimum prices: ice cube trays, plastic mixing bowls and flowers, long winter underwear. **A sort of secondhand Clover or K Mart,** it offered little that spoke of things fancy or fun, but then keeping your sense of humor when you're poor can be hard. This large, clean space is well organized and lit, with six or seven employees to keep it that way. Double that number of shoppers were rapidly grabbing and tossing garments over outstretched, already well-dressed arms doing double duty as clothing racks.
Look: BOTTOMFEEDER **Goods:** DOWN & OUT-STATUS QUO **Prices:** LOW **HOURS:** Mon-Sat 9-6. Call Ahead.	Men's Tidewater Traders trousers, original John Wanamaker tag of $35, here $2.50. $2.50 would also have bought a brand-spanking-new, white, all-cotton Saks Fifth Avenue shirt. There's a dirt cheap, large secondhand book and record section. Hardbacks 3/$l. Paperbacks 6/$l. Titles ranged from _The Prize_ to _Know Your Pomeranian_. Furniture has been relocated to the nether world of Bargain Thrift's second location farther down Germantown Avenue. In its stead, a glass-partitioned, **vintage, back-room boutique** displays clothing and objets d'(semi) art. Beware, hours posted on the boutique door aren't the same as the main shop. Because they've changed twice just during this research period, you'd best call first.
CLOSED: Holidays	**CONSIGNOR ALERT:** Donations only. Gives 10-15% of profits to Fox Chase Cancer Center and the American Cancer Society. 100%-10%=90% (?)

Bargain Thrift Center	$ P_F

4530 Germantown Ave. Phila., PA 19119 **843-1300** (P$)	The farther you travel down Germantown Avenue, the farther you travel down the economic slippery slope. Bargain Thrift's second location is a warehouse with aisles of furniture stacked like so much cord wood for the winter, some like wet pine, capable of giving off only smoke, some dry hardwood, **good enough to set any retro room ablaze**. None of it is priced. You'll have to find Tony, the manager, drag him around with you, asking prices. A maple dining room table with red formica top and two fold-out leaves, four chairs and matching hutch were only $150. Go ask Tony if you don't believe me.
Look: BOTTOMFEEDER **Goods:** DOWN & OUT–STATUS QUO **Prices:** UNMARKED	I half-expected to see a battalion of homeless pushcart scavengers pulling up to the back door, unloading their trash-pile treasures. Every imaginable household appliance is arrayed against the farthest right-hand wall, silent witness to "advancing" technology and fickle taste. An electric broom à la Bewitched, a Hoover for Harriet (Ozzie only swung clubs, never pushed a vacuum), a Kelvinator for Bess (50's TV queen of appliance commercials), and an Admiral for Archie (to tune out his family and any opinion other than his own). Center stage, cardboard
HOURS: Mon–Sat 9–5	refrigerator packing cartons are cut precisely in half like magic-act stage-set props, and used as toss bins to contain thousands of wrinkled, torn and boring garments. While the $1 bins are labeled, it could take the patience of a saint or the imagination of a genius (or both) to find one worthwhile item. Was this a transcendental experience or the preliminary staging area for Dante's descent?
CLOSED: Holidays	☞ **SHOPPER ALERT:** Furniture ⚓ ⚓ ⚓ **CONSIGNOR ALERT:** Buys outright.

Bird-in-Hand	$ L P$ P_F

8419 Germantown Ave. Phila., PA 19118 **248-2473**	...is worth two in the bush. Over 18 years of intrigue and gossip, civic pride, hard work and Mrs. Machiavellian power struggles of the nth degree have produced The Place for jewelry, art, occasional furniture, linens and chachkas. You can tell what day it is by the faces of the regulars and the all too regular dealers facing the turf-conscious volunteers who form the emotional tidal basin for the ebb and flow between customers on the shop floor, and the not-so-behind-the-scenes-powers-that-be and wannabe. Like basketball players on the foul line, not one inch over, not one inch inside the line between the front door of the shop and the public hallway, dealers wait for the second that volunteers release the just-ticketed treasures on their all too brief journey from consignment room to shop floor then pounce. A point **of entree for The Philadelphia Story "look."** Buy yourself the Ralph Lauren mystique
Look: CLASS ACT **Goods:** STATUS QUO–TOP DRAWER **Prices:** MODERATE–HIGH	**for real, for 'cheap.'** (It's all relative.) Disinherited, upwardly mobile? Buy yourself some well-heeled ancestors. Often a bit overpriced, occasionally balanced by being accidentally under priced by an unpaid, rotating staff with varying levels of experience and selfless and selfish
HOURS: Mon & Fri 9–4:30, Tue, Thu & Sat 10–4:30	vested interest. As a confirmed Bird Faithful, I bought the vast majority of finishing touches for my home here. Inventory of late, however, has been looking a trifle sketchy, or is it my imagination? There has been a managerial sea change over the summer. Will the internal political roil and boil subside, or will it continue to bubble over and into the profit margin? Stay tuned.
CLOSED: July & August	**CONSIGNOR ALERT: 70% You–30% Shop**. $5 fee. Monday-Friday 9-11, Tuesday & Wednesday 1-3. Benefits Chestnut Hill Community Fund.

The Clothes Closet	

500 W. Willow Grove Ave. Phila., PA 19118 **247-4343** 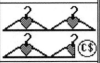	Step down a brief flight of stairs, duck under the overhanging porch, swing open the windowless door and travel down the long, display-hung corridor to 30 years "under the porch" at Chestnut Hill Academy. This obscure architectural beginning could have made for a gloomy bunch of staffers and shoppers. Instead, you'll discover a **cohesive, fun-loving volunteer crew** and their faithful coterie of regulars. A Bernie Seigal look-alike, but real-life school Director of Development, was delving into the men's rack on his lunch hour. Very dapper in his crisp clothing and suspenders. Did they come from here? The Old School team spirit is exemplified by friendly cross fire between here and nearby Monkey Business: "We're cheaper and better, period. We consign over 1000 items a week. It's here one day, gone the next."
Look: STATUS QUO **Goods:** HO HUM – TOP DRAWER **Prices:** LOW – MODERATE	The occasional fur, frequent bridal gowns, **constant supply of evening gowns and prom dresses**, seriously conservative women's clothing, a separate room for men and their **better than average children's** department make this a better than average, off the beaten track, Chestnut Hill institution. (Is this how everyone's affording private school tuition these days?) Finding the place open for business
HOURS: Mon–Thu 9-4, Fri 9-3, Sat 10-12:30	could be a challenge, unless you remember to follow a private school calendar. **P.S.** When CHA is open, so is the store.
CLOSED: CHA holidays, 2nd week of June till school reopens	**P.P.S:** $5 bag sale June 1-3, 10-12:30, 50% sale once a month. Call for details. **CONSIGNOR ALERT: 60% You-40% Shop.** $5 annual fee (school year). By appointment only. 4-weeks. Benefits Chestnut Hill Academy and Spingside School.

Cooper's Thrift Etc.	

7139 Germantown Ave. Phila., PA 19119 **247-3818** 	Always, always, always, the front window display had women's white work uniforms. Not blue, not green, not men's, but women's white uniforms. (Until I wrote this review last year.) Peek around the open doorway and you'll see thirty-some classic, basic-black, little old lady pocketbooks in patent, suede and leather, all lined up, neat as a pin, sans the requisite bricks. There's a table-top filled with new irregular socks from High Point, NC (according to the labels), in solids and argyles. Men's $1.50/pair. Lots of nondescript day dresses, none higher than $12, something a semi-retired bookkeeper for a strip joint might wear. This place's safe and boring but hey, maybe somebody you know needs a pair of new socks (or a used black pocketbook). For the less eccentric male, I found a size 46 cashmere topcoat, reduced from $80 to $40, and **any number of conservative but nice wool sweaters** for $6.
Look: STATUS QUO **Goods:** HO HUM - STATUS QUO **Prices:** VERY LOW	
HOURS: Tue–Sat 9:30-5	Don't panic if you don't see a shopkeeper. I was in the store for a full 5 minutes, thinking I was alone, when I heard a rustling sound off in the corner. Let your eye follow the wall of metal basement racks with relentlessly clean and organized jelly glasses, cheap florist vases, etc. to the cubby hole in back. That's where they seem to be hiding.
CLOSED: August	**CONSIGNOR ALERT:** 40 % You-60% Shop. $5 annual fee. By appointment only.

Corrie's

6389 Chew Ave.
(Chew & Johnson)
Phila., PA 19138

849-3190

Look: STATUS QUO

Goods: STATUS QUO

Prices: MODERATE

HOURS: Daily except Sunday. Owner comes and goes, but is usually there. Call first.

CLOSED: Holidays

Corrie's is the name on the front door. WoWo is the name on the business card. **Wowed is what you get.** Shipboard snaps, from every obscure port of call known only to the most restless traveler, adorned and papered the walls. A second section, sort of a lifetime tableau, included photos of obvious family members, a few local show business types like Hy Lit mixed in, smiling faces frozen in 45 RPM time. Another wall was a shrine to Rosa Parks and other pioneers of the civil rights movement. In the midst of all this personal memorabilia and eclectic assortment of the mundane to momentous, stood the commanding figure of a woman of a certain age, with an attention-grabbing hat, too-much-is-never-enough constume jewelry, and a show stopping personality big enough to fill Carnegie, but Chew & Johnson will have to do for now.

Shell out a modest $17 and you could take home an electrified ET. Plug him in and his heart lights up. The unwired twin had sold earlier and for less. Child-sized Chippendale clawfoot love seat and chair, with plastic covers protecting the white brocade seats, were displayed in the window. Underneath was propped a pair of pen and ink pictures of Valley Green and the Chestnut Hill area, $28 each. A riotously red leather dress and a doozie of a white and black stripped fur hung side by side. In the far reaches of the shop, behind all the collectibles and the memories, a practical beauticians station stood at the ready, waiting for the next do. Did W o W o learn this trade as a fall back, just in case show business was a chimera, or the demand for collectibles faded? Rich with jewelry and knickknacks and saga, it is all of a piece, like history. Come on in. Sit in the only collectible free chair. Get your hair done. Let your hair down.

CONSIGNOR ALERT: We buy. We trade. We?

Dandelion

7107 Emlen St.
Phila., PA 19119

247-9717

Look: STATUS QUO

Goods: HO HUM – CLASS ACT

Prices: LOW – MODERATE

HOURS: Mon–Thu 10-4, Fri 10-5, Sat 11-4

CLOSED: Holidays

The collective imagination of thrifters everywhere would have conjured up this place if it hadn't already existed, because it so clearly captures the mainstream image of **just how a thrift shop is suppose to look.** Hollywood on location in Mt. Airy.

Stuff is helter-skelter, stuff is everywhere, floor to ceiling. Handmade price tags, paper-clip display hooks. Rusty-dusty metal shelves usually found in someone's basement, storing supplies, here display a range of small households, all priced to sell.

Vintage, children's, a modest inventory of men's and a larger selection of women's clothing, all hung in push-and- shove proximity, converge to create a too-real-to-be-true movie set. **What a funky fun place this is.** Some shops cannot pull off this look. In the wrong hands the same elements combine into a looser. It's that certain something, that *je ne sais quoi*, that pulls it all together. Even more amazing is that this seemingly decades old, entrenched, funky charm (or charming funk, depending on your perspective) is all of about 4 years old.

CONSIGNOR ALERT: 60% You-40% Shop. $10 fee. Call first.

The Extra Hanger	
30 Maplewood Mall Phila., PA 19144 **844-3906** **Look:** STATUS QUO **Goods:** ? **Prices:** ? **HOURS:** Mon–Wed, Fri & Sat.12-5	What does one say? On the one hand, I had a fabulous time talking to Ruth, the 26-year veteran owner of this shop and her 19 cats. Yes folks, 19 cats. She's taken in all the strays of Maplewood Mall. Ruth is tiny, perhaps a size 2 or 4. The strays are all fat. On the other hand, I couldn't help but notice everything was covered with old sheets to prevent an avalanche of cat hairs and flea eggs from descending upon consignor's garments. A faint perfume of *eau de feline* was in the air, surprisingly faint considering the odds. **And then there was the white fur hat that moved**... It looked as if the inventory hadn't been disturbed in years, except by a pouncing paw. The only thing in the entire store that I wanted to buy wasn't for sale. She kept telling me it was broken. I kept telling her I didn't care. She kept telling me I couldn't buy it because it was broken. For those with an appreciation for the truly eccentric, wander in and have a chat with Ruth and her companions. It warms the heart. For those with allergies, don't come within a mile of this place, I kid you not! **Update: September, 1994.** Front door had a new protective metal grill. Feline "perfume" wafting through the screen packed a big wallop. Couldn't force myself to go in so soon after lunch. Rumor has it Ruth thinks I don't like her, or I wouldn't have written about her this way. How could I POSSIBLY dislike a woman who has the SAME sparrow sit on her shoulder every day while she waits for the bus home? I think she should create separate but equal accommodations for her cats and her business. "Church and State" don't mix.
CLOSED: Holidays	**CONSIGNOR ALERT:** 50%-50% split. No annual fee. Call before you come.

Ivy Hill Furniture	$ CC P_F
717 Ivy Hill Rd. Wyndmoor, PA 19150 **836-7676** 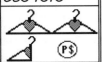 **Look:** HO HUM **Goods:** HO HUM– CLASS ACT **Prices:** HIGH **HOURS:** Mon–Fri 9-7, Sat 9-5	It could be a stage set for a small Mediterranean town. Add imagined olive trees baking in the midday sun and chickens scrabbling in the dirt to three very real old men in clean white shirts hunched at a kitchen table over an intense game of cards, saying little. They've known each other so long, played together so often, words aren't necessary. No one in this busy place disturbs them. You sense they wouldn't dare. One balding player, the owner, jumps up from time to time to help the man and woman behind the counter. It could be a roadside cafe or taverna. What it is is an **all-American combination deli and secondhand furniture store.** The card-playing, sandwich-making pinch hitter is also a secondhand proprietor. Cattycorner from the deli is the entrance to a furniture showroom displaying two used Delongi heaters $35 each. Brand-name, used refrigerators $200, lamps, bedroom sets and new hooked area rugs slightly cheaper than catalog price, small sizes only. A card table or two full of unmatched nondescript dishes and glasses completes the inventory. Drop in for a hoagie and a hutch. The owner appears to have a knack for the unusual commercial juxtaposition. He adds on a **third, entrepreneurial profit maker and stage set at Christmas.** We get our tree here every Christmas Eve. It's become a tightwad tradition, midst butt-warming barrels of burning, smoky pine boughs and encircling display of trees scenting the cold night air. Marvin insists on waiting till the last possible moment to pick out a beauty. It takes some of the sting out of financially and emotionally supporting me in my alternative holiday celebrations. At this late hour, the working (and I do mean, stiffs), are almost ready to give the darn things away.
CLOSED: Holidays	**CONSIGNOR ALERT:** Buys everything outright

Just a Second

7723
Germantown Ave.
Phila., PA 19118
247-7510

Look: CLASS ACT

Goods: STATUS QUO–TOP DRAWER

Prices: MODERATE

HOURS:
Tue-Sat 10:30-5,
Wed 12-6

CLOSED: July 15-
Labor Day

Owner, Kathleen Soup, many years a thrift shop volunteer on The Hill, probably did recognize me. Gloated on the phone months ago that she knew what I looked like, would spot me, and I wouldn't be able to shop undercover. She was right, but not in the way either of us expected. I couldn't get in to be recognized. Deepset awning made the all-too homey pink sign unreadable from the road and obscured the shop window. Forced me to park, get out and walk over, only to discover nobody unexpectedly home either Tuesday (today) or Wednesday. Second try? Peeked in the window, again. Small and neat and cute as a button. Not more than 60 feet of front room racks. A 'Back in Five' stretched to ten. Sorry, gotta go. Third try? I'm finally in. Undercover or not, you never know when TSM will strike. Was it my imagination, or did she begin straightening up as soon as I was spotted? Although it all looked fine to me. But what do I know? To treat me any differently would be like a restaurant owner recognizing a food critic, giving her better food and service than neighboring tables. Each customer is a maniac (or food critic) in disguise.

A real live, genuine, Patrick Kelly grey wool suit with red pin stripe and quirky signature buttons, this time dice size 6, and a back linen number with offset white satin collar, same size, same designer, no buttons. A little far away from Paris, *n'est-ce pas*? Tres cheap, *mais oui*? Alone and neglected, they hung smartly, dressing up the plain-jane pass-through hall between the small front room and the slightly roomier back room doing dressing-room double duty. **Show-off evening wear** was back here, and the tiny middle room, contained mostly markdowns. Kathleen: Raise the awning. Hang the Patrick Kellys in the window instead of all those nobody-home signs. Show us what you've got! That'll keep us coming back for more.
CONSIGNOR ALERT: 50%-50% split. No fee. Drop and run.

McDaniel Furniture

5301
Germantown Ave
Phila., PA
19144
438-4460

Look: WAREHOUSE SHOWROOM

Goods: STATUS QUO–TOP DRAWER

Prices: LOW

HOURS:
Tues – Sat 10-6

CLOSED: Holidays

Signage is obscure. A drive by potential customer can't tell what goes on here. I stopped because I caught a glimpse of a neighborhood oldtimer just inside the open front door, guarding and selling a small array of flea market-type merchandise. It's my duty and pleasure to sniff out possibilities, so I did a well-rehearsed, professionally executed, last-minute curbside swerve, parked, and went on in. Goes back for "miles," but you'd never know it from the Avenue. By comparison the relatively small, dirty, streetside window downplays splashy black lacquer, mother-of-pearl Oriental tables and cabinets, otherwise known in the overdecorator's trade as accent pieces.

I didn't expect much. Imagine my surprise when I ventured past the half-in-the-street, half-in-the-shop merchant and wandered up a brief flight of steps. I was greeted by the unexpected sight of an **enormous warehouse of furniture from every walk of the recycled good life**: posh, secondhand, sample home pieces and brand-new goodies damaged in transit, rerouted here (one label said Proper Brothers, a very upscale furniture store in Manayunk), superfly leathers and flashy orientalia, Ethan Allen hutches ($550) and huge Italian import armoires ($1200). There were many genuinely ugly to downright attractive, truly secondhand pieces as well. I wandered around alone for quite some time before a woman, as big and brusk as her business, greeted me with her huge white cowboy hat and her 10-gallon size personality, took me in hand and told me everything (and more) I needed to know. Put her in the window.
CONSIGNOR ALERT: Buys outright

Mix & Match

24 E. Armat St.
Phila., PA 19144
848-2150

Look: HO HUM

Goods: DOWN &
OUT–STATUS QUO

Prices: LOW

HOURS:
Mon–Sat 10-6

CLOSED: Holidays

Junk, Junk, Junk. Buttons to bowling balls! The mind boggles. To call this place a thrift shop is really much too highbrow. Pack rat's palace is getting warm. An overwhelmingly patriotic set of children's bedroom furniture painted in unrelenting red and bilious blue—but good wood and good shapes underneath the riot of color abound. The matching red, red, red deacon's bench, 6 to 7ft. long, was only $30. Imagine that! Inside the back room, packed floor-to-ceiling with <u>stuff,</u> was a jelly jar cabinet, the kind almost everyone used to have in the basement to store homemade canned goods.

A personal jolt down my own memory lane: lying amid all the relics and bits and pieces, a single aluminum hair roller from the 50's, the real skinny kind with a teensy red ball at the end where the gizmo locked. Remember those? Ouch! Hadn't seen one of those corkscrew-curl sleep tormentors in years. Really took me back. That lone curler told the story—**you can expect to find <u>anything</u> here.** There are clothes here, like the Bonwit Teller, soon-to-be and worthy-of-becoming, vintage quilted jacket, $20, **but junk is where it's at.** She gives away clothes to the homeless.

CONSIGNOR ALERT: Donations accepted. She also buys out estates and end lots.

Monkey Business

8624B
Germantown Ave.
Phila., PA 19118
248-1835

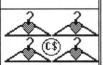

Look: STATUS QUO

Goods: STATUS
QUO–TOP DRAWER

Prices:
LOW–MODERATE

HOURS:
Mon–Fri 9:30-4:30,
Sat 11-4

CLOSED: Late June
thru Labor Day

This is where it all began for me. By age 12 or 13, I was finding all my Mme. Schaliff dancing-class and Lankenau-School prom dresses here. I still remember the yellow-tulle, the pearl-grey Grecian-goddess chiffon, and the blue-green irridescent number with rose-colored peony at the waist (and Joe, my first kiss). Years later, this is still a regular stop.

So many "lives" mingling here on the shop floor; so many stories hanging out side by side on the racks. If only the clothes could whisper. (But fortunately people do.) Very healthy young Chestnut Hill matrons pushing their very healthy babies. Aging society grande dames and glamour pusses who would simply die if their friends knew. Preppies from Chestnut Hill College looking for a good-girl punk outfit to wear to town when the nuns aren't looking. Cleaning ladies with tired feet and time between buses. Three-piece-suit types discreetly wingtip in during lunch. They all find their way here sooner or later--as many different types milling together in the narrow aisles as on the racks.

Conscientious volunteers stock an **enormous selection of brand-new, grand-entrance ballgowns and cocktail dresses** from a local boutique's overflow, many with the original price tags of $400, $800, still attached. None higher than $125 in this current reincarnation. **Lots of exceptional WASP hand-me-downs,** too. And by golly it's all back in vogue. Kilts and plaids and barn coats and wellies were shown everywhere this fall. To find this hidden, out-of-the-way Philadelphia tradition, look for the big black witch's kettle on Germantown Avenue, in the middle of the walkway sandwiched between a gift shop and an import boutique.
P.S. Monkeys and hat boxes are not for sale. But the Guide is.

CONSIGNOR ALERT: 60% You–40% Store. $7.50.fee+$1per/10 items. By appointment.There's usually a waiting list. Call early in the season.

No Name Really

711 Emlen St.
Phila., PA 19118
NO PHONE#

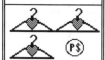

Look: HO HUM

Goods: HO HUM – CLASS ACT

Prices: LOW – MODERATE

HOURS:
Thu 10:30-2, Fri, Sat 10:30-4:30

CLOSED: Holidays

Spewing onto the sidewalk it shares with neighboring Dandelion, is this formerly anonymous store, now dubbed "No Name Really" by yours truly. When I asked Nick and Bob the name of their shop, one shrugged, off-handedly answering, "no name, really!" That's how "No Name" got its name. Out on the sidewalk, a slightly damaged gateleg table for $30. Eighteen dollars would get you a half-moon side table with ball and spindle legs. I used this one on AM Philadelphia, as a 'before' on the show I did about transcendental thrift. There was also a small, not-quite-antique, black lacquer, handpainted table with mother-of-pearl inlay. You could take it home for $35.

Walking into the store, leaving the sidewalk glare behind, my eyes began to adjust to the deep gloom. Peering down menacingly was a larger-than-life plastic snowy owl with one ear missing. This musty space with its old-time carpenter's workshop in the rear, sporting tabletops filled with cans of finishing nails and glue, clamps, shavings and bargains-in-the-making, also revealed an iron rooster weather vane mounted on a cupola. They have old stuff, new stuff, and, I suspect, some stuff just plucked from the trash. **They definitely have bargains and the guys are great**, each one a unique character, like the merchandise.

CONSIGNOR ALERT: They buy all items outright. They may or may not haggle.

Opportunity Shop

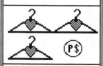

8835 Germantown Ave.
Phila., PA 19118
247-7299

Look: STATUS QUO

Goods: DOWN & OUT–STATUS QUO

Prices: VERY LOW

HOURS: Tue 9-1

Can you imagine in the real world of commerce a shop that can be open one day a week for 4 hours and still stay in business? Well, ladies and gentlemen, welcome to the real world of charity, because this is exactly what can, and does happen at the Chestnut Hill Hospital Opportunity Shop. Constantly playing a losing game of "Sharking For Parking", I was put off by what appeared to be an impossible task. The hospital lot seemed to be the only game in town, and it was full. Off-street isn't easy to come by either, because of restrictions put up to protect the tony residential neighborhood surrounding the hospital. Then one day it all came together. The brief window of opportunity opened just a crack. Eureka! I found a spot.

Set back from the street, under enormous shade trees, the shop gave every external appearance of being tiny. Appearances can be deceiving. Lo' and behold, inside, one small room zigzaged into another and another and another, revealing a warren of busy chat-you-up volunteers sorting the castoffs of the well-to-do. **It's quirky, it's intimate and it's full of life.** God knows what or who will turn up here from one Tuesday to the next. **I like the unexpected, I like this place.** House-wares and jewelry are better than clothes, but you never know. Rummaging around in the back, I unearthed two unpriced, hand-knit wool sweaters. A volunteer cast an experienced eye, seizing up the sweaters (and me), and announced "$3 each." Before she could blink, they were mine, all mine.

P.S. Some charity thrift stores donate to other charity thrift stores further down the pecking order. Monkey Business sends end-of-season leftovers here.

CLOSED: Holidays **CONSIGNOR ALERT:** Donations only.

Pandora's Box

821 Bethlehem Pike
Erdenheim, PA 19118
233-4008

Look: CLASS ACT
Outside &
STATUS QUO **Inside**
Goods: STATUS QUO
Prices: MODERATE

HOURS: Mon & Wed 12-4:30, Tue, Thu, & Fri 9:30-4:30, Sat 10-4:30

CLOSED: July & August

If you don't know to look for the bicycle store, its easy to miss the thrift shop sign. It took three passes on three different occasions to find out where this place was, and here I'm supposed to be The Thrift Shop Maniac, the expert, the pro. An old ad I clipped from the Chestnut Hill Local, tipped me off. At last! Pandora, a mythical Greek busybody and know-it-all (remind you of anyone?), ignoring good advice, once opened a box stuffed with all the ills of world, releasing them upon unsuspecting man. Beware lifting the lid and peeking inside, you never know what will be revealed in a person or a place, seemed to be the fable's life lesson. So the name of this shop is an anomaly, because lifting the "lid" causes pleasure, not misfortune, here.

The place is an interconnecting series of three small, poorly lit rooms, filled to overflowing. Clothing more often decent than designer, serviceable rather than sensational. **Labels were solid, very middle-class "citizens" with lots of life** left in them. I bought a new pair of Gap jeans, replaced the lid, so to speak, and left none the worse for wear. The jeans were in good shape too.

CONSIGNOR ALERT: 50%-50% split. No fee. No consigning on Wednesday or Saturday. 15 items maximum. 30 days. Whatever you do, make an appointment!

Past & Present

7224 Germantown Ave.
Phila., PA 19119
242-2908

Look: TOP DRAWER
Goods: STATUS QUO – TOP DRAWER
Prices: MODERATE

HOURS:
Tues–Sat 11-5:30

CLOSED: Wed in July & August

The debate raged on. Should this shop be included in the Guide or shouldn't it? Is it a thrift shop or isn't it? I wrestled with my sense of fairness, truth, justice and the American way. I decided you, my fellow maniacs, should have the opportunity to decide for yourselves. It is first-rate vintage: jewelry, hats, clothing, linens, and costumes. Past & Present has grown and prospered for so long. The U.N.-like cross-cultural, intracultural and just plain cultured staff is so **friendly**. Merchandise is so great, with top-of-the-heap garments and accessories from every era, I just couldn't leave it out.

Collectors, fashion design and history mavens, partygoers, eccentrics and the curious, **this is a must -see. The only one of its size in the Delaware Valley. It's clean, charming, well-lit, spacious, stocked to the rafters with goodies, and well-organized,** filled with bits and pieces of a multitude of lives long passed. Strangers in life, they mingle and become friends on the hangers, just as the customers do between racks.

The costume department, where they will **rent** out some of their treasures for a party, is located in the rear of the store. My little girl decided her life wouldn't be complete without a hula skirt and all the accoutrements. I didn't have to think twice about where to look; I didn't even bother to call. Sure enough they had kid-sized hula everything.

CONSIGNOR ALERT: 50%-50% split. No fee. Come in anytime, but call first.

St. Vincent's	
115 E. Price Street Phila., PA 19144 **438-2925** 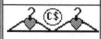	**This could be a picker's paradise.** Or it could be a dud. Depends on the day and the roll of the dice. Set back off Germantown Avenue on a residential-row side street, the church thrift shop is run by the inevitable cast of volunteer characters: dithering, well meaning ("sorry, I don't know anything, I only help out once a week") to hovering, overly involved, darling dearies, to one or two serious-minded regulars, the organizational get-up-and-go types. Wouldn't have it any other way. It's part of the charm of these places.
Look: HO HUM – STATUS QUO **Goods:** HO HUM – STATUS QUO **Prices:** LOW **HOURS:** Tue, Thu, Fri & Sat 10-2	As I roamed the austere shop flooded by a wealth of sunlight, a man so assiduously anonymous looking that he caught my attention poked and fondled and handled and inspected books and records and knickknacks. Cache box balanced by the register, he continually added this tidbit and that doodad to his groaning stash. Hard to appreciate any single item, mixed in with the dross on the shelves, till he selected it and placed it with the rest of his accumulated booty. Visual rethinking and reshuffling jacked up the perceived value in a twinkling. Jewels in the junk. Flea market dealer adding to his upcoming weekend inventory and profit margin, or a discerning pack rat? **Very, very low prices,** low profit horizons and all-but-hidden location produce a modest winner for this charity, a big winner for such a wily customer. Random acts of resale, or "hitting the big one," depend on how educated and patient a shopper you are, how often you're willing to stop in and what got donated that day. Timing is all. They have a lot of time on their hands here. So did our intent friend. And you?
CLOSED: Holidays	**CONSIGNOR ALERT:** Donations only. Benefits St. Vincent's Church social outreach.

2nd Hand Rose	
1006 E. Willow Grove Ave. Wyndmoor, PA 19038 **242-2095** **Look:** STATUS QUO	I can't tell you how many times I've tried to get in this place. Marvin and I drive by here at least three or four times a week, just never when it's open. I was feeling really frustrated. I was also feeling very sick. I was on my way back from the doctor's office, where I had just been diagnosed with some malignant-sounding form of pneumonia. Of course, the shop was open. And of course, I went in.
Goods: HO HUM - STATUS QUO **Prices:** LOW **HOURS:** Wed 11-5, Thu & Fri 11-6, Sat 10-5	The outgoing owner has managed to shoehorn **an enormous amount of stuff into a very little place.** Even she had to struggle to fit just one more item on the racks. I worry for her. There is some sort of ratio of floor space to profit, making it possible to calculate if a business is to be successful. I can't imagine there's much of a margin here. It's probably the smallest shop I know. Sidewalk display poured out onto the concrete slab where a lawn used to be, cluttered outdoor area as big as the inside. **Budding mystery reader alert?** I stocked up on 6 original, hardback, Nancy Drew mysteries for Morgan. **Student alert?** Outdated clothing, pointy collars. **Eccentric collector alert?** Sensible to weird household items, like an enormous pink plaster fish. To each his own. And with this much variety, most could come away from here owning something "new."
CLOSED: Holidays	**P.S.** Parking isn't great, with only two or three spots available curbside. Owner suggests you try across the street at the 7–11. **CONSIGNOR ALERT:** 50%-50% split. No fee. 60 days. No appointment necessary.

Village Thrift	

40 E. Chelten Ave. Phila., PA 19144 **No phone #** 	Imagine a *chain* of thrift stores located in failed supermarkets. Imagine that big. I love it! Employees all wear white, head to toe, including white gloves. They waft through the aisles leaving trails of perfume in their industrious wakes. I'm serious. Virtually the same as American Family Services minus the need for head hones. No calls to salvation here. Thank God. Add shopping carts. (Drag racing anyone?) Also add a daily 50% sale. It goes like this: Two enormous ever-changing color chips are posted high on the wall for all to see. Those two chips correspond to sales tags on some of the garments. You luck out if the ticket on your selection matches one of the color chips on the wall--50% off. Yeah! Whatever doesn't sell eventually
Look: BOTTOM FEEDER	gets sold by the pound for mattress felt or sent overseas to be re-resold in Albania or Tanzania or some such place. Hip hip hooray for recycling.
Goods: DOWN & OUT–TOP DRAWER **Prices:** LOW	Anxious moments happen here when stressed-out caregivers with little ones all get cranky, bored and tired. (I remember what it was like.) Create a small, user-friendly play area, **PLEASE!** The minimal amount of surrendered floor space will ultimately increase the shop's sales. Happier kids = happier shoppers = higher sales. Do you
HOURS: Mon–Fri 9-9, Sat 9-6, Sun 9-5	want our money, or don't you? Had to take away half a hanger. Store's still great, but inventory is down, an increasing phenomenon in charity resale. Are you guys consigning more, rather than taking a tax deduction? **P.S. Great place for upscale Wasp retro look** now in vogue. Holland American-stickered steamer trunk, fur lined 50's stadium boots, equestrian pants, etc.
CLOSED: Holidays.	**CONSIGNOR ALERT:** It must be donations (but how can that be, since it's a for-profit shop?). Trying to get information out of these people is like trying to get the CIA to open its files to the <u>National Enquirer</u>. What gives?

Whosoever Gospel Mission	

101 E. Chelten Ave. Phila., PA 19144 **438-3094** 	Downstairs? Old jelly glasses come here to retire. This is a place where you can find little old lady hats with crumpled silk flowers. Where whole shelves are taken up with one-of-a-kind saucers, cereal bowls and teacups. I never knew there was such a demand for jelly glasses and one-of-a-kind saucers, yet this place is almost always crowded. Wall-to-wall beds, bedpans, walkers, scaggy suitcases and an organized toy section. Brand-new ice skates for Morgan, $2. Archeological electronics--curlers, typewriters, office equipment, coffee makers--fill the room.
Look: DOWN & OUT **Goods:** DOWN & OUT–STATUS QUO **Prices:** LOW	Fertile digs for a history of early 20th-century household appliances. My advice? Spend no more than the time it takes to go from the front door to the back of the store and up the enormous dark brown steps to the second floor, even though Whosoever is much cleaner and better organized than last year. **Upstairs? Check**
HOURS: Mon–Thu & Sat 9-4, Fri 9-5:30	**furniture**. If you get there first, which almost never seems to happen (must be somebody showing up at this place at dawn everyday, grabbing all the good stuff). Anything worth buying almost always has a "sold" tag on it, needs to be stripped or repaired or re-finished. However, if you know what you are looking at, you can walk out of here with solid wood vanities from the 20's for $20, heart-shaped boudoir chairs, Victorian recliners, solid maple nursing rockers, deep-fringed, plush living room sets from the 40's and 50's, etc., etc., etc. **P.S.** Sleep out front in your car and get here **FIRST**.
CLOSED: Holidays	☞ **SHOPPER ALERT:** Furniture (If you like to refinish) **CONSIGNOR ALERT:** Donations only.

Worth Repeating 	It must have been worth repeating. Barbara, former partners with Jeannette at Second Editions in Bala, sold her half, and moved to the Southwest for R & R. Eventually recovered from whatever sent her into premature resale retirement, she returned to the East and to the biz, opening up Worth Repeating, a safe, noncompetitive distance across town from her former digs. **We're glad to have her back.**

5 E. Willow Grove Av. Phila., PA 19118 **247-1422** **Look:** HO HUM – CLASS ACT **Goods:** STATUS QUO–TOP DRAWER **Prices:** MODERATE **HOURS:** Mon–Sat 11-5 **CLOSED:** Holidays	Barbara displayed two hangers worth of au-courant kilts and in-the-know wool plaid scarves in her fish-tank-size, fashion-savvy, side-street front window on one of my many trips here. The window changes weekly, if not daily, and I always look to see what she's hung there to tempt and tease. Charmingly playful, the densely packed front room is the cutest, with the cutest stuff, mostly sizes 6 through 10. That's where the owner (a stylish size 8?), also hangs. By curious contrast, the second room's decore is early nondescript. Either Barbara can't see around corners, or ran out of interest and/or cash. Spotlight directed glare gets you right in the eye. Ceiling is cracked. Room needs paint. But bargains, afterall, are what we care about most, and this is a room full of seasonal or end-of-season bargains. The average Chestnut Hill first-sale boutique is not as up-to-the-minute as a Main Line Jules Botega, so Barbara doesn't have quite as many high-end glitzy garments in her evening wear department, but there is an 8-foot-long rack with **good-to-great party duds.** **Men** regularly but cautiously descend narrow, wooden steps to a dark, depressing basement with chalk bubbles percolating in the walls and exposed beam-and-pipe ceiling to reach an adequate to **better-than-most,** inventory in most inadequate surroundings. Open over a year, maybe now it makes enough profit to make boring to bad rooms as inviting as the front. **CONSIGNOR ALERT:** 50%-50% split. No fee. 60 days. Markdown after 30 days. No appointment necessary.

TOUR #6
STRANGE BREW

The Delaware are gone. **Conshohocken and Manayunk**, tongue-tying names on a map, are all that remain of that ancient, once powerful tribe. Ensuing generations of Irish, German, English, Polish, and Scottish families arrived and settled along the banks of the Schuylkill, attracted by river transportation, abundant energy and even more abundant natural beauty. The hillsides must have seemed like home away from home for the immigrants who flocked here, hoping to realize the promise of opportunity. Once thriving, turn-of-the-century breweries, spinning mills and factories underwrote working class neighborhoods; interconnecting canal and railroad systems linked these thriving commercial hubs.

Everything went bust after the Korean War. Beer, like many other products, became centralized big business. Small breweries, unable to compete, closed. Factory and mill work eroded, following cheaper labor "offshore". Workers who didn't flee to suburbia were left behind to struggle on as best they could. Yet the wheel has turned once again. Main Street **Manayunk** has gone through an amazing, and to some disturbing, gentrification in recent years. Their moment in history passed, the darkened mills and factories stand silent witness, a few converted into condominiums. Victorian mansions, once belonging to the industrial elite, still decorate the steep hilltops like so many wedding cakes, but now they house funeral parlors and drug rehab centers. Workers' row houses hold on to these same slopes for dear life, clinging to every twist and turn, as the cobbled streets and granite and marble stairways (and cars and buses that try to navigate on snowy days) course down to the Schuylkill.

Stubbornly insular, many of **Manayunk's** residents, much like **Roxborough's** and **Conshohocken's**, are members of the original workers' families, tracing their genealogy back three or four generations. My grandfather, William Turner, shopped Manyunk's Main Street in their shared heyday, dressed to kill in a laced, bone-riveting corset, cutting an elegant figure in his morning coat, waxed mustache, dove gray spats and bowler. My father, Hassie, and his older brother, Mills, worked summers in the mills and breweries of East Falls, just one canal barge ride or whistle stop, down river.

Unlike Manayunk, nothing much new is happening in Conshie. Except for the new bridge and hotel at the interchange, it's still the old neighborhood. Main Street Manayunk may be bumper-to-bumper Jaguars and BMW's, but the hillside hearts of both towns still belong to Chevy and Ford. Row-house-side street residents still scrub their front steps, train grape trellises into arbors on their tiny plots, and wear snap-front, shiny black or navy jock jackets with school names blazoned in yellow arches across their backs.

Why is any of this important to maniacs? Because of the earning and buying power of a neighborhood. The more expensive the neighborhood, the more expensive and expansive the secondhand trickle-down effect. Manayunk's tony shops and restaurants are a magnet for Center City, Chestnut Hill and Main Line consignors with their fancy dancy duds and doodads. Roxborough and Conshohocken aren't experiencing a similar revival. Boutique resale is missing from their vocabulary. More bang for your buck thrift (and its unintentional by-product, retro-neo) is spoken here. Style? Natives sensibly hold on to stuff so long, it's back in style without their ever noticing it went out. Like my three-piece twig porch set from Salvation Army for $60, worth $1500. Manayunk shopkeepers know from fad, and care about style, and charge accordingly. But they also display and preselect, providing shoppers with a cohesive fashion sense. (More bang for your time.)

Norristown is a similar brew, but one that can leave a bitter aftertaste. Like Conshie and Manayunk, Norristown has lost most factories and mills. Except for Conte Luna, crumbling red brick shells are all that remain. But Norristown is still a company town. Only what's manufactured is politics. High noon the streets are crowded with lawyers and politicos and office clerks. The wealth that enters Norristown comes by day and flees by night. The legal eagles that flock to the courthouse don't nest here. They takes their money and runs. Meaning poor old Norristown has neither the tax base nor consignor base to make much of a go of it. Are you listening, Harrisburg? Washington? A smattering of homeless people and druggies aimlessly wander Main Street, while the suits and the skirts come out just long enough to run from climate-controlled office to climate-controlled restaurant. They sleep, consign and donate elsewhere. Marshall Street's semi-historical secondhand shops are banding together, attempting a revival. The curbside scene, with its ethnic melting pot of working-class and welfare families, is vivid and vital and well policed, the sort of neighborhood were bargains can and do happen.

Breweries are back, only now they are called micro. Thank you, Dock Street and Samuel Adam's and the newly launched brew, Manayunk. Pubs, taverns (tappies, as Dad used to call them), pizza joints, mom-and-pop sandwich shops and groceries pop up on almost every corner in all three towns. But my favorite roast pork sandwich in the whole world was a Conshie culinary event. I gobbled it up sitting in the car staring back across the street at **Mastrocola's** 9th & Fayette Street window with its suckling pig, apple and all, rendered, if you'll pardon the bun, in red and blue neon. Working men trucked in, neighbors walked in, willing to stand eight deep in first one line to order, take out only, then a second, this time to pay.

Manayunk? Take your pick. But I'm especially fond of the vegetarian chili at **Le Bus** (I'm a nondenominational shopper and muncher.) The foam head on the mocchaccino at **Dean and Deluca** was the firmest and highest I've ever had, the pecan shortbread, divine. Sandwiches looked fast, cheap and très trendy. Mexican takeout at **La Cantina** at the **Manyunk Farmer's Market** is great! Munch on some of my buddy Rona's designer dark chocolate covered **Society Hill Nuts** for dessert afterwards.

Roxborough? People don't eat out often in Roxborough. Why should they when they've got stewed tomatoes, canned string beans with Durkee real fried onion rings, and Campbell's cream of mushroom soup-and-chicken casserole, or a Lipton's onion soup drenched pot roast to come home to? I can smell it now. But if you're traveling midway between the Roxborough and Norristown mindset, you might try the mindbending **Persian Grill** and **American Diner** on Germantown Avenue at Crescent Road in **Barren Hill**. Marvin said to be sure I fit this one in somewhere. And **Boardwalk Fries** if you get as far as the **Plymouth Meeting Mall** are a must!

My favorite lunch spot in Norristown closed over the summer. Driving by, with neither the appetite nor the time to eat, I spied the **Airy Street Cafe** and the **County Seat Restaurant**, one block up from Fayette near the courthouse at Swede & Airy. Through the opposing picture windows, I could see they were both packed. Try one, and let me know...

TOUR #6

5	Amazing Gracie's	Plymouth Meeting
12	Crossroad Gift & Thrift	Norristown
16	Debbie's Gift & Thrift	Norristown
7	Fairfield County	Conshohocken
8	Fayette Street	Conshohocken
19	Fred's Treasure Chest	Norristown
6	Girl's Night Out ★	Conshohocken
15	Larry's Thrifty Shoppe	Norristown
18	Marshall Street Used Furniture	Norristown
14	Salvation Army-Norristown	Norristown
4	Salvation Army-Roxborough	Roxborough
2	Second Childhood ★	Manayunk
11	St. Vincent de Paul	Norristown
10	Sugar Plum	Conshohocken
13	Thrifty Threads	Norristown
3	Wear It Again Sam ★	Manayunk
9	The Well	Conshohocken
17	Willie's West End Furniture	Norristown
1	Worn Yesterday ★	Manayunk

*Note: This list has a shop's entire name. Names in review boxes may have been shortened a tad to fit. Numbers before each shop name correspond to their numbered location on each map. **Shops with a star sold Volume II. Volume III? ASK!**

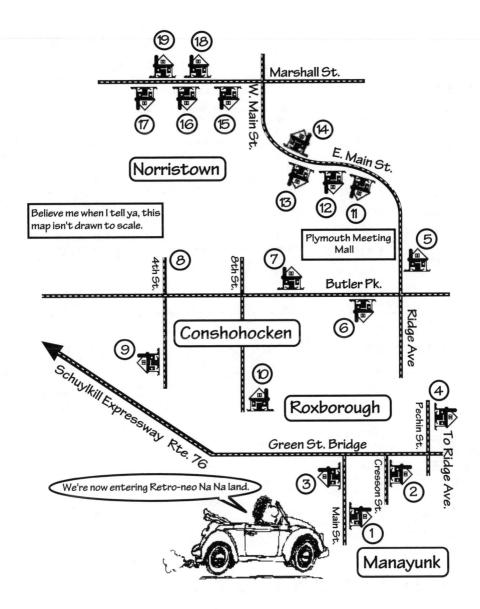

Marshall St.

W. Main St.

E. Main St.

Norristown

Believe me when I tell ya, this
map isn't drawn to scale.

Plymouth Meeting
Mall

Butler Pk.

Conshohocken

Ridge Ave.

Roxborough

Schuylkill Expressway   Rte. 76

Green St. Bridge

Pechin St.

To Ridge Ave.

We're now entering Retro-neo Na Na land.

Main St.

Cresson St.

Manayunk

TOUR #6 MAP Page 102

Amazing Gracie's	
NEW LOCATION! Plymouth Meeting Mall Plymouth Meeting, PA 19462 **610-397-1990**	I still get goosebumps when I remember my brother playing Amazing Grace on his bagpipes at my wedding. Bill Moyers once narrated a PBS program devoted to this old spiritual. Imagine the hand-me-down composer's empathic powers, still able to evoke such a timeless hold on the collective imagination. Then, so many generations later, that same God-given skill is rekindled in screenwriter(s) creative enough to script an entire television program embracing this hymn.
Look: CLASS ACT **Goods:** STATUS QUO–TOP DRAWER **Prices:** MODERATE –HIGH	Amazing Gracie's got its name because of the power and promise of this song. Owners Howie and Mimi, amazed at the continuing grace in their lives and the constant stream of amazing goodies that get dropped on their doorstep, selected this same song title as the name for their shop, to remind them, and their customers, of the universal ties that bind. **They feature unworn closeouts, reconditioned resale** (and come Spring, I'm told, its their own line), thanks to Mimi's design talent. Also projected are more Amazing Gracie's franchises, scheduled for opening throughout the Delaware Valley throughout the year.
HOURS: Mon–Sat 10-9	They've got some top-secret, biodegradable formula they use to clean, brighten and freshen every garment that comes through their doors, a computerized mailing list, sales promotions and their own logo on the cutie-pie price tags. Even more amazing? **They take returns up to 10 days**, so hold on to your receipt. How sweet it is. My mission? A play area in every kids' resale shop in the Delaware Valley. Let's show first-sale retail how to do it. With Grace.
CLOSED: Holidays	**CONSIGNOR ALERT:** Buys outright. See Tour #8 for details, as they have a second store in the Lawrence Park Shopping Center.

Crossroad Gift & Thrift	
14-16 E. Main St. Norristown, PA 19401 **610-275-3772**	Mennonites, a.k.a. The Plain People, have never been known for starting fashion trends. They're known for their practical humility and acts of charity toward their fellow man. Just as you might think, Crossroad Gift & Thrift is much better at giving than receiving.
Look: STATUS QUO – CLASS ACT **Goods:** HO HUM **Prices:** LOW	Discreetly peeking out from behind the gift and the thrift is **the untouched shell of a small downtown 50's-style department store.** The secondhand clothes concealing this remarkably beautiful classic are clean and cheap, endlessly boring, dated beyond belief. Put on any of these clothes and you'd instantly become invisible. The word 'gift' comes into play because while one-half of the store is thrift shop, the other contains crafts imported from over 35 developing nations all around the globe. The idea works this way: Mennonite missionaries buy up the crafts, reselling them in their stores throughout North America. A large percentage of the profits are returned to the producer groups or co-ops. The **crafts are great!**
HOURS: Mon–Wed 9:30-4:30, Thu, Fri 9:30-5, Sat 10-4	**P.S.** There are also Mennonite cookbooks, hand-made afgans and quilts for sale.
CLOSED: Holidays	**CONSIGNOR ALERT:** Donations only! Benefits Mennonite Central Committee.

Debbie's Gift & Thrift	

	Too cute for words, almost. If the display smarts that went into arranging all the little bits and pieces were what was for sale, Debbie would make a fortune as a window dresser of the woolly lawn-sheep school of design. Unfortunately, the 'gift wrapping' was better than the thrift. When you get right down to it, a crafty thrifter must ultimately purchase and take home the stuff, not the suggestion of stuff.
522-520 W. Marshall St. Norristown, PA 19401 **610-272-5005**	
	The corner-facing front room enshrines what looks like prized pieces of brightly colored glass and china from some nonna's or babushka's row-house, living room window. The **expanding furniture inventory**, ranging from darkly distressed neanderthal colonial to formica French to veneered semi-vintage, provides a backdrop of display shelves, nooks and crannies for all the chachkas.
Look: STATUS QUO – CLASS ACT **Goods:** HO HUM **Prices:** LOW	The architecturally dramatic, exposed brick, framing gallery, is hung with a preponderance of pre-fab poems and pictures with vaguely blissful, windswept maidens, cherubim, bunnies and such. Hippility-hoppity round my brain went the unanswered question: Who is Debbie? Is the centrifugal force amassing these divergent, seemingly unrelated forces a fake French colonial grandmother, a
HOURS: Mon–Fri 10-5, Sat 11-5	relentless hearts-and-flowers woman-child, or a brooding neanderthal cherub? Or a shopkeeper trying too hard to create a look with stuff not worth so much effort? Or a sensible woman doing the best she can with what she knows? You decide. I did.
CLOSED: Holidays	**CONSIGNOR ALERT:** Buys outright.

Fairfield County	

	When they had their grand opening, gas-station pennants were strung across the front porch. They're gone now. The neighbors may not have liked this boisterous bit of marketing Americana, but it sure helped me to find the store. The printing on the enormous sign out front is small, hard to read. Driving up or down Conshohocken's main street, you're on top of it way too soon. Speed-reading through binoculars won't be enough to decipher this microscopic essay at 35 mph. Big bold letters, curbside, so we can find you, please! Parking is tricky. One or two cars can fit in the driveway and then you're out on fly-by Fayette Street.
1514 Fayette St. Conshohocken, PA 19428 **610-828-1168**	
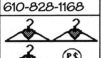	The obscure name choice could be explained by the fact that the owner moved here from Fairfield County, CT. If she accumulates possessions the way she does memories, that could explain how she got into this business. The shop is in the first two rooms of an ordinary house. My guess is she lives upstairs. Downstairs are limited, but usually **good quality, collectibles and housewares, priced right**. She tells you as soon as you enter, she's **willing to negotiate**. Unusual. The clothes are all very clean with a great deal of attention paid to display. It's a small, but solid little shop. If it's summer, bring a small personal fan. There was no A/C, no fan and no open window in the middle of a July heat wave. Too many Connecticut winters?
Look: STATUS QUO **Goods:** HO HUM – STATUS QUO **Prices:** LOW– MODERATE	
HOURS: Mon–Wed call first. Thu, Fri & Sat 10-5:30	
CLOSED: Holidays	**CONSIGNOR ALERT:** 50%-50% split. **Annual fee only $3 if you bring TSMG with you.**

Fayette Street

214 Fayette St.
Conshohocken, PA.
19428

610-825-6852

Look: STATUS QUO

Goods: HO HUM–
CLASS ACT

Prices: LOW–
MODERATE

HOURS: Call first
and listen to their
tape.

CLOSED: Holidays

Signage problems again. This sign, which states, Step Up To Quality, is big enough and bold enough. But it doesn't spell out shop hours. For that you have to **climb two sets of 18-steep, hill-hugging, granite and concrete steps** to check out the chalkboard at the tippy top. Five frustrating, heartpounding visits and four or five accompanying serendipitous hour changes later, I finally managed the requisite two shop visits. Phew. This is what keeps me in business (and in shape).

Watch where you walk when you first enter. An unexpected, small first step, then rolling folds of carpeting, which looked like the owner hadn't vacuumed in weeks, might just reach up and grab you. Stuff from every era and in varying degrees of quality and style hangs everywhere. Sewing room mountains of clothing exemplified the organized chaos. Just when I think I've come to understand her committed nonrelationship to neatness, I spy innumerable jewelry display cases with **antique to recent costume jewelry, pins and earrings immaculately ranged by color** and size. Inventory ranges from plain-Jane to **better-than-average contemporary** and **vintage** to almost-vintage. The owner, overheard chatting on the phone with a regular, explains: "I've got a mixed clientele because of the neighborhood". Her mix of inventory matches the economic mood swings. This shop may not be for everybody, but it suits me fine. It's one of those atmospheric messes that imply a potential find under every pile, jammed up against every askew hanger, behind the next rack, just around the next corner.

CONSIGNOR ALERT: 50%-50% split. $5 annual fee (200 items). 50%/30 days.

Fred's Treasure Chest

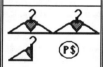

517 W. Marshall St.
Norristown, PA
19401

610-275-7742

Look: STATUS QUO

Goods: HO HUM–
STATUS QUO

Prices: LOW

HOURS:
Tue–Fri 11-4
Sat 11-5

CLOSED: Holidays

Only it wasn't Fred. It was Lynda, his daughter, who was positioned by the front door, guarding the treasure on my second visit. I browsed among the shelves of **Smurf** ($3) and **Tweetie Bird glasses** ($6), identical except for price and comic imprint. That steep difference may tell you something about the pantheon of collectibles, or it may not. Fred has obviously been listening to financial reports on new toy investment shopping. The idea is to buy up great gobs of the latest TV-induced kiddie fad frenzie, then sock them away like so many priceless jewels. So he also offers up new **toy trinkets**, those tiny **oh-so-collectible**, freestanding and wheeled plastic tidbits that will eventually be worth twenty times their weight in gold if you pick right and are willing to wait 40 years. If you don't, or aren't, you can always give them to your kids.

Mixed in among the oversupply of floral shop vases and like-minded inventory were two modest treasures: a shrimp cocktail serving platter, $9, and a Teleflora painted chicken and stuffed-egg platter, $5. (We finally have the answer to that timeless riddle: The plant, which we now know came first, is long gone.) The rear of the shop contains still servicable, but seriously broken-in cookwear and small electricals. There I spied a heavy-duty, double-hole cookie cutter I just had to have. At $1.50, it was overpriced by at least a third. I whined about it to the ever-patient, silently resilient Lynda, all the while keeping my identity to myself. An economic minimalist in her use of conversation, she silently reduced the price to $1. I stopped whining, and took home my treasure.

CONSIGNOR ALERT: Buys outright.

Girls Night Out	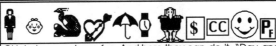
3022 Butler Pike Conshohocken, PA 19428 **834-1844**	Girls just wanna have fun. And here they can do it, "Day and Night, Night and Day," in show-stopping, grand-entrance beadwork, chiffon, velvet and satin, enough to make heads turn and growing boys and grown men faint. This feminine, yellow and white floral, resale paradise is one of the first places I think of when a special event looms large on my social horizon. Why plunk down hundreds, even thousands of dollars for a knockout outfit, worn once or twice, and destined to languish in the back of the closet like a fading showgirl lost in her memories? Instead, consign (or rent) your experienced **party dresses and gowns** here, recouping your investment to party again. When it's your turn to dance the night away, come back again and buy someone else's vision of loveliness for 20 to 30% of the original cost. It's a secondhand party clothes circuit.
Look: TOP DRAWER **Goods**: TOP DRAWER **Prices**: LOW– MODERATE **HOURS**: Tue–Fri 11-6, Wed 11-9, Sat 10-5	Volume II hit the stands, and prices here were slashed, as soon as the delightful threesome that owns and operates Girls Night Out saw how they stacked up in the pricing wars. **Branching out to sensibly increase their customer base, they recently added women's work (is never done) clothes** that are every bit as good as the evening wear, and a play clothes section (that needs a little work). There's also a full to bursting rack of sensational, never worn preteen and prom dresses, bought outright in New York, and enchanting, preowned fairy princess gowns for the little ones. Located across the street from the Plymouth Square Mall, the shop is bright, spacious and pretty with two enormous dressing rooms and tricky parking.
CLOSED: mid-end June–Labor Day	**P.S.** During Prom season, mid-March through mid-May they are open **Sundays 12-5**. **RENTALS:** Fee varies based on value + $10 dry cleaning fee. Damage it? You own it. **CONSIGNOR ALERT:** 50%-50% split. No fee. 60 day consignment.

Larry's Thrifty Shoppe	
406 W. Marshall St. Norristown, PA 19401 610-279-6387 	There's a chair by the register that's almost never empty, occupied by a steady stream of local gossips who have five minutes or the whole day to goof off. They spend this time at Larry's, swapping bits of neighborhood lore and describing contests of will and financial fencing matches. It's the usual picker braggadocio between shopkeeper and customer.
Look: STATUS QUO **Goods**: STATUS QUO– CLASS ACT **Prices**: LOW	Larry is a seasoned veteran, who **knows and carries everything from the whimsical to the practical to the curious**: William Nutting drawings, cupie dolls (if only I'd held onto all my cupie dolls), motorcycle helmets, old Mrs. Smith's pie tins, French poodle salt and pepper shakers, Heisey glassware. One favorite touch: puckered gingham doughnut-shaped circles, called yoyos in some quilting circles, strung together, then tacked to shelf edges, create a unifying force field of pattern and traditionally vivid colors amidst the clutter, visually holding it all together.
HOURS: Mon–Sat 10-4, Fri 10-5	This is one place I'd regularly come back to in Norristown. The chair beckons... but duty calls.
CLOSED: Holidays	**CONSIGNOR ALERT:** Buys outright. Tries not to deliver, but will if asked.

Marshall Street Used Furniture	
403 W. Marshall St. Norristown, PA 19401 **610-277-0442** 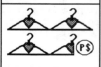	**Outsiders with deep pockets could turn up a bargain** or two here because many a neighborhood local's pockets have holes in the bottom. Consequently, the shop cannot command high prices. Norristown doesn't leap to mind when considering a fertile field for antiques. Nonetheless, one very expensive, but fairly priced item, too big to be put on display, and therefore represented in a color photograph, was a solid wood, glass and mirror bar front and cabinets, $15,000. Some lucky commercial decorator or architect will be only too happy to plunk down the big ones for such quality, still leaving plenty of financial maneuvering room to make a thirdhand profit. A solid oak, seven- or eight-drawer lingerie chest, badly in need of stripping (adding $50-75 to the cost if you can't or won't do it yourself), with glass pulls and casters, $65. Don't forget, Ikea or Caldor would charge $150 for something similar in all too flimsy, always unassembled, particle board.
Look: HO HUM–STATUS QUO **Goods:** STATUS QUO–CLASS ACT **Prices:** LOW	Lots of old kitchen implements, including a hand-cranked, 1926 pasta machine with cutting tines for fetuccini and spaghetti, $35. Tin scoops, bread pans, etc., with a timeworn patina, **very cheap**. Metal, multi-doored and -drawered, doctor's implement cabinet, circa 1930, only $35. A gracefully aging, fading paint and plaster rendering of Elvis, before time and gravity caught up with him, $70. Unlike his
HOURS: Mon & Tue (call), Wed 12-5, Thu & Fri 12-7, Sat 10-5	memory, the bust was banished to the relative obscurity of the second floor, with its handsome dark green walls and contrasting, stark white, pressed-tin ceiling and crown molding. And unlike the glory days, he kept a still and silent vigil.
CLOSED: Holidays	**CONSIGNOR ALERT:** Buys almost everything outright. Ask.

Salvation Army	
147-49 Main St. Norristown, PA 19401 **610-275-9929** 	Other than the Center City and Northeast locations, this is one of the weakest Salvation Army shops I've been in so far, probably explained by the fact that Norristown's wealthiest citizens come and go like so many shoebees, and the in-residence residents who actually spend the night have little to throw out, discard or recycle (except the incumbents?).
Look: BOTTOM-FEEDER **Goods:** DOWN & OUT – CLASS ACT **Prices:** CLOTHING LOW, FURNITURE UP & DOWN	As with most Salvation Army stores, the consistent **best bet is the furniture department**. Whoever scoops up, refinishes, and designs those nifty little chintz-covered tables consigned at Sweet Violet in Manayunk ($125-$250), could theoretically score the raw material here for a song ($20-$45). As in many bottomfeeders, all too predictable manic-depressive price swings go on here. A formica and particle board, reproduction pedestal table with two leaves was $185. While it was unused, it would have better served the community priced around $125. Ditto for the $75 (but should have been $15) mirror. $49.95 X two and you could have carted home matching white-wood trim and purple-upholstered deck chairs, supposedly from the Queen Elizabeth. On the other hand, an unused 12"rock maple salad bowl with 'Vermont' burned into its butt was only 85¢. Williams Sonoma catalog had the identical bowl listed for $39. I bought the Salvation Army version. That certainly served me better. Salad anyone?
HOURS: Mon–Sat 9-5	
CLOSED: Holidays	**CONSIGNOR ALERT:** Donations only.

Salvation Army 4555 Pechin St. Phila., PA 19128 **487-9993** 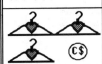 (C$) **Look:** BOTTOM FEEDER **Goods:** DOWN & OUT - CLASS ACT **Prices:** CLOTHIING LOW, **FURNITURE** UP & DOWN **HOURS:** Tue–Fri 9-9 Mon & Sat 9-5 **CLOSED:** Holidays	$ P$_F$ Like any bottomfeeder, they'll take anything you've got to give: The Good, The Bad and The Ugly. **I've heard many people swear by this place** as a family clothing resource. I haven't done as well. Notable, all too rare exceptions: a new pink girl's jacket, $5--identical to the one I had foolishly bought Morgan on sale retail the previous winter for $60. An al fresco summer picnic-scene, print silk shirt, $6.90 Marvin wore it till he tore it. Last trip, this time a find for me: royal blue corduroy shirt, $3.90. These few great buys kept luring me back to the clothing racks more times than I should have. The time vs. find ratio soon tilted against me. **Lady Luck has smiled on me big time in furniture.** $60 dollars bought a 3-piece rustic, bent-twig set, retailing in catalogs for $595. I've carted home a good-as-new, flower carved, solid wood armoire for Morgan's room, now repainted white, with chintz curtains behind the stylish wire-door fronts. I just missed the highly stylized, white-wire birdcage, a decorator's swoon at $45; fixed up it would easily bring $250. Someone else got to it first. Furniture finds turn up, ranging from good chair frames waiting to begin a chintzy new reupholstered lifestyle to only slightly damaged furniture-showroom floor models, ready to move right in. **The weird, wacky, and wonderful.** **P.S.** The longer furniture sits on the floor, the higher the percentage off. Check the sign behind the register. Check the price tag for the date. I saved 50% on Morgan's new armoire this way. Price tag: $225, I paid $112.50. ☞ **SHOPPER ALERT:** Furniture 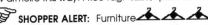 **CONSIGNOR ALERT:** Donations only.
Second Childhood 4369 Cresson St. Phila., PA 19127 **483-9703** (P$) **Look:** CLASS ACT **Goods:** STATUS QUO–CLASS ACT **Prices:** MODERATE **HOURS:** Tue–Sat 11-5, every 2nd Sun 12-3 **CLOSED:** Holidays	CC L P$_S$ P$_F$ Let your little light shine. Second Childhood is tucked under a bushel basket, one block back from Manayunk's burgeoning scene and just around the corner from Worn Yesterday in the gloomy shadow of the elevated train tracks that run parallel to Main Street. I wondered how this would work, having two children's consignment shops virtually a competitive stone's throw away from each other. But if current inventory emphasis and personalities prevail, this proximity will work to their mutual advantage. Having two similar, yet diverse shops can only draw more customers to both. Second Childhood is a **Tiny Tim of a place, a Tom Thumb-size warehouse** of here-today-gone-tomorrow boys' and girls' play and school clothing, up to size 14. Maternity is still minimal and still boring (clothing, silly, not the E-X-P-E-R-I-E-N-C-E!). **All clothing is super clean.** Some of it because it's brand-new, some of it because the owner scrutinizes consignments. I couldn't help but overhear a customer-shopkeeper confab on the latest spot-removing products available, comparing pluses and minuses. The play area in the rear of the shop was so tidy, incorporated into the inventory as it was, that I had to look twice to realize it was really there. Just like mom, a sign sensibly requests you put the toys back just the way you found them (if you find them). Awarded four hangers for equipment last year, they had very little in sight this time. An off day? This stuff is in high demand everywhere. Comes and goes fast. **P.S.** Donna has thought of everything. When the inevitable happens, there are free diapers and swipes for baby in the changing area. **P.P.S. Best of Philly Magazine 1992 for Children's Thrift Store** **CONSIGNOR ALERT:** 50%-50% split. $5 fee. Appointment preferred. 10% off for store credit.

St. Vincent De Paul	$ P_f
De Kalb Pike & E. Main St. Norristown, PA 19401 **610-275-5601**  C$ **Look:** HO HUM – STATUS QUO **Goods:** DOWN & OUT–STATUS QUO **Prices:** VERY LOW **HOURS:** Mon–Sat 10-5 **CLOSED:** Holidays	Masses of wayward, playful, irridescent soap bubbles floated by outside, propelled from a bubble-making machine installed over the doorway of a boutique just two doors down as a potential customer attention grabber. Inside St. Vincent's, one well-meaning, slightly less playful, overworked person was managing to run the store, doing everything for everybody. She was alternately manicked-out by the workload, then endlessly talking on the telephone. But help is on the way. They're getting someone to help out. Things should lighten up soon.

Most everything was very clean and cheap and should have been on its way to the rag factory to be turned into expensive paper or mattress padding. The signature piece, (one that I see over and over again in thrift shops), a used wine bottle with handmade white crocheted netting, had the requisite poodle head lopped off. One customer did buy a telescope to gaze at the heavens of a summer's eve. I turned up a $5, once $60, Esprit black-and-white wool sweater in mint condition. **Saturdays the shop is packed with local moms,** kids in toe, doing their best to keep it together for themselves and their families on a tighter than tight budget.

P.S. A sign in the window requests: "Do not drop off donations outside when the store is closed." Too direct a form of charity? Littering fines?

CONSIGNOR ALERT: Donations Only. A Catholic umbrella charity that benefits the homeless and the poor. |

Sugar Plum	 $ ☺ L P_f
244 E. 8th Ave. Conshohocken, PA 19428 **610-825-3266** P$ **Look:** STATUS QUO **Goods:** STATUS QUO – CLASS ACT **Prices:** LOW **HOURS:** Tue–Sat 11-5, Sun 1-5 **CLOSED:** Holidays	A low-slung, red brick addition, slap dashed onto a row house, it looks like it should be a corner grocery or barber shop, but it's **the best all-around secondhand store in the Conshohocken/Norristown area.** Even if I leave without buying something, I feel good about having been here. **There's so much good stuff to look at and handle,** to occupy my mind and get my imagination going. I can feel the bargain that's about to happen, even when it doesn't. That's O.K. And when it does, that's even better. I brought friends here twice and they cleaned the place out both times. This one goes on My List. If I'm in the area, I come here.

I had just been shopping at The Well nearby, engaged in shoulder-bumping competition with an obviously savvy old-timer. Walk into Sugar Plum, and who's there? The same Olympic-calibre thrifter. Turns out she's Sugar Plum's owner's sister. Turns out they recognized me. So did a customer, related in some way to Anthony's in Jenkintown. Glad they got good reviews. Phew. That was close.

Recent expeditions turned up a troll doll collection (put them away for a rainy-day investment), a men's quilted Stag Harbor red jacket, $20, and a man and woman, shopping for evening clothes. He was trying on the black beaded high heels.

CONSIGNOR ALERT: 50-50% split. $4 fee. 60 days. |

Thrifty Threads

26 W. Main St.
Norristown, PA
19401

610-275-4715

Look: STATUS QUO

Goods:
STATUS QUO

Prices: LOW

HOURS:
Tue–Sat 10-4,
1st & 3rd Sat 10-3

CLOSED: Holidays

Among the services provided by Hedwig House to its clients are vocational training and supervised employment experience, based on the belief that this will help restore the client to being a contributing member of the community. The person waiting on you behind the counter could be a client or a staff member. Whoever does wait on you is **competent and caring**. The store itself is dark and brooding, crowded and dingy. What lights it up are the people, and sometimes the inventory.

On one visit, there was a pair of American Eagle riding boots trimmed in blue and green plaid for the amazingly low price of $5. A Fisher-Price car seat could be taken home for $12, and the workmanship of a child's authentic French designer dress in white wool with hand-sewn beadwork blew me away. It only cost $5. Sorry, Morgan, it was too small or you would own it.

There's a posted price list behind the register. If an item isn't tagged, refer to this.

CONSIGNOR ALERT: Donations only. Benefits Hedwig House, Inc. of Montgomery County

---

Wear It Again Sam

4430 Main St.
Phila., PA 19127

487-0525

Look: CLASS ACT

Goods: CLASS ACT

Prices:
MODERATE – HIGH

HOURS: Mon–Wed,
11-6, Thu 11-9, Fri.–
Sat 11-11, Sun 12-5

CLOSED: Holidays

Really good secondhand shops, the survivors, the ones that are keepers, the ones whose names get passed around on the grapevine, seem to spawn spinoffs. Worn Yesterday proved to be a training ground for Wear it Again Sam's owner Kelly, a canny merchandising mavin, moved out of her original obscure basement location and up the street to her new digs, a stylish, retro mini-warehouse.

For those of you who like to cross eras, maybe mixing new punk, silver-toed backless cowboy mules with a 30's early-depression, draped-crepe dress, they've got the dress here. For those who just plain cross over, there was a Halston done up in cherry red sequins with silver and white cowl collar and cuffs that looks for all the world like something Judy Garland would have knocked 'em dead in: $120 firm. DJ types and ponytailed greying hippies alert: Guys they have authentic '50s Hawaiian tourist shirts and skin cowboy boots here! Kelly knows how to cross decades combining a LIZ Claiborne or a Banana Republic garment from the 90s with sensational 30's-40's-50's vintage.

Kelly is due with son #2 this Spring. Deep into maternity, wearing goodies hand-picked from her inventory, she maintains her stylishly fun, funky look.

☞ **SHOPPER ALERT: Best of Philly '92 upscale vintage, Philadelphia Magazine.** Featured on Discovery Channel's Home Matters, October of '94 with yours truly.2

CONSIGNOR ALERT: 40% You–60% Shop split. $5 fee. Appointment only Tue/Wed.

The Well

107 E. 4th St.
Conshohocken, PA
19428
610-825-3117

Look: STATUS QUO
Goods: HO HUM–
STATUS QUO
Prices: LOW–
MODERATE

HOURS: Mon–Thu &
Sat 10-2

CLOSED: Holidays

The Well was created 25 years ago by the Neighborhood Council. Their mission? To give food, diapers, etc. to the unemployed and impoverished of the community. This shop helps to raise the funds to do just that. The second time I was here, there was a half-price sale in effect for the week following the Fourth of July. A plainly simple, basic, two-piece navy blue Harve Bernard gaberdine suit could've been had for $2, down from $4. There was also a great, half-price black wool dress with the Nordstrom label inside. Yours for a buck.

On an earlier visit, a Black & Decker popcorn popper was an unbelievably high, $25. It should have been about $7. On the other hand, a Norelco water purifier was only $1. Go figure.

P.S. They'll accept returns with a receipt for store credit.
P.P.S. Call and keep asking for what you need. These kind folks will 'wish' a donation of just what you're looking for.

CONSIGNOR ALERT: Donations only. Benefits Colonial Neighborhood Council.

Willie's West End Furniture

614 W. Marshall St.
Norristown, PA
19401
610-272-0486

Look: HO HUM
Goods: DOWN &
OUT-STATUS QUO
Prices: LOW

HOURS: Mon–Fri
11-4, Sat 11-3:30

CLOSED: Holidays

Out on the street, a man and woman were fighting. She was unloading a flatbed truck full of kids' furniture. He was hanging around, watching, chowing down on a meal of fried chicken purchased at the oriental takeout across the street. I know where he got it, because I had been in the same place only moments before. His behavior had made me nervous enough to leave without ordering. He kept hopping around, looking out the door. I was so uncertain what would happen next, I bolted. The Marshall Street scene can be like that. People coming and going, fast and sometimes furious.

Willie has a **good, steady, secondhand furniture and appliance** business. Nothing fancy, mind ya. But we all gotta have a place to lay our head at night. And then sooner or later you gotta wash the sheets. Willie's got the bed and the wash-and-rinse cycle. Plus an easy chair to sit in while you watch the sheets go round and round. It ain't much. But it's home.

CONSIGNOR ALERT: 70% You-30% Shop until it sells, or he buys outright.

Worn Yesterday

4359 Main St.
Phila., PA 19127

482-3316

Look: TOP DRAWER

Goods: CLASS
ACT–TOP DRAWER

Prices:
MODERATE – HIGH

HOURS: Tue 10-3
Wed 10-8, Sat 10-5
2nd Sun 11-4

CLOSED: Holidays

Davida understands moms and kids and their needs. **Davida goes out of her way to be helpful.** Occasionally she'll even let a regular take home a garment to try it on their child and return if it doesn't fit. Unheard of!! **She has primo resale stuff for infants through teens and a larger-than-most inventory of mid-range maternity** (every pun intended), **manufacturers' samples, overruns and designer** slightly worn.

I'm often frustrated by too many tempting, as yet unopened, bags waiting to be consigned at the beginning of the fall and spring seasons. But call. and she'll let you know if a consignment with the sizes or consigning number you're looking for is just in. There's a basket of toys available to keep ankle biters busy while you shop, turning the whole place into a rollicking-good-time playhouse for the little ones. This is the location for the **AM Philadelphia** snowy day live shoot, where I went careening, off-camera down the Kamikazi steep slopes of Manayunk, making it to air time with only minutes to spare. I held up endless examples of outstanding kids' outfits to the camera, surrounded by racks and racks of goodies. Most of the stuff was sold over the phone before the show ended. Davida's life didn't return to normal for weeks. I'm not sure mine ever will.

We were having another one of our heart-to-hearts, when Davida and I realized we wanted to share something with you. As underhugged kids, we've both been given life's second chance, the opportunity as grownups to overhug our own kids (how can you overhug a kid?). In the process, we've come to realize one of life's bottom lines. Cherish your children, the child within yourself, all God's children. Clothing brings us together at Davida's. Love is what keeps the world together. When you shop, remember to pay loving attention to your little ones. Mommy's little well-dressed alter ego can still be miserably "dressed" inside. Only a well-hugged kid is a happy kid. When shopping becomes more important than nurturing, something's kaka, and it's not the diaper.

CONSIGNOR ALERT: 50%-50% split. $5 fee. By appointment only.

TOUR #7
SHOPPING ON THE RIGHT SIDE OF THE TRACKS

Ah, the **Main Line**. These folks have more dough-re-mi than most. While there are pockets of working-class folks, it costs more to live here than almost any other neighborhood.

In our pre-thrift shopping days during the closing moments of Reaganomics, after extensive searching, we wound up happily settling down across the Schuylkill in the Melrose Park area. We chose a gatehouse to one of the many estates built by families with names like Elkins and Curtis and Stetson. Delving into the history of the place, I learned from the well-informed LaMott librarian that our neighborhood was to have originally been the Main Line, lo those many years ago. Until one fine day when the cigar chomping, oyster guzzling, top-hat-sporting powers that be of the then Reading Railroad opted to lay tracks on the opposite side of the river. All the magnates and mini-magnates followed along, making their own tracks up and down the line, building country estates and commuter stations as they went.

Top-hat cigar-chompers and their ladies are not gone, simply new and improved. They've been reconfigured and updated into a diverse group of rare birds of distinct plumage, found predominately on the Main Line, their natural habitat. These days, no more open spaces connected only by horse-drawn carriages and rails leading only to town. These days the birds flock to one of the great suburban preserves of the 20th century, and shop till they drop in a series of charming communities lining Lancaster and Montgomery Avenues, each with its own cluster of shops and restaurants. By night, they go home to roost...with their own flight path, to their own preserve, feathering their own distinctly constructed nests and rookeries.
****

In Paoli on any given day you may spot the...inherit the Country Squire, great granddaddy's trust lives on, buys little but we're still proud, brand name only my-o-nnaise (never may-o-nnaise) frosted and frosty hunt breakfast scotch and marriage on the rocks while keeping up appearances as horse and show dogs run loose on The Family Kashans, while wearing (forced to sell off the) barn (to a developer) jackets and (un)cultured pearls to be seen at all the socially (in)correct charity balls SET. (Got that? Take a deep breathe and try it again.))

☞ SHOPPER ALERT #1: So, Maniacs, be on the lookout for sterling toast holders, monogrammed pickle forks and iced tea spoons, bone china egg cups, lead crystal highball and sherry glasses, linen tablecloths for Sheridan dining tables, set for 12, those funny little dog statues for the mantle and orientals with bare spots and moth holes. Lots of cashmere sweaters (moth holes again), riding boots and Gucci saddles (custom-made), French Creek shearling coats, estate jewelry, How To Train Your Labrador manuals and romance novels.
****

Then again, in Bala Cynwyd and Ardmore you may run across the...
HE: Over-manicured, work-free hands, overwhelmingly cologned and artificially tanned baby soft skin, sporting two day's growth that never once saw the

great outdoors framing petulant overworked mouth and underworked potbelly from overeating one power(less) breakfast too many, pal

SHE: Over-perfumed, made-up, manicured, coifed, and overwrought at all the right weight loss and work out centers, Evian and salad, (over)dressing on the side, white chocolate cheesecake for dessert, after one let's-do-lunch darling too many, darling.

THEY: Platinum Card-carrying members of the self-made and proud of it, two Jags to every four Rolexes, never be seen in the same outfit or decorator twice **CIRCUIT.**

☞ **SHOPPER ALERT #2:** Maniacs, keep an eye peeled for custom made shirts with initials on the breast pocket and French cuffs, diamond pinkie rings, Italian loafers, Jules Botega silk jogging suits, sequined evening gowns, strenuously modern leather furniture from Bloomingdales, Made in Japan bone china dessert plate sets, studs, gold-accent sterling services, German and Swiss gold watches with so many diamonds you can't tell time for the glare, important furs, size 46R silk double-breasted suits, contrived artificial flower arrangements, all-purpose wine glasses, oversized cocktail table ornaments, leather-bound books (unread), and cashmere overcoats.
****

Narberth is the favorite nesting place to observe the...homeo(unem)pathic natural-fiber hair weave, zany brainy, vintage Volvo dangling crystals from the rear view, vegetarian leather Birkenstocks on your tootsies and pot(ed) plants in every greenhouse growing chemical-free, made-from-scratch takeouts from the ain't-no-farmers-in-these-here Fresh Fields market, nuked in the spare-no-expense custom-made but seldom used kitchen, big enough to cook but not Save the Whales (and hold the anchovies) in, never dare to be square, recycled reflex(ology) knee jerk that goes around **CIRCLE.**

☞ **SHOPPER ALERT #3:** Maniacs, you won't have to search long for unbleached natural fiber, bamboo steamers, unused Le Cruset and Calphalon, terra-cotta planters, vine baskets and herb wreaths, hooked and chain-stitched wool rugs, car seats, Sporto mud boots, air purifying machines, salad spinners, vegetarian cookbooks, books on transformation, vintage hippie clothes, massagers, scratched, beaten up and chipped-on-purpose reproductions, old records, backpacks, strollers, yogurt makers.
****

Wayne is a stronghold for the...forever-fixed, republican tight-curled red-red smile and basic blue tint, Life Strides crossed to bare at the cut to the bone(y)-white ankles, while democratically sitting up front in the late model, wouldn't-dream-of tinted-glass, only go to Town (for the annual bored meeting) Car, with the not-required-to-wear-a-uniform chauffeur, while shopping for the Brussel sprouts and generic brand gin soaked (hold the twist) pot roast every Sunday after vespers crew cut, kilt and Brooks (he ain't my) Brothers' blazer, family crest emblazoned pinkie ring **CROWD.**

☞ **SHOPPER ALERT #4:** Maniac's, you'll be rubbing shoulders with oxford-cloth button-down shirts and Lilly Pulitzer dresses with Dorothy Bullit labels, trenched carving boards, bone-handled carving sets, electric carving knives, sweater sets, gray wool slacks, German beer steins with pewter lids, monogrammed martini glasses, gold wedding bands, wing tips, ice crushers, family portraits, war relics, moose heads, guns, ice buckets, butler trays, cocktail shakers, coaster sets, ashtrays, navy pin-stripe suits, walkers, twin beds, bridge anything.

****

Bryn Mawr has more than its share of the...Ivy League all terrine electronic ignition home home on the Range Rover, armed and dangerous with pager, car phone and portable fax ahead your pet laptop Patagonia to a beer and tequila chase your own tail, don't forget the lime, workout, with no apologies to Anthropology, Borders on Barnes & (if not) Noble decaf cappuccino, after a last minute Bertucci's designer pizza for brunch **BUNCH.**

☞ **SHOPPER ALERT #5:** Maniacs, seek and ye shall find your secondhand selves in this pick-a-pro-team, sweat-suit and backwards baseball cap dream of pizza stones, slip dresses, computer electronics and telephone equipment, margarita glasses shaped like cacti, espresso makers, zero degree camping equipment, stair steppers, ski poles and boots, juicers, athletic shoes and waterproof Vibram-soled boots, Colnago bicycles, silk turtlenecks, braided leather suspenders, designer vintage, Nicole Miller ties, books on tape about surviving corporate downsizing, leather attaché cases, and guy's diamond-stud earrings.

****

Whatever the cultural and social icons, the familial (and school) ties and brand names that bind these socio-scatological cartoon sendups, "They" (numbers 1 through 5) have more of much than most. Meaning we can shop here till we drop. Meaning great gobs of trickle-down goodies for us Maniacs, so we can assimilate, absorb, imitate (it's the best form of flattery, remember?) and reconfigure, but for far less, thereby creating our own infinite variety of sendups. Since turnabout is fair play, how about this for the maniac sendup:

Maniacs everywhere are a...never pay retail flea market fortune of secondhand clothes enough to insulate the attic, basement and got them at the porch sale, Reeboks, half size too large, but all the better to triple store coupon shop longer, then press pedal to metal in your previously owned, government auction scratch and dent van, on your way to consign at the thrift shop after dumpster diving, après membership shopper club aisle flatbed wheelies at the outlets forever, all the while filling (Hold) Every(thing catalogue) room is a potential storage closet in your bought at bankruptcy auction, home sweet This Old House forever-unfinished **CREW.**

☞ **SHOPPER ALERT #6:** Maniacs sooner or later do, own, and/or are most or all of the above.

****

I've broken the region down into two, more manageable flight paths or halves. There's the **Eastern Main Line: Ardmore, Bala, City Line and Narberth,** and the **Western Main Line: Bryn Mawr, Berwyn, Paoli and Wayne.** To help you organize your thoughts and time, I've separately listed Eastern and Western Main Line in the shop lists, but tossed them together alphabetically in the review section.

Good cheap-eats places abound. I like the **Wayne and Ardmore Farmers' Markets** (see homeo(unem)pathic natural fiber). But they aren't open every day of the week. Sooo, there's also **Bala Pizza** in Bala. Try the whole-wheat vegetarian torta. It's fabulous. Ardmore used to be a culinary wasteland with only **Rittenhouse Deli** as a place worthy enough and cheap enough for the Maniac to chow down. Good, but not nirvana. Try the newly opened **Cafe Paradiso** for a fast trip to paradise. Coffee shops at **Borders and Barnes & Noble** in Bryn Mawr (where you can buy The Guide--just thought you'd like to know) are also great places to grab a midafternoon mocchaccino pick up. **Peche Mignon** on Lancaster Avenue in Bryn Mawr has good soup and sandwich takeout. **Walter's Swiss Pastries** directly across the street at 870 Lancaster Avenue, although distinctly European, got started in the days of America's developing, adolescent taste buds. Hence, they haven't caught on to our newly acquired rage for espresso with pastries. Here, it's coffee only. Villanova has a **diner** at the intersection of 476 and 30, then there's also **Minella's On The Main Line** at 320 W. Lancaster Ave. in Wayne. The short order genius in the kitchen prepared me a picture-perfect late-afternoon breakfast. Every detail was correct, and there were a lot of details. (I'm fussy, remember.) Last, but not least, if you're all the way up by Alexandra's, As They Grow, or Palm Tree, try **Our Deli** on the train-station side of the street near Paoli.

Two last, non-foodie tips: **Calico Corners** in **Wayne** is a great place to get yard goods for reupholstering and coordinating windows, pillows, etc. They sell discounted brand names like Schumacher and Waverly. I made all my curtains and drapes and lots of pillow covers and got the fabric to recover several chairs here. The staff is super trained and super polite. Also, did you know **QVC** has outlet stores? Neither did I. There's one located in the same strip mall as the Rediscovery Shop in **Frazer**. Check it out.

P.S. O.K. You can take a deep breath now.

TOUR #7
EASTERN MAIN LINE
(Bala Cynwyd, Narberth, Ardmore, Gladwyne)

4 Baby's Berth
8 Block's
13 The Browse Around
11 The Clothes House
5 Donohue Used Furniture
3 Expecting One
6 Hamper Shop
2 Hey Little Diddle
10 Nearly New Shop
7 Pennywise Thrift Shop
1 Second Editions
9 Sylvia Berkow's
12 Treasures & Trifles
14 Village Boutique ★

WESTERN MAIN LINE
(Bryn Mawr, Berwyn, Rosemont, Wayne, Paoli, Frazer)

17 Alexandra's
7 The Alley Door
14 As They Grow ★
1 Bryn Mawr Hospital
8 The Clothing Sales Shop
10 Consignment Galleries ★
4 Good Shepherd
3 Junior League ★
11 Marigolds Resale Shop ★
9 Neighborhood League Shop
18 New Life Thrift Shop
6 Noah's Ark
16 The Palm Tree
5 Play It Again Sports
19 Rediscovery Shop
2 Renaissance
12 St. Jude's Thrift
13 The Trading Post
15 Yesterday's On the Main Line

*Note: This list has a shop's entire name. Names in review boxes may have been shortened a tad to fit. Numbers before each shop name correspond to their numbered location on each map. **Shops with a star sold Volume II. Volume III? ASK!**

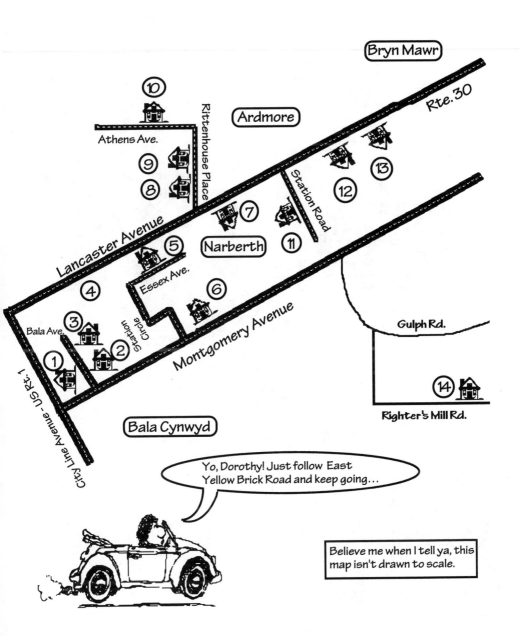

TOUR #7 MAP Page 118

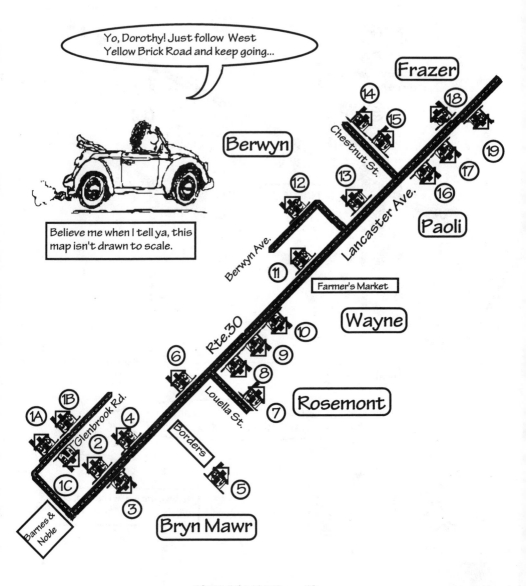

Alexandra's

Paoli Village Shoppes
Rte. 30 & Valley Rd
Paoli, PA 19301
610-640-4627

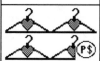

Look: TOP DRAWER

Goods: STATUS QUO – TOP DRAWER

Prices: LOW – MODERATE

HOURS:
Mon–Fri 10-6,
Sat 10-3

CLOSED: Holidays

Lull-you-into-shopaholic-complacency, classical music was aiding and abetting in the background. A far-reaching expanse of newly installed charcoal gray wall-to-wall lured me through **two floors of brightly illuminated, graciously decorated rooms**. Enormous pine mirrors flanked the dressing area. (That's area, my dears, not just rooms.) My heart swelled with the visual pleasure of it all. Alas, too many garments didn't live up to the classy decor. Very good stuff, mind you, just not enough of it among safe, middle-of-the-road designs with labels like Cambridge Dry - Goods, Spree, Heirlooms, Land's End, Terrazia.

Each and every day, (graciously) facing off with every would-be consignment appointment standing before them, resale owners must reinvent themselves and their store, flexing their fashion muscle by putting the shop's image on the line as they accept or decline part or all of a consignment. They must pick out the "cherries" and leave behind the 'pits' to make a 'pie' with neither too little nor too much filler, the ripest cherries, the shortest crust, thereby attracting customers who know and appreciate the difference between canned and fresh fashion. I'm being hard on this shop, because it so clearly has **all the peripherals and most of the requisites of the uppercrust resale world down pat, like decor, bridal salon, and service.** But there is enormous, well-established competition all up and down the Main Line.

Mixing yet another ingredient into my metaphoric pie: Like attracts like, like bees to honey, and there's just so much "honey" to go around. Higher honey yield? Pull a few weeds, then plant a few more flowers in their garden.

CONSIGNOR ALERT: 50%-50%. $10 annual fee. 90 days. By appointment only.

The Alley Door

8 Louella Court
Wayne, PA 19087
610-688-8352

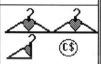

Look: STATUS QUO

Goods: HO HUM – STATUS QUO

Prices: LOW

HOURS:
Mon–Fri 10-4,
Sat 11-4

CLOSED: End of June-August

Unsold items from the Clothing Sales Shop and that motherload of them all, the Neighborhood League of Wayne, get one last chance to strike it rich, as **everything under the sun and over the rainbow from A to Z, except furniture**, left unsold after the end of the two shops' grace periods, is brought here. Time-intensive shopping investment for low yield, but the low yield could be a single, fabulous find.

We gave a High Tea Hoot before Christmas. Guests were gently requested, but not required, to come in costume, dressed as any historical or literary persona ever to have partaken of High Tea at any period, anywhere in the Empire. Champagne (on sale), tea, cucumber and watercress sandwiches, shortbread and lemon curd tarts(all homemade), a butler to serve (Matthew, wearing thrift-shop tails and his sense of humor). Guests sang along to our one-man, electronic keyboard orchestra. The connection to all this secondhand elegance...?). Panning fool's gold here, I turned up a 14K gold nugget: Marvin's costume essence, a white linen, double breasted dinner jacket for $5. Adding a black silk shirt and ascot, he came as...James '007' Bond. Morgan's floor-length, peach satin underskirt and cream lace dress was purchased across the street at Noah's Ark for half price: $1. I cut faded velvet roses and netting from an old hat, then reattached them at the throat and hip. Her copper hair piled high, and her even higher voltage personality tuned in and turned up, Morgan was transformed into the young Sara Bernhardt. I was Lady Ottoline Morrel, turn of the century Bloomsbury hostess extraordinaire.

CONSIGNOR ALERT: Donations Only. Visiting Nurses Association in West Chester.

As They Grow

37 Chestnut Rd.
Paoli, PA 19301
610-993-8180

Look: TOP DRAWER

Goods: STATUS QUO–CLASS ACT

Prices: LOW–MODERATE

HOURS:
Mon–Fri 9:30-4:30,
Sat 10-4:30

CLOSED: Holidays

One of the prettiest, one of the largest and one of the choicest children's consignment stores in the Delaware Valley is just a hop, skip and obscure jump off Rte. 30 on a retail and residential, tree-lined street. (Look for the Gulf Station.) Keep your eyes peeled for the car seats and carriages all lined up outside the front door in good weather. I'm sure this stuff goes out as quickly as it comes in, which may explain why equipment here fluctuates in quantity but not quality from one of my undercover shopping trips to another. There's ample parking in the rear. If you're pushing a baby carriage or have a couple of toddlers in tow, you might want to walk back around to the front, because the rear entrance has a steep set of (well-constructed) stairs.

Big, well-lit and cheerful with a play area added over the summer, it has tons of **great clothing for babies and anklebiters.** Upstairs there's a wall-to-wall rack of **fashionable maternity** ranging in mood from day to evening wear and in size from We've-Only-Just-Begun to Who's Sorry Now? Larger children's, up to size 16, are also up here. Two walls have floor-to-ceiling display shelves of shoes and boots. This is also where the **bathroom**/dressing room is located. I remember just how useful this information can be to a parent with a desperate little one. Or to a parent in the same knee-clamping, foot-hopping fix. After play areas in every shop, how about (public) bathrooms? Now wouldn't that be civilized?

CONSIGNOR ALERT: 50%-50% split. $10 annual fee. 90 days. Unlimited drop offs. No appointment necessary.

Baby's Berth

2 Station Circle
Narberth, PA 19072
610-668-4224

Look: CLASS ACT

Goods: CLASS ACT

Prices: LOW–MODERATE

HOURS:
Tue–Sat 10-5

CLOSED: First 2 weeks in August

If you find the Narberth train station, you'll find Baby's Berth. Birth, get it? There's even a choo-choo in the logo. If you've never been to Narberth, use this as your excuse. It's a charming, walk-everywhere, everyone-knows-everyone kind of town. This shop fits right in.

I haven't seen an ugly baby's secondhand store yet, and this one is **another cutie pie**. Whatever you do, don't be distracted by the **huge assortment** of "Mommy, I want it" toys and fit-for-a-princess, "Mommy I'll just die if I can't have it," party dresses filling the window. (A happy distraction for me? Seeing her Maniac's review blownup and hung up in the front window.) WATCH YOUR STEP, as you enter. The store's steps are très steep. Safely inside, note the bulletin board with pictures and prices of larger sale items. (As this is a small place, there's not much room for big stuff, so this is a good solution.) For the limited amount of floor space available, there's also **lots of maternity**! Now, that is unusual!

The shop owner has a B.A. in Elementary Education, and did window displays for The Limited. It shows! She's great with the kids AND the clothes. Carefully selected merchandise including goodies from the 50% off rack, fly right out the door.
CONSIGNOR ALERT: 50%-50% split. $5 annual fee. 60 days. 20%/30 days. No appointment necessary.

Block's

27 Rittenhouse Pl.
Ardmore, PA 19003

610-649-9388

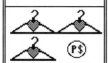

Look: STATUS QUO

Goods: STATUS QUO– CLASS ACT

Prices: MODERATE

HOURS:
Mon–Sat 10-5

CLOSED: Holidays

What's this? The front is filled to overflowing with street-vendor quality new-new jewelry and new-new pocktbooks. I inhale deeply and begin to wonder if the shop is wandering out of the domain of thrift and into some other, as yet unknown, marketing concept. I take a few steps farther. Racks reveal extensive secondhand men's and women's clothing, including ladies size 1X to 3X. Exhale...yes it's thrift.

Recently, the owner renovated the rear of the store, knocking down the wall to what had once been the open-only-by-customer-request back room, where their top-of-the-line resale items had been stashed. Now its lighter and brighter. The only hitch: the dressing rooms are 2 feet deep. Take another very deep breath going in. The burning question: Which half of yourself do you want hanging out in the wind? Front or rear? Left or right side? as you attempt to contain all of yourself in the (lack of) space?

MEN! Go to the back of the store. With so many thrift and resale shops in Ardmore competing for donators and consignors, Block's seems to have made a small, but significant niche in menswear. If you're a regular, **they'll call you when a likely consignment in your size comes in.** Nice touch. They did it for my husband before they knew he was married to the Maniac.

SALE ALERT: 2 blowout sales at the end of winter and summer seasons.

CONSIGNOR ALERT: 50%-50% split. $5 annual fee. 60-days. By appointment only.

The Browse Around

323 W. Lancaster Ave.
Ardmore, PA 19003

610-649-9793

Look: PACK RAT

Goods: HO HUM– STATUS QUO

Prices: LOW

HOURS:
Mon, Tue, Fri & Sat 10-3, Wed 10-3:30, Thu 10-4

CLOSED: Holidays

You can browse, but there's little room to turn around. And most of the space is taken up by jelly glasses, sour cream glasses, saucers, too wide ties, Bing Crosby-era ornaments with fake White Christmas flocking. **It's pack-rat heaven.** Yuppie hell.

Margaret, all peaches and cream and eternally young at 86, is by now the resident, 15-year volunteer angel. She used to work for pay at a top men's shop. She missed a few fashion fads in menswear in the ensuing years. She was advising a middle-aged customer, shopping for her husband, to purchase the wide-wide silk ties for $1, as "they were back in style." She did this with the lightest touch, the sweetest of smiles, the merriest eyes. Maybe she knew something I didn't, after all.

The basement (this time I found it) looks just like the basement in any old house where the family stayed on for years, amassing and collecting. When something passed from use, they carted it downstairs to become one more well organized, long forgotten family possession. Only difference? Here you have to pay if you want to take it back upstairs and out the door. Like the $10 wicker baby's hamper. Closed, it's a stacked set of four boxes, two to a pair of legs that open by spreading them apart to reveal staggered storage. The top box's lid flips up. I spray painted it all white, cut leftover wallpaper and lined the box bottoms, glue-gunned upholstery trim, mimicking the four boxes' outside shape. Et voilà. It's a $150 lingerie chest! Heaven.

CONSIGNOR ALERT: Donations only. Benefits Missionary Sisters of the Holy Rosary.

Bryn Mawr Hospital

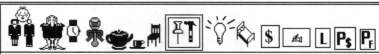

820 Glenbrook Rd.
Bryn Mawr, PA 19010

610-525-4888

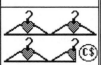

Look: STATUS QUO

Goods: HO HUM–TOP DRAWER

Prices: LOW–MODERATE

HOURS: Mon–Fri 9:30-4:30, Sat 9:30-3

CLOSED: First 3 weeks in August

Main Line institution. **So big its practically a mini thrift shop mall**, spread out over five (three for selling, two for processing/consigning) separate buildings on the same side street, all stocked to the rafters with children, men's, women's, furniture and household. **This place gets everything sooner or later**. Remember the old-fashioned word "emporium?" Well here's the working definition of that word. Every smart thrifter comes here sooner or later. Hospital employees spend their lunch hour and their pay checks. Locals spend their days. Dealers descend in droves. Come here early and often to get a jump on the very regulars.

SALE ALERT: Terrific sale goodies that didn't find a new home upstairs are relocated to the basement and given One Last Chance. Thursday, there's a dollar bag sale.

 SHOPPER ALERT: Furniture & chachka department:

CONSIGNOR ALERT: 67% You-33% Shop. $10 annual fee (August-June). Original pricing marked down after 30 days. **CONSIGNING HOURS:** Monday, Wednesday, Thursday 9:30-12:15. Donations also accepted. Benefits Bryn Mawr Hospital.

The Clothes House

11 Station Rd.
Ardmore, PA 19003

610-642-8785

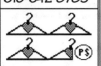

Look: STATUS QUO

Goods: STATUS QUO–TOP DRAWER

Prices: MODERATE

HOURS:
Mon–Fri 11-6
Sat 10-5

CLOSED: August

Regina Porter was in the window. A linen 3-piece number in palest pink with abalone shell buttons. Yours for $65. An Albert Nippon was hanging out by the dressing rooms. Again in linen, this time white! The usual, slightly girlish charm peek-a-booing through hip-hugging laser-cut "lace." Again priced $65. Then there was the bejeweled black chiffon number for $175 hanging out by the dressing rooms...

I've bought here. I've consigned here. Turns out Marvin (the *King*) bought here before we were married, before he even knew me. This shop has been here for ages, bought out by the current owners some 23 years ago. Bruce has the marketing vision, and wife Florence puts in the day-to-day effort, following through on his schemes. A winning combination. She's one of the prettiest, best-dressed owners, a walking testament to just how top drawer secondhand can be. **Men's department here is very good and growing.** Check it out. Larger women's sizes too, up to size 24.

SALE ALERT: Participates in Ardmore's sidewalk sale, last week in July.
CONSIGNOR ALERT: 50%-50% split. $8 annual fee. No item limit. 90 days. No appointment necessary.

The Clothing Sales Shop	
187 E. Lancaster Ave. Wayne, PA 19087 **610-688-8712**  **Look:** STATUS QUO **Goods:** HO HUM– CLASS ACT **Prices:** LOW **HOURS:** Mon–Fri 10-5, Sat 10-4 **CLOSED:** Late June –Labor Day.	Sandwiched in between shops as it is, you just might miss the obscure front door if it weren't for the awning and the sign. Once you've found it, follow the vining, deep rose-and-green floral border up the steep, wide stairs to the pale mint-green, airy expanse at the top. Generally the women's sun-drenched front room, the larger of the shop's four, is **filled with practical, good quality stuff.** I know right down to my secondfoot-shod tootsies, that if I lived nearby I'd have a much better ROI. As it is, I have found good stuff here over the years. On my catch-up review for this edition, I was dutifully checking out the larger size rack, only to discover someone had accidently or in–tentionally mishung some very choice stuff, just right for my size-twelve bod. I got an olive green quilted silk, 3/4 length KIKIT's jacket for $30, a pale pink satin floor length nightgown, never worn and only $15, and a bubble gum-pink Benetton cable pullover for $12. While the two racks at the top of the stairs by the register are where the preselected, and therefore more expensive, women's stuff hangs, with a regu-lar shopper's regular attention, probably weekly, the other three rooms are worth a look-see. I've done well by Morgan and the family budget in the kid's room. **SALE ALERT:** Big sale at the end of the Spring season, as (yes, you guessed it) they close for the summer and go fishing. **CONSIGNOR ALERT:** 67% You-33% Shop. $8 annual fee. 12-item limit. Consigning phone #:**610-688-9350** 10-2pm (except Wednesday 10-noon). Saturday by appointment only. Donations benefit the local visiting nurse association.

Consignment Galleries	
163 W. Lancaster Ave. Wayne, PA 19087 **610-687-2959** **Look:** TOP DRAWER **Goods:** CLASS ACT – TOP DRAWER **Prices:** HIGH **HOURS:** Mon–Sat 10-5 **CLOSED:** Holidays	Come to Wayne and take a trip through time. Flash back and forth between the 20th century and Wayne's historic past. A catalog-current, dark blue, two-door chest with hand-painted rabbits on the front; at $775, it captures the cachet of contemporary furniture displayed on the shop's floor. Only 4 feet away, have a 40's flashback to a Daphne Du Maurier novel. Envision Rebecca brushing her hair while seated at the $350, drop-dead, hand-carved vanity. Porcelain and fine china are handsomely displayed on highly-polished tabletops. Crystal and silver safely tucked away behind beveled glass doors. Antique white wicker cozies up to austere Danish modern. Linens and lace set off fine jewelry with a beckoning wink in the display case by the owner's perch. Golf balls overflow from floor-level toe-tapping buckets and bowls. Golf balls? Here? And I quote: "Why not? They sell like crazy." **Everything here sells like crazy.** The good citizens of Wayne, Paoli & Bryn Mawr paid more when they bought 'it', and therefore expect more when they turn around and sell 'it.' A shop owner must negotiate the gap between consignor's profit expectations and marketplace reality. **Mary Beyer has the three basic requisites of a successful shop nailed: 1)** Pick the right stuff for the neighborhood and **2)** charge the right price. 'Right' meaning generous enough to satisfy the consignor and low enough to convince the shopper it's a deal. And then **3)** manage to be pleasant enough with both parties to keep 'em coming back for more (or less). **CONSIGNOR ALERT:** 60% You-40% Shop. No appointment. No fee. Will arrange for delivery of large items for a small fee. Willing to make house calls.

Donohue Used Furniture Outlet

106 N. Essex Ave.
Narberth, PA 19072

610-664-8175

Look: STATUS QUO

Goods: HO HUM –
CLASS ACT

Prices: FLUCTUATE
WILDLY

HOURS: Tue–Fri 10-
5:30, Sat till 5

CLOSED: Holidays

Scavenging about for additional, quirky pieces of furniture for my home, **I keep this shop on my circuit.**

Here are some of the items I've seen over several visits: A maple gateleg, drop-leaf table, $185; a pine chest of drawers with great brass pulls, $125; a three-piece, grass-green Fenton china set for $40, cast-iron hand-cranked cherry pitter for $20, a braided rug for $25, a mounted widemouthed bass for $65, and a simple, sturdy one drawer table desk, $90. Sometimes the prices, however, are way too high. For instance, a scaggy brown-plaid sectional sofa was $150 (I would have paid the trashmen to take it away), and an equally ugly medieval Mediterrranian mutant oak hutch was vastly overpriced at $800. An old-fashioned secretary below, glass enclosed double-door bookshelf above, teetered at $500. The $750 price tag for the otherwise austere double bed also seemed inexplicably steep, just like the steps leading through the painter's supply-strewn warehouse where there's a **whole unoccupied house full of the weird and wonderful.** (Leave the rear of the shop and turn right, travel through the parking lot, and up the stairs.)

So, fellow maniacs, **I recommend you come here and buy here**, but I also recommend you cast a very hairy eyeball on the prices.

CONSIGNOR ALERT: Buys outright. House & estate liquidation.

Expecting One

115 Cynwyd Road
Bala Cynwyd, PA
19004

610-668-1246

Look: TOP DRAWER

Goods: CLASS
ACT–TOP DRAWER

Prices:
MODERATE–HIGH

HOURS: Mon, Tue,
Thu–Sat 10-5,
Wed. 10-8

CLOSED: Holidays

Expecting two? Expecting none? Come anyway. Finally we've got what we've all been deserving and expecting, but not finding up till now: **chic maternity**, firsthand and secondhand, all in one place. And the place is gorgeous, coming and going.

Upstairs is first hand maternity with oodles of high waisted, flowing, high fashion, nice enough to wear even if you've hung up your ovaries. (Or they've hung up on you.) Most of the clothes look like designs you'd see in high-profile Manayunk boutiques.

Downstairs is secondhand maternity, every bit as good and half the price. I told them, obviously past my baby-making years, I was scouting for my newly pregnant daughter-in-law, who was coming to town to join me in a shopping excursion. On my way out, all smiles, they handed me a promotional mug, one with their name, address and phone number. Not just any promotional mug, mind you. The bowl portion was shaped like a 9-month belly 'bout to burst, sporting an anatomically correct and humourously reproduced "outtie." It was the cherry on top of the cake.

CONSIGNOR ALERT: 50%-50%. $5 annual fee. 90 days. Appointment preferred.

Good Shepherd

Lancaster & Montrose Ave. Rosemont, PA 19010 **610-525-7634**	Pull in the circular parking lot on the church grounds, past the startlingly orange traffic cones and bobbing balloons, and nip down a few steps to the thrift shop in the basement. Walk through the door, and you're greeted with a bevy of angelic faces. With only one paid employee to comprise the "work force," and everything else done by volunteers, **this sweet place looks like a rummage sale that just kept going**. Most of the displays have a tentative quality to them.

Card tables, folding tables, everything hip height. Common floor space with no visual or physical separations. Clearly well-meaning, probably profitable and charmingly amateurish. Still, it's **very well organized** with none of the negatives of being in a basement. On one of my many trips, I found a white cotton Nancy Heller top, a Lands End white-pique lady's polo for $5, a Vittadini floral dress for $25, a Rare Editions blue-and-white polka-dot frock for $8, four Limoges luncheon place settings for $125. Not bad for a 'rummage sale.'

Look: STATUS QUO

Goods: HO HUM – CLASS ACT

Prices: LOW

HOURS: Wed & Sat 10-3

P.S. Check the bulletin board inside the door for ongoing sales.

CLOSED: July and August

CONSIGNOR ALERT: Donations only. Benefits Church of the Good Shepherd.

Hamper Shop

714 Montgomery Ave. Narberth, PA 19072 **610-664-8772**	Growing up, I attended a Lankenau namesake, The Lankenau School for Girls. Remember it? It used to be located in Germantown, before Philadelphia College of Textiles swallowed it (and Ravenhill Academy whole). This Lankenau Hospital affiliate is very much alive and kicking. At 10am the lot can be completely empty and in the space of a half hour, cars are jockeying for position, trying to get in or out of the now completely filled lot. It's amazing!

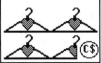

The best bet for me is housewares, immediately inside on the first floor. It's **packed with the eccentric and useful, all competitively priced.** Furniture is in a separate part of the building with its own entrance. Because of this, I occasionally forgot it was even there. (Now you know.) I also managed to miss the basement, until this most recent undercover excursion. While it is certainly not something you'll ever read about in Roy Campbell's fashion column, it's a great place to load up on dress-ups and costumes. Vintage is generally sky high. Down here, it (and the other stuff that didn't sell upstairs) is bargain basement cheap: $3 a bag.

Look: STATUS QUO–CLASS ACT

Goods: HO HUM– TOP DRAWER

Prices: MODERATE

HOURS: Mon– Fri 9:30-4:15, Sat 10-2

CLOSED: July & August

For the real thing, go upstairs ladies. The better stuff lines the center hall walls, the best stuff is behind the 4-foot counter at the very end of this hall. I'm sure security measures are necessary, but it takes away some of the spontaneity to find a volunteer free to pass the stuff over the counter, one delectable item at a time. Four rooms are set aside for clothing, with a disproportionately high number of stained, torn and moth-nibbled disappointments scattered among them. Although I did take a $20 gamble and bought a Dunhill dark green evening jacket, resplendent with the previous owner's last meal. My dry cleaner worked her magic. Marvin is looking forward to wearing his "new" $750 treasure. Can't wait till he works *his* magic in it.

CONSIGNOR ALERT: 75% You-25% Shop. $10 fee. 30 days. Tue–Fri 9:30-2:00pm.

Hey Little Diddle	
118 Bala Ave. Bala Cynwyd, PA 19004 **610-664-1228** **Look**: TOP DRAWER **Goods**: STATUS QUO–TOP DRAWER **Prices**: MODERATE **HOURS**: Tue–Sat. 10:30–4:30 **CLOSED**: Holidays	The sun, the moon and the stars that are painted in play-room vivid white, yellow and sky-blue tickle your fancy and your tootsies, gently guiding and cajoling them up the curving concrete steps and into Hey Little Diddle (HDL) Bala's newest entree in the baby boom retail wars. Inexplicably, Bala is rapidly becoming an attractive and attracting galaxy of shops, new sale and resale, for moms, going-to-be-moms, and their newest nebbulae. An otherwise delightful, undercover shopping expedition was interrupted when a customer, immersed in conversation with an HLD partner, remarked, "The shop up the street told me there wasn't any children's secondhand in Bala. Why would they have said that?" Why indeed? The green-eyed monster must have snuck up and bit them on the tushie. The more HLD's owner thought about the slight, the more distressed she became. "I gladly refer customers to any shop in the neighborhood if I don't have what they need," she repeated over and over. But cooperative competition is a game that takes two to play. Growing up, if you weren't taught to share, all grown up you'll still be trying to keep all the marbles for yourself. Guess what? Eventually you'll find yourself up in your room, playing marbles all alone. Nobody wants to play with a bad sport. And word gets around. **The word here is all good**. Come on in and play. **They're nice, and they've got great toys and dress-ups**. And they share. **CONSIGNOR ALERT:** 50%-50% split. $5 annual fee. 90 days. Drop and run.

Junior League	
1111 Lancaster Ave. Bryn Mawr, PA 19010 **610-525-8513** **Look**: STATUS QUO **Goods**: HO HUM – TOP DRAWER **Prices**: LOW-MODERATE **HOURS**: Mon–Sat 10-5, Wed 10-9 **CLOSED**: Week between Christmas and New Year's	Which mythological figure was born full grown from the head of Zeus? I can't remember. But what can you expect from someone who walks into a room and forgets why she's there? The good ladies of the Junior League felt they deserved to be in the first edition of the TSMG, and couldn't imagine why they weren't. Truth be told, who gets in is based solely and randomly on the shops I serendipitously unearth. Truth be told, way back then, I just didn't know about the Junior League shop. Like ancient Dianas, they drew a bead. Instead of arrows, they used carefully aimed words through the telephone line to let me know not to miss them next time around. I took their call seriously. After my second undercover visit, I usually, but not always, reveal my identity. This time, instead of the usual fanfare and trumpets, I was greeted with, "Oh, you're the one." Ah well. They have every reason to be proud. **Most donated, high-end Main Line stuff winds up here**. Big, plain, **easy to shop and fun to poke around, massive amounts of merchandise** and a fast turn-over. Everything but chic. That's left to the 600 volunteers and the merchandise: Laura Ashley, Woolrich, Ann Taylor, Brooks Brothers, Vittadini, Bill Blass, Gap, St. Laurent, Ralph Lauren, Mousefeathers, and Calvin Klein. Fashion label luminaries enough for a celestial soiree. I pounced on a Benetton blue and white V-neck Shetland, very reasonably priced at $15. Just down the street at Renaissance, they were asking $24 for the same sweater. A $12 green and multicolored floral-strewn Gap blouse I admired here, but left behind, also hung on the racks at Renaissance, but dangling a $7 price tag. Pricing at both shops averaged out to be **reasonable**. Finding identical garments within blocks of each other was mind-bending. Pssst...Now I remember—Athena. Those days they were all maniacs! **CONSIGNOR ALERT:** Donations and consignment. **67%You-33%Shop**. $8 annual fee. Consign Tue–Thu 10-11:45, Wed 6-7:45, 1st Sat every month 10-11:45.

Marigolds Resale Shop

380
W. Lancaster Ave.
Wayne, PA 19087
610-687-2808

Look: TOP DRAWER

Goods: STATUS
QUO –TOP DRAWER

Prices: MODERATE
–HIGH

HOURS: Tue–Sat
10-5:30, Wed 10-7

CLOSED: First two
weeks in August

Due to a large pool of carefully coddled, well-heeled consignors, Marigolds in Wayne takes up a whole house, yet even that's not nearly big enough to contain the place's energy and inventory. Peak shopping hours can mean lining up and waiting for a dressing room. Racks crowded to overflowing. Wonderful stuff in too small a space. I'd love to have problems like this more often.

Good to excellent men's. Good to excellent children's. Good to excellent women's clothing and accessories. Household items an afterthought. Computerized inventory system. Very friendly, very well-dressed staff. Very well run shop with a country chic look. **This has been and continues to be one of my favorite places**, well worth the hour round trip in the car. I consistently come away from here with wonderful buys.

P.S. Featured last summer on one of Orien Reid's continuing series on thrift shopping, this time men's, with Marvin modeling the clothes. What a hunk!
SALE ALERT: Sometimes an entire room upstairs is set aside for sale merchandise, depending on how much end-of-season leftovers they have to unload. Come hungry.

 SHOPPER ALERT: Women's evening wear is awesome.

CONSIGNOR ALERT: 50-50% split. $5 fee. By appointment only.

Nearly New Shop

26 E. Athens Ave.
Ardmore, PA 19003
610-642-0431

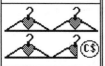

Look: CLASS ACT

Goods: HO HUM–
CLASS ACT

Prices: MODERATE

HOURS: Mon–Fri
9:30-4, Sat 9:30-2

CLOSED: Mid–June
thru Labor Day

A happy accident led me to Nearly New. Last-minute research prompted a Yellow Pages check for any missing Ardmore listings. Nearly New popped off the page. Now why didn't I know this one? I'd shopped Ardmore for years and thought I knew them all. How could I have missed it? The reason was simple. Nearly New is tucked around the corner, just out of sight from all the others lined up like obliging ducks along Lancaster Avenue and Rittenhouse Place. So close, yet so far.

Certainly, Nearly New is no stranger to the community or the press. Once inside, I saw favorable newspaper mentions and photos from over the years, tacked to the wall near the register, all aglow in their praises. Indeed it's become a regular stop, as I cut my well-worn swath through Ardmore. **Furniture and housewares are my favorites.** Designer-quality, cast-iron twin white lamps with fringed shades (don't bother, I bought both), $18 each. An unused Italian, peach trimmed, hand-painted punch bowl, $20, reminded me of Roman summers gorging on succulent lemon and brown sugar-encrusted, tree-ripened peaches, brimming with fragrant juice.

Upstairs in clothing, things aren't quite as exciting. Generally more sensible than glamorous, with some treasures mixed in. There's a sizable area set aside for larger sizes and children's also had maternity. Men's, as usual, was the weakest section. Theresa, their second-floor "guardian angel," and all the **volunteers under Barbara's wing are experienced, friendly and forthcoming**, making this converted house a home.

CONSIGNOR ALERT: 75% You-25% Shop. $8 annual fee. Tuesday–Thursday 9-12:30.

Neighborhood League Shop

191 E. Lancaster Av.e Wayne, PA 19087 **610-688-0113** 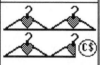	The Main Line version of Bird-in-Hand. (Or is Bird-In-Hand the Chestnut Hill version of...?) Most very wealthy communities have one of these, whispered about, highly coveted but poorly kept secrets. **Grandma's attic on sale, cheap.** Limoges, Waterford, high-tea silver service, Irish linens big enough for tables that sit 12, estate jewelry, original watercolors and etchings.
Look: STATUS QUO **Goods:** HO HUM – TOP DRAWER **Prices:** MODERATE –HIGH	Stuff upstairs, the chachkas, still seem to be of better quality and more competitively priced than the furniture downstairs. More than once I have been mildly jolted by the contrast of merchandise and prices between floors. Upstairs, yes. Downstairs, maybe. The good ladies are aware of this gentle disparity, and are on the case.
HOURS: Mon–Fri 10-5 Sat 10-4pm	**SHOPPER ALERT: China, silver, crystal, jewelry, linens** 
CLOSED: End of June to Labor Day	**CONSIGNOR ALERT:** 67%You–33% Shop. $8 annual fee. 12 items limit. 60 days, 33% off after 30 days. Consign Monday–Friday 10-2pm, Saturday by appointment.

New Life Thrift Shop

Church of The Good Samaritan Lancaster Avenue. Paoli, PA 19301 **610-647-0248**	Faced with a steady stream of customers lined up for the half-price sale, the experienced, still cheerful, lone male volunteer held the fort at the frontdesk. Overhead, steam pipes were hissing in one room, while pass-through fans whooshed hot air along aluminum ducts in another. I don't know if the shop is located near the church kitchen (churches always have a kitchen), but eau de one-church-potluck-dinner-too-many lingered, blending in with the residual whiff of previous ownership. Decoratively, the shop is held together, midsection, by an on-going band of blue-stenciled, traditional Boy Scout emblems, with the words "Be Prepared."
Look: HO HUM– STATUS QUO **Goods:** HO HUM– STATUS QUO **Prices:** LOW	The one item to jump off the rack and into my hands was a navy blue wool Brooks Brothers blazer with a gold thread nautical emblem on the breast pocket and all its expensive embossed-gold buttons present and accounted for. I knew it wouldn't fit Marvin, and I'm not one for wearing men's blazers, no matter how handsome. Within a heartbeat of my returning it to the rack, a young mother snared it,
HOURS: Tue, Wed Thu 10-3	whilemanaging her delightfully rambunctious tooth-free, wide-angle-smile son, accompanied on a shopping tour de force financed by Grandma's deeper pockets. Eat your heart out all you Main Line Brookies (and the Maniac). The $18-reduced-to-$9 jacket's patch and buttons alone were worth $40. He, She Or It W h o Hesitates...Ah well. Over the enormous bright red church doors is carved **"Peace**
CLOSED: June– Sept	**To All Who Enter Here."** That's a good motto, too.
	CONSIGNOR ALERT: Donaltions only. Annual June Fair benefits Dakota Indians.

Noah's Ark	
104 Louella Ave. Wayne, PA 19087 **NO PHONE** 	Another church, another basement, but this time it's called the undercroft, and it does have a lot of the liabilities of being located in a basement. And rather than a rummage sale, this looks more like a sidewalk bazaar with stuff being displayed…well, displayed is too intentional a word. Bring a flashlight or miner's helmet. It's so dark in some places down here in the undercroft, you might wind up trying to buy your own shoes.
Look: HO HUM **Goods:** HO HUM – STATUS QUO **Prices:** LOWEST of LOW	**The prices, like the ceiling, are so low that if anything good does turn up, boy have you got a bargain.** Like the pink and cream lace dress for $1 (they were having a half-price sale--it had been $2) that I transformed into an Edwardian costume for Morgan for a shindig we had this Christmas (see The Alley Door review). **P.S.** On second thought, the miner's helmet would be best. Watch out for the overhead pipes, occasionally doing double duty as clothing racks.
HOURS: Wed, Fri & 1st Sat of month 10-1	
CLOSED: Jan-Feb, July-August	**CONSIGNOR ALERT:** Donations only.

The Palm Tree	
255 W. Lancaster Pike Paoli, PA 19301 **610-647-2775** 	Find the Paoli Hospital, follow the signs up the hill and turn left. This place is so **well run** and the building so new that it speaks for itself. They even have a public bathroom near the dressing rooms, and a blue bean-bag chair, reading cubby in the rear for bored, broke or blistered shoppers.
Look: TOP DRAWER **Goods:** STATUS QUO–CLASS ACT **Prices:** LOW–MODERATE	Better household items are locked away behind glass doors, past the register after you enter. To find the second, lower, level is trickier. Boy do I have egg on my face. I've been coming here for years and never saw the overhead sign--among the forest of other signs etching store policy in melamine, if not stone--that directs shoppers to the **Lower Level**. There they sell men's, sporting equipment, furniture, electronics, etc. **What a revelation**. When I finally finished wiping off my second, unexpected breakfast, I individually asked four volunteers if any of them had heard of anyone else who whined, complained and sniveled about what they'd been missing for so long? Each of the dears, after racking up all those 100 hour volunteer pins for dealing with the public, like startled does caught in the headlights, pleasantly passed the buck. I pass this info on to you in case you too have missed the second level, or previous reviews led you astray.
HOURS: Mon–Fri 9-4, Sat 9:30-2	**SALE ALERT: Bag sale end of June, right before summer closing.** **CHECK WRITER'S ALERT:** Ask about their check preapproval card a la supermarkets. Shops that currently don't accept checks might want to look into this.
CLOSED: June –3rd week in August	**CONSIGNOR ALERT: 65%You-35%Shop.** Annual fee $6. Monday-Wednesday 9:30-11:45. Thursday by appointment only.

Pennywise Thrift Shop	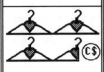 $ L P$
57 E. Lancaster Ave. Ardmore, PA 19003 **610-642-7239** 	**Fabulous floor-to-ceiling front-window displays** lure us inside. Walk right into the regionally acknowledged heartbeat of the shop, where recent renovations have made for a more user-friendly atmosphere. **Enormous, well-lit** and locked display cases packed with precious jewelry, crystal and china line the room. Furniture and oddities stacked in the center, unintentionally create a consumer's race (against the starting gun and each other) track. Main Line, **occasionally estate-quality**, it moves out as fast as it comes in. Sometimes I feel like I'm playing an adrenaline intensive version of musical chairs, as I and my fellow thrifters and competing, deliberating dealers circle the room, covetously eyeing the furniture in the center. Who has the fastest thrift-shop reflex in town? Who will find the treasure first and pounce?
Look: STATUS QUO **Goods:** HO HUM – TOP DRAWER **Prices:** MODERATE	The room to the left of the register as you walk in contains family clothing, linens and accessories, more thrifty than nifty, with the occasional designer label. Quirky. **SHOPPER ALERT:** Household and furniture
HOURS: Mon–Fri 10-4:30, Sat 10-3	**SALE ALERT:** End-of-season bag sales in June, one week before they close.
CLOSED: End of June--mid-August	**CONSIGNOR ALERT: 75%You-25%Shop.** $8 annual fee. Tuesday–Thursday 10-12, 2-3:30, Saturday 10-12. Proceeds and donations benefit Jefferson Hospital.

Play it Again Sports	🚲  $ P_F
1149 Lancaster Ave. Rosemont, PA 19010 **610-519-9530**	Cleverly attached at the architectural hip to high-traffic, high-demand Borders, it's just the team-building to attract mutually coveted customers looking to keep their bods and brains in shape. So there I was, standing outside the glass-enclosed display case-type first-floor entrance, trying to figure out how to get inside. (Use the door stupid!)
	While there is a sign directing would-be customers to "the stairs," for some reason I just couldn't figure out if the stairs were around the outside far right of the building, or if the shop had already gone out of business. Unlikely. Finally I put it together. I know this sounds dumb, but you would have to be standing in my secondhand sneakers to appreciate my confusion. Somehow the display and my aging eyes had been
Look: A WINNER **Goods:** OLYMPIC CALIBRE **Prices:** COMPETITIVE	playing visual tricks on me. I finally realized that the enormous steps I could plainly see through the glass door led up to secondhand sporting goods heaven. I would suggest something clearer be posted for those of us who are not as swift. I would also suggest that all Main Line jocks and jockettes check out this place as a **reasonably priced** alternative to paying retail or disposing of outgrown equipment and fading glory.
HOURS: Mon-Fri 11-9, Sat 10-6, Sun 1-4	**Play It Again Sports is an excellent chain of secondhand sporting goods shops throughout the region. This one is no exception.**
CLOSED: Holidays	**CONSIGNOR ALERT:** Buys outright? You get 1/3 appraised value. You take store credit? 40%. Items priced over $100 or special item, then its **60% You-40% Shop.**

Rediscovery Shop

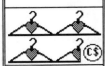

Route 30 Malin Rd.
Frazer, PA. 19355
610-644-8626

Look: CLASS ACT
Goods: STATUS QUO–CLASS ACT
Prices: MODERATE
HOURS:
Mon–Sat 10–4

CLOSED: Holidays

On our trip here, with a little help from mom, Morgan used the car phone to successfully ask for directions. "Hello, this is Morgan," she began in her best little-girl voice. "Do you have any landmarks?" Nevertheless, we arrived just at 10 o'clock. Three men entered to shop, two dropped off donations. I saw long-sleeved silk shirts, $6, original price tag attached, handsome suits, silk ties $4, a Mexx sweater, never worn, $10. **Definitely better than average.** Somewhere between the Norma Kamali, red flannel snap-up dress, $12, blue-and-white checked GAP cotton pants, $8, and the $25 Bichon, red crepe and black-trimmed dress, my cover was blown.

After hiding in all those racks, whispering in all those corners, trying to look relaxed enough not to be mistaken for a shoplifter, I finally got caught taping review notes into my hand-held recorder. Politely, but firmly, the vigilent volunteer wanted to know just what was I doing? So I told her. Eyebrows shot up, jaw dropped, but she registered no further questions. Fellow maniacs, doing last minute Christmas shopping, overheard us. Taking advantage of the opportunity, they inquired, "Have you seen any gold (they had to be gold) ornaments? Morgan told them of her last such sighting, while shopping nearby Bring and Buy (Tour #9). Off they dashed, laughing all the way. Ho! Ho! Ho! I, however, was left with spirits dashed and spirits soaring. Red-faced and embarrassed at getting 'caught', heart swelling with pride and amazement at Morgan's quick recall. That's my girl.

CONSIGNOR ALERT: Donations only. Drop off 10-4. Benefits American Cancer Society-Chester County chapter.

Renaissance

850 Lancaster Ave.
Bryn Mawr, PA
19010
610-525-7743

Look: CLASS ACT
Goods: STATUS QUO–CLASS ACT
Prices: LOW–HIGH
HOURS: Mon–Sat
Call for hours.
CLOSED: Mondays
in summer

Hard to give a read on this place. Walk in and it seems to have all sorts of goodies. **Spacious, well thought-out floor plan and displays** visually draw you in. The place is immaculate and fresh-smelling, not stale and stuffy or worse, like some. A young woman was spritzing surfaces, even as I prowled. But I kept walking out empty handed. Better at display than consigning? Inventory was good. It just didn't live up to the stylistic promise of the place. Last visit, I did see a simply elegant and elegant in its simplicity, Carolina Herrera wedding gown for $900. And I ran into an old chum. I never knew *SHE* secondhand shopped.

High ratio of good to great chachkas mixed in with furniture in the back and along the front wall behind the register. But the prices on some seemed more antique shop than thrift.

The hours on this place are constantly changing. A new handwritten sign greets me every time I come. Call first and check, especially if you're traveling a distance.

CONSIGNOR ALERT: 50-50% split. No fee. **Single item selling over $100: 60% You-40% Shop.** Consign any weekday. Call ahead for appointment. Mover available.

St. Jude's Thrift	
637 Berwyn Ave. Berwyn, PA 19312 **610-644-8509**	**Go straight to furniture and household, and stay there. Such good buys!** I always make certain the back seat of my van is out before I go to this one. Sharing the first floor with furniture, smaller items such as the engagingly sentimental, $75, engraved silver loving cup, circa 1902, and the pugnaciously priced plaster bowwow ($65) attract and amuse. Volunteers, however, know a good thing when they see it, have a good chuckle, and price accordingly.
	If you are in a hurry, forget the cramped basement. It's like a bad-news (re)birthing experience, plummeting headlong down the narrow stairwell, only to push and elbow your way through the small, gloomy spaces filled with pipe racks hung with
Look: STATUS QUO **Goods:** HO HUM– CLASS ACT **Prices:** LOW – MODERATE	too many dated clothes and floor-to-much-too-low-ceiling shelves of understandably cast-off housewares. Back upstairs, a quartet of ladies of the parish huddled around the big old-fashioned oak desk in the back room, smoking, swapping post-Thanksgiving turkey-stuffing recipes, eating lunch. Drove me wild. I got so hungry, I had to leave and go straight to lunch. I had a smoked turkey sandwich. Domestic.
HOURS: Mon–Fri 10-4, Sat 10-3 Summer: Tue, Wed, Thu 11-3	
CLOSED: Last two weeks of June	**CONSIGNOR ALERT:** Clothing and electrical, donations only. Bric-a-brac **67% You-33% Shop**, furniture and antiques **80%You-20% Shop**. $4 fee June-May. 10 items/visit, 30 max. Tuesday and Thursday 10-3.

Second Editions	
155 Bala Ave. Bala Cynwyd, PA 19004 **610-664-8508**	This shop is tres chic. Jeanette, the owner, has a cool, slim, European-elegant, former model's appearance that sets the tone. Once the other half of a partnership and now sole proprietor, she has a firm, Swiss border guard's sense of who and what belong, and don't belong in her shop, a shop with a dizzying concentration of high-end merchandise. **Only the best labels hang out here.**
	Need just the right pocketbook or piece of jewelry to complete your look? There are very good quality accessory buys here. Planning a special evening out? This place has first-class formal wear. Top it off with a primo fur. Cocktail party, afternoon tea or luncheon? Come here. Tennis or pool lounging? This is the place. Something new for your executive woman's wardrobe? Jeannette's got it.
Look: TOP DRAWER **Goods:** CLASS ACT –TOP DRAWER **Prices:** MODERATE –HIGH	Sometimes you have to wait for one of the dressing rooms. Sometimes the jazz music, if you're borderline about jazz, is a little outré. Jeannette is definitely not borderline about jazz. Avoid the shoes unless you're smitten—too expensive. Same labels, but new, for almost the same price, go to Dan's (1733 Chestnut 568-5257). But hey, this is picky—**the place is great.**
HOURS: Mon–Fri 10:30-6, Sat 10:30-5	**P.S.** Watch for limos pulling up and chauffeurs making consignment drop-offs. **PP.S. Featured with yours truly on <u>Home Matters</u> on the Discovery Channel.**
CLOSED: Holidays	**CONSIGNOR ALERT:** 50-50% split. No fee. Appointment very much preferred.

Sylvia Berkow's

49 Rittenhouse Pl
Ardmore, PA 19003
610-896-5020

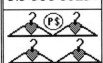

Look: STATUS QUO

Goods: STATUS QUO –TOP DRAWER

Prices: MODERATE-HIGH

HOURS: Mon–Sat 10-5

CLOSED: First week of July–3rd week August

In response to my best incognito voice, they told me over the phone in mid-November that they couldn't handle any new consignors for the fall/winter '94 season. Multitudes of the faithful get first dibs. I had barely begun my December in-person undercover shopping expedition, when Mildred, a very regular regular, dressed in expensive black leather pants, sailed in without an appointment, an armload of about-to-be consigned goodies thrown over her arm.

Berkow's owners are exprienced, second-generation, professionals, who know their business and run it well, hiring similarly qualified and friendly employees. **Back-room designer merchandise is great!** There's also a very large selection of coats, jewelry, shoes, furs and leather. While the decor is a throwback to the times when clean and well organized were a milestone in resale, this is one of the larger women's-only clothing shops with good lighting and space to move between the racks. A picture in memoriam of Sylvia, the founder, hangs over the register, as a guiding presence. She is sandwiched between two awards presented over the years by KYW and Philly Mag. Here's another!

SALE ALERT: Watch for Ardmore's Sidewalk Sale every year in early July and November. Call for information.

CONSIGNOR ALERT: 50%–50% split. $5 annual fee. By appointment only.

The Trading Post

1536
E. Lancaster Ave.
Paoli, PA 19301
610-644-6122

Look: CLASS ACT

Goods: STATUS QUO –TOP DRAWER

Prices: LOW

HOURS: Mon–Fri 10-4:15, Sat 10-2

CLOSED: Holidays and Summer

Two floors big. Main Line spoken here. Conservative, reasonably priced clothes. Dealers regularly sharking through the place, looking for a score in the locked glass-cabinets that hold the best and costliest bric-a-brac. Sooner or later, you can find anything here: salad spinner? lacrosse sticks? baby stroller? bicycles? ballroom chairs? real copper pots? heirlooms and sort-of-heirlooms.

Volunteers have their shop so well-organized, it seems almost to run itself.They say you can't teach an old (or new) volunteer new tricks. This place makes a lie of that old saw. They've also gone and computerized their operation. Nothing charmed me more than to see someofthese 60- and 70-year-old silver-haired, silver-tongued volunteers interfacing with the 21st century. Some were scared, some were hesitant, but they dared.

A favorite thrift-shop memory: The portrait of a man's head bowed in prayer over a poor man's lunch of soup and bread, hung alongside that of a great crowned and enthroned King, enrobed in ermine with arms outstretched to all of his court. **P.S.Channel 6 Evening News and I did a Thrift Shop Maniac segment here. PP.S. Men! The second floor has a fairly steady supply of formal wear**

SALE ALERT: Pre-closing summer closeout sale.

CONSIGNOR ALERT: 66% You-34% Shop. $5 annual fee. By appointment only. Benefits Fox Chase Cancer Center.

Treasures & Trifles	
43 W. Lancaster Ave. Ardmore, PA 19003 **610-896-1676**	Sweet tidbits of life's leftovers, all reassembled and rethought, scattered across antique lace and linen-draped dressers and tabletops. Charming lace-, and velvet-, and fur-, and netting-, and floral-, and sequine-trimmed, elegant old hats. Cottage to castle caliber pictures, hung high and low and every which way, all across the walls. Curious handmade vintage and contemporary vintage reconfigurations filling a rack in the rear, so full it's hard to get a peek. If you're a collector of the old and unusual and ideocyncratic, or just plain unusual and ideocyncratic, **I double dare you to walk out empty-handed.**
Look: CLASS ACT **Goods:** STATUS QUO–CLASS ACT **Prices:** MODERATE	**SHOPPER ALERT:** Vintage hats and clothes
HOURS: Mon–Sat 10-5	
CLOSED: Holidays	**CONSIGNOR ALERT:** If they like it and know in their bones it will sell, they'll buy it.

Village Boutique	
351 Righters Mill Rd. Gladwyne, PA 19035 **649-4790**	To find Gladwyne, you have to intend to go there. You don't just pass it by on your way to somewhere else. Except for time. In some ways, time did pass it by. This very high-ticket crossroads of a community goes way back. I'm told the ancient, moldy records, still kept in someone's attic, indicate that back in 1836 for example, a local woman charged a pound of butter on account at the local grocery, and how much much she paid was also entered in spidery black ink. Now Super Fresh is in town, but it is probably the only retail establishment that doesn't operate here on a charge-account, first-name basis with all its customers. Gladwyne is that kind of place.
	Wrapped in history and the surrounding vibes, Village Boutique is housed in a large, white colonial-era building. But inside, it's all charcoal grey with sharply contrasting white paint on the wood trim and the gigantic Victorian mirrors, which reflect the light inside this pretty shop. Stapled all around the top of the walls are artificial long-stem pink roses, forming a glamour-with-humor border, their playful positioning playing against the grey, very with-it interior.
Look: TOP DRAWER **Goods:** CLASS ACT –TOP DRAWER **Prices:** LOW- HIGH	Center stage, a sewing form figure sports pins and other costume jewelry. A whole rack of tiny Nippons, a second rack of new Italian knits at great prices. Ultra Pink, BB, Ann Taylor, Nan Duskin, Anne Klein, DKNY Saint Laurent, Missoni. Behind the modern white metal tower display of shoes, shoes, and more shoe? **The famous $5 sale**
HOURS: Mon–Sat 10-5	**rack.** Behind that? **Men's.** Added since last year's review, poor dears, they're stashed in the back on the wrong side of a door purposely kept shut for privacy's sake, but also leaving them out in the cold. **The quality, like women's, is excellent.**
CLOSED: Holidays	**CONSIGNOR ALERT:** 50%-50% split. $10 fee. 60 days. 20%/30 days. No appointment necessary.

Yesterday's
on the Main Line

35 Chestnut Rd.
Paoli, PA 19301

610-993-3355

Look: TOP DRAWER

Goods: STATUS
QUO–TOP DRAWER

Prices:
MODERATE–HIGH

HOURS: Mon–Fri
9:30-4:30.,
Sat 10-4:30

CLOSED: Holidays

Displays incorporating label-strewn steamer trunks and old-fashioned wooden laundry drying racks and wall pegs scattered throughout the two selling floors were as good as any Bloomie's or Ralph's window dresser, maybe better. So were the clothes. Traditional upscale labels like Pappagallo, Paraphernalia, Talbot, Brooks Brothers, Alexander Julian, Sisley, and Ralph Lauren were also scattered throughout the two floors of the shop, competing for your attention.

As They Grow, the infant-to-preteen and maternity shop next door, grew too big for its britches. It's birth two years ago carried the seeds of inception for Yesterday's, a very grown-up shop for moms and dads. The caliber of the **au courant clothes** match the charm of the single-ownership twin resale shops housed side by side in a pair of immaculately restored white-stucco and moss-green-shuttered houses. Rum-flavored pound cake and coffee were available by the register. The comforting fire in the mantel-framed fireplace and the classical music playing in the background set the mood. **Shopping here was almost as refreshing as spending a romantic weekend at some Bed & Breakfast.**

If the owners here ever decide to give up the resale biz, there's always interior decorating, or running an inn, or doing window dressing, or personal shopping, or This Old House-type restorations, or...

CONSIGNOR ALERT: 50%–50% split. $10 fee. 90 days. 50%/60 days. No appointment necessary.

TOUR #8
A LITTLE ZIG, A LITTLE ZAG or THE NEUROBIOLOGY OF THRIFT SHOPPING

Media. Swarthmore. Lansdowne. I always knew they were around here somewhere. I had never actually seen them. Perhaps they moved around under cover of darkness. Of course, it was really my mesmerized mind, darting between the anxiety of going from the known to the unknown, rubbing up against the 'rumored' certainty of their existence that stimulated all this angst. Heading south on Rte. 1 for Longwood Gardens, I always had the vague, slightly disconcerting notion that if I were to simply turn left, these out-of-time towns would obligingly appear on the horizon, etched in silhouette. My left-brain self knew it would take a few more turns, a little zig, another zag, to actually find these good citizens going about their daily lives. It's never been easy for me to close the gap between hearth, home and uncharted destination. Unless the intention is there. After all, I didn't wake up one morning, sit up in bed and realize I wanted to be a cab driver or a coast-to-coast trucker. I guess I just needed a good enough, what's-in-it-for-me reason to draw these lovely places out of the mists of my own myopia and into the forefront of the ol' frontal lobe. The Guide was reason enough. Ironically I've become something of a tour guide in the process..."Over to your left you'll see the oldest thrift shop in America, begun over 200 years ago..." So I set out to slam-dunk Media, Swarthmore, et al. four square on my mental grid. Of course, they've always been there. Silly me. And, of course, they're worth the journey, real and imagined.

Media. It's dawning on me that there seems to be something statistically alluring, even magnetic, about a town with a name beginning in M. Medford. Moorestown. Lots of good M energy. (H's and R's and S's are usually good, too.) What is it? And then there's the fact that I am surrounded by M's. Marvin. Morgan. Muffy. Millie. Marjorie. Matthew. Media is darling. At least to the casual user. I have little or no idea what it's like to sleep, eat and work here, I can only infer. But to sup is divine. Try **Sweet Potato Cafe** at 4 W. State Street (the main drag). They have mountainous configurations of fruit piled on crust, mundanely referred to as pie. Apple, lemon meringue...drool-inducing. The everyday muffin is also transmogrified into something otherworldly. Try the peach slump. Sit down or take out. Your choice. But definitely pig out. There's a crossover lunch menu with enough choices to make veggies and carnivores alike happy. Also in town, the **Lion & Ram**, a handsome new antique shop that serves cappuccino in the huge sunburst front window, where you can sit on Gardener's Eden-genre, bright green enamel bistro chairs, sipping, chatting and generally hanging out in high style. For a faster tempo, **Hometown Kitchens**, almost next-door to Yesterday's Child and across the street from The Attic, serves soups, salads and sandwiches. Order take-out lunch, and nail dinner at the same time.

Swarthmore is a place of surprising, gentle contrasts. For all the high density of high-impact real estate values, and the world-renowned college near by, I couldn't believe how small the town is. I never would have imagined the slightly hidden, off to the side, irregularly shaped, innocuous looking core of shops and restaurants. It adds a subtle shading to the concept of low profile. College founded in 1863, a Quaker community (a stop on the underground railroad?) incorporated in 1893, a dry town, discreet as a length of grandmother's pearls, the tiny shops huddle up against one another, clustered around the train station. **Occasionally Yours** at 10 Park Avenue has a few sit-down tables and a long list of takeout and catering options. The chili was very good, but needed a jolt of hot pepper. The fresh, marble-swirl rye sandwiches more dainty than dude sized, suited me--Left Marvin, who ordered soup and half a sandwich, wanting more. Next time he'll order up. Patrick Flanigan, **Booksource, Ltd.'s** owner, located just around the corner, and a regular at Occasionally Yours (everyone knows everyone) has a wonderfully quiet, elegant secondhand bookstore with a well-worn, inviting couch. Marvin and I lingered longer than we should have, chatting with the affably outgoing bookworm.

Lawrence Park doesn't look like a neighborhood. It's a strip mall surrounded by houses. BUT, it does have a very good deli right next-door to the Acme--**Mrs. Marty's**, where I wound up getting advice, opinions, potato pancakes and good directions from Sally, our waitress, whose mom lives in Allentown and is a fan. (Hi Sally's Mom!) I also got a freebie 50%-off lunch coupon from the ladies at the next table, after briefly describing to them how they lived in the thick of things, surrounded by the world of secondhand, even though they had been unaware of it till I got hold of them over lunch. The coupon they handed over was their way of saying thanks. Now that was neighborly.

Lansdowne is an unexpected revelation of small town life within view of Willy Penn and his perch atop City Hall (assuming he's using binoculars). If you stand at the front door of the **Lancaster County Farmer's Market** at the corner of Baltimore Pike and Lansdowne Avenue, you'll get a drop-dead spectacular long shot of the far-off, glistening, high-rise energy of city life, as you stand surrounded by the sweetly prosaic background charm of Lansdowne. Once you've finished taking in the slackjaw view, turn around, close your mouth, and go inside. But get ready to open it up again, soon. Try the Market for lunch. It's open Thursdays and Fridays from 8am to 7pm, and Saturdays till 4pm. Take your take-out with you, and roam all the way to the rear and check out **Noreen's Nook,** a mini junque shop over in the corner by the dining area.

Better yet, there's **Doyle's,** just up the street. I was told to come here in no uncertain terms by Ann, owner of Ye Olde Thrift Shoppe. Roaming her delightful store, I asked if she knew any good place nearby for lunch. I was starved. She got all warm and fuzzy just thinking about it, and said "I wish I could close up and join you. It makes me hungry just to think about going there. I'd eat there every day if I could." Sure enough, it was fate. My absolute favorite waitress, Betty, from the days when I used to regularly eat at Glassman's Deli just off City Line works at Doyle's now. She delivered the most wonderful BBQ sparerib sandwich (sans ribs) to my table. We caught up on the last fifteen years or so, while I nibbled. Ann, you were right. It was great!

City Line and Haverford Avenue, home to S'ORT and Sheila's has an old time **Deli** where I used to eat frequently, and a **Kosher Bakery** in the mini shopping area. Boogie on down City Line/Township Line a little further and there's another **QVC** outlet right next to **Loehmann's.**

TOUR #8

6	Amazing Gracie's	Broomall
13	The Attic	Media
5	Consigning Women	Broomall
4	C.R.C.	Newtown Square
8	Delaware Co. Memorial Hospital	Lansdowne
10	Heidi's	Clifton Heights
12	My Cousin's Closet	Swarthmore
7	Play It Again Sports	Springfield
15	The Riddle Hospital Thrift Shop	Media
1	Sheila's	Philadelphia
2	S'ORT of New Shop	Philadelphia
11	Trinity Thrift Shop	Swarthmore
3	Wee Exchange ★	Havertown
9	Ye Olde Thrift Shoppe	Lansdowne
14	Yesterday's Child	Media

*Note: This list has a shop's entire name. Names in review boxes may have been shortened a tad to fit. Numbers before each shop name correspond to their numbered location on each map. **Shops with a star sold Volume II. Volume III? ASK!**

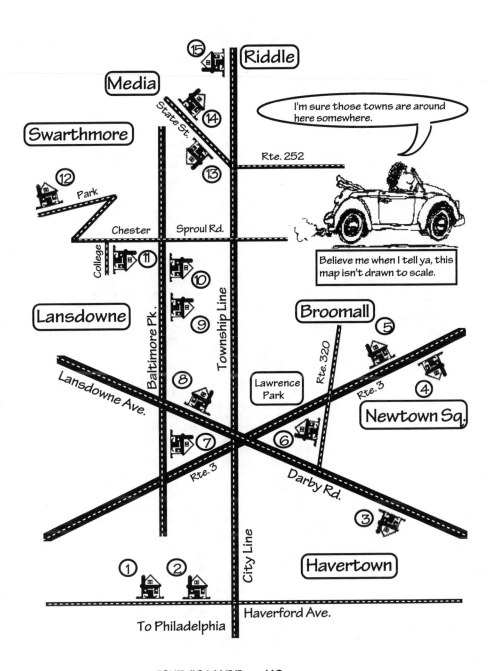

TOUR #8 MAP Page 140

Amazing Gracie's

    CC L P_F

Lawrence Park Ctr.
Broomall, PA 19008
610-353-5400

Look: CLASS ACT

Goods: STATUS QUO–TOP DRAWER

Prices: MODERATE–HIGH

HOURS:
Mon–Fri 10-9, Sat 10-7, Sun 1-5

CLOSED: Holidays

A chrome wall rack had gone bump in the night and dumped its burden of boys' duds smack dab on the floor. The clerk had a cold. Morgan, getting too big for little-kid play areas, got stuck in the playhouse. I had to pull her out, writhing and squawking. The music was too loud. A fellow customer's kid was wailing. Life. There was lots of life going on in this place. Lots of primary colors and activity and room for the little buffaloes to roam while you decide which of the great clothes to buy.

Every bit as good as the sibling shop in the Plymouth Meeting Mall, prices for some closeouts seemed a tad high side: (like the new dress-up coats, Doren Girl label, (comparable to a $135 Rothschild's), $59.95. Very reasonable for others: Mousefeather's hearts and flowers cotton dress, $29.95 ($80 new?). New Flapdoodles dresses, $19.95 (Identical to ones in Bryn Mawr. Bought in quantity?) Prices for secondhand are competitive, Gap, dark green corduroy dress with self-covered buttons running up the front, $15.95, assembly-line twin but for color (red) to the one I had seen in a West Chester resale store for $14.95 only the day before. Boy's red plaid flannel-lined, denim toggle coat $16.95, and Polo dress shirt $4.95. There was even a toddler-size navy blue tux.
P.S. Located near the Acme, with free bumper and fender parking, at the opposite end of the same strip from Barnes & Noble (where, bless 'em, they sell The Guide).

CONSIGNOR ALERT: Buys outright. Bring any and all kids clothes, any season, any amount. Condition determines your 25% to 33% share of projected resale price. Choose immediate payment or store credit (worth twice the amount of immediate payment). Which would you choose? Stuff they cannot use is donated.

The Attic

  $ L

42 E. State St.
Media, PA 19063
610-566-1502

Look: STATUS QUO

Goods: HO HUM – STATUS QUO

Prices: LOW

HOURS:
Mon–Fri 10-4, Sat 11-3

CLOSED: Holidays

Friend Jody and I were on the prowl. January this year, instead of pneumonia, I got mono. My coordination wasn't so hot, so Jody was driving. Don't worry, she won't get it unless we share glasses or forks, and I've sworn off kissing anyone till Valentine's Day. Suited me just fine. We ambled on a-around Havertown, Media and Lawrence Park. All the while, in the back of my mind, I held a growing desire to retrace my steps to this little corner of the world. My first visit here, someone else was driving, too. Odds are, unless I'm behind the wheel, recreating a return visit can get dicey. But we pulled it off. Glad we did too, because even though it wasn't our toniest stop of the day, it was where we had the most fun.

Check out the **good selection of books** in the back, paperbacks 25¢, hardbacks $1. But even at $3 a bag, the price was still a little steep for what was left of the winter doldrums hanging on the racks. Volunteers kept trying to get people to fill 'er up, but customers kept hangin' round housewares instead, jockeying for a vantage point, just like us. Belly up to the counter, we acted like kids in a candy shop, having a run on flavors. "I'll take one of those." "Oh, I've gotta have that picture frame." "Please, pass me the little oriental vase to the left. The one with the blue flowers. How much is it?" Only $1? "I'll take it." So it went, over and over, till we had exhausted ourselves and the volunteers and our mad money for the day. I got two pyrex laboratory-looking vases, just right for forcing bulbs, $1 each, down from $2. The sweetie-pie volunteer lowered the price when I explained I'd paid the lower amount only days before for identical stuff in another shop. Two for one. Goodie, Goodie.
CONSIGNOR ALERT: Run by the Bernadine Center, donations benefit a blood bank and charity work done with unwed mothers.

Consigning Women

2546
W. Chester Pk.
Broomall, PA 19008
610-353-6475

Look: TOP DRAWER

Goods: STATUS
QUO–TOP DRAWER

Prices: MODERATE

HOURS: Mon 10-5,
Tue–Fri 10-8,
Sat 10-4, Sun 1-4

CLOSED: Holidays

Little girls, big girls, bountiful beauties, precious petites, brides and bridesmaids, party girls, play girls, jockettes, working women, and expectant moms. Did I leave anyone out? Consigning Women doesn't in this **pretty in pink, hearts and flowers place**. Deep set, hand-carved, floor-to-ceiling, Victorian, fabric-draped mirror reflected boudoir and hatboxes and sachet scattered about, all for sale. The detailed, color coordinated pink consignment sheet outlines their high expectations of "making you happy enough to come back."

Accessories, work clothes and separates were half a hanger down in overall quality of design and fabric from evening, bridal and kids' wear departments, but shared the same high degree of fastidious cleanliness. Notable exceptions popped out and grabbed my attention, but they were ultimately overwhelmed by one too many sensible, middle-of-the-road labels. I know, I know. Some of you jump on my bones for being too label conscious. Hear me out. Labels are a great benchmark. They bespeak a well-known manufacturer's pricing, quality and design strategy. I utilize them with some reservation, certainly. Even the best designers turn out a turkey or two. Overall, however, they are a reliably consistent, almost universally understood language in the ratings game. Experience your own economic and esthetic reaction reading MY preferred label litany, so YOU can form YOUR OWN opinions about a particular shop's inventory. Get it? **P.S.** MAC ACCEPTED!

☞ **SHOPPER ALERT:** Bridal and party dresses ⬧ ⬧ ⬧ ⬧

CONSIGNOR ALERT: 50%-50% split. $2 fee/appointment. 42 days. 25%/28 days.

C.R.C. Thrift Shop

3729
West Chester Pike
Newtown Square,
PA 19073
610-353-8012

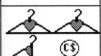

Look: HO HUM-
STATUS QUO

Goods: HO HUM–
STATUS QUO

Prices: LOW–
MODERATE

HOURS: Mon–Fri
10-3, Sat 10-2

CLOSED: June–
Sept.

A Fred Flintstone doll sat in a rocking chair, big as life, with a senseless grin on his famous puss. Nearby, a small closet was converted into a book-lined reading cubby, complete with chair. A regular, wrapped in hat and coat in the too warm shop on a too warm December day, was slumped over, facedown, asleep. Worried volunteers checked on her from time to time. Eventually she woke up and left. Fred's still there. The shop has that ragtag, slightly disheveled, slept-in-your-clothes look, which I find promising. Most stuff is a yawn, but there was an authentic aviator's hat for $1. All it needed was Rocky, Bullwinkle and friends. But they had probably been put to use in the fabuously shaped, 40's, brown fake fur. It was a $15 collarless wraparound, 3/4 length number with deeply rolled cuffs. I put the hat and coat on Morgan, prematurely preparing myself for when she comes home in something similar once she reaches her teens. She hated the look, I loved it. Give it some time. Or maybe she'll have some kind of reaction formation, skip the fashion rebellion stage and go firsthand retail, only. Oh God no, not that, anything but that!

Glass-enclosed jewelry cases held two 3'-long Madame Alexander dolls. $200 and you could take home the documented one, or pay $80 for the slightly prettier one without 'working' papers. I bought a $1 handknotted, fringed, white silk evening scarf for Marvin for New Year's to go with his $20 Dunhill/ Boyd's dark green velvet evening jacket. Quite dashing! That will make everyone sit up and take notice.

CONSIGNOR ALERT: Furniture & housewares **60% You-40% Shop**. 30 days. $5 fee, 9 mos./20 items. All else donations only. Benefits Children's Hosp. Dept. of Oncology.

Delaware
County Memorial

20
N. Lansdowne Ave.
Lansdowne, PA
19050

610-623-1662

Look: STATUS QUO

Goods: HO HUM–
STATUS QUO

Prices: LOW –
MODERATE

HOURS:
Mon–Sat 10-4

CLOSED: August

Marble facing, brass grates and trim, copper roof, terra-cotta roof tiles, hand-set black-and-white miniature hexagonal tile walkway, glass-enclosed storefront window with mahogany doors and backdrop, immaculate gold, pressed-tin ceiling, built-in cabinets leading to a mahogany-paneled office, in the middle of downtown Lansdowne, in the middle of the block, at the close of this century. A former five and dime, it's also a **perfectly preserved marvel of American retail history**, very much like Second Act in West Chester (former grocery store) and Crossroads in Norristown (former department store).

And as if that weren't enough, staff and merchandise were a **quirky delight.** One very pleasant young woman with a deep, graveley voice big enough to reverberate throughout the cavernous place, could be heard exhorting and encouraging staff and customers alike. Another, older, but very local woman efficiently performed her volunteer tasks, all the while wearing her meter-maid hat.

Barry Manilow warbled "Trying To Get the Feelin' Again."I'd lost mine two stops back. I wanted to go home. Marvin wanted to make just one more stop, PUHLEESE. Foot dragging, I regained my Maniac's wide-eyed wonder the minute I got inside. I gawked, like a tourist eyeing the Sistine Chapel. I found a three-tiered PuPu with "Hawaii" carved into the wood, topped by a 6" pineapple, all for $28, the pink flamingo plaster statue, $5. Handblown, pale blue fruit dish, $5. And an **enormous selection** of unintentionally camp to seriously servicable clothing.

CONSIGNOR ALERT: 67% You, 33% Shop. $8 fee Sept.-June. Mon–Thu 10-12:30. Sat. by appointment. 12 items/week, 30 days. Sponsored by United Auxiliary of Delaware County Memorial Hospital. Donations accepted anytime.

Heidi's

219
E. Baltimore Pike
Clifton Heights, PA
19018

610-259-8664

Look: STATUS QUO

Goods:

STATUS QUO

Prices: LOW–
MODERATE

HOURS:
Mon–Sat 10-5

CLOSED: Holidays

Gloriously typical junk shop jumble. Frank Rizzo's in his glory days as Cisco the Cop, his enormous chest pushed out far enough to seemingly overwhelm his head, standing tall on the cover of a yellowed copy of the Inky's Today Magazine atop a pile of old Life magazines. A black cast-iron ashtray with a gold, S-curved dragon looming large over the match holder/ash catcher. A blonde-veneer highboy with a typical machine-carved floral design typical of the 20's on what was probably a 50's chest of drawers, $60. Calendar pinup beauties and Hollywood starlites, alluringly posed in peekaboo and see-through decoupage decollete, a crazy quilt of pictures pasted on a pair of 5'-high brittle cardboard. One femme fatale was either peeled off or punched out, creating a huge hole in the otherwise perfectly preserved twin panels.

Feet up on a desk, a woman with short blonde curly hair was hypnotized by the T V to-do over O.J. One man rushed in and out, then plopped himself on a nearby sofa. A second scurried about pricing incoming furniture. He cut me a deal ($5 down from $8) on a weird and wacky pen and ink drawing of a naked woman surrounded by a halo of cosmetic company names dating back to the Twenties. Straight black lines lead from the products to that portion of the woman's full-figured anatomy where Kleinert Shields, Lady Esther, Woodbury, Zoto's Hairwave, Winx, Tangee, Hump Hair Pins, Kurlash and Ipana would be applied. The caption read: "Where The American Dollar Goes." I plan to have her, half too-true commentary, half sexist cartoon, (wry) mounted and framed, then hang her over my desk as an irritant and an inspiration.

CONSIGNOR ALERT: Buys outright.

My Cousin's Closet

104 Park Ave.
Swarthmore, PA
19081

610-543-1999

First impressions? My mind's eye was riveted by the freshly sanded, high-gloss floorboards, the pristine paint job and the high-spirited, hand-done stenciling visually unifying the shop's interior, then repeated on business cards and consignment agreement. **Visuals were as great as the goods.** It Must Be Love, pink velvet dress with lace collar, $14. Gap purple shirt with silver rose buttons, $6. Jeans $7, jean jackets, $7.50. Spoiled BeBe, spotted brown and tan, fake fur jacket, size 4 to 5, $35. (Now take 40 % off all those prices. They were having a Mid-January winter clothing sale.) Scoot-around seat, $9. Baby carriage $30. (Where does she get these relatives? My cousins won't let me look inside their closets.) All the parts hung together and were equal to the sum of the whole.

Look: TOP DRAWER

Goods: STATUS
QUO–TOP DRAWER

Prices: LOW –
MODERATE

Looking back? My only 'Mom" regret has been wishing I had known about secondhand maternity. Unlike my last, infamous trimester, **maternity here was limited, but choice.** Had I only known then what I know now...I could have saved myself a bundle trying, and failing, to keep external pace with internal growth spurts. It was kinda like being a Mrs. Watermelon Belly, second cousin twice removed from Mr. Potato Head. Interchangeable head, arms, legs, and feet, growing disproportionately smaller day by day, the dominant body part became the disproportionately enormous belly. Parting words of wisdom? Lead with your brains and not your belly. Buy low. Sell high. (And get your husband to rub your feet.)

HOURS:
Mon–Fri 10-5,
Sat 10-3

CLOSED: Holidays &
August 7-11

CONSIGNOR ALERT: 50%-50% split. $10 fee. 45 days. 20%/25 days, additional 10% off after 35 days. Clothing with defects automatically marked 50% off.

Play It Again Sports

500 Baltimore Pike
Springfield, PA
19064

610-543-2008

A tremendous (over?) supply of ice hockey equipment. A few snow boards propped up against the back wall, one new $239, with a "sex wax." (Is that anything like a bikini wax?) Mid-afternoon on a cold, rainy mid-January day, three young men had all they could do to keep up with the demands of their mostly younger customers. Members of a local team were walking out the back door with an enormous order, while newcomers were streaming in the front.

Good wife that I am, I tried to pick out a pair of ice skates for Marvin as he waited out in the car. The young man who patiently assisted me, in the midst of this pregame buzz of activity, checked his computer screen for inventory (**very organized, up to the minute techno wizzardry**). Nothing. Then plowed through bin after bin trying to unearth a size 12 or 13 EE. Seems that most ice hockey skate size markings wear off after brief use. The only way I could get Marvin properly fitted was to lure him out of the warm, dry car and into the shop. Next time.

Look: TOP DRAWER

Goods: THINGS
SPORTY

Prices: MODERATE

HOURS:
Mon–Fri 11-9,
Sat 10-6, Sun 1-4

Next season? I look for the first snowdrops poking up their delicate white heads in my garden to herald spring. Around here? Right before the attention span of sports fans everywhere shifts from hockey and basketball and skiing and figure skating, Play It Again Sports will have a limited sale on leftover winter equipment. Then its on to golf, tennis, baseball...Wonder if they have anything in a size 12EE golf shoe?

CONSIGNOR ALERT: Buys outright, consigns and trades. See Tour # 19 for details.

CLOSED: Holidays

Riddle Thrift Shop	
1068 W. Baltimore Ave. Media, PA 19063 **565-0383** **Look:** CLASS ACT **Goods:** HO HUM–CLASS ACT **Prices:** LOW **HOURS:** Mon–Fri 9:30-4, Sat 9;30-12:30 **CLOSED:** Sat June–September	Cheryl Squadrito, reporter for the Inquirer, intent on doing a story about my adventures, played Guide For A Day. A local, she turned me on to her secondhand stomping grounds. We had a rollicking good time, shopping, doing lunch, yakking. Wrapping up the photo shoot (with a photographer who was also an avid, international thrifter) I felt happily obliged to include Riddle in my next opus, but I had not been paying attention, and had no idea how to get back here. Christmas vacation and Morgan, home from school, was riding reluctant shotgun. We were doing our mother/daughter thing, her present buying thing, and my Maniac thing, all in one. Lost, we stopped at the Lawrence Park Barnes & Noble to say hi and get our bearings. A nun appeared as if out of nowhere. One look and I knew she knew how to get us to Riddle for a return visit. Using her lucid directions, we found the shop on Rte. 1, right across from the Granite Run Mall, no problem. Divine intervention? Morgan and I looove charity thrifts. And she has her opinions, too. No surprise here. We both felt **housewares and furniture were more exciting and serendipitous** than the enormous selection of good solid-citizen clothing. Morgan happily frittered away her hard-won dimes and quarters on ladybugs and teddy bears, while I admired the matching cherry buffet $150 and china cabinet $275, the $250 solid oak dresser with all but one of its original brass pulls, a fireplace fan $4.50, and the amusingly Escher-like animal, cast-iron candy mold, $5. Halfway-to-antique embroidery with Johnathan Livingston Seagull flapping over a bunch of colorful flowers quoted in profoundly coy fashion "There's a reason to life." Here, it cost $5. **CONSIGNOR ALERT:** 67% You, 33% Shop. $2 fee/20 items/week. Tue–Fri 9-11:30 am, or first 40 people. Appointments available. Proceeds benefit Riddle Hospital.

Sheila's	
7401 Haverford Ave. Phila., PA 19151 **877-3113** **Look:** STATUS QUO **Goods:** STATUS QUO–CLASS ACT **Prices:** LOW–HIGH **HOURS:** Mon–Sat 10-5 **CLOSED:** August	The first time I ever came here, there was a beyond-middle-aged woman alone, managing the store. Not a shopper in sight. Not another employee at work. Heavy metal was blasting from the radio in one room, competing with a second station offering elevator music in the other. I wonder which station, if either, she had selected? Had some much younger employee just left? Thus possibly explaining the pulsing rhythms. Did this woman actually like hard rock? Or was she hard of hearing? Such are the unanswered questions of life. What is easier to explain here is the inventory. It's **good, with a sprinkling of great pieces**. The neighborhood ladies were out in full force on my post- Labor Day visit. They were shopping, comparing, gossiping and competing. A happy crew. Lots of go-to-church hats and matching shoes. A Victor Costa black two-piece $125. A hot red, Ildi Marshall dress, $75. Several new Cotton Express tops in sherbet colors, a little steep at $15. Carol Little two-piece, too high at $80, but renegotiated to $50. A beautiful pink-wool wrap coat, $95. A pure cotton, shell button, hacking shirt, $10. The front room had been home to Kids Korner, a mini business within. But after less than a year, it's only a memory. Such is the restless nature of resale. Sheila keeps the front room filled with her own kids' consignments now, sort of like a mother waiting for her grownup children to come home between semesters (or after a messy divorce). Unworn outlet stuff was good, but overpriced. End of winter play clothes had seen one playground too many. **CONSIGNOR ALERT:** 50%-50% split. $5 fee. 90 days. By appointment

S'ORT of New Shop

7592A
Haverford Ave.
Phila., PA 19151
473-5590

Look: STATUS QUO

Goods: STATUS QUO - CLASS ACT

Prices: MODERATE

HOURS:
Mon–Fri 9:30-5,
Sat 10-4

CLOSED: Holidays

It's almost too friendly. One petite volunteer kept telling me *everything* looked pretty when I held **any number of very nice department store-quality dresses** up in front of me, inspecting them in the mirror. Lots of I.D. Marshall, Regina Porter, Gap. One customer working the racks one secton down clutched her newfound Blue Fish with fervor. She joined me for a stroll and a chat to the corner MAC so we could cough up the loot for our catch. Told me she worked nearby and was a regular.

Virginia, the manager, had written and phoned me several times, nudging, making sure I wouldn't miss her shop. She wanted me to know they had **recently moved** from their old location in Ardmore to the new one, right next-door to the Kosher bakery and across the street from a good Deli. Glad she was so persistent. I had it that I just couldn't miss this one. I'd be letting her down. It sure didn't let me down. I got two new dresses, both linen. One is a hot pink, $50 two piece with three enormous self-covered buttons running from the neckline to that secret place where we all put a dab of perfume. The top was tunic length over a tight skirt, scrolled, same color embroidery making a luscious curving pattern overall (I know that kind of embroidery work has a name. What is it?) The other was a $35 black lined linen, V-necked, dropped waist with box-pleated skirt, fake gardenia pinned to the shoulder. For a total of $85, I walked out with $450 worth of knock 'em dead dresses. Anyone recognize their donations? I'll be wearing them to the next crop of booksignings, fashion shows and speeches. See you there.

CONSIGNOR ALERT: Donations only. Proceeds benefit Women's American ORT.

Trinity Thrift Shop

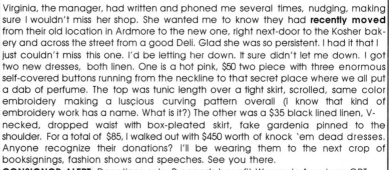

Chester Rd. &
College Ave.
Swarthmore, PA
19081
610-544-2297

Look: STATUS QUO

Goods: HO HUM – STATUS QUO

Prices: LOW

HOURS: 1st & 3rd Friday of every month 8:30-1:30

CLOSED: Holidays

Just as grades in school don't always give you a complete picture of a students' abilities, this hanger system has its limits. I bumped up against those limits doing this review. **I loooved this place.** In my heart it's a four-hanger all the way. I'd come back here every other Friday, just like a faithful congregant, if they'll let me in the fold. I'm distressed at the rating I must give this happy, loving place. The work they do with their outreach program is so important, and the women volunteers such a happy lot that I found myself wishing I could join up.

Grades don't always profile the student. They didn't with me. Grades might tell you someone's a good student, but what happens after graduation? Are they good at life? Some of those same Honor Roll kids turn out to be mediocre or life's "losers". On the other hand, my college freshman English professor said I couldn't write, and here I am. A 2 1/2-hanger rating can sometimes mean the same thing.

Big, bare basement school of design, with people's personalities creating the vivid interior decor. An **eclectic jumble of goods with the possibiliy of discovery** just around the corner. **Each volunteer a burst of light.** Every conversation came from the heart. I bought nothing, but I came away with a great deal. I plan to return and continue the search. Here, they've already found what we're all looking for.

P.S. Morgan goes to a Friends school. They do not give out grades. Twice a year, each classroom teacher, in conjunction with gym, art, music and science teachers write a three page evaluation on each and every lower school student.

CONSIGNOR ALERT: Donations only. Benefits a variety of charitable causes.

Wee Exchange	
1617 E. Darby Rd. Havertown, PA 19083 **610-446-6668**	The two owners here are the happiest pair of friends imaginable. They go way back, so far back they seem to have blended into a sort of twinship. Or perhaps it was similarities that attracted them to each other in the first place. They are both tiny, both very pretty, seemingly smiling at the same thoughts at the same time. Both wore matching **rhinestone**, heart-shaped, earrings. Yes, even their manicures --clear to white, with white underscoring the nails, emeried to a finely pointed, short arch, indicating precision and delicate detail.
	So what happened to all that precision and detail? It certainly didn't carry over into basic store management 101. The place is early lived-in. Boys' clothes are inter-
Look: STATUS QUO **Goods:** STATUS QUO–CLASS ACT **Prices:** LOW	mingled with girls' in a kind of retail recess. This system works in a shop with a small inventory, but I was ready for nap time halfway through, facing down something like eighty feet of comingled rack. Men's and women's clothing is negligible. **Kids are what they do best and most.** But their hearts are in all the right places and they know their labels. I did very well by Morgan here on two visits. She got several new bathing
HOURS: Mon–Fri 10-3, Sat 10-3	suits and a really cute, floral, suspendered jumper. I endured sorting through boys' clothes and the crowded racks because the state-of-the-art **play area is huge.** A bulletin board is packed with information, and they seem to know every customer on a first-name basis. A more than fair trade. (And besides, I want to know where they get their nails done, and where I can buy those earrings.) **PS.** Ask about their **Frequent Buyers Club.** After 5 purchases, you get $5 off the sixth.
CLOSED: Holidays	**CONSIGNOR ALERT:** 50%-50% split. $5 annual fee. Monday-Wednesday 10-2.

Ye Olde Thrift Shoppe	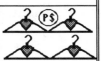
213 W. Baltimore Ave. Lansdowne, PA 19050 **610-623-3179**	Ann's been in the biz and somewhere in the area, one place or another, for over 23 years. **She knows her stuff.** A cream-colored bedspread with vivid, immaculately done, show-your-stuff embroidery work in cottage colors and design, whipped stitching around the hem, echoed the tones in the big, overall design, $75. A shadow box frame displayed Goode's Victorian women modeling clothes. The twist? They had real fabric clothing superimposed over the etchings, $105. Very well done and unusual. There were pictures scattered all over the walls and on the narrow passageway leading to a **treasure trove of antique tools, postcards, old magazines and books, and vintage clothing dating as far back as the 1880's.** Really fine.
Look: STATUS QUO **Goods:** STATUS QUO–CLASS ACT **Prices:** LOW – MODERATE	So was Ann. She either busied herself in the small room behind the register area that she's turned into a personal haven, complete with work space, sofa and fridge, or stood at the jewelery display case, one elbow propped on the glass top, chatting amicably, remembering...
HOURS: Wed–Sat 10:30-4:30	
CLOSED: Holidays	**CONSIGNOR ALERT:** Under $50=**67% You-33% Shop.** Over $51=**75% You-25% Shop.** No fee. 2 mos. All items returned or donated after consignment period ends.

Yesterday's Child	

27 E. State St. Media, PA 19063 **610-892-9211** **Look:** TOP DRAWER **Goods:** STATUS QUO–TOP DRAWER **Prices:** MODERATE– HIGH **HOURS:** Mon–Thu 9:30-6, Fri 9:30-8, Sat 9:30-5	A child's silver tea service was balanced in the store front window, $24.99. "It's A Boy" announced the blue and white wind stocking, same price, same playful mood. New Dakins peeked and poked and piled everywhere in their **adorably cozy**, temporary home. The blankie concept formalized by these clever folks in a cream colored blanket topped by a draggable, huggable bear's head, $20.99. Tiny, tiny new windbreakers circled the rack just inside the front door, their $18 (or was it $16?) price tags flapping as each new customer breezed in. A secondhand Sara Kent dress, $24.99. A baby carriage in great condition, but nonetheless high at $49. Heartstrings boy's blue-and-white strip top with chevron over the breast, $8. A gorgeous wine and black brocade party dress with black net petticoat, $79. Fisher Price swing seat $24.99, the requisite Snuggli $9.50.

Half of the goods were new, half secondhand. Quality was so high, it was hard to tell at first glance which was which. Only complaint? Both visits, neither woman behind the high-density, mini computerized, consignment command center at the rear of the shop looked up from their pressing work to welcome the steady press of customers. It must be hard to juggle all the responsibilities of operating a resale shop, do it in such a small space, and manage a smile. I'm sure the square-footage-to-profit margin equation dictates only one employee at a time to consign, greet, straighten, answer the phone, etc., etc. etc. I'm also sure that a cheerful word or two to each shopper informing them of the blue line sale, new consignment season starting, whatever, will go a long way toward ensuring a healthy growth in repeat business. Blankie, afterall, is only an internalized, but necessary substitute for Mommie's reassuring warmth, a beginning step toward independence. It can wear thin from overuse, but losing it would be a real tragedy.

P.S. They accept MAC. |
| **CLOSED:** Holidays | **CONSIGNOR ALERT:** 50%-50% cash or **60%You-40% Store credit**. 45 days. 20%/25 days 30%/35 days. No appointment necessary. |

TOUR #9
ISSUES AND ANSWERS

West Chester has been featured on the evening news lately. Homeless people have been using the downtown area's benches as an address for the day. Residents, causing quite a ruckus, are engaged in time-honored, civic debate over the yea or nay value and values of removing the benches. Ongoing lack of sufficient parking has been another pain in the lower extremity of the body politic. Residents must use zoned parking stickers. Big-city problems, like the ones I thought I was leaving behind when we moved from 10th & Clinton Streets in Center City Philadelphia to the relative calming green of Melrose Park, are spreading. Now before I get angry calls from the Mayor and the Chamber of Commerce and well-meaning taxpayers, know this: West Chester, with its brick walks, spreading shade trees, adorable storefronts, gracious Victorian and colonial homes and offices and fine restaurants, shares these problems with every small town and big city in America. **I am not singling out West Chester. We are all in the same leaky ship of state.** Too much of some things, not enough of others, all at once, all in one place. What to do?

One solution immediately at hand is to support your favorite charity thrifts, especially those that benefit the illiterate, the abused, the hungry, the homeless and those without work. There are several in this area, and numerous ones throughout our region. Donate your goods. Volunteer your time. Lend a hand. All too many volunteer thrift shops are running short on man-and woman-power. I see hand-lettered signs in shop windows wherever I go. They need volunteers. They need us. Wherever possible, I list where the proceeds go, so you can choose where you want to send your time, money and goods and begin to make a difference, begin to plug the leaks.

As to parking, as Center City residents, we owned one car and had to negotiate (sometimes arm wrestle) over who got it and what for and when and why and how long and what counted the most. I walked or rode everywhere on my three-speed secondhand bike with saddlebag wire baskets clamped on the back. I was a lot thinner then, too. Even in the burbs, even with the hassles it can cause, we still own only one car--a van big enough to schlepp kids, dog and curbside treasures. Biking is out. You'd get killed trying to toot around on two wheels on Routes 611, 309 or 73. But we fill in with cabs and trains. It's a lot cheaper than a second car, too. We've even considered moving to a more urban area (like Chestnut Hill or West Chester or Haddonfield or Moorestown), where we can walk and bike around more. I miss it.

Walking around West Chester is a charming experience. There are two main streets. Gay Street leads into town with one-way traffic going West, and Market Street one way going East. The 100 block of East Gay alone has five restaurants. **The Spare Rib, Dinon's, Kustom Kuts, Clemente's and DeStarr's.** I have eaten in the **D-K diner** near Bring and Buy, where Morgan wolfed down bow-tie noodles and enormous chunks of chicken and carrots in broth, and I had a yummy grilled cheese and pork roll sandwich. **Vincente's**, with it's more sophisticated and therefore more expensive menu, was delightful on both occasions. I looooved their pasta dishes. I'm dying to try **The Cafe**, located near County Seat on the opposite side of Gay, and **a coffee shop** near the Women's Exchange over on Market.

You know you've hit **Downingtown** when you spot the one-room, whitewashed log cabin, circa 1701, with its single electric candle shining through the window, welcoming the weary traveler. You also know you've missed St. James Thrift if you've gotten this far into town without finding it. Head back east on Rte. 30. It's on the end of town closest to Rte. 113. At the extreme western end of town is a painted to-the-extreme **diner**. It's retro-neo, glow-in-the-dark paint job of pink and turquoise echo those of Detroit, circa 1954. It's the limit. Happy Birthday Elvis and Home of the Blob (a sandwich, I suppose) shouted from the portable marquee at Viaduct and W. Lancaster.

Caln, Thorndale and Coatesville are linked by Lancaster Pike (Rte. 30). Remnants of the once powerful railroad system still run along the left-hand side as you head west, forming a sort of Chinese Wall effect. With no noticeable bridge access, I haven't a clue as to what lurks on the other side of this formidable impediment. The right-hand side is a loosely formed series of strip malls, some in better shape than others, each with a single thrift or resale shop, held a competitively safe arm's distance apart. The area is struggling. Empty businesses stare back with some windows vacant, others boarded up, completely expressionless. Fairygodmother's owner Camilla is in the forefront of an effort to restore her little corner of the world, the Wedgwood Shopping Mall. New landscaping, a new roof and a new coat of parking lot blacktop to repair the ravages of last winter are scheduled. Way to go, Camilla! Headin' on down the road, Goodwill is the amazing antithesis of every mainstream misconception of what it's like to shop a charity bottomfeeder. Check it out. If you're hungry right about now, there's a **pizza parlor** (eat in) and a **Master Wok** (take out) located in the mall Goodwill shares with Acme. Another very very very 50's-looking, very pink **diner** is just past Thrifty Fox, but before Memories and Consignments up by the Ford dealership.

Depending on your whim and time constraints, you can either head north on Rte. 100 out of West Chester or take 113 East out of Downingtown and wind up in the **Exton & Lionville** section of our little extravaganza. The area is one of those unsettling visions of semi-suburban, semi-rural, and semi-urban life. Cud-chewing cows are silhouetted against high-tech office buildings. Cornfields surround major hotel chains. Winding two-lane roads that were originally nothing more than Indian trails and pioneer blazed ruts lead straight to the interstate turnpike system. Gigantic shopping malls crowd out white farm houses and red barns. Strip malls and housing developments are surrounded by woods. What a curious muddle. Commercially developed land lies, going to economic seed, just outside Downingtown, while we dig up virgin earth in Exton and Lionville. Let's start recycling people and communities as well as clothing and curiosities, shall we?

Coatesville lost its economic heart when Lukens Steel closed up shop. Like many former industry-based towns all over America, it has yet to regain it's vitality. Perhaps it never will. Some shops are hanging in there, others are boarded up and abandoned. Some blocks are better than others. Just like their citizens, neighborhoods also have a life cycle. One resident at a time, one shopkeeper at a time, this one is looking for the way back.

TOUR #9

10	Brandywine Thrift Shop	Downingtown
15	Bring & Buy	West Chester
21	Christine's	West Chester
14	County Seat ★	West Chester
6	Fairygodmother ★	Downingtown
5	Goodwill Fashions Etc.	Downingtown
23	The Growing Years	West Chester
11	Inch By Inch	Exton
2	K.C.'s	Coatesville
3	Memories & Consignments	Coatesville
12	Michele Rose	Exton
17	My Best Junk ★	West Chester
22	Play It Again Sports	West Chester
1	Reuzit	Coatesville
16	J. Ryans	West Chester
18	Second Act	West Chester
13	Second Thoughts	Exton
9	St. James	Downingtown
7	Tiny Tots	Downingtown
4	Thrifty Fox	Thorndale
8	The Unforgettable Woman	Downingtown
19	Westminster Thrift Shop	West Chester
20	Women's Exchange	West Chester

*Note: This list has a shop's entire name. Names in review boxes may have been shortened a tad to fit. Numbers before each shop name correspond to their numbered location on each map. **Shops with a star sold Volume II. Volume III? ASK!**

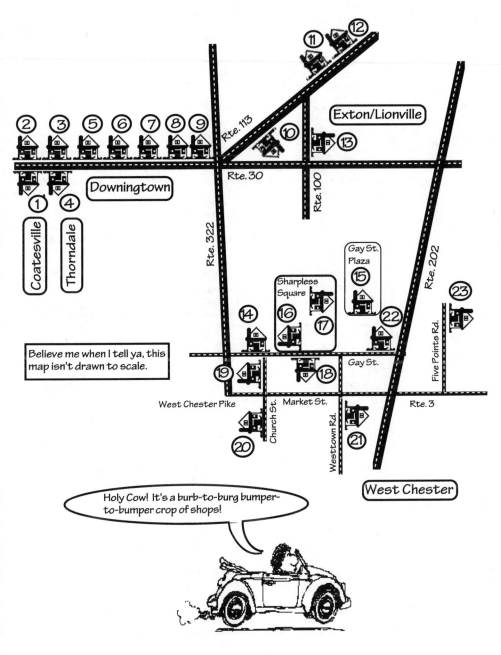

TOUR #9 MAP Page 152

Brandywine Thrift Shop	
368 W. Uwchlan Av. Downingtown, PA 19335 **610-269-8622**	First visit? Couldn't get in. No sign. Closed for the day? The week? Christmas vacation, don't you know. Volunteers, everywhere, must still believe in Santa. They're all at home, staring up the chimney, waiting. Morgan and I were very disappointed, noses pressed against the chilly windowpane, staring at the darkened shop, sniveling. (Me especially. She loooves charity resale. They're usually within her budget.) The unexpectedly thrift-free day was growing too long to keep her waning interest much longer. Far from home, we're headed for an Excedrin moment.
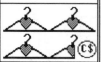	Determined, I returned weeks later, alone. Stressed out again, this time because I was coming down with something sinister and my day had been filled with one too many two-hanger-and-under experiences. I reached for the Excedrin, again. What I got when I reached the shop was far better. What a relief. **Brandywine was bright as a new penny, clean as a whistle, happy as a lark, and organized up the kazoo.** Ladies scurried around, busy as bees, gleefully dusting, sorting, folding, and rehanging as they went. I could almost swear I heard one whistling while she worked. Final undercover visit, the week before Valentine's Day, the snowplowed lot was filled. I had to hover like a plane at the airport, waiting for my turn down the
Look: TOP DRAWER **Goods:** STATUS QUO–TOP DRAWER **Prices:** LOW–MODERATE	
HOURS: Tue–Sat 10-3	runway. This place is very popular with the locals, and me. Neither rain, nor snow... **P.S.** They have a 24-hour hold policy.
	SHOPPER ALERT: Women's & men's clothing 
CLOSED: Mid-June – Mid-August	**CONSIGNOR ALERT: 67% You–33% Shop.** $8/15 items Tue–Thu & 1st & 3rd Sats 10-12. Donations: Tue– Sat 10-3. Benefits Brandywine Hospital.

Bring & Buy	
The Gay St. Plaza West Chester, PA 19382 **610-696-2576**	Last winter, fire destroyed Bring & Buy. But "God," as one volunteer reminded, "works in mysterious ways." They may not have risen as magnificently as the Phoenix from the proverbial ashes, but after the initial shock wore off and the ensuing frenetic scramble to relocate and reopen was behind them, volunteers now can't help but look a little like the cat who got to eat the proverbial canary.
	New digs, costing every penny of their $15,000 insurance settlement, are **sunny and spacious with plenty of free parking**, a treasured commodity in these parts. I saw labels every bit as good as any three-hanger, privately owned shop. Mom could be decked for the holidays in a Jennifer Moore hot, black velvet, backless cocktail $15. Or how about a peaches and cream, two-piece, Jessica McClintock cocktail suit, $6, if she can get out the stain dead-center on the bodice? For $10, a navy velvet and pink satin-trimmed party dress by Rare Editions would temporarily transform your tomboy into a princess. Dad, as long as you're no larger than a size 48, you could purchase any one of the reasonably priced, conservative suits, and no one need be the wiser about its origins. Boys' looked played in, slept in, but scrubbed behind the ears. Except for the enormous old trunk, underpriced at $135, plentiful housewares and minimal furniture were underwhelming. Mary and Mildred, the Wednesday volunteers womaning the register, were **awesome**.
Look: STATUS QUO **Goods:** HO HUM–STATUS QUO **Prices:** LOW **HOURS:** Mon–Fri 10-4, Sat 10-1	
CLOSED: Saturdays in June, July & August	**CONSIGNOR ALERT: 67% You-33% Shop** . $5 fee. 15 items/week. Monday–Thursday 10-1. Donations accepted. Benefits Chester County Charities.

Christine's

Westbrook Center
105B Westtown Rd.
West Chester, PA
19382
610-692-9375

Look: CLASS ACT

Goods: STATUS QUO

Prices: LOW-MODERATE

HOURS: Mon–Fri 10-5:30, Wed & Thu 10-7, Sat 10-4

CLOSED: Holiday weekend hours vary

Morgan wanted to know just how much everything in the store was worth if the owner were to add it all up. "A million dollars?" These days everything is either a million or her latest fad number, a googolplex. The amused owner obliged, estimating $20,000 was more like it. "Why, are you interested in buying it all?" she playfully shot back. Morgan was more pleased by the prospect than I. My dressing room closets are already bursting at the seams, so Marvin keeps reminding me.

And I'm too easily bored to stay put in one place. Traveling long distances in a car every day and writing the Great American nonnovel at 4am, while folding laundry, planning an ad compaign and worrying how the bus tours will work (and is there any dog food left?) is a cinch compared to what shopkeepers go through. Besides, this way I get paid to shop. And I can talk on the phone whenever I want without someone spying on me.

This owner was customer-involved. She discreetly offered assistance. She pointed out upcoming sales. Unflustered, she fielded several telephone questions, arranged a pickup time for a consignor's leftovers, and respectfully answered all of Morgan's many questions. I appreciated that. So did Morgan. The selling floor is everything you would want in a privately owned, neighborhood resale boutique. **clean, bright, well organized and friendly.** Just as the consignment guidelines instruct, clothing was clean and pressed and either current (mostly) or classic (mostly). Nothing was said about designer. Often, what is not said, is just as important as what is.

CONSIGNOR ALERT: 50%-50%. $5 annual fee. 60 days 30 items max./consignment. On hangers. Appointment preferred.

County Seat

Church & Gay Sts.
West Chester, PA
19380
610-696-0584

Look: CLASS ACT

Goods: STATUS QUO–TOP DRAWER

Prices: MODERATE– HIGH

HOURS: Mon–Fri 10-5, Sat 10-4, Sun 12-4

CLOSED: Holidays

Three dealers under one roof, on a busy corner of the main shopping drag. Handsome red-awninged windows display everything from the ridiculous to the sublime, hinting at what can be found inside. Well, sublimely ridiculous like the Paul Bunyan-sized twin, carved and paneled, curly maple headboards, probably standing 6' high, definitely $1400. Intricately boxed, tooled and machined gizmo by Thomas Walker & Sons of Birmingham, England, to calculate yacht, motor launch fishing craft speed, $225. Locked and cubbyholed Empire-style butler's desk, circa 1825, $750. A corner and wall full of clocks, all a tickin' and a tockin', a table full of paperweights, sitting pretty. 1890 dentist's chair, menacing enough to double for executions, $325. A saddler's bench, sans saddle, sans saddler, sans horse. $350. Cosc's Farmer's Accounting Book, $100, firm. Betsy Wetsy, $90 and Tiny Tears $100, dry. Don't sulk, Pouting Patty was there, too, $55--one for every year.

Sublime? Ridiculous? It's all in the eye of the beholder. As I behold this **freely associated inventory,** I am briefly transported out of my values and into those of many others. This journey, a sort of esthetic role-playing, can bring a good giggle at the very least and revelation at best. Climbing into someone else's values, however briefly, can enlarge our own. The wild ride from ridiculous to sublime often makes life worth living and this store well worth the visit.

P.S. Some dealers take credit cards, some don't. Ask. All pick up and deliver. Charges are distance-based, i.e., 15 miles = $20.

CONSIGNOR ALERT: 65% You–35% Them. No fee. No appointment. 20%/6 weeks.

Fairy-godmother	

Fairy-godmother

Rte. 30
Downingtown, PA
19335
610-269-8127

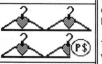

Look: CLASS ACT
Goods: STATUS
QUO–CLASS ACT
Prices: VERY LOW

HOURS:
Mon–Sat 10-6
CLOSED: Holidays

"Whether you are in the market to buy or sell, you need a fairy godmother." Ain't it the truth! Move over, Shopper Lady, here comes Fairygodmother. I can't remember the last time I saw such low prices for kids' stuff outside of a bottomfeeder. Here we are out in the boonies, where the idea of New York style is downright silly. And yet, there are some **really cute duds for kids** here. Not runway-caliber high fashion, mind you, but real life stylish kids' clothes. Labels included Rainbow Creek, Jet Set, You Babes, Silver Unicorn and Sister Sister.

There were scads of kid's new accessories and underwear. They also have a really **well thought out buying procedure** that tells you everything you really need to know about consigning children's clothing here, or anywhere else for that matter. It includes not only the niceties (like, remember to remove the smell of cigarette smoke and mothballs), but also Pennsylvania laws (such as those forbidding the resale of secondhand stuffed toys or car-seats because of the substantial number of recall notices on these items). It also tells you that they won't consign cribs.

P.S. There's a **map** on their brochure. If you've got the piece of paper, you've already found the store, but it could prove useful to help a friend know where to find a new fairy godmother. A clean, well-appointed **bathroom** awaits you and your baby. **Also note their 10-day cash return policy.**

CONSIGNOR ALERT: By appointment only. **Clothing, toys and furniture are purchased outright. You get paid immediately.** 12-item min., 100-item max/appointment.

Goodwill Fashions Etc.

3953-3955 Rte. 30
Downingtown, PA
19335
610-873-9797

Look: UPSCALE
BOTTOMFEEDER
Goods: HO HUM –
CLASS ACT
Prices: VERY LOW

HOURS: Mon–Sat
10-9, Sun 12-5
CLOSED: Holidays

"...and of course there's the Goodwill up by the Acme." When I finished shopping at St. James Thrift Shop on the outskirts of downtown Downingtown, I asked, as I always do, where are the other thrift stores in town? Well, there's nothing 'of course' about it. Driving around for a while I find the mall. There's the Acme. Where's the Goodwill? It's not here. I scan the street. I look for a sign. I look for signs from heaven, any sign, from anywhere at all. No Goodwill. I pull into the parking lot in front of the Acme. First person I ask, looks at me like I'm from Mars. Points to the new brick-front building abutting the Acme. The one where we are standing. The one with the huge picture windows. **The one as nice as any Caldor or K-Mart.** The one with no sign. The Goodwill. Of course!

How times have changed: two dressing rooms, credit cards, and pinch-me-if-I'm-not-dreaming business cards with a fax number, no less, on the desk by the register. Right about where color-coded racks and mass-marketing display techniques end, the old Goodwill is spotted lurking in the racks. For all its 90's splendor, make no mistake, this is still a bottomfeeder. Prices are posted by item. For example, all women's dresses $3, all men's shirts $2.50. Children's department is strong; furniture is weak. A sign begs, "Supervise your children, please". Even better? A play area, please.

CONSIGNOR ALERT: Donations only.

The Growing Years

1 N. Five Points Rd.
West Chester, PA
19380

610-430-7601

Look: CLASS ACT

Goods: STATUS
QUO–CLASS ACT

Prices: LOW–HIGH

HOURS: Mon–Sat
10-5, Wed 10-6

CLOSED: Holidays

Snag #1. Some prankster rotated the intersection sign 90 degrees. Couldn't find the correct street. **Snag #2.** Found the strip mall, only to prowl parking lots and driveways for ten minutes. **Snag #3.** Morgan, growing weary of the hunt, wanted to know "just when are we going to find this shop?" Increasingly anxious myself, but the grown-up, afterall, I patiently explained. " Helping find shops is one reason people are willing to buy The Guide." She nodded with growing, first-hand appreciation.

We jump up and down with relief when I finally pinpoint our open-for-business, 10am target. All thistrouble despite the big pink and blue, hanging, storefront sign and the yellow one straddling the sidewalk. Look for Jefferson Bank and the Gulf station. The shop is sandwiched between two buildings, around the corner from the chiropractor, catty-corner from the ophthalmologist. There, now you can find it. The The friendly sales clerk was snipping food coupons while fielding phone questions. (We're always trying to save a buck, aren't we?) **Nice and new and cubbyhole cute, it's very strong and reasonably priced in children's up to size 8**, with a few equally good but too-few-and-far-between sizes 10-14. There were lots and lots of new clothes, too, labels like Mousefeathers and Rompers with original price tags still attached, a sort of **mini-outlet** for several children's clothing manufacturers. Prices are about 1/2 the origional. High for resale, average for outlet.

CONSIGNOR ALERT: 55% You-45% Shop (45% if not on hangers). $8 annual fee. By appointment, especially first-time consignors. Drop-offs for regulars.

Inch By Inch

Lionville Business
Center
Rte. 113
Exton, PA 19341

610-594-6844

Look: TOP DRAWER

Goods: STATUS
QUO-TOP DRAWER

Prices: MODERATE

HOURS:
Mon–Sat 10-4,
Thu 10-8

CLOSED: Holidays

Rack by Rack might be more like it. A baker's dozen, most double-sided, looking for all the world like miles and miles of **good to great kids' resale**, stretching all the way back into the deepest recesses of this adorable shop. Pooh Bear and Rabbit danced across the pale yellow walls, as happy kids and moms played tag in the open green-carpeted spaces, hide-and-go-seek in the angular maze of racks.

Lots of party dresses and boys' suits to choose from, right before the holidays. Pretty new hair accessories were on display near the register. Pre-pirouette, pristine white skates, steep at $18.95 but still much better than $40 before-sale retail or the usual $24.95 after. Cheapest ever? $2 at Whosoever Gospel in Germantown, new but without laces. Average? $10-14, new, $5-$12, used. I'm up on secondhand ice skate prices because Morgan takes lessons. Only nine, she grows one size every year. Her dad wears size 12EE. Uh oh. Tip: stick to one brand that works for your kid's feet. Buy ahead. I've already got next year's size-7's stashed in the bottom of a closet. If she grows out of skating, I'll consign them away at an expensive resale and just get my money back.

I'm now sore and weary but still restless, trying to get to the last scheduled shop on the day's olympic-caliber route. I ask the two young women behind the counter if they know where it is. Recognizing neither me nor the shop, they pull out a well-worn TSMG, put their heads together, and look up the name. Now why didn't I think of that? Knowing full well it is unreviewed and unlisted, I wait, nevertheless, to see what will happen. When they can't find it, they seem to think that means it doesn't exist, shrug their shoulders, and close the book. Next time...
P.S. 48-hour return policy with receipt!

CONSIGNOR ALERT: 50%-50% split. $5 fee. 30 items/week/consignor. Reduced by 30%/61-90 days. On hangers. Drop-off on Mon, Thurs or Sat only. Call ahead.

K.C.'s Bookstore	
217 E. Lincoln Hwy. Coatesville, PA 19320 **610-384-7021** (P$)	Well it's called a bookstore. Indeed, it used to be a bookstore. But now there are almost no books. It used to be a store for collectibles. That didn't work out. Then she tried dolls. Dolls are almost all sold. Now dolls are on the way out, too. Now they're trying clothes. Clothes are in. Clothes are selling. Stay tuned.

Because of this let's-try-it-and-see-what-happens-approach to marketing, a little bit of everything lingers here, there and everywhere. The stuff in the locked glass cases, the leftover **dolls, houseware, collectibles and books are the best stuff** in the place in my estimation. A signed, framed and autograph photograph of Richard Nixon, looking presidential, looking heavenward, heaven help us. Bear

Look: STATUS QUO

Goods: HO HUM - TOP DRAWER

dolls, each one individually dressed, each one with a name and an identity. Expensive but well worth it, when you consider all the care and work that went into making each one.

Prices: LOW - HIGH

I understand the entrepreneurial process going on here, all too well. As a fellow business person I admire and empathize with the owners' responsive survival in-

HOURS:

Mon–Sun 10-4

stincts. That old door-to-door salesman's/carnie, side-show hawker's/medicine show motto: "Give 'em what they want,"still rings true. If clothing is what they want, give it to 'em. But as a customer, I left wondering which bear doll's identity she would most closely resemble next time around?

CLOSED: Holidays

CONSIGNOR ALERT: Buys outright.

Memories & Consignments	
270 E. Lincoln Hwy. Coatesville, PA 19320 **610-384-1770** (C$)	The **best stuff was costume** items fit for a Hollywood studio wardrobe department. A floor-length black sheath from The Kollection, a Lord & Taylor label, packed the biggest retro-fashion wallop. It had enormous long-stem roses scattered over the dress and matching tight-fitting, longsleeved jacket, with a long leg-revealing slit. $15 and you could compete with any bleached, bosom-enhanced, glamour-puss outfits Heather Locklear wore in her TV murder mystery set in the 70's. I also spied a brown suede, hooded, patch jacket stitched together with matching brown yarn, holding on almost by rote, just like the one an old flame used to wear. Didn't like it

Look: STATUS QUO

Goods: HO HUM– STATUS QUO

Prices: LOW– MODERATE

then either. Wedding dresses of a similar place and time ranged up to $50. Some had fabric...worthy of consideration, if you know how to do alterations. Otherwise...The best bet was a stainless steel sink, $8, and an orange nylon backpack with gold-colored frame, $5. Scattered about: lidless sugar bowls, a purple plastic box filled with wooden drawer pulls, a seashell-encrusted plastic plate, matching pillows with hearts, very odds 'n ends of the road.

HOURS: Mon–Fri 9-6, Sat 10-5.

The man behind the counter seems to be popular with the ladies, especially those who peaked right around this same era. Each and every time I entered, he was deep in tête à tête with one such customer, friend, whatever. Each time, he stopped long enough to greet me, announce general 'here's-how-it-works' info about the store, and then return to the local legend with lore in the making.

P.S. Planning on a shift to a half-and-half split between clothing and housewares.

CLOSED: Holidays

CONSIGNOR ALERT: 50%-50% split. No fee. 60 days.

Michele Rose	
310 Gordon Drive Exton, PA 19341 **610-594-8084**	**Lovely**, with lots of space and light and mirrors, located in the corner of a relatively new strip mall. They innovatively created a second dressing room by hanging blinds between the big picture window and the wall. A few hooks or a stand outside the room for try ons would be a great help. Posted on the wall was a unique sales calendar, one sale item for every day in the month of December. A significant portion of the shop is **evening wear and bridal, and that they do very well** indeed. Bridal hovered around $170-250 with one beaded extravaganza topping out at $900. They have some sort of pipeline to Doncaster, with some of their never-worn dresses mixed in the racks. Marked half price, they're still too high for resale. Some work clothes and play clothes, especially those above size 10, were uninspiring. Sweaters and suits played it safe. Furs were just plain UGLY. I was perplexed. Why two sets of hours on the front door? Why the fluctuating inventory?
Look: CLASS ACT **Goods:** STATUS QUO–TOP DRAWER **Prices:** LOW–HIGH	This could be a great shop. As it is **it's very good.** Here was another owner, phone grafted to ear, deep in heated, who-did-what-to-whom. This time there were two friendly, proficient salesclerks working the floor and the customers. Thank you. I suggest, however, that next time she consider looking closer to home to reach out and touch someone. You never know who's unintentionally listening in on the party line. Hello? **P.S.** 24-hour return policy with receipt.
HOURS: Mon & Tue 10-6 Wed & Thu 10-8, Fri & Sat 10-4	 **SHOPPER ALERT:** Bridal and evening wear
CLOSED: Holidays	**CONSIGNOR ALERT:** 50%-50%. $10 fee. 25 items/week. 90 days. By appointment only for first-time consignors. Afterwards, drop and run.

My Best Junk	
323 East Gay St. West Chester, PA 19380 **610-429-3388**	Unbeknowst to them, Salvador Dali, the very late surrealistic capitalist, and Mario Buatto, interior decorator to the stars, still very much alive and specialist in all things English and chintz, have formed a working partnership. They've come together in a sort of interior design by seance, held daily in a West Chester strip mall. These two spirit guides are trapped in the creative sensibilities of Linda, medium and entrepreneurial provocateur extraordinaire. **The beautiful and bizarre, the ordinary and the sublime**, from color-coordinated display settings of china and pottery and linens to soaring swallows and dangling gorillas, all swirl together in a profusion of color, mood swings, camp style and a fully formed sense of humor.
Look: SURREAL CHINTZ **Goods:** TREASURES – TUPPERWARE **Prices:** MODERATE–HIGH	**The sheer volume and visual complexity of the merchandise is overwhelming.** A deviled-egg dish, two eggshells holding snippets of yolk-yellow yarn, startle and amuse. Aluminum frying pan, hand-drawn fried egg glued to the bottom, hangs on the wall. Why so many eggs? Ah well Dali had his watches, Linda has her eggs. Paper breadsticks jut jauntily out of a jar. A topless sugar bowl with hand-painted violets is used to hold sachets. And then there are the grottos: two are reincarnated closets, the third, a former powder room, all shrines to our lady-of-the-secondhand. A hand-lettered sign, one of many posted helter-skelter, goes straight to the point: Even junk looks nice in the right place. Busloads of tourists will be pulling up soon.
HOURS: Mon– Fri 10-5, Sat 10-4	**Ya gotta see it to believe it.** Words fail. Even moi. **P.S.** Linda **added two rooms** to her wildly successful enterprise, sub-letting to similarily inclined visionaries. Leaded glass thingies, gift shop caliber perfume, jewelry, hand-painted sweats, and repainted, transformed thrift shop treasures like the
CLOSED: 1 week summer & Mondays	cream-coloured 40's end table, garnished with hand-painted fruit. **CONSIGNOR ALERT:** Buys outright. Drop in. House calls by appointment.

Play it Again Sports

507 E. Gay St.
West Chester, PA
19380
610-429-9764

Look: TOP DRAWER

Goods:
YOU TELL ME

Prices: MODERATE

HOURS: Mon–Fri
10-8, Sat 10-6,
Sun 12-5

CLOSED: Sundays
July 4–Labor Day
& Holidays

My idea of aerobic exercise is walking down thrift shop aisles. I used to ride horseback, I used to play field hockey, I used to high jump. I still swim, the only equipment I need for that is a suit. I may not be the best person to tell if the quality of the stuff here is primo. After some of you sports' fiends shop this place, please call or drop a line and give me some feedback. I'm out of my league here. What I *can* tell, and the basis for the four hanger rating, is **the store looks like any other sporting goods store in any other strip mall, anywhere USA.** I'm making the assumption that merchandise is primo, too. Inside, there were bins of ice hockey skates, bins of all things golf, racks of bowling balls, and a whole ice hockey section. Midway, there was a large area dedicated to weight lifting equipment. The young man at the desk seemed very well-informed. He was certainly patient and polite.

While I was there, a pro golfer/amateur consignor was trying to sink a sweet deal. The clerk said that since it was the end of the golf season, and the club had a nick at the base, he'd pay $18 outright. $20 if it had been the start of the season and had no nick. $25 if he was selling it on consignment. Signs everywhere state that **they buy, sell, trade and consign new and used sporting equipment.** Quote of the week: "Our business is based a lot on kid's feet; they grow out of them so quickly."
P.S. Lot entrance is one-way only. Miss your layup shot? Circle around for another.
PP.S. One of a 500-member franchise, locations include Paoli, Marlton & Horsham.
CONSIGNOR ALERT: Your take depends on which category you choose and how much risk you tolerate. Consigning riskier but more profitable than selling outright. Trade-in can be very profitable. 20% more in store credit, than cash upfront. For example, a trade-in of $20 worth of merchandise = $24 in store credit.

Reuzit

228 W. Lincoln Hwy.
Coatesville, PA
19320
610-383-5473

Look: STATUS QUO

Goods: DOWN &
OUT– HO HUM

Prices: LOW

HOURS: Mon–Fri
10-4, Sat 10-2

CLOSED: Holidays

Enormous trucks rumbled by, shaking the neighborhood almost as much as the loss of Lukens Steel did several years back. The streets still hadn't been cleared of snow, leaving only two lanes for traffic. I nervously circled looking for a chair-free spot, then plowed through mounds of snow hoping I wouldn't get stuck when it came time to leave, praying I wouldn't get killed just trying to get out of my car. Row upon row of simple brick houses huddled together for comfort. Smack dab in the middle sat this **little haven of quiet solicitude.** I only wish I could give out hangers and hearts for human kindness. The lady at the register was the brightest, sweetest soul. I really enjoyed talking to her, even more listening to her stories. This shop is part of the Mennonite Central Committee. She explained that their first mission back in the 1920's was to help feed the starving in Russia. Now they are spread all over the world, trying to make a dent, trying to make a difference. Then she explained the difference between a heffer and a calf, and what the word freshen means in the cow biz. I must have seemed like such a city slicker.

Gifts made abroad for sale here in this country, the proceeds sent back to the country of origin, were far superior to the local secondhand clothing and goods. The best local product was the five butternut squash, clustered and sitting on the floor under a clothing rack near the register, 25¢ each. If I hadn't been so tired, dreading the long ride home, I would have bought one to cook for dinner. No, better yet, I should have taken her home and had her cook it. Even though she was much older, she looked and sounded like she knew how to do almost anything, and would or could with a smile.

CONSIGNOR ALERT: Donations only. Benefits the Mennonite Central Committee.

J. Ryans

323 E. Gay St.
West Chester, PA
19380
610-436-0967

Look: STATUS QUO – TOP DRAWER

Goods: STATUS QUO–TOP DRAWER

Prices: MODERATE –HIGH

HOURS:
Mon–Sat 10–6

CLOSED: Holidays

Midsummer. A heat wave. No air conditioning. I was in one of those "Why am I doing this?" moods. Understandable. The shop was rating a 3 or 3 1/2, while the thermometer was registering around 93 1/2. Then, after all that sweat (no blood), they up and moved, never making it into Volumn II. Edit. Delete. Midwinter. Linda, of My Best Junk, was hosting a Bigger and Better Digs For More Junk Party. Invited to autograph copies of my opus, I arrived underdressed, far from home, after a day on the road reviewing. What to do? Shop, of course. I stopped in J. Ryans, now relocated to Sharpless Square, at the opposite end of the same strip mall from Linda. I bought a Carol Little outfit for under $40. I asked to keep the price tags on, choosing to remain undercover when I made my request. They were curious, but obliged. I left them on, hoping to get a laugh from fellow party goers back at the soiree, while still managing to look glamorous. It worked. (Now, J. Ryans understands the who and the why of it all.)

Absolutely great front room, packed with average-to-sensational women's work and evening clothes. They've taken care to create a glamorous setting, with merchandise vignettes scattered about. Just a few steps shy of a heart, here's what could put them over the top: Get rid of men's and some of the casual stuff. It takes up space and your heart's not really in it. And what is that sheet-covered mound of layaway or pending consignments doing in the middle of the back room, taking up even more valuable space? A glamorous screen instead, perhaps? Friendly owners spend their days in the far-prettier front room, meeting and greeting. You however, must see and shop both rooms. Right now, it's as if you'd checked in the mirror before going out--hair, dress, jewelry just so--then ignored your back, and missed a drooping hemline and a runner. Turn around gorgeous!

CONSIGNOR ALERT: 50%-50% split. $7 annual fee. 42 days. Drop and run.

Second Act

142 East Gay St.
West Chester, PA
19380
610-431-2905

Look: CLASS ACT

Goods: HO HUM – STATUS QUO

Prices: LOW

HOURS:
Tue–Fri 10–6,
Mon & Sat 10–5

CLOSED: Holidays

Housed in what was once a grocery store, its huge picture window framed by the handsome, dark green marble facade. There, three enormous cardboard vintage-car cutouts are parked. They grab your attention and won't let go. The **interior is equally unforgettable,** with dark wood paneling, built-in displays and twelve original Deco ceiling lights. Lending a whiff of authentic atmosphere if not actual aroma of French Roast, an old-fashioned coffee roaster filled a darkened alcove with its enormous girth. Overall, vintage was more exciting than the contemporary resale, and architecture was more exciting than anything. Although any students worthy of their cherished worn-torn jeans and reinvented recherché resale would probably disagree with me on this one. And so they should.

Former manager, Abigail, certainly disagreed. She thought to write, eventually, almost a year to the day post-publication, and tip me off to several factual review booboos. I changed hours and consignor policy accordingly. I cannot, however, include a bride icon, because I only saw two or three gowns, once. Two vintage, one merely old. Pictures aren't numerous enough here, either, to qualify. A minimum of 10% of DEDICATED floor space is required per icon. We do a last-minute research phone call to every shop checking facts, right before going to press. Don't know how, but we messed up some on this one. Sorry, Abigail.
P.S. They will accept returns for store credit. P.P.S. 10% discount to students with ID.
CONSIGNOR ALERT: Donations only. Proceeds benefit Goodwill Industries.

Second Thoughts	
Brentwood Shoppes 225 N. Pottstown Pk. Exton, PA 19341 **610-594-9111**	The pretty, pleasant-sounding young owner chatted on the phone, making numerous birthday party plans, describing ice cream cone cakes she'd baked. Cute recipe, bad idea. A bad idea to ignore real-live customers for personal reasons during business hours. It wasn't as if the shop was crowded, making it possible for an owner to lull herself into complacency. The entire time we were there, surrounded by mall-induced bustle of the last day's countdown before Christmas, no one else entered. The gigantic intersection for this place, Swedesford Road and Rte. 100, was one of the most frenetic, time-consuming ones I'd ever encountered. Strawbridge's and Pier I and K Mart and Goodyear, every retailer imaginable, are clustered around here. Everyone, it seemed, was either trying to get to or from them all at once. Second Thoughts lies in the shadow of Color Tile.
Look: CLASS ACT **Goods:** HO HUM– STATUS QUO **Prices:** LOW	There was a line of cosmetics and locally made jewelry in display cases by the register. A nice touch, helping to set them off from other secondhand shops in the area. **Maternity rack was better stocked than many. So was the double rack of larger women's clothing.** Too many eye-popping, hey dude, attention grabbers, or clean, neat, and tidy yawns among the better skirts and blouses. Way, way too much big-hair, mall-crawler or safe safe safe, make-you-invisible suits and dresses scattered among the few big name recognition labels. It just wasn't *my* favorite
HOURS: Mon, Wed, Fri 10-6, Tue & Thu 10-6, Sat 10-5	flavor. But that's why they make vanilla *and* chocolate. Hold the cone. **P.S.** Second visit? She was busy curling her hair in one of the dressing rooms. This time I did get a hello, though.
CLOSED: Holidays	**CONSIGNOR ALERT:** 50%–50% split. $7 annual fee. 60 days. By appointment only.

St. James	
409 Rte. 30 Downingtown, PA 19335 **610-873-7812**	Another church, another basement. This time **well-lit and friendly**, but very little else going on, except the intense smell of popcorn competing for air space with the local grassroots public opinion poll and gossip channel going full blast. Both packed a wallop. Two women, self identified as formerly abused, tried to decide just how much corporal punishment was O.K. to inflict on their kids. Their vote: Spanking with a hand on a fully-clothed butt. Mine: Never, ever, under any
Look: STATUS QUO **Goods:** STATUS QUO–CLASS ACT **Prices:** UP & DOWN	circumstances, anywhere. There are other, user-friendly methods that are even more effective. Theoretically, at least, when was the last time one grown-up got to legally smack another grownup if they disagreed with what the other was doing or saying, and didn't also Go To Jail? Why should a child be any different? Because you're bigger and they can't hurt back? Just how do you suppose 'bad" kids learned to use fists first, hearts and minds second (if ever)? The BIGGIES have a habit of popping up even when we're 'only' shopping.
HOURS: **Summer**: Tue–Thu 10-3 **Winter**: Mon–Fri 10-3	Caught up in the daily grind of making a living, the congregation here is either economically struggling, or personally consigning elsewhere, donating only the leftovers here. An Izod two-piece lady's cotton pants set, washed once too often. A Chaus cotton knit, only $3, but stained. Lots of men's flannel shirts and low-end linens. Because it was such **a happy place**, filled with the bustle of four concerned volunteers, who truly wanted to help, I feel bad, not being able to give this place more hangers. But a Maniac's gotta do what a Maniac's gotta do. And I know such nice folks would want me to play fair, play by the rules.
CLOSED: Holidays	**CONSIGNOR ALERT:** Donations only. Benefits St. James outreach program.

Thrifty Fox

3524 E. Rte. 30
Thorndale, PA 19372
610-383-9943

Look: HO HUM

Goods: HO HUM – STATUS QUO

Prices: LOW– MODERATE

HOURS: Mon, Tue Thu, Fri 10-4, Wed 10-6, Sat 10-3

CLOSED: Holidays

A little house by the side of the road with faded, weathered paint. So small and in such an unexpected location, it's easily missed. The smart-like-a fox-owner hung attention-grabbing spangled and sequined, twice-marked-down, but-still overpriced professional dance costumes from the front porch. That worked almost as well as the old sled holding weather-beaten stuffed animals and bedraggled Christmas presents. Inside, chock full of not much, racks are crowded, the lighting so low it's hard to see. Twice the price in a tenth of the space of Goodwill Fashions, with basically the same assortment. The inevitably steep and narrow steps lead to the basement, where end-of-season sale items are kept waiting for the coup de grace (processing into mattress felt and rag paper to put them out of their misery).

Going to a costume party? Try the top floor, Its **bursting at the seams with inexpensive vintage and costumes** and overpriced, unintentionally camp, definitely dated party clothes that could do double duty as serious, retro funk.

P.S. They gladly accept donations. Benefiting whom? I found $6 in the pocket of a costume I'd bought here. I put the money in Morgan's charity jar. I know she'll figure out where it will be used to the most benefit.

CONSIGNOR ALERT: 50%-50% split. $2/30 articles. 42 days. By appointment only.

Tiny Tots

835 Rte. 30
W. Lancaster, Pike
Downingtown, PA
19335
610-269-6621

Look: STATUS QUO

Goods: HO HUM - STATUS QUO

Prices: LOW - MODERATE

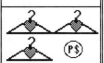

HOURS:
Mon–Sat 9:30-5

CLOSED: Holidays

I liked her enormously. Even if she did figure out who I was after I had finished my first undercover visit. Tom-toms originating in another part of the resale jungle carried THE WORD back home, almost before I got back there myself. Such is secondhand life. Tuning in to the old word-of-mouth channel still works faster than any TV or radio or newspaper.

Pulling up for the second go round, Shopper Lady told me to park off to the side. But would I listen? Whenever I don't, I get into trouble. Of course, this time the owner spotted me almost immediately because of the van. I had just enough time to scramble downstairs where the larger kids' sizes are hung before her gray matter kicked in. It is clean and bright down here. But there's some sort of impromptu sheet-draped office and sorting area taking up the rear. The best of the inventory was average. The end-of-season last-chance sale stuff should have been on the way out the door, headed for the carpet pad factory. Upstairs, on the other side of the kiddie-proof security gate, is **a bountiful selection of little kids-stuff and a simply wonderful room set aside for them to play in**, filled with a table and chairs, toys and plenty of room to roll around.

When I emerged from the basement, she nailed me. Yes, I'm the Maniac, I fessed up. We chatted. We swapped stories. More good grist for the mill. She is a California transplant ("Seasons? What are seasons?") who followed her husband here and now wouldn't dream of returning. She's taken marketing courses, traveled around using The Guide to check out the competition, making all the right moves. Oh, and yes, on slow snow days, she's on the phone to Growing Years, Fairygodmother...the hand-held Internet of resale.

CONSIGNOR ALERT: Buys everything outright except maternity.

The Unforgettable Woman	
151 W. Lancaster Ave. Downingtown, PA 19335 **610-269-7997** 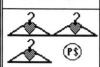	Well, it will be a long time before I forget this one. Son did TV & movie wardrobe, makeup and hair consultation, out on The Coast. He's back on the small 'c' for East coast, fully pancaked and coiffed, selling closeout and secondhand clothing to local "Divas and Dames." He could easily upstage either. Mother was no slouch in the Make-a-Grand-Entrance department, either. Fresh from a new do and a dab, she manned the register, while her son roamed the shop, fixing this, straightening that, chatting all the while. There I stood in my usual undercover, mousy disguise, hat pulled down over a nondo, no makeup, wearing your basic don't-look-at-me outfit. He sized me up in one of those top-to-bottom, stem-to-stern, professional 10-second assessments, registered the data, and wisely kept his opinions to himself.
Look: TOP DRAWER **Goods:** HO HUM – TOP DRAWER **Prices:** LOW – HIGH	Of course, I've never been able to keep my opinions to myself. Here's the dish. Son and Mother, both large in size and personality, claim to stock sizes 4–48. I saw a goodly amount up to and including, size 18; then inventory took a nosedive. Divas outdid Dames. The frontroom was stocked with unworn closeouts, mostly sizes 10-14. Even with 25%-off, prices were still steep (90-$120). I did see an **unusually large selection of evening wear that I liked**. You'd get to wear the dress, not the other way around. Two rooms worth of consigned clothing weren't nearly as good. Some, like an old Pringle pullover, an even older gingham dress from the 50's, had me scratch-
HOURS: Tue- Fri 9-5, Sat 9-2 Call ahead for evening hours.	ing my head. What were *they* doing here? Vintage wasn't splashy enough to be a send-up. Real-life clothing was safe and boring, prices low. They've made quite a few fashion statements, some better than others. If I'm confused…
CLOSED: Holidays	**SHOPPER ALERT:** New evening wear  **CONSIGNOR ALERT:** 50%-50% split. $3 fee/20 items. 60 days. 25%/30days, 50%/60days. Appointments preferred.

Westminster Thrift Shop	
200 S. Church St. West Chester, PA 19382 **610-692-9298**	It would seem that churches can change ownership and names as fast as resale shops. This one did. Once Westminster Presbyterian, now Emmanuel Baptist, the thrift shop has kept the name of the original denomination. I have no idea what such a changeover has wrought, as I came upon this place after the fact. What is timeless is the glorious tree filling the annex courtyard. In summer, its long curlicued branches conceal the shop entrance. Revealed now, in all its winter-bare, linear splendor, it made me gasp out loud in admiration. The shop was another matter.
Look: STATUS QUO **Goods:** HO HUM **Prices:** VERY LOW	A lone, pleasant enough, but lonely volunteer sat at her folding card-table post, guarding the entrance at the top of steep metal and concrete fire steps. Bright yellow cinderblock rooms, brown marble linoleum and alternating brown and gold 70's floral-intense carpeting were design-by-committee bright, clean and organized, lacking warmth or real-time decoration. Inventory matched all to well, like a middle-aged man sporting a white, belly spanning belt, white summer shoes
HOURS: Tue, Wed, Fri 10-3, Sat 9-12	and black socks. Three delightful girls, just out of diapers, with plenty of food and naptime and love to sustain them, played together and sang about happy families. "You be the mommy and I'll be the daddy," instructed one brown-curled little one,
CLOSED: June–August	as she gently cradled a doll so wrinkled and bald and naked only a 'mother' could love it. This shop serves a useful purpose. It just needs a little more lovin'. **CONSIGNOR ALERT:** Donations only. Layaway 20% down/ 2 weeks.

Women's Exchange	

<table>
<tr>
<td>

10 S. Church St.
West Chester, PA
19382

610-696-3058

</td>
<td>

I was happy here. There's a great deal of stuff to see. The small Dickenesque shop held any number of expensive antiques culled from the town houses of West Chester and surrounding gentlefolk farmer's estates. I was surprised that the seemingly tiny shop was actually quite large. An involved volunteer inquired whether I had been in their basement yet. Good thing she'd asked, it might have passed me by. Go to the rear, through a small landing doubling as work room and selling floor. Downstairs, meandering through multi-layered household artifiacts, time warps colliding, a gentlemen who identified himself as a regular, allowed that he had never before been in the shop's **basement**. He'd no idea it was there. She must have clued him, too.

</td>
</tr>
<tr>
<td>

Look: STATUS QUO

Goods: HO HUM –
TOP DRAWER

Prices: LOW–HIGH

</td>
<td rowspan="2">

I was startled here. Downstairs, where items of lesser value are kept, shoplifterproof so to speak, I was startled to unearth three separate long forgotten household objects, identical to those in my mother's home. A Stengle turquoise and gold hors d'oeuvre platter, missing its rescrewable gold handle, a stainless steel kitchen canister, the one remaining piece from a set of five, and a teacup saucer in the same pattern as our everyday china. In all my years of thrift shopping and of all the stores I've ever shopped I, never experienced such a high concentration of personally evocative flotsam and jetsom. Do we ever really own anything?

</td>
</tr>
<tr>
<td>

HOURS: Mon–Fri
10-4:30, Sat 10-2

</td>
</tr>
<tr>
<td>

CLOSED. Holidays
and end of June
thru Labor Day.

</td>
<td>

I was thoughtful here. The good ladies of the Women's Exchange operate as if they have time on their side, and maybe they do. I have never seen sales reduction policies stretch out over a period of months and even years. Founded during the 1940's as part of the war effort, this place harkens back to another way of living and doing business. I suspect little has changed since those densely concentrated days. Has anyone let them know the War is indeed over? And we won? Sort of.

CONSIGNOR ALERT: 67%You-33%Shop. $5 annual fee. No time limit. 10%/42 days, 20%/180 days, 50%/270 days. Becomes donation/1 year. Consign 10-3 daily.

</td>
</tr>
</table>

TOUR #10
ROLLING IN RESALE CLOVER

Only an hour and fifteen minutes from home but worlds apart. I was beginning to think we'd never get around to doing this tour. Marvin and I were just getting comfortable with the mysteries of the New Jersey road and sign system, when it became time to abruptly switch perspective and head south, rather than east. 'Doing' Swarthmore and Media, and having a great time in the process, helped me realize it wasn't such a big deal getting here after all. This next region waiting to be 'discovered' was just one more geographic hop, skip and jump over the horizon.

Think of each tour as one stepping stone leading to the next, rather than 'Oh my gosh, it's over 40 miles between here and....". Take one baby step (tour) at a time. Positive mental preparation, rather than a self-defeating attitude of sooo many shops, sooo much distance, sooo little time. Overnight you'll be conditioned into MARATHON MANIAC. Phone calls from Resale Boutique's obliging owner had enlarged the database. Forays last year to The Encore (Rtes. 1 & 52) and a sprint over the state line to Rags to Riches in Centreville, Delaware, were rewarding enough to make me want more. I'd hit the wall and passed through. I'd gotten my secondhand wind. My endorphins had kicked in.

Bopping down Rte. 1 toward **Kennett Square**, I get the first major clue to what this tour is all about: there's a branch of the **Franklin Mint** set up high on a hill. No surprise. Most folks around here have deep pockets, allowing plenty of room for jingling all that small change. Turning on to Rte. 52 and heading south toward **Centreville** (shops spell it Centreville, maps spell it Centerville), I pass by small side roads with horsey-set names like Paddock leading to the real thing. Split-rail fences define the edges of just how much of what belongs to whom. I just know I'm going to be rolling in resale clover. Sure enough. At every momentous crossing of every state line all over America, we've come to expect the requisite markers with the usual cautionary info like 'Fasten Your Seat Belts' and 'Radar Monitored by Airplane.' Elks to the left, Moose to the right. Commingled in and among, signs announce the population, founding date of the town (if you're about to enter one), and usually the State motto. A catchall collection of official and historic 'Hi, how are ya?' little ditties that let the traveler know he's left one state (of mind) behind and entered another. Sort of sets the tone for things to come. The marker for Delaware? **HOME OF TAX-FREE SHOPPING.** Hot diggity!

The most dignified of the bunch is, as usual, the historic info sign in heavy, dark metal. It reads: Centreville Founded 1750. OOOLD MONEY. The town is an esthetically correct, strip-mall precursor of 32 charming antique shoppes and galleries and interior decorators and such, atonally suitable businesses like a realtor's office and a financial house, and one tony (reservations a must, I'm told) restaurant called **Buckley's Tavern**. The town is worth a day's walkabout all on it's own. Some enterprising soul printed up a list of the "Centreville Business and Professional Community", but no one, as yet, has caught on and begun offering it to the public. Too overtly commercial for the group to manage? I spotted it hanging behind the register at Rags to Riches. Ask.

If you're hungry right about now, there are two restaurants back in **Chadds Ford**, one on either side of the intersection formed by Rtes. 1 and 100. **Hank's** is the local greasy spoon. Stick to sandwiches, etc., avoid anything requiring frying. First stop? Eggs and undercooked potatoes were taking an impromptu swim. Second stop? Sandwich was great. The **Chadds Ford Cafe**, written up in the New York Times no less, according to a 30-year local (who for her own reasons prefers to remain anonymous), says it's great! Back in Centreville? There's a carryout place called **Troll of Scandinavia**. Honest.

It's oozing with history and culture around here. Bucolic Rte. 52 will take you straight to **Winterthur**. **Brandywine Battlefield** is nearby. **Chadds Ford** has wineries. World-renown **Longwood Gardens** is back by the **Mint**. You can be a Thrift Shop Maniac Atypical Tourist (TSMAT) for the day. Do a little sightseeing, do a little thrifting. Eat. Do a little sightseeing, do a little thrifting...you get the idea. All of the other thrift and resale shops are along Rte. 202. Double back, and head south. There are long, random stretches of old and new businesses at some distance from each other and then sudden clusters of very upscale, newly constructed shopping malls. Threading through all this are some all-too-surreal, random sightings. A highway staging area with a showroom-type lineup of 20 parked-on-the-bias orange earthmovers and bulldozers perched precariously on a man-made, bare earth ridge. An abandoned blue-and-white helicopter, ancient and rusting, its side propped up against trees lining the very edge of the the field where it lay, belly down. A classic stainless steel diner stacked on top of enormous beams in the middle of an empty, razed field. Right next-door to a BMW dealership right next door to a mulch supply business with a brown mountain of the stuff piled high. Road testing? Just north of **Wilmington**, in an equally surreal forest of everyday fast-food chains and gas stations (gas up you and your car?) is Baby & Me, across from the **Charcoal Pit**. Keep following 202, now called Concord Pike, which leads to--Philadelphia Pike, leading to Claymont if you take a left at the Church--or hang a right and follow Market Street into downtown Wilmington.

Philadelphia Pike, leading into **Claymont,** has three great shops and two great places to eat. The **Queen Bean Cafe** at Commonwealth and Philadelphia Pike, right next-door to Lamb's Loft, is absolutely devine. I got the biggest, friendliest greeting and best service I've ever gotten anywhere. The menu is fun and fab. They. also serve a two-page menu of coffees, Italian sodas, cappuccino and tea. I plan to take Marvin and Morgan back here for a busman's holiday during spring break. **Dreamer's Cafe** comes highly recommended by Merel, owner of Resale Boutique as "they have the best sandwiches anywhere." It's just up the road from her shop. She should know.

I was trying to figure out the best way to describe **Wilmington** to you guys. Here's what I came up with. Take Philadelphia's historic district and its downtown, neck-craning, ("Look! It's a bird. No, it's a plane. No, it's Superman") buildings and broad streets, then stir in some of Washington D.C.'s semi-southern style. The bridge coming into town looks just like the ones that link D.C. to the rest of the world. Big white arches with a sense of grandeur about them, black 'gas' streetlights at either end. No lions, though. The downtown district is very much Big City. Enormous clean streets filled with a sense of purpose and power, surrounded by pockets of urban blight and poverty. March winds blew through small side-street caverns. Parking was a bear.

The **Hotel Du Pont** is only one block away from the **Shipley Grill** and **Talkin' Turkey**, both of which are next-door to the Junior Board Thrift Shop and not far from an excellent Goodwill. The Hotel has a world-class restaurant, but it's nosebleed expensive. I ate there once, years ago. It was wonderful. Buy enough copies of The Guide and maybe I can afford to go there again sometime. **Mary's Kountry Kitchen** on Main Street in **Stanton** just south of Wilmington is a good bet if you're near Family Thrift or Gingerbread House.

Alone, traveling home in the car with time on my mind and the attendant freedom to simultaneously venture far and wide on another inner journey, I was appreciative of the local wealth that has created such a great pool of secondhand shops. But I also found myself wondering if the Du Pont, Sharpless and other branches of the local got-rocks-clan ever get to thrift shop? Money has its rewards, and its punishments, don't ya know. Poor dears, it's not all fun and games being rich.

TOUR #10

3	Baby & Me	Wilmington
9	Brandywine Treasure Chest	Wilmington
1	The Encore	Hamorton
13	Family Thrift Center	Newport
12	The Gingerbread House	Wilmington
7	Goodwill	Claymont
10	Goodwill	Wilmington
11	Junior Board Thrift Shop	Wilmington
6	Lamb's Loft	Claymont
2	Rags To Riches	Centerville
8	The Resale Boutique	Wilmington
4	Second Source	Wilmington
5	Treasure Chest	Wilmington

*Note: This list has a shop's entire name. Names in review boxes may have been shortened a tad to fit. Numbers before each shop name correspond to their numbered location on each map. **Shops with a star sold Volume II. Volume III? ASK!**

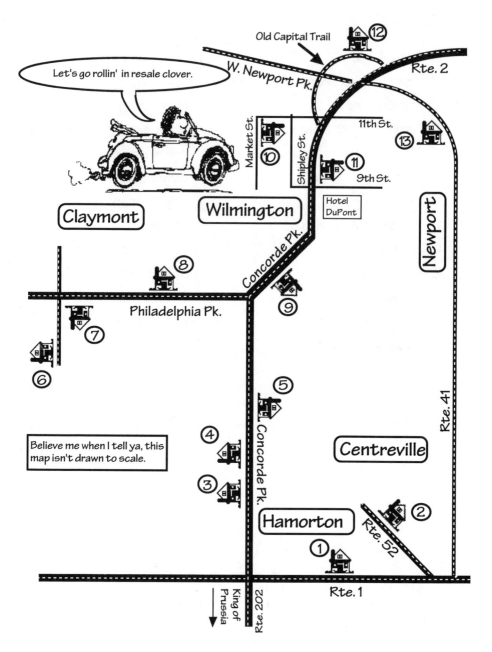

TOUR #10 MAP Page 169

BABY & ME Consignments	
2415 Concord Pike (RT. 202) Wilmington, DE 19803 **302-478-8240** (P$)	Knock. Knock. Who's there? jokes are very popular in secondhand. Short staffed, short-sighted owners sometimes fail to show up, with or without the answer. Too often I pull up, only to find, nobody's home. Just to heap hyperbole a little higher, know we had driven for over an hour to get here. It was raining and cold. I was sick. Sign said open at 10am; it was 10:45. One by one, a steady stream of only slightly more sanguine local maniacs tried the door to Baby & Me, then left. Reason? Owner away on a well-deserved vacation. Person in charge of opening had sick-ness in the family. Know we have a car phone. Know this was our first stop. W e would have passed by, no matter what. We could have called from the road. For me, it's all in the game. Cat and mouse. Sylvester and Tweetie Bird. (I always loooved Tweetie Bird.)
Look: STATUS QUO **Goods:** STATUS QUO **Prices:** LOW–MODERATE **HOURS:** Mon 10-4, Tue–Sat 10-6	Toward the end of the day, retracing our steps, we found them open. Small from the street, **three rooms big** in fact, we hit them at the end of their end-of-season, 50%-off sale. Good news? There were **some real buys** in the back room. A Nippon, bias-flared, velvet-skirted dress with floral satin top, very smart. A patch pocket, brown plaid, Italian chemise, button vents over each leg, could do double duty as a tunic. Very chic. Skyr cardigan with 'pewter' buttons, pastel winter scene of polar bears, penguins and pine trees, a tad steep at $18, an instant keeper at $9. Morgan had been noodling me for a Christmas sweater, "just not red and green, please Mommie." Second visit? Same scenario. Opened 2 hours late at noon. The spring rush was on. I saw **lots of great kid's clothing**. Do come, but call first, if you want the answer to your knock, knock. No joke.
CLOSED: Holidays	**CONSIGNOR ALERT:** You: 40%/clothing, 50%/nursery, **60%/bridal**. $5 fee. 60 days. Appointment preferred.

Brandywine Treasure Chest	
1913 N. Market St. Wilmington, DE 19802 **302-656-4464** 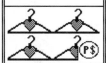 (P$)	"Do you know the difference between VHF and UHF?" was the burning question. I was greeted by this Q&A and the sight of the owner kneeling over a chair used to prop up a small TV. She was peering into the back of the set, her back to the door, trying to make the !@#^ thing work. "Rabble rousing feminist that I am, I still refer all electrical and mechanical repairs to me husband," was my reply. From there we switched channels to, "Oh, what does he do for a living"? "He's a shrink," was my reply. "Oh, that's interesting, I used to be a psychotherapist," was her's. (Does one ever really stop?) We stayed put on this channel, discussing the value of a book called "Men Are From Mars, Women Are From Venus" and the one about hatrracks (you'd have to be in the biz to know that one.) The owner here knew the guy who wrote the hatrack's book. Met him at a professional to do she said. I hadn't gotten inside the doorway, and I felt like I knew her from forever.
Look: HO HUM **Goods:** HO HUM–TOP DRAWER **Prices:** LOW–HIGH **HOURS:** Tue–Sat afternoons. Call ahead. "I'm unreliable."	The place looks like it's been here that long, too. You know how those Hollywood-types aerosol spray cobwebs and dust around to give a movie set that authentic decrepit look? Well, they've been here. I think she's having a reaction formation to possessing such a neat and orderly mind. But I liked the shop in spite of (or because of?) The Look. An entire wall is taken up with household, china, glass, silver, etc. in the front room, the middle, matching wall--musty, dusty books. Scattered hither and yon are archeological peels from over the decades and centuries, up to and including ours. Furniture, mirrors, curiosities. Lost of curiosities. The pump organ in the front room was high-Victorian Gothic, and only $900. Needs work. Should I say it? O.K. So does the shop. But so what. It, like the owner, is a piece of work in progress. **P.S.** She does furniture repair. (No TV's.)
CLOSED: Holidays	**CONSIGNOR ALERT:** Buys outright.

The Encore	
Rtes. 1 & 52S Hamorton, PA 19348 **610-388-6269** 	Have I accidently stumbled into a museum, or perhaps the gift section of Bailey's? Enter, and you are immediately surrounded by wall-to-wall, built-in shelves and cabinets and a room-dividing bank of glass-enclosed jewelry cabinets, **contents of the first order.** This is the kind of neighborhood where they have to spell out: No horse tack or monogrammed clothing on consignment. Entire rooms, each busy, **sunny, clean and well-organized,** are given over to men's, children's, furniture and household. One room is ladies only. Eavesdropping over the racks (as usual), over-heard two locals discussing art classes and the pros and cons of various thrift shops. They rated The Encore--Very Good. Art class? So-so.
Look: TOP DRAWER **Goods:** STATUS QUO–TOP DRAWER **Prices:** LOW–HIGH	No one had to eavesdrop to hear the raucous gang joyously acting out yet another drama-filled day-in-the-life of the Thrift Shop Volunteers Everywhere Soap Opera. They prowled the racks and shelves, spotted for each other at the counter, gossiped about life experiences, all the while helping customers. The peak moment came when the gang gathered, taking turns describing their fantasy about a pale, sea-green quilted bathrobe with "look, they're real" ostrich feathers at
HOURS: Mon–Sat 10-4	the cuff of each long sleeve. "Just what I'd wear to clean the pots and pans," one quipped. I exchanged knowing looks with another customer over the racks. Smiling, we both agreed we came for the stuff *and* the staging.
CLOSED: Mid-June–Labor Day	**CONSIGNOR ALERT:** 67% You-33% Shop. $5 annual fee. 20 item limit. Mon, Wed, Fri 10-12pm, Sat 10-12. Benefit Chester County Hospital.

Family Thrift Center	
2012 W. Newport Pike Newport, DE 19804 **302-999-1416** 	This one practically fell on us. Driving around trying to find Gingerbread House My disbelieving eyes ever on red alert (and just plain bloodshot from burning the midnight oil over a hot keyboard) looking for the next shop and the next, they practically fell out of their sockets. Instead of a shop, how about a billboard? Family Thrift uses this road-hugging (Rte. 4), bigger-than-life, all-American-way of advertising to oh so subtly remind you of their existence. Worked for me. Took an abrupt U turn and a quickie side trip. A 'bird' in hand is worth two still waiting to be bagged.
Look: BOTTOMFEEDER **Goods:** DOWN & OUT–STATUS QUO **Prices:** UP & DOWN	**Lots of action in the aisles. Early Saturday morning, this place is bust-out city.** Occupying an old A & P with the familiar cupola, shoes on top of every seemingly mile-long rack are the signature now. $6.99, bright hunter's-orange rubber-soled bucks, unworn, size 10. Acres of overwashed linens, rows of techno-curiosities, too old even to be taken for parts, an actual TV room à la Silo, where anything over $99 comes with a 30-day warranty. Could find something here.
HOURS: Mon–Sat 9-9, Sun 11-7	When they get something good, the price skyrockets (relatively speaking) like $9.99 for a Cobbs Creek banana-colored, extra-large men's polo. A mundane shirt, an everyday label, but in excellent condition. The same shirt at a Goodwill costs $3-$6. Vastly outnumbered by over-worn, over-washed, $2 and $3 T's. For the ambience and pricing structure here, it should be $4, $5 or $6 tops. This "gotcha" pricing structure reverberated throughout the cavernous store just as consistently as the scores of shoppers milling about in the aisles, filling their carts. I left empty-handed.
CLOSED: Holidays	**CONSIGNOR ALERT:** Another anomaly. Obviously for profit, but with some unstated portion of the proceeds diverted to The Cancer Federation.

Gingerbread House	
3810 Old Capital Tr. (Marshallton) Wilmington, DE 19808 **302-995-2742**	Boy did we have to work to find this one. Tucked away off the main highway, nestled in a crook in a bend in a back road, off the beaten trail, out in the middle of what seemed like nowhere. Obscure location, dynamite shop. Gingerbread House is stretching it a bit. More marketing will power, than architectural actuality. But boy does she understand the power of concept. Layered on an otherwise sweetly plain white clapboard house, some icing pink bows and sineage here, a few feet of inexpensive garden mart trellis there, and you've got instant zip and zing. Inside she really went to town. **The place is adorable. So are the contents.**
	In addition to an **excellent selection** of secondhand children's clothes are quantities of **everything you need to keep the kiddies safe** and happy. Electric light covers, out-of-sight cupboard locks, Snugglies. The underlying, extra special something that pulls it all together visually and functionally? The owner will gladly use these same talents at display in your house. Staple, glue gun and imagination at the ready, she'll use whatever is within her secondhand wherewithall to transform your baby's nursery into a childhood delight at a cost that is well within most family budgets. How about--chintz skirt tacked around a used bassinett? Nursing rocker with cushy coordinated and bowed, Mommy nuturing, butt-and-back soothing pads? Matcing curtains? Call or come in and discover the possibilities
Look: TOP DRAWER **Goods:** STATUS QUO–TOP DRAWER **Prices** MODERATE	
HOURS: Tue-Sat 10-5	
CLOSED: Holidays	**CONSIGNOR ALERT:** 50%-50% split. $3 fee. 60-days. No appointment needed. 20 items or less. Evening appointments available

Goodwill	
2701 Philadelphia Pike Claymont, DE 19703 **302-798-9047**	What's going on at the Goodwill stores in Delaware? I've had a pleasantly and **unusually high ROI in the clothing department** at both shops, both times. What gives? To the best of my knowledge, these places use a central distribution point. How does it happen that the quality seems so much higher just over the state line? Well, whatever the reason, you can bet I'll be back on my dime. My very first stop here, I spent $12 and came away with a brand-new pair of Gap chintz and floral flats for Morgan, the original price tag of $26 still on the sole. She also got two nice cotton dresses. One was mostly purple and pink roses with long sleeves and a short skirt, the other a sleeveless sundress with an ankle-length, tiered skirt, empire waist and big patch pockets all in a delicate overall pink and pale yellow floral. I got a cotton sweat jacket by Guess with a tiny snippet of lace circling the throat and wrists, hems, and pearl baby buttons running up the front. WOW!
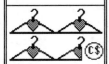	
Look: CLASS ACT **Goods:** BOTTOMFEEDER **Prices:** LOW	The snappy-looking male clerk working the customers, the floor and the register was **super friendly** and got complimented by a shopper on how well-dressed he always looks. Now we know the how and the why of it. If I were **rating them on the clothing/price/grab factor alone, they're a 4.** I just wish they would get the quality of donations in housewares and furniture to have as much zip and zing as clothing. They're so gol darn tedious. With fully 25% of the floorspace caught up in these go-ing-nowhere categories, it brings the rating low. I know they'll keep cranking 'em out because they're moneymakers. They're doing their best with what they've been given. Just as we all do.
HOURS: Mon–Fri 9-8, Sat 9-6, Sun 11-5	
CLOSED: Holidays	**CONSIGNOR ALERT:** Donations only.

Goodwill	
Market Street Mall 7th & Market Wilmington, DE 19980 **302-654-6926** 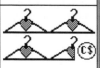	Long before I learned that the manager was a woman, a unique experience in male-dominated chain charity stores, I had decided this one had the **best selection of women's clothing of any Goodwill I've ever shopped.** Way to go, Juanita. First trip? Carol Little shorts, size 10; top, unsized; and culottes, size 14, hung together, priced as a set, $10. The top could conceivably fit either bottom piece, wear two, consign one, you're in the black and way ahead of the game. Keep in mind this was was last year's Carol Little, never worn. Remember the multi-colored floral, with white dots embossed, superimposed on a white field? I'd seen it just last spring and summer on the racks at John Wanamaker's. (Remember: Do your research at the malls, your buying secondhand.) The total bill there would have been around $175 pre-sale big ones, or $105 at 40% off retail. $10 for three unworn pieces was a real coup. Amazing. Also spotted a long-sleeved, navy and small
Look: UPSCALE BOTTOMFEEDER **Goods:** HO HUM – CLASS ACT **Prices:** VERY LOW	white polka-dot, cotton dress by LIZ, worn but still vivid, and a two-piece black-and-white dot LIZ and probably from the same season, again, $10 each. **I can't remember the last time I was in a bottomfeeder, having a hard time choosing between all the stuff I had found.** Kids', men's and housewares was standard Goodwill, lowering the curve. Juanita and staff, keep up the good work. If you can manage to bring those currently average departments up to the same excellent standards as women's (or how about making it a women's only?), you'll be wearing two hearts next year, the one
HOURS: Mon–Sat 9-6	you've already got on your sleeve and a second one in your review. **P.S.** For a complete listing of Delaware Goodwills call 302-761-464 **CONSIGNOR ALERT:** Donations only. Larger donations go to 300 E. Lea Blvd. Mon-Sat
CLOSED: Holidays	9-6, Sun 12-5. No mattresses, please. Benefits Goodwill's rehabilitation programs.

Jr. Board Thrift Shop	
907 Shipley St. Wilmington, DE 19801 **302-658-6268** 	Toward the end of the business day, they perform the most thorough, ritualistic vacuum-cleaner-intensive job per square foot of any shop, anywhere. The volunteer doing the ol' back 'n forth whoosh and swoosh must have reached a state of bliss available only to those who've been meditating on their mantra for eons. I, on the other hand, a slightly less advanced creature, was ready for the loony bin by the time she deemed the job finito. We're talking two sections of 10' by 4' carpeting here. We're talking 15 minutes per. We're talking thorough.
Look: CLASS ACT **Goods:** HO HUM– STATUS QUO **Prices:** LOW– MODERATE	The shop is also a thoroughly old-school, charity thrift. The label likes of Neiman Marcus and Saks were a good read, but they were mostly social register has-beens from a decade-old, out-of-print edition. There were few current possibilities. An apricot cotton house or beach dress for warm weather days with a collarless neckline, a gently shaped bodice slowly opening downward to a breezy flounce of tiered skirt. One size-8, black sheath, evening dress was a $50 knockout! The sweater bins behind the evening wear (quite a few **tux and tails** priced around $50) were extensive, but only one called out to me. An end-of-season, unreduced, he-man XLarge Pringle with 3 pastel chevrons on a field of cream, $12. Surprisingly, there was quite an extensive selection of toys, no equipment and little or no child-
HOURS: Mon–Fri 10-2:45	ren's clothing. Housewares was scant. They gladly accept any and all donations in good, working condition (how about a new vacuum?), but **women's clothing is their largest resource.**
CLOSED: Holidays	**CONSIGNOR ALERT:** Donations only. Benefits the Junior Board of the Medical Center of Delaware Inc.

Lamb's Loft	CC L
16 Commonwealth Ave. Claymont, DE 19703 **302-792-9620**	**40 dealers big**, they all rent space from the Loft. Atmospherically and stylistically it reminds me most of My Best Junk (See TOUR #9) in West Chester (or is it the other way around?). In fact, I've promised Morgan a post-printing, mom-and-daughter day where we do both with lunch at Queen Bean sandwiched in between. She loooves My Best Junk and has been constantly noodling me for a return visit, so I know she'll looove this one, too. I can't wait! I'm not going to bore you with hyperbole on this one. **It's simply great. Go.**
Look: TOP DRAWER **Goods:** STATUS QUO-TOP DRAWER **Prices:** LOW-HIGH	
HOURS: Tue 11-4, Wed 11-8, Thu & Fri 11-6, Sat 11-4	**P.S.** Speaking of food, they do an occasional afternoon high tea here. Ask. **P.P.S.** Soon to be opening a new 1000' big furniture space behing the cafe.
CLOSED: Holidays	**CONSIGNOR ALERT:** Buys outright. Lamb's Loft sells for 40-45 individual dealers. To sell your things, bring them in and Lamb's Loft will work out a deal with you.

Rags to Riches	CC L
5714 Kennet Pike (Rte. 52) Centreville, DE 19807 **302-654-6011** 	I made it over the border, just. Barreling down Rte. 52, engines thrust in overdrive, trying to bag this one before it's pumpkin time again back at Morgan's school. Can I make it all the way from here to Jenkintown by 3pm, leaving enough time to whirlwind through the shop, get my hit of impressions and get back in the saddle? It's 1:30 already. Ouch. And as always, the burning question, "Will the shop be worth all this?" My hunch is, yes. Where is it? This country lane business is taking too long. It better show up NOW. Ten minutes deep into Delaware, the state with no income tax, at the edge of a small, too-cute-for-words clutch of touristy shops with a crazy-quilt patchwork of signs, the name Rags to Riches jumps out. I almost fly by. I zoom in, tires spinning, gravel flying, and park, dashing inside to--**fabulous evening wear**
Look: CLASS ACT-TOP DRAWER **Goods:** STATUS QUO-CLASS ACT **Prices:** MODERATE - NOSEBLEED	with fabulous prices. Original price tags from $398 to $765, now hovering around half-price. Too high! Should be more like 60-75% off to fit in with resale pricing. Customers seem to agree, cause these fancy dancy dud sits here till it's marked down further. What booty! If you've got a special event and live in this part of the world and have big bucks, come. Last year I reluctantly returned a too-hot-to-handle-the-price-tag, hot pink sheath to the racks and dreamed about it every night. This year it was still here, reduced enough now that it's mine, all mine. Yippee! **Everyday stuff is sensational** with the usual assortment of name-dropping labels. These prices are
HOURS: Mon-Sat 10-5	more in line with my budget, too. I bought a $48 pair of velvet Hollywood 'pajama' pants by Nippon Night (originally $248) and a second pair of black, but this time wool slacks by Vittadini for $68. Both were never worn, with the original price tag intact. The hunch paid off. It's great. Gotta go. (So do you.)
CLOSED: 1st 3 weeks in February	**CONSIGNOR ALERT:** 50%-50% split. No fee. 60 days. No appointment needed on first 6 Mondays starting March 1 (spring/summer). 10 items max. Fall/winter consigning starts first Monday after Labor Day.

The Resale Boutique

818 Philadelphia Pk.
Wilmington, DE
19809

302-764-3646

Look: CLASS ACT
Goods: STATUS QUO–TOP DRAWER
Prices: UP & DOWN

HOURS: Mon–Fri 10-5, Sat 10-4, Fall Thu till 8

CLOSED: Saturday July-mid August

Orien's coming! Orien's coming! Orien Reid of Channel 10 fame had scheduled a taping for the following week, resuming her very popular Maniac-inspired series on local thrift shops. The shop owner and cohorts were deep in preparation for the big day, while I roamed the aisles undetected for my second undercover trip midst already underway decorating and cleaning. Orien doesn't get to go undercover. She sees shops at their face-to-the-camera best. I get to see them as everyday customers do, and it isn't always facial features in my lens finder.

Circumstances had it that my first visit came at the end-of-winter sale season. Second visit? Spring consignments were just beginning to trickle in. I took this all into account when I assessed the racks and allotted hangers. Relax, ladies. Just like a grande dame rising to face her dressing table, your good bones could be seen underneath the early morning disarray. Two floors big, the top, and largest had frequently **good, occasionally excellent women's and children's** clothing. Downstairs is a full, **one-stop-shopping bridal salon** with an **enormous selection** of plastic covered gowns and all the accessories. Prices ranged from $100 up up and up. Bridesmaids and mothers-of will be happy here, too. Both visits, everyone at the counter had their heads together recipe swapping, all the while processing consignments, racking up sales and answering the phone. I want those recipes.

 SHOPPER ALERT: Bridal

CONSIGNOR ALERT: 50%-50% split. $5 annual fee. **Bridal gowns: 60% You-40% Store.** 60 days. By appointment. Mon-Fri 11-3.

Second Source

Rt. 202
1601 Concord Pk.
Independence Mall
Wilmington, DE
19808

302-656-3943

Look: TOP DRAWER
Goods: HO HUM – CLASS ACT
Prices: LOW
HOURS: Mon-Fri 9-6, Thu 9-8, Sat 10-5

CLOSED: Holidays

"A part of the expanding network of Second Source locations" and "Your First Choice for New & Used Computers," it says on the card. On Vol. I, I was so computer-phobic that I actually stood behind Marvin and dictated the entire opus, even pointing out where each star should be in the galaxy. Now, I'm finally using The Thing, an Apple Macintosh Duo 230 with a Mini Dock and a full-page monitor, but only as a word processor. So, I'm going to have to defer to Marvin's expertise on this one. I can tell you the store is slick, modern, with the inevitable wall-to-wall charcoal grey carpeting. The salesguy behind the desk was cute (Marvin probably wouldn't have told you that) and helpful (no doubt he would have mentioned that). O.K., take it away, Marvin...

The Word, according to Dr. Maniac: "The store had lots of old Sega and Nintendo games on the racks with some older versions of Lotus and WordPerfect. The hardware was exclusively PC (386 25s); not an old Apple, aging Mac or moldy Amiga to be seen anywhere. Printers were mostly HP inkjets of the last 3 years' vintage with te odd HP Laserjet and 24-pin models."

P.S. They have a second location in a strip mall on Rte. 3 just outside of West Chester **(Tour #9).** 5 store franchise. This store is the smaller of the Delaware stores.

CONSIGNOR ALERT: Buys outright, trades and consigns. Go negotiate your own deal. 30-day minimum consignment. **90-day warranty on all used items.**

Treasure Chest	
2205 Jefferson St. Wilmington, DE 19802 **302-654-3391** **Look:** HO HUM **Goods:** HO HUM **Prices:** UNMARKED	I can attest to the randomness of the hours here. First stop was around 10:30, nobody home. I swung by again on my way out of town, mid-afternoon. An ironing board, office chair and some other items I can no longer remember, circling the skirt of sidewalk just outside the door, told me they were open for business.

Bright and sunny outside, it took my eyes a few minutes to adjust to the gloom inside. Blinking and groping I practically fell into bed. Just inside the door, stacked and stored, a bedroom set from the 20's, its blond paint chipped and worn. Some of the superimposed carving needing a touch of glue, one pull missing. But, by golly, it was really beautiful! And cheap! A double bed, two night tables, a round mirror, bombay dresser and high chest of drawers, all for only $300. I'm dying to own it. I plan to put it in the guest room. But to do that I'd have to sell what's already there. Then I'd have to either pay to refinish the set, or do all that work myself. |
| **HOURS:** By 11, after 7, or "When I get here" | Unfortunately this all too rare, all too reasonably priced find was the only treasure in an otherwise well-organized but unimaginative collection of dishes, jelly glasses, old bed linens and clothing. Except for **Liz**, the owner. Sitting behind her enormous desk and sporting a black velvet hat adorned with a rose at right angle. She **practically glowed in the dark with good energy.** |
| **CLOSED:** Holidays | **CONSIGNOR ALERT:** Buys outright and consigns. Works it out as she goes along. |

TOUR #11
SWAMP GAS, SECRET UFOS AND TURKEY BUZZARD SIGHTINGS

Brooklawn is little more than a U.S. Postal letter drop, a dot on the map where lines converge. It's what 'they' call a bedroom community. And a very small one at that. Think of it as the vestibule to **Gloucester City**, which rates a little blob of color on all the maps. It also rates the distinction of having (according to the Courier Post) the best thrift shop within its circulation's boundaries. So pass through Brooklawn, stopping only for a brief visit to Rags and Riches, then drive till you reach the corresponding wide swath of blue on your map, the one separating Gloucester City from the U.S. Naval Base and the Sun Oil monolith dominating the opposite shore line. You've arrived in Gloucester City. Take note: That substantial chunk of color marked Tinicum Wildlife Preserve, hemmed in by Philadelphia Airport farther west, is all that regionally remains of what was once an extensive estuary ecosystem, draining into a watershed of naturally thriving marshland.

Backed up against the banks of the Delaware River as it is, with nowhere left to go, Gloucester City has little left to show for the Divine plan drawn up back in the dawn of creation. Concrete sidewalks, road ways lined with telephone wires, nearby refineries, passing tankers, and white clapboard storefronts turned grey from the industrial fallout, dominate. Gloucester City is not a worker's paradise. Streets are clean. Cyclone-fenced lawns, telephone company 'pruned' shade trees, and garden variety garden center shrubs decorate and separate the small cottages, certainly. But there is a sense of disconnection, an unreality about the place, as its people go about the business of life. Inspiration has been blacktopped. Beauty trampled.

Every time it rains around these parts, over on the Philadelphia side that evening, the local 3, 6, 10, and 29 photographers are inevitably sent to tape live footage of flooded Rte. 130, and anchor men and women inevitably have the task of reporting this river and that stream have overflowed their banks once again. Small wonder. Lord knows, endless small-town planning commissions, charged by their constituencies over the decades with promoting growth, growth and more growth, have tried. Inevitably, however, you can't fool Mother Nature. Or keep her down. She keeps bubbling up to the surface. Ready to move on? (Just not to California, where the very hills are sliding into the sea. Any connection do you suppose?)

Tool south on Rte. 130. Keep an eye peeled for Rte. 47. It leads right to **Woodbury** where the two-lane highway becomes a wide main street called Broad. You have to wonder about the level of imagination of our founding fathers and mothers. Broad Street. Market Street. Main Street. High Street. These now all-too-familiar names, repeated over and over again on street signs in almost every small town U.S.A., grew out of cumulative, off-handed, day-to-day repetition, and stuck. **Like:** Honey, let me pack some hardtack and embers for you on your day's walk over to the general store at the broad bend in the highway. Buy me some ribbon and a bobkin. **Or:** Dearest, It's *market day*. On your way home from plowing the back 40, stop and pick up some isinglass. **Later:** Sweetheart, I could really use a new flint...Ride over to the trading post over on the *mainroad* and swap pelts for one for me. So it went, and so it goes...

Now it's more like: Cruise down to the Goodwill on Broad and grab a pair of closeout running shoes. Or: I need an evening gown, and I need it yesterday. Hang a left on Broad, but don't go over 20 or you'll miss Worth Repeating on Hopkins, a small, one-way side street. Or: Dash around the corner to Curtis, another one-way, and see what's new in donations at the Leprechaun.

Woodbury has a parenthesis of diners one each at the northern and southern ends of town. There's the **Colonial** on Rte. 47, (or North Broad St. as it's called in these parts) and Edith Ave. Or try the **Woodbury Heights** at Griscomb Lane and Rte. 47. It's pink and grey and good. I've eaten here, sandwich in one hand, pen in the other, scribbling thrift-shop phone numbers and addresses out of the local yellow pages, chewing.

We found **Pitman**, thinking we wanted Glassboro. The Glassboro fantasy: College town. Spreading oaks, climbing ivy, brick sidewalks, mossy walls, great consignments. Reality? The one consignment shop on the data bank print out for Glassboro had gone bust. No trees, eroding tax base, empty streets, empty stores. We blew town. Hunger-cranky (passed up **Angelo's Diner** in Glassboro, very small and very full with a serious chow-down lunchtime crowd), tired and disappointed after the long drive, wandering around a residental community, we alternately tried to fight our way out of a growing funk and the twisting thicket of lookalike streets. Up ahead, two police patrol cars were pulled over. We needed a local hero in a big white hat, only to accidently stumbled upon two in brown stetsons. Cautiously, we approached, thinking it might be a crime scene. It turned out there was an ENORMOUS turkey buzzard lunching on road kill. Fair game in the wild, a curiousity among the split levels and cape cods. The officers gawked. We gawked. We waited a respectful period of time, then asked for directions to Pitman. Of course we were only two blocks away. The buzzard, satisfied, flew off to a nearby rooftop, this time a rancher.

Pitman is great. It has a local movie theatre with an old-fashioned marquee, a fully stocked hobby shop, the accordian music school, a great news shop, a recording studio, and teal and chartreuse banners flapping in the wind, inviting shoppers to Experience Pitman. Saturday afternoon, kids biked and roller bladed by, practically dressed crowds hung out on the sidewalk or just inside where it was warm, and caught up on news. Some of the absolute best (remember, dark only) chocolates I've ever had came from the **Nut House**, here on South Broadway. The 'factory' is in Woodbury, where they have a second location, as well. Try the turtles.

Sadly, little Pitman has been in the national news lately. The Landfill scandal has finally hit the front pages. Would someone please tell me just what do the words "Clean up a Super Fund Site" mean? Think about it? Ask any housewife or any husband who's ever wielded a mop or a broom. If you only move the dirt around and sweep it under the rug, it's still there. Just moved to a different spot where you can't see it. It doesn't take a couple of Ph.D's to figure out we have to stop creating these poisons in the first place. Moving it around isn't cleaning it up. And it never will be. The community is banding together, seeking solutions. How about the rest of us?

Researching My Fair Lady and Kid Stuff, our undercover assignment completed, we stumbled upon another in progress. The hobby shop on the corner, remember that? Inside a round, bespectacled, seemingly introverted clerk, sitting on a low stepstool, was stocking the shelves. Replenishing dwindling supplies of model airplane kits, he and Marvin (in his youth, an avid fan of anything that was held together with rubber cement and flew), struck up a lively, insider's conversation. Soon he had the clerk talking up a storm about UFO's, and planes that can go seven times the speed of sound. He had 'friends', said the now-loquacious clerk in hushed undercover tones. "Well placed friends in high places." He knew "these aircraft really existed," he whispered. I could almost see the trench coat appear around his shoulders, collar up, and the microphone-in-a-lighter and camera-in-the-fountain-pen put into action (though he seemed more Maxwell Smart than Sean Connery). Turkey buzzards going in. UFO's going out. What a trip.

Bookin' south on Rte. 55, headed for **Vineland** and a noon rendevous with fellow maniac Adrienne P, local jewlery designer for 23 years. Her jewelery is made out of bits and pieces and buttons found in local junk and thrift shops. (She wore one of her creations. It was pretty enough for our waitress to remark on it and wnat to know how to get one for herself.) We're due to meet up in the parking lot of the Ramada Inn. She wrote to me back in December, asking if we could do a secondhand shopping excursion together. She'd play 'shotgun', pointing out all the local sights. I'd do my undercover thing, giving out pointers. What a great idea. It gets lonely on the road some days.

The drive is a long one. Last fall's not-yet-fallen oak leaves, still cling to grey branches. Dried marsh grasses bob and weave in the wind-driven sleet. Symetrically spaced bushes, their roots holding on for dear life to manmade hills and valleys, planted by highway work crews in a partial pay-back attempt to undo what they've already, unintentionally done to rob Mother Nature of her mantle of earth. Rigorously prunned orchard tree branches reach up and tickle the grey canopy of low-hanging clouds. Rythmically interspersed baby evergreens, sprayed, the signs warn, with noxious chemicals to prevent them from becoming a free, impromptu landscaping or Christmas tree resource are the only color hit in this monocromatic world, a world that seems to stretch on and on. For a while there I lost all sense of time and space.

Then just outside town the flat, fertile region of scrub pine and oak yielded to truck farms which in turn give way to light industry and one zoning curiosity after one strip mall after one defunct business after one fast food restaurant after another. It's all glued together by a broad, bustling Main Street shopping district, surrounded by newly constructed, start-to-finish communities and older neighborhoods with (un)zoning concepts not unlike the outlying business/shopping strip--a brick colonial here, an abandoned(?) hovel there, a well-built, well-maintained standard issue split level beside a homemade, cinderblock, learn-as-you-go architectural eyesore.

As we drove around Adrienne's stomping ground, she pointed out all the restaurants. I asked her to pick one from the bunch, my treat. We were near **Verona** (1231 S. Delsea Drive), so that's where she told me to pull in. There was a gas log fire going, a welcome sight on such a miserable day. We shared a really good smoked turkey and melted provolone sandwich on an Italian roll. I ate French fries. Adrienne watched.

Other likely looking spots included **Coffee Time** on Landis Avenue near Goodwill. They sell cappuccino! As we flew by in the van, **Bill's Lunch**, just up the street, popped out and caught my attention and got Adrienne's nod. I'll probably also get around to trying the Greek restaurant, **Olympia**, and **Joe's BBQ** chicken, closer to the Salvation Army when I come back again. I'd independently checked out the **coffee shop** back at the **Ramada Inn** while waiting for Adrienne. It was clean and bright and cozy and friendly, very busy and centrally located.

☞ **Maniac Tip:** Gas is much cheaper on this side of the river. I've seen it as low as 99¢ a gallon. Fill 'er up just before leaving New Jersey, coming or going. You can save $5-$10 this way. And while we're at it, some bridges are $2, others only $1.

TOUR #11 Page 179

TOUR #11

8	Bear-Ly Worn	Vineland
4	Goodwill	Woodbury
10	Goodwill	Vineland
6	Kids Stuff	Pitman
3	Leprechaun Shop	Woodbury
7	My Fair Lady	Pitman
1	Quality Thrift	Gloucester City
2	Rags To Riches	Brooklawn
9	Salvation Army	Vineland
5	Worth Repeating	Woodbury

*Note: This list has a shop's entire name. Names in review boxes may have been shortened a tad to fit. Numbers before each shop name correspond to their numbered location on each map. **Shops with a star sold Volume II.** **Volume III? ASK!**

TOUR #11 MAP Page 180

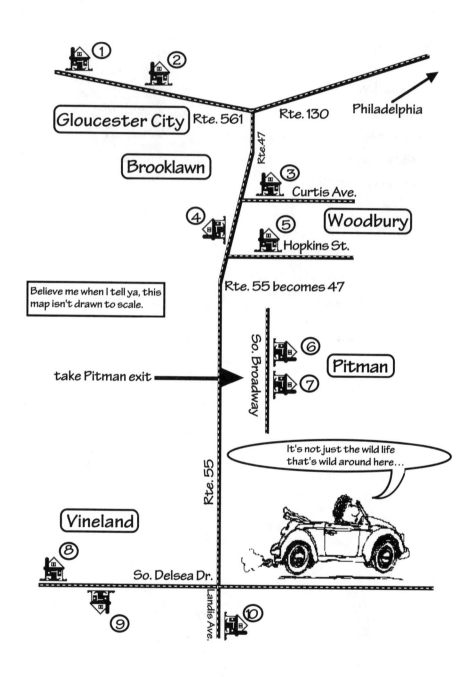

TOUR #11 MAP Page 181

Bear-ly Worn	
3370 S. Delsea Dr. Vineland, NJ 08360 **609-327-WORN**	She called me. I didn't call her. Nice when that happens. Shows I'm making a dent. (I don't have to 'work' quite so hard trying to find 'em this way either.) Shopkeepers are beginning to get IT--What's in it for me to put my head under the blade?--that sort of thinking went on a lot last year. Well last year, 10,000 readers bought this little ditty and used it. And they voted with their dollars. Lots of shops reported an upsurge in business. Maniacs walked in with The Guide under their arms or in their
Bearly 6 months old so I don't bestow hangers till next edition.	purses and pockets or waved it in the air, or just plain flat-out told owners what brought them there. Others kept mum, did their thing, but did it. The **Channel 3** spot a few weeks ago with **Paul Moriarity** produced **1,000 phone calls** and stripped the racks at the Pennsauken Goodwill and Back to the Rack, according to the managers. "Wow! I didn't know you could get clothes *that* good for *so* little!"
Look: CLASS ACT **Goods:** STATUS QUO -CLASS ACT **Prices:** LOW	went the drift. Even after all the TV and radio work we did last year, there's still lots to do out there. Gotta get The Word out, there're millions of new folks to 'convert.' Stay tuned.

And stay tuned to this little newcomer, too. I think she's gonna be a winner. It's a sweet gray and white cottage-style house by the side of the road at the far end of Vineland's crazy-quilt zoning on your way outta town. A tiny beginner model, only two rooms big, nicely done. Looks like mom/owner took over the front porch area of the family home, put in new carpeting, painted the walls, hung some racks, et |
HOURS: Mon-Sat 10-5	voilà--she's in business. **Clothing and equipment were cute and clean and current. I'm pleased to be able to tell you about the shop,** but because she' only been open a few months, I can't and won't bestow any hangers. Just wanted to get the tom-toms going, and let you guys know she's **arrived.**
CLOSED: Holidays	**CONSIGNOR ALERT:** 50%-50%. $3 fee per consignment. 45 days. 15 days/20%, 30 days/50%. 45 days/outta here or store property.
Goodwill	
117 S. Broad St. Woodbury, NJ 08096 **609-848-9834**	A father has taken his little ones thrift shopping. Must be a first, as I overhear him answer the littlest one's question "what's secondhand, Dad?" He gently and clearly answers, "That means someone else loved it before we did." Bring 'em up right, and they'll do right.
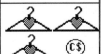	Nearby, two pubescents on their way to being beauties, but still at the awkward stage, pick through bins, rummaging for **"cool"** outfits. (A whole generation and a half later, and they still say cool.) Picking through bins and rattling through racks, the duo intermittently emit a randomly shared **"awesome,"** the fav slang just one TV sit-
Look: BOTTOMFEEDER **Goods:** DOWN & OUT- CLASS ACT **Prices:** LOW	com generation ago. Awesome T's. Awesome sweats. Awesome jeans. Why on earth should after-school wage-earning, allowance-pinching kids pay hundreds of dollars at the mall, when they can come here, acquire the requisite peer-group look for 10% on the dollar, feel like they've discovered thrift, and think it cool and awesome to boot? Oh yea, you can also get combat and hiking boots here. Real ones. Awesome. And how about the Sasson sneakers, brand new, enough to outfit five typica "13.9" families, are lined up behind the register, behind hardworking, friendly Sis, the store clerk. Original boxes with original prices written in marker big
HOURS: Mon-Sat 8-9, Sun 10-6	enough and bold enough to be seen from my side of the counter. $60, now $20. **Peachy keen.**
CLOSED: Holidays	**CONSIGNOR ALERT:** Donations only.

Goodwill	

618 Landis Ave. Vineland, NJ 08360 **609-696-9824** 	Near the register area a clerk was picking up "yet again" after the kiddiwinks who had availed themselves of the toys, yet again. She was not pleased. When I broached the subject, she too wondered why there was no official play area...
	Basically your upsale bottomfeeder. Well lit, spacious, clean and clean-smelling. Two floors huge. Lots and lots of everything, including a surprise cache of evening wear. Some weird prices for a Goodwill or even an upscale boutique in an upscale neighborhood. Please explain to me the reasoning behind the price on an exquisitely classic unworn Bill Blass. White bodice and black lace sheath, street-
Look: UPSCALE BOTTOMFEEDER **Goods:** THE GAMMUT **Prices:** UP & DOWN	lenght cocktail dress, two enormous bows holding the peekaboo top together in the back, only $30 (size 8). As opposed to a $120 price tag on a worn, irridescent, floor-length gaudy taffeta number, designer unknown, with sparkling beadwork over the bodice (size 16). More fabric? If this had been an anomaly I wouldn't carry on. But this inconsistent, reaching-toward-nosebleed pricing was consistent throughout **three racks of what were in most instances upper echelon gowns,** many of which were damaged. What gives? **MEN: Downstairs there were 12'-worth of After Six tuxedos! Also downstairs: a huge book department with old shoe-store-clerk benches for reading.** **P.S.** Every Goodwill has a printed list of nearby branch stores. Ask. **P.P.S..** Each Goodwill can and does charge different prices. Example: Store to store men's shirts can range from $2.69 to $4.99.
HOURS: Mon–Sat 9-8, Sun 10-6	**SHOPPER ALERT:** Evening wear
CLOSED: Holidays	**CONSIGNOR ALERT:** Donations only.

Kids Stuff	

44 S. Broadway Pitman, NJ 08071 **609-589-7171** 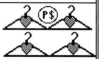	It's unavoidable. Lots of times I'm forced to undercover shop during one of the off seasons: January and February, or July and August. Aren't enough months in the secondhand year to squeeze in all the trips I have to make. They're called off-season because we're pooped from the winter holidays, or off somewhere on our summer vacations hiding from the heat. When we're between frenzied closet-, attic-, basement- and garage-cleaning episodes, thrift and resale shops are between the old supply-and-demand rock and a hard place. But some of us valiantly struggle on, doing our maniac thing, out here shopping anyway, in spite of the odds. Shopkeepers only want ME to shop in the peak months, when they're at their best. I say, "if you're open for business, you're fair game." They never tell cust-
Look: TOP DRAWER **Goods:** STATUS QUO–CLASS ACT **Prices** LOW–MODERATE	omers not to bother, come back in October or May only, now do they?
HOURS: Mon- Wed 10-5:30,Thu & Fri 10-8, Sat 10-4. Jan, June, July 10-4	The inside of someone's fridge can often show how good a meal they had the night before. What's left on racks can tell the story about the consignment quality of the previous season (forensic thrifting?). Here, what was left was better than some shops ever hope to have during peak months. I saw (along with all the other good- ies) a purple, citron and teal Pacific Trails jacket for $18. Luckily, I managed to swing by on my second visit at the beginning of the spring season. **Enough little-girl lace and ribbon and chintz floral dresses to replant every bulb at the Flower Show.** How sweet it is. Bigger kids' sizes 10-14 trailed off in quantity and quality. More to come?
CLOSED:	**CONSIGNOR ALERT:** Undergoing reappraisal. Call after February 1 for new policy. Was 50%-50% across the board. To be split more in consignor favor. Up to 50 items by appointment. Or drop off 10 or less Mon - Fri only. Will supply hangers.

Leprechaun Shop	
18 Curtis Ave. Woodbury, NJ 08096 **609-845-6224**	**1994:** Some naughty leprechaun must have been playing tricks again. Surely this dingy, depressing place could not be named for such mischievously fun-loving creatures as the Little People. No pot of gold here.
Look: BOTTOMFEEDER **Goods:** DOWN & OUT–HO HUM **Prices:** 25¢– $5	**1995:** Couldn't get in. It was 1:08 in the afternoon, the first Saturday of the new year. The shop was darkened and closed, a bundle of donations in brown paper bags leaning up against the doorway where some well-meaning contributor had left them. No shop hours posted in the window, no note telling why they were closed or when they would reopen. Seconds after I tried the latch, another disappointed customer did the same. Who or what was responsible for this mischief?
HOURS: Mon–Sat 10-3	**P.S.** For those of you wondering why this review is so short, you never see big leprechauns, do you?
CLOSED: Holidays	**CONSIGNOR ALERT:** Donations only. Benefits St. John of God, a school for the developmentally disabled.

My Fair Lady	
62 So. Broadway Pitman, NJ 08071 **609-256-0111** 	Large Leading Ladies. My Fair Mom. Talk about theme park. Here in this fashion playground, signs were posted everywhere above racks and bins with spin off messages from that perennial Broadway and Hollywood favorite, My Fair Lady. Sizes ranged from those small enough for Audrey Hepburn, all the way to leading ladies with bountiful physical atributes, **providing as well for every possible fashion type and age, and every stage in a woman's life.** Juniors, seductive lingerie, maternity and work and play wear were in the front room. Here I found a pair of black patent-leather rain boots on sale for 40% off. Translate that to $15 (originally probably $60) marked down to under $10.
Look: CLASS ACT **Goods:** STATUS QUO - CLASS ACT **Prices:** MODERATE	They were having their end-of-year biggie. Yippie! I bought them even though I had two other pairs at home, one leaked, both rubbed. Time to donate.

Further back was a pretty, intimate space **filled to bursting with evening wear and bridal.** Classy shopping bags with even classier names were tacked to the upper walls, tissue paper peaking out. An enormous mirror and dressing room tempted me to stay for the afternoon and play out my fantasies, but alas, the curtain was rising for the next act. The (road) show must go on. Besides, Marvin had run out of computer mags to devour at the news stand just down the street. Time to hit the road. |
| **HOURS:** Mon–Fri 10-8, Sat 10-4, Sun 12-4 | |
| **CLOSED:** Holidays | **CONSIGNOR ALERT:** 50%-50%. No fee. 90 days. Appointment required. |

Quality Thrift	 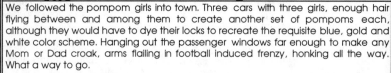
124 S. Broadway Gloucester City, NJ 08030 **609-456-8170**	We followed the pompom girls into town. Three cars with three girls, enough hair flying between and among them to create another set of pompoms each, although they would have to dye their locks to recreate the requisite blue, gold and white color scheme. Hanging out the passenger windows far enough to make any Mom or Dad croak, arms flailing in football induced frenzy, honking all the way. What a way to go.
	Quality Thrift wasn't quite as exciting as the girls. Although it's the recipient of **Best Resale Shop for 1994 by the Courier Post**, I would have cast a negative vote had I been on the selection committee. It's not bad, mind you. It truly looks, acts and feels like a consummate thrift shop. It's just not, in my opinion, nearly the best resale shop New Jersey has to offer.
Look: BOTTOM FEEDER **Goods:** DOWN & OUT—STATUS QUO **Prices:** MODERATE	They have a work space for the owners right inside the front door that is larger than some shops. This should indicate just how much stuff gets processed in and out of here. The owners were talkative and helpful, really tried to assist the customers. There was an entire wall covered with a NFS display of quilted primary-color, nursery room balloons and bears and such. The owner felt it contributed to making them different from other thrift shops. I thought it just made them weird. Even stranger were
HOURS: Tue–Sat 9-5	the **600+** pairs of shoes displayed at eye level on top of every rack of clothing. (Yes, I counted them.) (OK, I'm weird, too). I would definitely have voted them the **Imelda Marcos Award for Most Secondhand Shoes In One Thrift Shop At One Time For 1993, 1994, 1995** and beyond.
CLOSED: Christmas week	**CONSIGNOR ALERT:** Buys outright. Call first for an appointment.

Rags to Riches	
114 New Broadway Brooklawn, NJ 08030 **609-456-7734**	Almost every single garment in the place is protected by a dry cleaner-type plastic sheath. As a consignor, I would appreciate the gesture. It certainly helps to prevent merchandise from being handled and soiled and possibly rendered unsalable. (I've seen this happen more than once.) As a shopper, I found it silly and frustrating. This overzealous fastidiousness kept me from being able to touch the fabric which frequently enters into my decision whether to buy or not to buy, that is the question, whether 'tis nobler... Well anyway, this strategy also made it impossible to see what was what without lifting the bag each and every time I found a dress or blouse to be even remotely interesting. The bags randomly reflected light into my eyes and decreased visibility, creating an overcast layer of gray film between me and the garment. Either way, I couldn't see a darn thing. Those bags have got to go.
Look: HO HUM— CLASS ACT **Goods:** HO HUM— STATUS QUO **Prices:** LOW	Thank heavens the stapled-to-the-wall blue, restaurant-quality-tablecloth, room divider is gone. It's been replaced by a large white bookcase filled with sweaters, put there to prevent access from the third and final room to the owner's sanctuary just on the other side. Much nicer, thank you. Gone, too, are bridal gowns and bustiers. Instead, this appears to have become an all-purpose secondhand shop
HOURS: Mon–Wed 9:30-4, Thu, Fri 9:30-6, Sat 9:30-2	filled with clean, serviceable family clothing and whatever else turns up on the owner's step, making for a mixed bag of the expected and the unexpected, like March weather, the month I blew in, did my undercover thing and blew town.
CLOSED: Holidays	**CONSIGNOR ALERT:** 50%-50% split. No fee. 60 days. No appointment on Mon or Thu.

Salvation Army	 
2279 S. Delsea Dr. Vineland, NJ **609-794-2491** 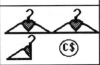	Housed in a former skating rink, stucco walls painted a color of green usually only seen in the tropics, it had a roof with that familiar elongated curving slope. Smooth wooden floorboards stretched on for forever. Bring your in-line skates. You could save a lot of time and get some exercise as you work the racks to the rythmn of 98.6. Imagine the marketing mileage that could be made out of this one if it were privately owned. I'm sure staid old Salvation Army's generals, captains, sergeants and privates wouldn't go for the idea, though (neither would their liability insurance carrier). Too bad. It's just the thing needed to give this place a goose. The basics are here, but after you've seen one...Of course, I want to see 'em all.
Look: BOTTOMFEEDER **Goods:** DOWN & OUT–STATUS QUO **Prices:** LOW	Moldy oldies playing in the background, I toe-tapped my way around to the no-strains-no-gains of "Volare", having **a grand old time**. Two well-dressed, handsome guys paired off, then separated, looking for new duds. They would converge from time to time, compare successes, put something back, swap, then resume, solo. Very intense, very well-dressed maniac pros.
HOURS: Mon-Sat 9-6	Furniture and housewares were dreadful. Clothing was safe and clean, with the random find. A pair of new stretch pants for Morgan for the summer, with watermelons and palm trees and pineapples and a zigzag pattern for only $3.99, and the weirdest pair of Wrangler jeans I've ever seen. I bought them for upcoming bus tour show and tell. Almost X-rated waist-to-hem, vivid depiction of a Greek epic complete with nubile, naked maidens coyly peeking out of well-placed foliage. Satyrs and helmeted warriors lusting after them. Amazing.
CLOSED: Holidays	**CONSIGNOR ALERT:** Donations only.

Worth Repeating	
6 Hopkins St. Woodbury, NJ 08096 **609-384-9022**	When I come home grumbling after a particularly odious shopping experience, wondering out loud how this could have happened, Marvin likes to put on his management-consultant guru's hat, reminding me that senior management's worldview filters down like drip coffee, creating corporate culture. Or, being bummed out while thrifting is most likely to occur if the owner or manager is a tight-ass, hostile creep. Odds are that staff are likely to have such an attitude and anatomical configuration as well. **This shop is every bit as sunny, pleasant and well-organized as the owner and her staff.** Like attracts like.
Look: STATUS QUO **Goods:** STATUS QUO **Prices:** MODERATE	In my line of work, innersoles in shoes (not upper management myopia) tell the story. Cheap leather and man-made soles on some of the secondhand shoe inventory here, indicate clientele that is not used to custom-made. A cynical, hard-as-hobnails job interviewer might include a glance downward, forming a superficial, on the QT assessment of the quality of the applicant's shoe leather. Favya? (lower-class underachiever) Florsheims? Naturalizer? (middle management, and likely to remain such) Soft, highly-styled Italian leather? (salesman) Church's? Ferragamo? (upper management or on the way up, knows how to play the game) The shop? It's somewhere around Florsheims and Naturalizer, with a Favya here, an Anne Klein there. Color-coded price tags hang from mostly rayon, polyester and cotton blends belong to **mostly mid-range mall clothes like Gap, and mail order catalog houses like C&W**. Like attracts like.
HOURS: Mon 9-3, Tue–Fri 10-5, Sat 10-4	
CLOSED: Holidays	**CONSIGNOR ALERT:** 50%-50%. No fee. 60 days. Tue-Sat 10-5. Drop and run.

TOUR #12
ON LOCATION AT THE GREAT WALL

My family went to the shore every summer, all summer. We flew past signs for **Collingswood, Haddonfield, Berlin,** and a slew of other small New Jersey towns I never once saw. Growing up in the Delaware Valley, I found those names as familiar as Bristol, Downingtown and Lansdowne, towns I had heard about but never seen, on the Pennsylvania side of the Delaware moat. Did they really exist, or were they like the tree that falls, unseen and unheard in the forest?

Then there's what I call the Great Wall factor or falling off the edge of the known world. Innumerable Pennsylvanians are afflicted by this narrow, regional view, as are their New Jersey counterparts. We truly believe, as an act of faith, that there is nothing on the other side of the Delaware River. There really are no small towns in New Jersey, only signs. I don't know how the locals manage to hide whole towns from drive-by view, Hollywood set, East Coast-style. Instead of storefronts that have nothing behind them but wooden two by fours propping them up, there are those signs to nowhere. Jug handles and soon to be obsolete circles, and innumerable small towns ebbing and flowing into one another, don't help either. Especially for one such as I, driving-permit weaned on Willie Penn's sensibly laid out, center-city grid.

So, take your time, take the day, take two, driving leisurely from one shop to the next. Don't take these tours too seriously. Once you get your bearings, you can do crossovers. A little Pennsauken (TOUR #13) stirred in with a little Collingswood/Haddonfield. They practically bump shoulders with one another. Circumnavigate, especially if you prefer bottomfeeders--Village Thrift, Back to the Racks or Goodwill. Haddon Avenue is the Collingswood/Haddonfield, New Jersey, thrift-shop treasure-trove equivalent of Easton Road in Glenside, Pa.

Tacked on top of the original colonial and Victorian architecture, most store fronts in **Collingswood** are dated, time warp '50's motif from the last great wave of commercial success before everyone left town for the malls. No uniform signage or window-box gentrification here. It's a middle-class working-stiff neighborhood with faint stirrings of boutique-type revitalization. The malling of America may have peaked. Or perhaps there are now two economic trends running parallel in a race for our money, as folks rediscover the pleasures of connection, neighborliness, shopping and walking right in their own backyard, right in their own town. Imagine that!

Books in the local library reserve stacks attest to Collingswood's all-American past. As in every settlement up and down the East Coast, pre-colonial founding fathers and mothers, arriving on a narrow sterned, 46-foot-keeled fishing boat, The Pink, proceeded to push, shove, buy and sell the Lenni Lenape and Delaware Indians into historical and cultural oblivion. Time travel fast-forward to Centennial archival photos of Kiwanis, Christian Scientists, Boy Scouts, Eastern Star and Rotary members captured forever in time and all their hard-won prosperity. Living, breathing repository of local lore, author Doug Frambs, retired reporter for the Courier Post, hangs out mornings at the Corner Cafe, eating two eggs sunny-side up, remembering...

Work the shops, only needing your car to schlep and warehouse finds. Then lunch at my favorite, the **Corner Cafe**, or one of the many **neighborhood sandwich shops**. Alternative lifestyle shopping might include the **Book Trader**, a secondhand book store on Haddon Avenue, and there's one new first-sale, drop-dead-beautiful 'thing' boutique in town owned by the Corner Cafe people. Good for window shopping and transcendental-thrift flash points of the imagination ("Oh, I can do that, only it doesn't have to cost $125. I saw just the same thing at Goodwill for only $5. All I have to do is...") or falling off the secondhand wagon. You can "do" Collingswood on foot in a day or in a few hours, depending on your pace and where your fancy leads. And Collingswood is definitely worth doing. One of the best, larger-size women's boutiques, The Plus Closet, is in town. There's Our Lady of Lourdes for whimsical bottomfeeder charity, and several very good women's and family resale clothing shops.

Then it's back to the car for a hop, skip and jump down Haddon Avenue with stops at The Exchange, Nifty Thrifties and Raks Thrift Avenue, clustered near each other in and around a mini strip mall. If hunger strikes, next door to The Exchange is an inexpensive soup, salad and sandwich place, **The Bread Board**. They make a mean chili, and the taste memory lingers. Or try **Food For Thought**, the fancier, more **expensive vegetarian restaurant** up near Nifty Thrifties' end of the strip mall. Let me know.

Haddonfield, New Jersey, Philadelphia's Chestnut Hill equivalent and then some, is every entrepreneur's dream come true. One tastefully correct colonial era house after another sports brass nameplates of this doctor and that lawyer, interspersed with chic shops and low-key cafes. This sort of place takes zoning SERIOUSLY. Wheelchair-accessible bathrooms and boutique-quality interior design cost big bucks. This is a rich resource. But you pay for it, because shopkeepers here must pay higher rents, have low key, hand-painted signs, pay this tax and conform to that regulation. Hard to believe this Mecca of upscale posh has its fair share of secondhand shops.

Secrets and Consignment Galleries, and several good-to-better resale shops, are all tucked away down an "alley" or just around the corner, as they ever-so-discreetly blend into the scene. They must. The local esthetic police wouldn't have it any other way. Nor would I. Hungry by now? Try **Remi's Cafe** for a sit down lunch, or the **Cheese Shop** across the street, where you can either teeter on bistro chairs in a cramped dining alcove, or do an expansive, takeout picnic, after scanning shelves packed with deli imports. Right across the street from the Children's Exchange is **Frank's Pizza Place**. I like a crisp crust (which it had), pillow-soft, real mozzarella (ditto), and tangy, acidic sauce. (This one was too sweet for me). But there was an amazing-looking sandwich on a pedestal pizza plate. It won "Best of Philly for Steak in a Blanket on Homemade Bread". (They must invent these bizarre categories to match the goodies as they turn up.) Anyway, it looked great, as great as Frank's selection of homemade bread and just about as good as his Old World accent sounded.

Back in the car for **Audubon** and **Haddon Heights**, only a hiccup down Kings Highway from Haddonfield. Ready? On your mark, get set, go. Don't blink. (Even for the purple house. You can't mistake it. You'll know which one I mean.) Oops, we passed 'em. Just kidding. But, it can seem like that. I don't grok all the town names and city limits bumping smack up against each other so suddenly, only to flow into one another, end, and pop up again. I'm from the big city. And yes we do have all those different communities with all those strange and wonderful names, but it's all just one big happy city. (Yes, I'm kidding again.)

Follow the Haddonfield-Berlin Road (still Rte. 30) past burgeoning big-business malls and fly-by intersections of **Voorhees**, just long enough to reach the outskirts of semi-rural New Jersey, where brick split levels and strip shopping malls are rhythmically separated by truck farms, nurseries, roadside stands and decrepit bungalows. Distances between points on the map increase exponentially, the farther south we travel. Franks gives way to Agway, city sidewalk life to scrub pine and sandy soil. The **Berlin Farmer's Market**, just around the corner from St. Vincent's is a great, unfettered hunk of Americana, open Thursday through Sunday.

Hungry? Something more upscale, but still 'diner'? In **Voorhees**, try **Echo Pizza's Fabulous 50's** black-and-white tile and linoleum checkerboard dream with a jolt of red and a jive sound blasting from a juke box. The wings were great. Choose carefully. They really are Mellow to Semi-Scorcher to Lethal. They're still working on the fries. (No place, nowhere, no how is as good as Boardwalk Fries, so far.) As we go to press, I haven't eaten here yet, but the **Country Club Diner**, right across the street from an Encore Book Store (yes, of course, they sell The Guide), looked like a good bet. Traveling further south to **Berlin**? Try the **New Berlin Diner**. It's cheap, fast, and friendly. Or there's the **Pallas Diner** just outside of town on Rte. 561 at the wacky intersection where eight roads converge and then lead to a circle. Weird.

TOUR #12

16	All My Children	Haddonfield
5	B Thrifty Shop	Westmont
15	Barbara's Bargains	Berlin
11	The Children's Exchange	Haddonfield
18	Consignment Galleries ★	Haddonfield
6	The Contact 609 Exchange ★	Haddonfield
10	Deja Vu	Haddonfield
4	elite	Collingswood
13	Joan's Closet	Voorhees
20	Main Line Boutique	Haddon Heights
8	Nifty Thrifties	Haddonfield
3	Our Lady of Lourdes	Collingswood
1	The Plus Closet ★	Collingswood
7	Raks Thrift Avenue	Haddonfield
2	Second Showing	Collingswood
17	Secrets & 9 The Backroom ★	Haddonfield
21	Short Stuff	Haddon Heights
14	St. Vincent de Paul	Berlin
12	Trading Places	Voorhees
19	Treasures in the Attic	Audubon

*Note: This list has a shop's entire name. Names in review boxes may have been shortened a tad to fit. Numbers before each shop name correspond to their numbered location on each map. **Shops with a star sold Volume II. Volume III? ASK!**

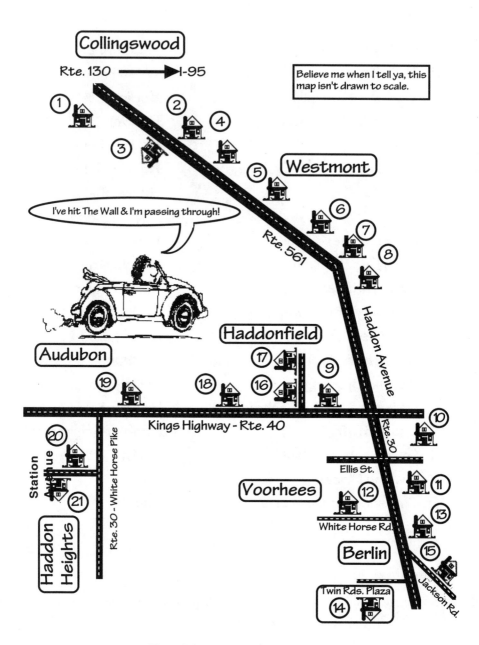

TOUR #12 MAP Page 191

All My Children

4 Mechanic St.
Haddonfield, NJ
08033

609-429-9000

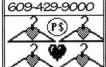

Look: TOP DRAWER

Goods: CLASS
ACT–TOP DRAWER

Prices: HIGH

HOURS: Mon–Fri
10-5:30, Sat 10-6

CLOSED: Holidays

Marcy Halpin has it aced. Rarer than a platypus, she's a newcomer 4-hanger. Attending 'University of Secrets' as paid 'intern' she eventually 'graduated' with an advanced degree. Working for Secret's owner, long tenured 'Professor' (Ph. D.T.) Kathy Murtha. part-time, paid off big-time. Kathy moved two doors down this summer. Marcy stayed behind, opening her own complimentary shop in the old digs. Use-what-ya-got school of decorating cubbyholes, chiseled out of the warm-toned terracotta brick wall, are filled with treasures and trifles that charm and amuse. A la Secrets, unproductive space where wall meets ceiling has a display border of pintsize, frilly gossamer, and snappy black tie in miniature, with matching suspenders, of course. A happy row of rainbow-color kids, lovingly hand-painted by Marcy's family, cavort in sunlight splashing through the big picture window. The narrow, staggered-step, three-tiered space is packed with infant through size 14. With no room for a "real" play area, supply has found demand. The lowest level has kids crawling over toys, grown-ups climbing over kids and other grown-ups to get to the clothes and furnishings, fishing out their kids from the bottom of the wriggling heap only when it's time to leave. And they get the right one every time. **Amazing!**

Only peeve? Prices match the neighborhood. But that inevitably attracts well-to-do consigners' well-to-do consignments, like Pooh Bear to honey. A pink confection, (originally $500) hung by itself like a work of art. It's soul mate sold only days before for $125 to a professional child-beauty-pageant contestant. Originally bought for twin flower girls at a posh wedding, they were worn all of 4 hours. **Pull out and inspect any garment, any piece of kiddy furniture or equipment. Top of the line all the way.**
CONSIGNER ALERT: 50%-50% split. No fee. 180 days. 50%/180 days. Drop and run.

B Thrifty Shop

225 Haddon Ave.
Westmont, NJ
08108

609-854-1003

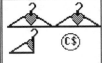

Look: STATUS QUO

Goods: HO HUM–
STATUS QUO

Prices: LOW–
MODERATE

HOURS: Tue–Fri
10-4, Sat 10-2

CLOSED: Holidays
and August

In what was a 100-year old private home, the recycled residence now does double duty: kitchen? Thrift shop office and drop-off. Parlor and front porch? Household and kid's. Dining room and second floor bedrooms? Clothing. The carriage house, referred to as The Barn, is cinder block ugly on the outside, a revelation of vaulting rafters inside. When an overly-eager, well-meaning volunteer started using "estate quality" to describe furniture inventory, I felt myself contorting into a Ralph Nader under the Hyde-look-alike. Dr. Nader and Mrs. Maniac?

Major moments in thrifting occurred at this organize-to-the-max hive of much ado about little. 1) Dusty pink metal hospital dressers, carbon-dated to the 30's or 40's. (I'm not as up on hospital furniture styles as I should be.) Anachronistic relics holding similar reliquary. Drawers labeled Girdles, Aprons. Long ago and far away, hospital acquisitions was very proud indeed to be so farsighted buying such modern, unusually colored dressers. 2) Matching desks in unique pinque in receiving. Lots of "what did you say?" shouting goes on, as some are hard of hearing. 3) Primary painted, 50's ceramic wall-mount telephone lamp, glass ginger jar lamps holding pastel plastic flowers, and nearby 'matching' overblown and functionally useless pillows in lace and face scratching-glitter, with a pink silk rose dead center. One serious goodie? A handsome red hunter jacket and khaki bullet holder, a $45 buy and a serious candidate for Northern Exposure's costume department.

CONSIGNOR ALERT: 60%You–40%Shop. $3 fee. 20%/30 days. Tue & Thu 10-noon.10 items. First Saturday by appointment. Benefits West Jersey Hospital.

Barbara's Bargains

75 Jackson Rd.
Berlin, NJ 08009
609-768-8777

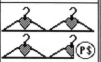

Look: CLASS ACT

Goods: STATUS QUO–CLASS ACT

Prices: MODERATE

HOURS: Mon, Tue, Wed, & Sat 10:30-4:30, Thu & Fri 10-6

CLOSED: Holidays

Training manuals still don't get handed out when you wheel your newborn out of the hospital. **Shopping here, at least you'll know your infant's dressed right from the get-go. Every growth spurt, every special occasion is covered.** When Morgan was born, I had one three-pack of undies from Bloomies, of all places. That was it. I'd gone brain dead in the store every time I picked up a rattle or a bib. Stepdaughter Erica, who had a hand in helping her mom raise twins and a third, solo daughter all born within two years of each other, took Marvin in hand and bought the basics, while I lay dazed in the hospital. Back then, I wouldn't have dreamed of putting anything secondhand on my immaculate princess. Now, I can't imagine anything else. High fallutin' attitudes changed radically when confronted by the bottom line.

Men are a no-no, little boys are tolerated, commingled in the infant section, with one circular rack of equally good, but minimal, duds for toddler through preteen. Swimsuits, aerobics, baptism, jeans, first communion, ski jackets, prom dresses, flower girl and bridesmaid dresses, bridal gowns, layettes, play clothes, go-to-business suits, it's all here. After all, Barbara's approach is very familiar. Just like most day care centers these days, the shop is an addition tacked onto her home, a substantial brick rancher on a small residential side street. Think of Barbara's as day care through post-graduate level course work on How To Enjoy Being A Girl, with in-depth concentration through middle school. Sorry. You'll have to go to Mom, Dad, Grandma and Grandpa, your local bookstore, your pediatrician for everything else.

☞ **SHOPPER ALERT:** Party and communion dresses

CONSIGNOR ALERT: 50%-50% split. $3 fee. 60 days. 14 items/appointment.

Children's Exchange

110 Ellis St.
Haddonfield, NJ 08033
609-428-8688

Look: HO HUM–STATUS QUO

Goods: STATUS QUO–CLASS ACT

Prices: LOW–MODERATE

HOURS:
Mon–Sat 10-4:30

CLOSED: Holidays

Calling ahead, we got directions. (Getting smarter!) Even with static on the car phone, it was a cinch. We did just what Grace said, went just were she told us. Children's Exchange was clearly printed on the sign with three other names. Where was the store? Ahh. Grace was right. She is here. The giveaway? Boxes of kids' clothes on the sidewalk. But those could have been explained away by the cleaners next door. Customer discards? Nope, too many. They were one more of Grace's space savers: end-of-season sale items. It's not a particularly pretty place, one of the smallest, ever, but what with rents in Haddonfield...Standing amidst the cockeyed, stacked and triple hung jumble, my heart sank. Take heart.

What's in a name? Everything. Cheerfully, efficiently, Grace explained how to work her store. 'Pull up' a balloon, one of the many woven into the rug, and park 'it'. You're going to be here awhile. Stacked piles of jeans and sweaters, boxes of shoes, party dresses and boy's suits three and four deep, hang along 6-foot poles in the back. Pull out a pile, any pile. Unfold. Take a peek. Fold. Unfold. Take a peek. Fold. Following their directions, once again, within two stacks I excavated three long-sleeve cotton shirts with tiny buttons marching up the front to the neckline, one floral with pale lavender background, the others magenta and purple, I couldn't leave those $4.25 cutie pies behind. Headed for the car to hit up Marvin for more cash, I spied a new pair of Nikes, white with purple and aqua trim in Morgan's size, only $8.50. Sold. And **I'm sold on this place**. Don't be put off by appearances. Besides, there's always Grace to guide you.

CONSIGNOR ALERT: 50%-50% split. $5 fee. 90 days. No appontment necessary.

Consignment Galleries	
43 Kings Hwy. E. Haddonfield, NJ 08033 **609-429-4290** 	In the bustling midst of veddy veddy upscale Haddonfield's veddy veddy posh shopping district, the unblinking eye is left undisturbed, the daily downtown parade of shoppers' well-heeled footsteps never miss a beat. Nothing to suggest anything amiss, anything less than the best. Not a whiff of thrift or a suggestion of secondhand. And yet that's exactly where droves of shoppers are headed. The footsteps of the local (and not so local) cognoscenti beat a path to Consignment Galleries' front door. A Scarecrow lady seated on a Gardener's Eden-caliber wooden park bench. She grasps some very slightly rumpled upscale shopping bags with logos of Godiva, Harrod's Food Hall and Henri Bendel. **We've arrived.**
Look: TOP DRAWER **Goods:** STATUS QUO–TOP DRAWER **Prices:** MODERATE –HIGH	So have Steuben, Mikasa, and Haviland. Or how about the oak armoire with hovering gargoyles flanking the mirrored door ($1000), colonial pie chest ($500), Welsh cupboard ($700), Victorian brass mirror with parenthetical, light-reflecting gas lamp globes ($500), and a statue of Father Christmas ($250). Miniatures and collectibles, fine linens, oils and watercolors, silver tea service, everything and anything Madam or Sir require to set up upper-class housekeeping and keep the investment banker busy investing the money you didn't spend. Or impress the wellies off friends and neighbors with **one-stop hostess, housewarming and birthday shopping.** Box and
HOURS: Mon–Wed, Thu, Sat 10:30-5, Fri 10:30–6:30, Sun 12-4	bow these great goodies with top-drawer greeting cards and wrapping paper. No one need ever know they didn't come from the best "firsthand" gifty shoppe in Haddonfield. 'Cause they did. **P.S.** Free Parking on Saturday & Sunday
CLOSED: Holidays	**CONSIGNOR ALERT:** 50%-50% on items < $150. **60% to You** on items > $150. 90 days.

Contact 609 Exchange	
605C Haddon Ave. Haddonfield, NJ 08033 **609-795-6604** 	Like moi, they had no experience in the thrift business. It could be argued they had no business getting into it either. But fools and angels dare to tread. I'd love a dollar for every time a fool approached me and opined: "I love to cook. I want to open a restaurant someday." As if home cooking skills, professionally undemonstrated at that, have much to do with running a successful restaurant. What about accounting and stamina (110° heat, 14-hour days, 6-7 days/week) and knife-wielding, coke-snorting perverts in the walk-in?
Look: TOP DRAWER **Goods:** STATUS QUO–TOP DRAWER **Price:** MODERATE	One day, while undercover, I decided to buy a sweater. The volunteer snipped the tag. Only then did I realize it was more than I wanted to spend. She graciously put the tag back on without a whimper or a snarl. The dear lady, and I do mean lady, rose to the occasion. No knives here. The Exchange is a tele-help service for Camden County. Contents and decor reflect the upper middle-class donors' cast-off wardrobes and dearly won, cherished lifestyles. **Clothes are beyond immaculate, arranged just so.** Protective makeup face nets and chintz-covered
HOURS: Tue, Wed & Sat 10-4, & Fri 10-5, Thu 10-8	chairs in the two dressing rooms exemplify the thoughtfulness and standards of the shop's movers and shakers. At the top of their flyer, and I quote: "Where the elite meet to browse, barter and to benefit..." Golf? (clubs and duds) Cocktails at the club? (glitter and glitz) Gallery opening? (subtly successful suits, paintings and prints) Dinner for six at 8? (crystal and china) Hostess tribute, birthday or anniversary? (small antiques, objets d'art, seasonal gifts) Tennis, anyone? You can argue with success, but why should you? **And here they are a huge success.**
CLOSED: Holidays	**CONSIGNOR ALERT:** 50%-50% split. $5 fee. 60 days. Wednesday 10-2, Thursday 5-7 and by appointment.

Deja Vu

9 S. Haddon Ave.
Haddonfield, NJ
08033

609-429-5059

Look: RECHERCHÉ
Goods: STATUS
QUO–CLASS ACT
Prices: MODERATE

HOURS: Tue & Wed
& Sat 10-5, Thu &
Fri 10-4:30 & 6-9.

CLOSED: Holidays

It's tempting for me to go off on a writer's riff. There's the portfolio-quality lingerie catalog by the register, and reclining seminudes in rapsodic rayon splendor. It would be easy for me to pan the latex and spandex and fake and bunny furs and the terrible lighting. It is difficult to resist being a smart-ass member of the fashion police. This is most definitely not my stylistic milieu (or is it?). It is, however, a viable niche in the marketplace.

Touches abound. Dressing room curtains are reminiscent of Ballard Designs, an ever so tasteful catalog that comes to my house several times a year. Deja Vu in diagonal handwritten gold ink lettering scrolled across taupe burlap-type fabric. Trés recherché. Trés curious when viewed in raging juxtaposition to the racks of filmy wedding-night seduction-quality boudoir and evening wear hanging on the overwhelmingly fake brick wall. I am told the image they wish to capture, the clientele they hope to attract is the a)divorced woman, b)who dates, c)after work. Their business card tag line: Chic and Unique Clothing With A Past. Me? I'm married and I work after work. Perhaps I should send Marvin here to shop out some male fantasy. But he wouldn't catch me in it. (Or would he?) I wound up buying against type, plunked down $105 and walked out with a shearling coat, two tops and a slit front dark green skirt by Ellen Tracey. It was the end-of-season sale. I either spent or **saved a bundle**, depending on your perspective.

While I am unclear how or why they decided to locate in tastefully correct Haddonfield, of all places, where would we be if we all thought, ate and dressed the same, or even if we wore the same style every day? So all you gay divorcees with big hair and bigger social calendars, this is the place. No demure dos (or don'ts) allowed. (Or are they? I got in.)
CONSIGNOR ALERT: 50%-50% split. $3 fee. 60 days. No appointment.

elité

829 Haddon Ave.
Collingswood, NJ
08108

609-858-4121

Look: CLASS ACT
Goods: STATUS
QUO–CLASS ACT
Prices: MODERATE

HOURS: Mon–Wed
& Sat 11-5, Thu &
Fri 11-7

CLOSED: Holidays

Its peaches and cream "complexion" makes it the prettiest secondhand store in Collingswood with little competition from neighboring firsthand stores, either. The interior is the same ladylike color scheme as the exterior. All alone, I blissfully shop my way towards the back of the store where the ball gowns are hung, humming along, until I realize I am becoming morose.

The farther I wander from the papered-over front window, the gloomier the long narrow room becomes. What light there is isn't shopper friendly. Fixtures are hung at either the wrong height or angle, light bounces off the garments, almost blinding me. I try holding garments at varying angles, this way and that. **Talbot, Esprit, Evan Picone, Collection, The Gap,** etc. Are they faded? Are they stained? What color is it, really? More wattage, please. I believe in showing off what you've got. And what they've got peaks out somewhere around a $40,000-a-year lifestyle. No big-time spenders consign here, no slumming, either. Good solid-citizen stuff. There is the beginning of a play area and a rack for plus sizes. Curiously, what few plus-size garments they had were the most consistent, best overall quality in the shop.
P.S. Get a **Frequent Buyer Card.** 10 purchases gets you $5 off the next item.

CONSIGNOR ALERT: 50%-50% split. $5 fee. 60 days. 20%/30 days, 40%/60 days, Wednesday–Friday by appointment.

Joan's Closet

561 Plaza
Voorhees, NJ
08043
609-768-5504

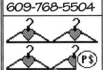

Look: CLASS ACT

Goods: STATUS
QUO–TOP DRAWER

Prices MODERATE

HOURS:

Tue–Fri 11-6,
Sat 11-4

CLOSED: 2 weeks in
August. Call ahead.

Privately owned resale boutiques are owned and operated by women. Entering a shop is tantamount to entering some portion of their imagination, their character, their private lives. As customers, we are invited inside to take a peek, lift the curtain, unintentionally gaining a sense of the person. Clues are scattered everywhere, obvious and subtle. Read the little signs scattered behind the register and those just as clearly 'written' without words. What has she chosen to consign? With what colors did she choose to surround us and herself? Is the place crowded and askew? Bare, each hanger spaced just so? Romantically dimmed, or just plain gloomy? Sunny, or glare-you-in-the eye bright? What does she pay attention to most: organization, or customers? Is the store a happy place, easy to use? Or uptight and inhibiting?

Owner aura comes through so clearly in some shops, that it's like entering a tangible force field. I 'felt' Joan and liked her immediately. I liked her energy: dainty, precise, poised, professional, yet feminine. Her being had a light touch. She knew just when to speak, just how long to let me roam around. She answered all my questions quickly and clearly. **The shop was organized, bright, and shiny as a new penny.** The clothes and accessories were hung just so, not a stain or wrinkle or tear in sight. **Labels were good to better. Evening wear and dresses, best.** Joan, thanks for letting me enter your world, however briefly. It's a good place to be.

☞ **SHOPPER ALERT:** Evening wear and dresses 🖋🖋🖋🖋

CONSIGNOR ALERT: 50%-50% split. $3 fee. 2 mos. 15 articles max. By appointment.

Main Line Boutique

613 Station Ave.
Haddon Heights, NJ
08035
609-547-5504

Look: STATUS
QUO–CLASS ACT

Goods: HO HUM–
CLASS ACT

Prices: LOW–
MODERATE

HOURS:
Tue–Fri 10-5,
Sat 10-4

CLOSED: Holidays

Familiar with the promise of the high economic impact of the same moniker (Main Line) on my side of the Delaware, and with the shop address abutting ever so prosperous Haddonfield, I was sure we were headed for greatness with this next one. And as if those weren't indication enough, there, prominently displayed in the window, was a small framed certificate stating this shop had been awarded Best Resale & Consignment Shop of South Jersey for 1994. Whoops. What we got instead was **a good, solid-citizen, three-hanger with lots of heart,** and yet another strong difference of opinion with the Courier Post's award system. (You may be surprised to learn I always *want* them to be fours. I hate it when they're not.) Very much the neighborhood shopkeeper, she knew her clientele. She willingly and pleasantly dashed and darted between, among, and around us, answering questions, pointing out a possible match between customer size and her inventory, all the while answering the phone, ringing up sales, all with a smile. (I have trouble not turning into a snarling hag if the phone rings just once when I'm writing.)

Men's had a few real possibilities. Several suits from Boyd's, and two unusually colored, striped, custom-made shirts with French cuffs were very attractive. There was also a Byblos shirt for $7 and an Alexander Julian sweater for $8. (If I were a local hunk, I'd drop in here from time to time.) Women's and children's, on the other hand, had little that even remotely attracted my attention. All was clean, and neat and tidy, but either dated or safe, like the prototype Laura Ashley for $14 or the Lillian Albus sequined jacket, also $14.

CONSIGNOR ALERT: 50%-50%. $5 fee. 60 days. 20%/30 days. By appointment only.

Nifty Thrifties	
413 Haddon Ave. Haddonfield, NJ 08033 **609-795-9085** **Look:** STATUS QUO–CLASS ACT **Goods:** HO HUM–TOP DRAWER **Prices:** MODERATE **HOURS:** Mon–Wed & Sat 10-4, Thu-Fri 10-7, Sun 12-4 **CLOSED:** Holidays	Rumor has it that Ellen, Nifty Thrifties' owner, originally bought out a preexisting shop. Experienced art teacher and speech therapist adds inexperienced entrepreneur to her resume. Persistence, hard work, savvy and the passing of time resulted in two locations. Entrepreneur does very well indeed. Recently, the former owner took it into her head to return to the resale biz, opening Raks Thrift Avenue several doors down in the same strip of shops. Customers like it, getting two shops with one stop. Ellen responded like any good shopkeeper would: Upgrading with new lighting, carpeting and stereo system. There's little of that Jersey flash-and-trash school of design here. The sort you see Saturday night on South Street: the steroid-enhanced, dude and his overdone everything doll. Mostly it's the **discreet and stylish** that crowd the trash to steam off the sidewalk, so to speak. Or in this case, off the racks, the overcrowded racks. This store is bursting at the seams with all the right labels, like the LIZ Claiborne pink sweater set, marked down to $28. Tons of belts, bags and shoes. Some of the racks in the front and back rooms are pushed against the wall, hard to reach. I wouldn't like to be a consignor whose clothes are stuck in the back, out of sight and out of the running. Except for this one snafu it's a very user-friendly shop. Perhaps because of the proven success of The Plus Closet in Collingswood, a **small rack of plus sizes has been added** since last year's review. **CONSIGNOR ALERT:** 50-50% split. $3 annual fee. 60 days. 20%/30 days, 50%/60 days. By appointment only.
Our Lady of Lourdes	
740 Haddon Ave. Collingswood, NJ 08108 **609-858-4204** **Look:** HO HUM–STATUS QUO **Goods:** HO HUM–STATUS QUO **Prices:** VERY LOW **HOURS:** Mon-Fri 10-4, Sat 10-3 **CLOSED:** Holidays	Filtered light passing down from the skylight on high. Reliquary and used white uniforms, Our Lady of the Secondhand. My first visit here, summer of '93, Bing Crosby, the large-eared, smooth-faced crooner, who portrayed numerous pious Father-So-and-Sos back in the 40's and 50's, and who we all now know in real life was a so-and-so of a father, was singing White Christmas in the back ground. It was mid-August, mid-heatwave. Pinky swear. As I skulked about researching Vol. III, the boisterous chatter of women deeply involved in backroom negotiations was the syncopated sound du jour. Bing had been excommunicated. I missed the kitsch of it all. Old time-thrift shops and old-time religion are going through revolution and renewal. This one may be living on borrowed time. **Prices are very low**, but could be even lower, considering. Ladie's dresses, $3. Children's tops, $5 Men's jackets $5. I was struck by the disparity in inventory, before I uncovered the reason. Clothing is 100% donation, everything else combination donation/consignment (on white bread). Shops tend to screen consignments much more carefully than donations. Consignment usually, not always "uplifts" quality as well as prices. So stick to rummaging around **china and housewares**. Keep your eyes peeled and your wallet folded until you are sure. I saw a hideous 2'-foot brass lamp which caused my eyes to water from the glare of its $35 price tag. $5 would've been more like it. Unused but seriously dated Sears ladies' ice skates in original box, slightly overpriced at $10. **CONSIGNOR ALERT:** Clothing donations only. Everything else donated or consigned. **60% you-40% shop.** $5 annual fee. 10 item limit. Tue, Thu, Sat, 10-noon. 20%/30 days.

The Plus Closet

602 Haddon Ave.
Collingswood, NJ
08108
609-854-8828

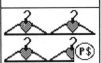

Look: STATUS QUO
Goods: STATUS QUO–CLASS ACT
Prices: MODERATE

HOURS: Tue–Fri 10-5, Sat 10-4

CLOSED: 1 week every Summer

Found myself wishing I were a size or three larger. Zaftig maniacs, you should come and shop here...yesterday. Women already in the know flock here from all over the Delaware Valley. Last year, I managed to keep my cover by pretending I was scouting the store for some generously endowed girlfriends. And in a way, that is just what I was doing. So listen up, girlfriends. This place is pretty, with lots of room to move around. **It is clean, bright and well-organized, the staff friendly and helpful. Sandy, the owner, is one of the nicest people you'd ever want to meet.** Wherever I go, and her name is mentioned, shopkeepers and customers alike say the same.

Chock full of Nippon, Elizabeth, Chaus Woman, Spencer Alexis, sizes 14-32, there was not a single "slipcover" in sight. You know, the old "If it's big it's gotta be ugly, with a price tag to match." No way! Here, there was **everything an attractive, stylish woman would need** to carry her through a busy day and a busy life. An in-depth assortment of scaled-to-size accessories to complete your look and the store's inventory. A MAC machine across the street, a **Frequent Shopper Discount Card,** and a blow-out sale twice a year make it easy to part with your hard earned dollars.

CONSIGNOR ALERT: 50-50%, $5 fee. 90 days. 50% off last 30 days.

Raks Thrift Avenue

421 Haddon Ave. N.
Haddonfield, NJ
08033
609-429-6777

Look: CLASS ACT
Goods: STATUS QUO - CLASS ACT
Prices: UP & DOWN

HOURS: Tue, Wed, Fri & Sat 11-5
Thu 11-7

CLOSED: Holidays, 1 week winter & summer

Prowling Haddon Avenue, scoping the scene, I came to a sudden, unexpected, screeching halt. Where I had come to expect Nifty Thrifties' familiar name in the window, there appeared at first glance to be a newcomer, instead. On the scent of a newsworthy "dish," I lurched into the first available parking spot, eyes desperately darting back and forth between traffic and curb. Mind's eye full of questions: What happened? Answer: Nothing and everything. Where's Nifty? Just where it's always been, several doors down the street.

Raks is a new shop that opened over the summer. The owner, having once sold out to Nifty Thrifty, decided to make a resale comeback, opening up almost next-door to her now competitor. **She obviously knows more than most beginners.** The shop is organized and clean, consignment sheet at the ready. And less than others, as two women (owner? clerk?) nibbled on lunch and chatted away behind the desk, ignoring customers. An eye-catching Tahari half navy/half white gabardine dress, hung on a headless sidewalk mannequin, caught my attention. Closer inspection revealed a faint yellow stain and a wallet-grabbing $100 price tag. Inside the front door I walked into the arms of a $950 bridal gown in flowing satin and pastel beadwork. Smiling from a wedding day snapshot tacked at a right angle on the neighboring wall, facing her gown, the original bride models for us. An inducement to potential secondhand brides trying to imagine what they might look like in it, or was she smiling because she knew she was going to consign her gown the next day? The Tahari and the $950 wedding gown skew the curve. Decor, garments, and pricing are mainstream, not these high end, high ticket exceptions to the rule.

CONSIGNOR ALERT: 50%-50% split. No fee. 60 days. 20%/30, 50%/60 days
Appointments encouraged.

Second Showing

685 Haddon Ave. Collingswood, NJ 08108 **609 854-0520**	I tried six or seven times to get my two undercover visits completed to include them in Vol. II. They closed for the summer, then their fall hours didn't jibe with the times I happened by. Well, Lord knows I tried. I didn't want 'em left out either. But with only one shopping expedition under my secondhand belt, I couldn't include them.

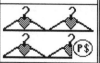

Look: STATUS QUO
Goods: STATUS QUO–TOP DRAWER
Prices: LOW

HOURS: Tue–Fri 11-4:30, Sat 11-4

CLOSED: Mid-July–Labor Day

One year later, we've got a match. I hung around at my favorite spot, Corner Cafe, pacing and networking and munching on orange muffins, watching the overcrowded, unpromising front window for any sign of retail life. Finally they opened, 25 minutes later than the posted 11am. I dashed across the street, greeted by the affectionate "Hi, dear" everyone gets when they enter. Another customer in flowing, dyed-ever-so-black, shoulder-length hair, full stage makeup and matching wardrobe, was a living, heavy-breathing example of what I call Jersey flash point fashion. A satisfied regular, she had returned to her favorite hunting ground for more. But there were also multitudes of ever-so-tasteful Anne Klein and bosom buds hangin' out on the racks. I was **absolutely delighted at the very high quality** of at the least a third of the clothing and **extraordinarily low prices**. I found a Dana Buchman red paisley jacket for $38, immaculate, cut in the latest silhouette. $400 new, give or take $50. Extraordinary. **The men's department had more inventory than usual and was also reasonably priced.** Glad I was so persistent.

CONSIGNOR ALERT: 50%-50% split. $3 annual fee. 80 days. By appointment only.

Secrets & The Backroom

4 Mechanic St. Haddonfield, NJ 08033 **609-354-9111** **The Backroom** 13 Haddon Ave.	are no secret anymore, thanks to Orien Reid of Channel 10 fame, and high energy, high profile owner Kathleen Murtha, the epitome of housewife turned outrageously successful busines woman. With wide-eyed wonder and in-depth inexperience she murmured in her husband's disbelieving ear those now oft-repeated, immortal words: "Honey, I want to open a secondhand shop."

Look: TOP DRAWER
Goods: STATUS QUO–TOP DRAWER
Prices: MODERATE–HIGH

Hours: 10-6 Daily, Thu & Fri till 8
Backroom:
Thu, Fri, Sat 12-5

CLOSED. Holidays.

Old digs: What did she know? Closet design. Who did she know? Everyone in Haddonfield, it would seem. What's her husband say to this wild 'n woolly scheme? "Certainly, dear, just as soon as you write me a business plan." She researched her size-8 (?) butt off for a year. Like everything else she does, she was so thorough and intense that when her plan was complete, several businessmen in the area were ready to sign on the dotted. Her husband relented, and dug deep, keeping the money and the idea in the family. Just when the poor man thought the worst was over and he could finally get a good night's sleep, Kathy tried a little more pillow talk. This time it was, "Honey, I've got to move. No, no, dear, don't panic. Get back in bed. It's the business. I simply must have more space." **New digs:** Kathy has successfully proven she knows upscale resale inside out and upside down. The new shop is **drop dead spectacular.** Surrounded by exposed, rosy pink bricks, white cubbyholes, gently circling ceiling fans and green shaded factory lights, **I've died and gone to resale heaven.** She's created one of the top secondhand shops in the Delaware Valley. My hat box is off to you Kathy. **With two locations, a block apart,** Secrets carries the first wave of elegant consignments. The Backroom functions as a "thirdhand outlet." Whatever didn't sell at Secrets comes here, immediately marked down 50%. Since quality is so high at Secrets, The Backroom is every bit as good as most three- or three-and-a-half- hanger shops.
P.S. Backroom Secret: Thursdays the 'new' stuff comes over from Secrets.
CONSIGNOR ALERT: 50-50% split. No fee. 60 days. Unsold? 50% off at The Backroom.

Short Stuff	

612 Station Ave. Haddon Hgts., NJ 08035 **609-547-2878** **Look:** HO HUM– STATUS QUO **Goods:** HO HUM– STATUS QUO **Prices:** LOW	While I worked the racks across the street at Main Line Boutique, Marvin dashed over here to begin scoping things out. When he left to fetch me, the owner closed up shop, thinking no one else would be coming in so late in the afternoon on New Year's Eve. I stood outside with my disappointed nose pressed against the frosty, darkened window. Seeing me stranded outside, looking so dejected and forlorn, she changed her mind and unlocked the door. **Bless her.**
	Bringing up the lights revealed fading, stained bunches of wallpaper violets and roses hung in ribbon-gathered stripes, trailing down the walls of this hobby-grown-into-a-business. Ruth does it for the fun of it, to get out of the house, cover expenses and meet people. She got here first, she pointed out, four years before Main Line moved in across the street last year. Originally a noncompete, now both shops carry children's clothing, although Short Stuff has far more. Appropriately enough, just as the name implies, she specializes in little kid's stuff, topping out around size 10, with only a few pieces of baby equipment tucked under the racks. $4 jeans, enough to match every penciled notch on a home-made growth-spurt yardstick for three generations' worth of a family that produced only sons. A $20, faded-glory Nicole, blue-grey party dress with equally faded purple-grey bows, matched the wallpaper.
HOURS: Mon–Sat 10-5	If only inventory were as solid and amusing as Ruth's personality. She's an avid Al Albert's fan. His show was turned on during my second visit. Ruth interrupted her hypnotic reveries to regale me with stories of her granddaughter's 'failed' first T V performance (age 4), and the difficulty of getting a tiny rising star to toe the mark. Thanks, Ruth, for letting me get my big toe in the door. Sorry the reviews were only lukewarm. She wants everyone to know "how **charming** she is." She is.
CLOSED: Holidays	**CONSIGNOR ALERT:** Buys outright, unless it's an expensive item like party dresses or a coat. 50%-50% split. $5 annual fee. No appointment necessary.

St. Vincent de Paul	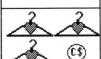

Twin Roads Plaza 17 Clementon Road Berlin, NJ 08009 **609-767-7391**	Lying at the tail end of the ocean's food chain as they do, bottomfeeders must share the same, take-what-comes eating habits and habitat. Subtle and profound differences exist, however. Few look and act alike. With a nod to Gertrude, a Goodwill is not a St. Vincent's is not a Village Thrift. And a St. Vincent's is not always a St. Vincent's.
Look: BOTTOMFEEDER **Goods:** HO HUM– CLASS ACT **Prices:** LOW	Sorrow hovers over the charitable spirit of each and every St. Vincent's I have visited until now. This one is the exception. Located hard by the Berlin Farmers' Market, and with room to breathe between businesses and homes, the climate of charity and tides of donation in these parts agree with our honored Saint. I'm told his mission among the poor began in France, and these shops bearing his name are now worldwide. **First trip?** I found an unused Melitta stovetop coffeemaker for $2, a leather-embossed beige belt with large gold buckle, 50¢, a whimsical Kleenex box-cover disguised as a chintz sofa, throw pillows and all $1, and a new pink, long winter undershirt with lace trim for Morgan, $1.50. **Second trip:** A new Gap, ancient paisley patterned cotton blouse, $1.60, a white stretch skirt, also Gap, $2, and a pair of Italian stretch crossover lace up white snow boots, $3. Well lit and well stocked,
HOURS: Mon–Sat 9-5	with bargains aplenty, it was more like following the warm, planketon- and algae-rich waters of the Gulf Stream than the usual storm-tossed journey, attempting to round the Cape of (Good) Hope (Springs Eternal), and coming up empty handed.
CLOSED: Holidays	**CONSIGNOR ALERT:** Donations only. Tue, Thu, Sat 9:30-3 only.

Trading Places	

200-14 White Horse Rd. Echo Shoppes Voorhees, NJ 08043 **609-772-1237**	As soon as we pulled up in front of the strip mall just down the road from Fudwruckers I was attracted by several sensational looking white polyester outfits hanging in the window. Inside, I asked the owner to bring down the two piece white tunic pantsuit with the white irridescent sequins and beads down from the suction cup that was holding it in place, just out of reach. She obliged. There was that label again:Caron. In the past two weeks, I'd seen it as far away as Downingtown. Brand- new, with original price tags attached, here marked at $80, reduced to $68, but she'd sell it for $60. Turns out, someone recently went out of business and has been hawking the leftover label from here to Jabib.

So it goes in resale. There were a number of garments as good as these, but none better. They exemplified the best this shop had to offer. Great design, but the too-thin fabric was one tier down from Top Drawer A knock off of a knockoff. I asked her to, please and thank you, return it to the window. Second visit? The exact moment I entered, there she was again, taking the outfit out of the window for another customer, who also tried it on and left without buying. (Gosh darn, but didn't I feel like I had just been Trading Places with the other customer.) Hurry, the outfit might still be there.

Look: CLASS ACT **Goods:** STATUS QUO–CLASS ACT **Prices:** MODERATE **HOURS:** Mon–Fri 11-6, Thu 11-8, Sat11–4 **CLOSED:** Summer hours differ. Call ahead.	

CONSIGNOR ALERT: 50%-50% split. $3 fee. 60 days. By appointment only.

Treasures in the Attic	

57 E. Kings Hwy. Audubon, NJ 08106 **609-546-1444**	An ultrafeminine, interconnecting maze of back-room hideways full of the most beautiful, drop-dead dynamite vintage I've ever seen in one place at one time outside of NYC: Stacked navy and white 40's spectacular spectator shoes, a tossed muff or three, a century-spanning wall of hats worthy of a Diana Vreeland caliber retrospective, rosy red velvet wrap coat, fox collar and cuffs, it's pricey, royal-blue counterpart sold only hours before. What woman would ever dream of buying two coats, identical but for color, so long ago? Me, in another life?

Revel in this sensual overload, so extravagant, it threatens to short-circuit your sensibilities. Hearts and flowers, draped chintz and curiosities, reproductions of old-fashioned greeting cards, custom-made, mink-coat teddy bears. Dreamy floral watercolors. Occasional tables holding beautifully useless, absolutely necessary objects. A room full of ever so slightly usual, women's here-and-now, everyday clothing in subtle but noticeable contrast, to **a to-die-for rack of sequined, feathered, tulled, velvet and satin evening wear.** All of it held together by the owner's profoundly personal sense of place and time. Perhaps she lived this era in another lifetime, only to unconsciously but meticuously recapture the experience in this one. (She looks normal.) (But then, so do I.)

Look: TOP DRAWER **Goods:** STATUS QUO–TOP DRAWER **Prices:** LOW–HIGH **HOURS:** Tue–Fri 10-5, Sat 10-4 **CLOSED:** Holidays	

CONSIGNOR ALERT: 50%-50% split. $5 one-time fee. Consigning times vary. Appointment preferred.

 **MANIAC NOTE:** I know this is an empty page. PLEASE **don't** write and tell me. We goofed. So take the lemons and make lemonade, I always say. And use this page for notes.

HAVING FUN?

ARE YOU A MANIAC YET?

WANT TO TURN ONE OF YOUR FRIENDS INTO A MANIAC?

OR DO YOUR HAVE A FRIEND OR RELATIVE WHO IS ALREADY A MANIAC, BUT DOESN'T KNOW ABOUT THE GUIDE?

WOULDN'T WE MAKE A CUTE PRESENT?

Make out a check or money order for **$14.95** (includes thecover price of the book plus shipping and handling.) Send it to:

Thrift Shop Maniac Enterprises
P.O. Box 27540 Philadelphia, PA 19118
Tell us where you want us to send The Guide and we'll do the rest.

OOPS! Page 202

TOUR #13
CHEAP EATS AND CHEAPER DUDS

We had a hard time at first. Jug-handle turns make it tough, median strips make it impossible. Flying by at 50 mph, incomprehensible signs lead to street names, rather than towns. The first New Jersey-intensive day of exploration saw Marvin as driver, me, poring over divergent maps, and Morgan as reluctant back-seat eyewitness to Maniac history in the making. She got to see firsthand, just how crazed grownups can get.

As a former New Jersey resident, truck driver and deliveryman in those good ol' working-himself-through-college days, and possessing a man's spatially inventive mind, we had it that if Marvin were to drive, it would expedite the hide-and-go seek process of locating the next shop and the next. Alas, he was having almost as bad a time as I would have. But because he was willing to endure the stress of driving, it allowed me to have just enough reserve energy to write reviews and play co-pilot. Cellular phone clutched ear-to-shoulder, laptop jiggling on my knees, ranting and raving in rhythm to the keys, screen open to the database, I call ahead to get directions. Some shopkeepers were no better at giving directions than sticking to hours or locations. Others must surely have been perplexed by the relentlessness of a shopper so determined to find them she was willing to make three or four such calls in a matter of minutes. But we were just that lost and just that driven to rack up more New Jersey shops.

If you've grown up around here, it's probably a cinch. I'm convinced residents are encoded at birth with the ability to integrate and translate the peculiar (only to residents of other states) mindset of generations of New Jersey's transportation engineers and highway planners. I worried over how to make these tours comprehensible to non-residents and the spatially challenged, like myself. One rosy dawn I awoke abruptly and sat bolt upright in bed, simultaneously throwing Nibs off my butt, where he had been perched, sleeping. (Morgan wanted a dog. She got a cat. An all black, adolescent Tom. His nickname is longer. It's Niblett.) Startling Sweetpea (the all-white, got-here-first-and-don't-you-forget-it female) into consciousness, I yanked my hair out from under her. I had the answer.

Rather than try to describe innumerable small towns, ebbing and flowing into one another in this tour, I would describe only those with something really special to offer, like Medford, for instance, (Hi!, Medford.) and tie the rest together just the way most New Jersey residents do. By diner. Every small town, every big town, every major intersection, every remaining traffic circle has one of these institutionalized community landmarks along the way. Get lost. Go in. Eat. Call ahead for directions, or ask the waitress (they all thrift shop). Get directions. Get to the next thrift shop. Shop. Get going. Get lost. Go in. Eat. Call or ask the waitress. Get directions. Get it?

Here's the Cheap Eats and Cheaper Duds Diners for Dollars List. This is incomplete, of course. There are almost as many diners as secondhand shops around here. As you tool around, you'll add your own to the list. Let me know.

Homer's, Rte. 30 & 130, Collingswood
Hollybrook Diner, Rte. 38, Mt. Holly
Olga's, Marlton & Medford where Rtes. 73 and 70 converge at the circle
Ponzio's, Ellisburg Circle
Sage, Rte. 73, Marlton
Weber's, White Horse Pike, Audubon & Haddon Heights
Medport, Rt. 70 leading into Medford
Drexel, Drexel Avenue, Rte. 130
Royal Garden, Rte. 73, Marlton
Mt. Laurel Diner, Rte. 73

Merchants of **Merchantville** must once have done very well indeed. Victorian-era houses are huge, surrounded by even bigger lawns. The whipped cream on top of this pie-shaped town center is a large red brick building with white trimmed double bay windows housing **Aunt Charlotte's Chocolates**. Yummie! A Courier Post-recommended cheap-eats award is posted in the window of **The Towne House Restaurant**, just around the corner from Irena's. An old fashioned coffee shop and luncheonette. You know the type--eggs over easy, gossip to go.

Tiny **Medford** has a lot going for it. The **Medford Village Gourmet Coffee Shop** at Union & Main is one of them. Eat in or take out, it's great. Quaintly colonial, with goats grazing in the fields just outside town, only half an hour from Philadelphia. Take the two or three block long post-luncheon sightseeing walk-about worth of precious shops. Work off lunch, then get back to 'work'.

Marlton's surrounding Rte.73 suburban sprawl includes must-see **Zagara's**, a fabulous food emporium. You can eat in, take out, and even buy dinner to go. They have a huge, upscale soup and salad bar, pastries, delicacies, produce, meat, fish, pasta, bread etc. displayed and sparkling like the jewels in Tiffany's window. Don't miss **Border's** bookstore in the same strip mall. They sell The Guide (and a few other titles) to strains of classical music and a whiff of cappuccino. Shop and eat. Shop and...

One of **Pennsauken's** most noteworthy landmarks is the **Mart**, a great, pre-mall sprawling, ramshackle mass of construction right off Rte. 130. On Rte. 70 almost directly across from the Garden State Race Track is a cafeteria style restaurant called **Chow Wagon**. I know, I know...with a name like that...be brave! It's a little dark from low-level lighting and even darker wood paneling, but the food is good, cheap and filling. I could only eat half of my egg salad sandwich on real marbled rye. I took the other half home for Marvin. The cameraman from Channel 3 (Did you ever buy that red shearling coat for you wife at Sophisticated Seconds?) turned me on to the place the Thursday he, Paul Moriarity, his producer, Karen Titlebaum, and I spent out and about taping at Pennsauken Goodwill and Back To The Rack, just down the street. Last minute addition--**Sagami**, a Japanese restaurant, also on Rte. 130, just after Village Thrift (on the same side). We were taken there for dinner by friends Andy and Gary. We had the freshest sushi and sashimi, ever. Great tempura, too! Go. It's touted as the best of its kind in the region. I believe it!

TOUR #13

2	Back to the Rack	Pennsauken
11	B Thrifty II	Medford
5	Debra's Closet	Pennsauken
10	Designer Consignments	Maple Shade
12	Encore	Medford
7	Goodwill	Marlton
1	Goodwill	Pennsauken
4	Irina's Closet	Merchantville
9	Kids Consignments	Marlton
8	Play It Again Sports	Mt. Laurel
6	Sandi's Sellar	Cinnaminson
3	Village Thrift	Pennsauken

*Note: This list has a shop's entire name. Names in review boxes may have been shortened a tad to fit. Numbers before each shop name correspond to their numbered location on each map. **Shops with a star sold Volume II. Volume III? ASK!**

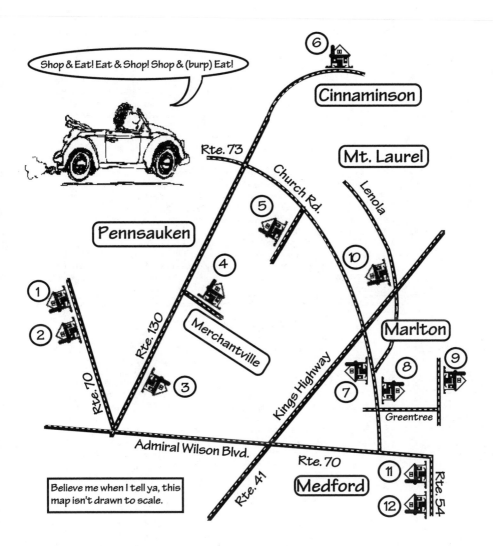

Shop & Eat! Eat & Shop! Shop & (burp) Eat!

6

Cinnaminson

Rte. 73

Church Rd.

Mt. Laurel

Lenola

5

Pennsauken

4

10

Rte. 130

1

Merchantville

2

Marlton

9

8

Kings Highway

7

3

Rte. 70

Greentree

Admiral Wilson Blvd.

Believe me when I tell ya, this map isn't drawn to scale.

Rte. 41

Rte. 70

11

Medford

Rte. 54

12

Back to the Rack	
5245 Route 70 Pennsauken, NJ 08109 **609-488-8070**	Tax time. Basements, attics, closets and garages all over this great land of ours are scrounged and emptied for that one last write-off. The flood of donations threatens to swamp volunteers. Signs on the foor-to-ceiling, greenhouse-effect storefront window implore, beg and cajole donators not to leave bags outside after hours. A teal green Accura and it's 33% estimated-income- bracket-dressed driver, pull up and park. Driver slings the equivalent of one week's worth of upper-income dry cleaning over his arm, walks in, throws his load over the growing pile. Knowing from experience the 'river' will rise every year right around now, two sanguine workers fortify themselves with mozzarella curly fries and gossip while slowly, methodically conquering flood-stage in reverse, unloading trash bags, leaf bags, shopping bags in a turtle race against the rising tide. It may well be April 15 by the time they're done, but they'll win, eventually. There's a predictable rhythm to this river.
Look: HO HUM – STATUS QUO **Goods:** HO HUM – STATUS QUO **Prices:** LOW	There's a rhythm to the store, too. Sort of post-flood-stage. Like when seasonal rains are heavy, water flows over the banks, then receeds, leaving behind natural and manmade debris. First visit? Hangers askew, racks packed, a logjam of furniture blocked customers from shoes, pre-processing donations littered counter-
HOURS: Mon–Sat 10-6, Sun 12-5	tops, a scrawled white poster-board sign listed prices: ties $1, shirts and slacks $3, socks 25¢, sweaters $5, blazers $6, skirts $4. Second visit? You'd never know there'd been a deluge. Order was restored. New clothing, bought to restock after an honest-to-God flood last July, crowded the front. Most secondhand was better, cheaper. I snagged a Le Creuset orange casserole for $2.50 ($120 list, lowest sale
CLOSED: Holidays	price $69), an oval vine basket, $1. Marvin got a fantastic new Ungaro silk tie, $1, and a paperback book he'd been searching for high and low, 25¢. Time and the river... **P.S. This is the place where Paul Moriarity of Channel 3 fame took it ALL OFF.** **CONSIGNOR ALERT:** Donations only. Benefits Jewish Community Center with cosponsor, Caring Hearts, a ministry for children with AIDS.

B Thrifty II	
4 South Main St. Medford, NJ 08055 **609-654-7495**	Yo, Phyllis. While you were chatting on the phone, I did my undercover Maniac thing. It wasn't till we were leaving that Morgan spotted The Guide on the counter. The autographed copy. The one I signed for you and your sidekick the day you came to a book signing. I was sure Morgan would blow it, dancing around like a Mexican jumping bean. Nine year olds can't sustain undercover shopping as
Look: STATUS QUO **Goods:** STATUS QUO **Prices:** LOW– MODERATE	discretely as as (?) year olds. You didn't remember me, but I remembered you. Hi! Here's looking at you. Again! And look I did. At the sweetly intimate shop on Medford's adorable hiccup of a Main Street. **Sweaters, blouses, suits and especially dresses were fairly priced.** Labels included a Talbot khaki dress, straight skirt with kick pleat, belt missing, $28. At that price, buy a new Talbot replacement belt and you're still ahead. A handsome navy, white and gold-trim $30 Jones, two- piece knit caught my eye, but the stain on the front should have been dry cleaned out, the outfit never accepted, or the price lowered by half. A mint-condition Fenwright & Mason V-neck, raspberry, mohair sweater was only $6.
HOURS: Tue–Thu 11-4, Fri & Sat 11-2 **CLOSED:** Mid–June to Mid August.	Winding up the winter season in preparation for their big year end sale, they were getting bags of unsold stuff ready for Animal Welfare, one paw step further down the resale chain. Morgan, managing to keep her cover, walked out with a freebie necklace and a great big grin on her puss. To her child 's mind, purple plastic was as good as gold. Thanks, Phyllis. **CONSIGNOR ALERT: 60% You–40% Shop.** $3 fee. 60 days. 20%/30 days. Tue 11-3 or by appointment. 10 items/visit. Benefit West Jersey Health System.

Debra's Closet

2673
Haddonfield Rd.
Pennsauken, NJ
609-486-9636

Look: CLASS ACT
Goods: STATUS QUO–TOP DRAWER
Prices: MODERATE

HOURS: Mon–Sat 10-5, Sun 12-4

CLOSED: Holidays

Saturday was coming to a close. The day was shutting down. So was this store. With just under an hour left, we frantically zigzagged over the Ben Franklin, up I-95, back over the Betsy Ross, wandered around Pennsauken making four car-phone calls, ("Hello. Yes. We're still lost, but we're getting closer. The road just dead ended. We're in the Pennsauken Mart lot. Do we go left or right?") Tearing into the strip mall lot with 15 minutes left to shop, all this seemed sensible at the time. So exhausted we were laughing and arguing all at once, we raced inside. Marvin knocked 'em dead at the register with stories, while I worked the racks, keeping out of sight.

Secondhand is mixed in with closeouts and overruns like the beautiful, see-through white Bonnie Strauss poet's blouses, only $20 a pop. These little charmers would cost more like $200 at Saks, commanding $29 to $45 at the Saks' outlet. It's left to the imagination what you'd possibly wear underneath. There are three or four other comprable labels in the same design league, like the Dana Buchman jungle-floral jacket and black pants set. Evening wear had possibilities. Jewelry, handbags and most day wear, though, were a different zip code, and it wasn't mine.

Second trip? Morgan and best buddy Nina are usually well behaved, but just for good measure they were WARNED. But irresistible nine-year-old energy overcame them, and for one buoyant moment they began running around. I opened my mouth to nail 'em, only to have the deep in inventory-taking owner beat me to it, pointing to the sign at the register "Misbehaving Children Will Be Sold." What's funny to grown-ups hurt Morgan's child's heart deeply. Nina wanted to know, "Can they do that?" I assure you they didn't hop, skip or jump out the door.

CONSIGNOR ALERT: 50%-50%. $5 fee. 90 days. 20%/30 days. 50% /60 days. Mon-Fri Drop-off .

Designer Consignments

Kingsway Plaza
Kings Hwy & Lenola Rd.
Maple Shade, NJ
08052
609-231-1500

Look: CLASS ACT

Goods: STATUS QUO–TOP DRAWER

Prices: MODERATE –HIGH

HOURS: Mon–Sat 10-6, Wed 10-8

CLOSED: Holidays

Looking like every brother retail team ever to enter the rag trade, well-dressed, well-groomed, they smiled out at me from reams of flyers. Certain this would be a four-hanger, heart-stopping shop, unconscious chauvinism caught up with me. **Kids' was consistent, coherent, right on the money. Some great menswear!** A gorgeous, rust-colored houndstooth, three-button, very hip Valentino, paisley-lined sports coat at $75 was stashed among one-too-many filler suits. A two-piece, black linen, $75 Sue Baseman suit, representing the best of many excellent woman's consignments here, was rubbing shoulders with flash-and-trash vinyls, fringe, and rhinestones on look-at-me butt-and-bust stretch fabrics in too-hot-to-touch colors.

Magnificent evening gowns were sandwiched between random, hallucenogenic (on its way to being phased out?) vintage, like the lime green two-piece, angel-wing pleated sleeves and pantlegs all a flutter, its empire bodice outlined in rhinestones, all yours for $38. Still there, second visit, this time its grey ticket meant it was marked down by half. Enough arch 70's vintage to stock a rampagingly hip (too hot for the burbs?) mini boutique within this otherwise traditional resale. Here's my mixed message: Marketing, organizational skills and many garments are a clear four. But up-and-down prices, quality and mixed-message consignments startle and confuse. Two, maybe even three, shops are trying to coexist as one. Cut the Siamese twin loose. Separate out the fashion signals, please.
P.S. They rent evening wear and wedding gowns.

CONSIGNOR ALERT: 50%-50% split. $12 fee. 120 days. By appointment.

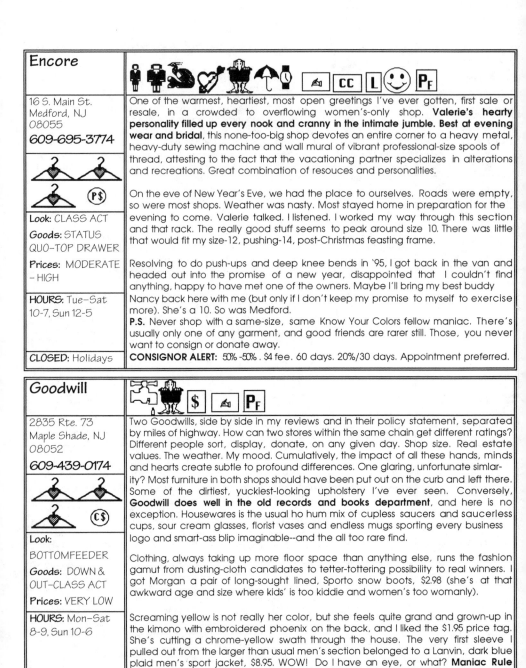

Encore

16 S. Main St.
Medford, NJ
08055
609-695-3774

(P$)

Look: CLASS ACT

Goods: STATUS QUO–TOP DRAWER

Prices: MODERATE – HIGH

HOURS: Tue–Sat 10-7, Sun 12-5

CLOSED: Holidays

One of the warmest, heartiest, most open greetings I've ever gotten, first sale or resale, in a crowded to overflowing women's-only shop. **Valerie's hearty personality filled up every nook and cranny in the intimate jumble. Best at evening wear and bridal,** this none-too-big shop devotes an entire corner to a heavy metal, heavy-duty sewing machine and wall mural of vibrant professional-size spools of thread, attesting to the fact that the vacationing partner specializes in alterations and recreations. Great combination of resouces and personalities.

On the eve of New Year's Eve, we had the place to ourselves. Roads were empty, so were most shops. Weather was nasty. Most stayed home in preparation for the evening to come. Valerie talked. I listened. I worked my way through this section and that rack. The really good stuff seems to peak around size 10. There was little that would fit my size-12, pushing-14, post-Christmas feasting frame.

Resolving to do push-ups and deep knee bends in '95, I got back in the van and headed out into the promise of a new year, disappointed that I couldn't find anything, happy to have met one of the owners. Maybe I'll bring my best buddy Nancy back here with me (but only if I don't keep my promise to myself to exercise more). She's a 10. So was Medford.

P.S. Never shop with a same-size, same Know Your Colors fellow maniac. There's usually only one of any garment, and good friends are rarer still. Those, you never want to consign or donate away.

CONSIGNOR ALERT: 50% -50% . $4 fee. 60 days. 20%/30 days. Appointment preferred.

Goodwill

2835 Rte. 73
Maple Shade, NJ
08052
609-439-0174

(C$)

Look:

BOTTOMFEEDER

Goods: DOWN & OUT–CLASS ACT

Prices: VERY LOW

HOURS: Mon–Sat 8-9, Sun 10-6

CLOSED: Holidays

Two Goodwills, side by side in my reviews and in their policy statement, separated by miles of highway. How can two stores within the same chain get different ratings? Different people sort, display, donate, on any given day. Shop size. Real estate values. The weather. My mood. Cumulatively, the impact of all these hands, minds and hearts create subtle to profound differences. One glaring, unfortunate similarity? Most furniture in both shops should have been put out on the curb and left there. Some of the dirtiest, yuckiest-looking upholstery I've ever seen. Conversely, **Goodwill does well in the old records and books department,** and here is no exception. Housewares is the usual ho hum mix of cupless saucers and saucerless cups, sour cream glasses, florist vases and endless mugs sporting every business logo and smart-ass blip imaginable--and the all too rare find.

Clothing, always taking up more floor space than anything else, runs the fashion gamut from dusting-cloth candidates to tetter-tottering possibility to real winners. I got Morgan a pair of long-sought lined, Sporto snow boots, $2.98 (she's at that awkward age and size where kids' is too kiddie and women's too womanly).

Screaming yellow is not really her color, but she feels quite grand and grown-up in the kimono with embroidered phoenix on the back, and I liked the $1.95 price tag. She's cutting a chrome-yellow swath through the house. The very first sleeve I pulled out from the larger than usual men's section belonged to a Lanvin, dark blue plaid men's sport jacket, $8.95. WOW! Do I have an eye, or what? **Maniac Rule #10,001: Use your EYES MORE, and your HANDS AND ARMS LESS. This way you'll have the stamina for the next Goodwill, and the next, and the next.**

CONSIGNOR ALERT: Donations only.

Goodwill

5461 Rt. 70
Pennsauken, NJ
08109

609-486-0300

Look: UPSCALE
BOTTOMFEEDER
Goods: HO HUM–
CLASS ACT
Prices: VERY LOW

HOURS: Mon–Sat
8-9, Sun 10-6

CLOSED: Holidays

Early hacienda school of architecture. Cream-colored stucco, red tile roof. Could be a huge fast-food Mexican restaurant. But it isn't. **It's state-of-the-art Goodwill.** Five dressing rooms big, with processing and storage bigger than most shops. No price tags stuck on with hole-rending staples; rather, pricing signs hang over women's dresses, children's sleepwear, etc. Helpful in this vast space. Amenities included shopping carts and baskets, extra parking behind the shop, and a half-hearted attempt at window display (Mother Russia school of design?). Lighting was excellent. The only negative? Bottomfeeder overkill. They overprice anything even remotely upscale. Stuff on the rack by the register set aside for such a purpose was a cruel hoax. Price can't transform streetwalker or Halloween-caliber goods into a Bill Blass or an Anne Klein. Price does not a lady (or a gent) make.

Most stuff was cheaper than cheap. I got three cotton play tops for $3.87. Another day I handed over $2.89 and left with an as-yet-unread Caldecott Award book; a pair of girl's size 10, Penny's, pink winter P.J.'s, unworn, and one grl's all cotton, purple, size 10, play dress, manufacturer's sample tag still attached. People were hanging out in the aisles, swapping shopping tips. Men's department was big and crowded with guys doing their early Saturday morning thing. I hated to leave. So I came back again. **Former Miss America, Susan Powell, and I taped one of three shows for Discovery Channel's _Home Matters_.** I called it Transcendental Thrift. Perfect in pink but boring $2.98 prom gown tossed over a rickety, $1.98, fit-for-the kindling wooden stool, et voila, transformed by the mere wave of a staple gun into a $225 boudoir bench. Eat your heart out, Bombay & Co. Third time? **Paul Moriarity, Channel 3, got a week's worth of $50 duds here with me for his 11o'clock TAKE IT ALL OFF.** Back at the station, they can't believe how great he looks DRESSED.

CONSIGNOR ALERT: Donations only.

Irina's Closet

19 W. Park Ave.
Merchantville, NJ
08109

609-488-5866

Look: CLASS ACT
Goods: STATUS
QUO-TOP DRAWER
Prices: MODERATE

HOURS:
Mon–Sat 11-6,
Fri till 8

CLOSED: Holidays

Deep in tete-a-tete, heads together, cross-pollinating cultures. The seated customer thoroughly American from her accent and attitudes right down to her shoe leather. The shopkeeper, hair piled high, hand on her model-slim hip, elegantly European. Up-to-the-minute opinions on all things American, filtered through a charming accent as thick as the snow of a Russian winter. Baubles and bangles glittered like icicles against the hard surface of the large rectangular mirror hanging behind Irena's desk. A prettily profuse display of pins was mounted on fabric under a white fur cape. Pocketbooks, one after another, hung from an extended wall display, just so. (She was a mechanical engineer in her homeland.) Not surprisingly **I felt as if I were standing in the midst of a petite, European, jewel-encrusted boutique.** Displayed center stage was a circular rack just for women up to size 20. Half the shop had standard-issues labels chosen for their unique flair. More glamorous, name-dropping labels had class, quality and flair.

Labels read like a Who's Who of commercially accessible, successful designers: Vittadini, Ann Taylor, Bill Blass, Krizia, Jenny, Laura Biagiotti, Danny Noble, Tapemeasure, Diane Gillman, Perry Ellis, Kikit, Kenar, Claudez, Shelli Segal, Tahari, and Eileen West. Kids' clothes, their twelve-foot-long rack curiously mounted on the wall at grown-up height, range from infant up to size 12, with labels like Rothchild and Knitwaves.

CONSIGNOR ALERT: Negotiable split. $3 lifetime fee. 60 days. By appointment only.

Kids Consignments	 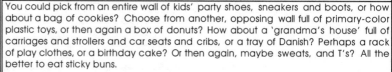
Greentree & Church Rds. Marlton, NJ 08053 **609-596-6139**	You could pick from an entire wall of kids' party shoes, sneakers and boots, or how about a bag of cookies? Choose from another, opposing wall full of primary-color plastic toys, or then again a box of donuts? How about a 'grandma's house' full of carriages and strollers and car seats and cribs, or a tray of Danish? Perhaps a rack of play clothes, or a birthday cake? Or then again, maybe sweats, and T's? All the better to eat sticky buns.
	That's what happened to us. This kids'-only shop is in a strip mall two or three red lights off busy, busy, busy Rt. 73, right next-door to Randolph's Bakery. (Greentree Road is at the Ultra Market.) But why choose one or the other? Both had **plenty of colorful treats.** As I prowled the racks, Marvin, Morgan and her friend Nina prowled the bakery, noses hungrily pressed against the glass display cases. I darted greedily back and forth between the two stores, snarfing down a tasty treat from one, scouting secondhand treats in the other, all the while secretly talking into my hand-held tape recorder, undetected, trying to outdo the blasting radio. The clerk (owner?) stood in the back by the register, making it impossible for her to meet and greet. It also flys in the face of current anti-shoplifter security wisdom to be located so far in the rear behind all those racks. All the better to be positioned by the front door...all the better to see us. As it was, all the better to 'eat' emboldened by the forest of racks between us.
Look: CLASS ACT **Goods:** STATUS QUO **Prices:** LOW	
HOURS: Tue, Fri & Sat 10-5, Wed 10-6, Thu 10-7, Sun 10-3	
CLOSED: Holidays & Sundays in summer	**P.S.** Ask about their Rent-a-Stork service. **CONSIGNOR ALERT:** 50%-50% split. $4 fee. 90 days. By appointment only.

Play It Again Sports	
Ellipse Shopping Ctr 4201 Church Road Mt. Laurel, NJ 08054 **609-235-2573**	**This is one location in a large and growing chain offering very attractive new and used sporting equipment.** Seasonally weighted to ice hockey and ice skates and all things winter, golf clubs and balls sold in egg cartons by the dozen, while basketballs and tennis benched on the sidelines, patiently await their turn of seasons. A lineup of weight-lifting equipment and going nowher- in-place, indoor electronic track equipment could tide you over till spring.
	The young man at the counter, optimistially wearing a navy blue baseball cap, was was friendly, happy to help, big enough and sturdy enough to know firsthand any sport except maybe gymnastics.
Look: TOP DRAWER **Goods:** STATUS QUO–TOP DRAWER **Prices:** LOW–HIGH	
HOURS: Mon–Fri 11-8, Sat 10-6, Sun 11-5	
CLOSED: Holidays	**CONSIGNOR ALERT:** Buys outright, consigns, trades.

Sandi's Sellar

2110 Church Rd.
Cinnaminson, NJ
08077

609 786-7562

Look: CLASS ACT

Goods: STATUS QUO–CLASS ACT

Prices: LOW–MODERATE

HOURS: Mon–Fri 10-5:30, Sat 10-6, Sun 12-4

CLOSED. Holidays

A merry punster housed in an under-lit, over-decorated basement. Screaming magenta and riveting blue in sharp juxtaposition to delicate vining garlands and dried floral wreaths. Tattoos and toddlers. Leather and lace. Rhinestones and chintz. In what could have been a popular location for an oh-so-discreet, there-goes-the-neighborhood adult book & video shop, it is instead a hard-to-find secondhand shop, nestled behind a shopping mall, just off very busy Rte.130.

Duck under the overhang and follow the downward-curving steps. The front door opens directly into the infants' and toddlers' section, which takes up a large percentage of the floor space. **Nice, inexpensive stuff.** Back in the rear of the shop, where women's clothing is kept, it was so dark I could not determine color on some of the is-it-navy? or is-it-black? garments. Beyond unusual, hand-sequined and beaded sunglasses were reduced to $15. They weren't selling, but I liked them. There was lots of costume jewelry that I didn't like.

All of this accessory merchandise is located in a peculiar can-I-go-back-there-or-can't-I? area behind the register. You may. The shop is as clean and organized as it is decorated. Sandi really wants to succeed, you can tell. There are good ideas and intentions here, even some good merchandise.

CONSIGNOR ALERT: 50%-50% split. $3 annual fee. 20%/30 days. Before noon, call for an appointment. Nothing accepted after 5:30. Appointment preferred.

Village Thrift

Airport Circle
Pennsauken, NJ
(no phone)

Look: BOTTOM FEEDER

Goods: DOWN & OUT to TOP DRAWER

Prices: LOW

HOURS: Mon–Sat 9-9, Sun 10-6

CLOSED. Holidays

Huge, huge, huge. One of my favorite bottomfeeders. But don't get smug. There's always a new thrift store just around the corner or ready to open up down the street. And some of the cashiers here have a capital A for ATTITUDE...them against us.

Outside the front door, a posted sign states:

> **NO FOOD**
> **NO DRINK**
> **NO FLEAS**

All 33,000 square feet are swept, waxed and polished. The floor gleams. The paint job is new. The lofty, high-tech, warehouse-style ceiling arches over an enormous inventory, made easy to shop by the equally enormous suspended signs directing you to BOYS, GIRLS, MENS, etc.

Twenty workers, minimum wage all, and eating a steady diet of Kentucky Fried, unload, sort, price, distribute. A hot dog vendor has positioned himself and his umbrella-shaded cart outside on the sidewalk. There are enough customers and employees to keep him in business. Village Thrift is a magnetic financial anchor for right-in-their-own-backyard Camden community.

P.S. Mondays, seniors 10% off.

CONSIGNOR ALERT: Donations Only.

TOUR #14
SEEK AND YE SHALL FIND DOWN BY THE RIVERSIDE.

Author-turned-delivery-driver, I gleefully slung another box or six in the back of the van, getting ready to make yet another book drop to my super-duper-best-ever-without-whom-the-TSMG-wouldn't-be-the-local-best-seller-it-is-today, capital D for Distributor. Grumbling down Cottman Avenue through stop-and-go traffic, crawling through the Greater Northeast shopping corridor, dashing over the Tacony, burning rubber up the ramp to Rte. 130 had became a regular, wheel-gripping run.

Arriving at the loading docks, I'd line up the family van and wait my turn for a bay, surrounded by 18-wheelers. This of course, caused no small amount of merriment among the workmen loading and unloading boxes of books by the thousands. I could almost hear them wondering: "Just what is this middle-aged woman DOING here?" After a half dozen reenactments, they began to take me for granted. I thought I saw a supportive twinkle or two in the eyes of the women in receiving. All this because you guys had stripped the bookstore shelves bare again. Thank you, devoted (and pissed off) readers. Mission completed, I wandered up and down the Jersey side of the river, searching for more you-know-what shops, sometimes finding more than I expected.

River Road is a good bet. Probably an animal track adopted by Indians, deepened and widened by settlers' horses, herds and wagons, paralleled by railroad tracks, the ol' 'if it ain't broke, don't fix it' mentality was at work. Referred to today as Rte. 543, this highly evolved footpath links Palmyra, Riverton, and Riverside, one small historic town after another, as it courses north along the Delaware to Burlington.

Palmyra almost lies under the struts of the Tacony Palmyra Bridge. Just who was this Palmyra dude? Or Tacony, for that matter? Palmyra the town is a sprawling collection of small clapboard, brick and siding bungalows with contrasting oversized vehicles, one to a block if not one to a driveway. One such homeowner had two stretch limos parked, side by side, sporting for-sale signs in the windshields. Only blocks away, a weekend camper loomed large. In a third stood the rusting hulk of an early-model red cement mixer. Some yards had that authentic backwoods of West Virginia look with more randomly discarded appliances and cars than shrubs, others were so well-manicured that weeds wouldn't dare. Industrial strength railroad tracks slice through the heart of town, creating an inescapable esthetic. People certainly thrift around here, but where do they eat out? I tried the local Chinese takeout. Don't.

Riverton isn't here, unless you know where to look. I stumbled upon it following my intuitive nose for news. Searching for authentic local flavors and color, I've taken to driving around communities, seeing what there is to see, tasting what there is to taste, reading local newspapers and real estate guides, then reporting back to you in these tours. There were three previous, uneventful visits to what I thought had been Riverton, which is to say, the crossroads of River Road and Howard Street. What made this day different? Why did I suddenly choose to follow the unassuming road past the tightly knit cluster of attractive, but equally unassuming houses? "Just one more block" went The Voice (Shopper Lady, again). "Just see what happens." Of course, when I get this tickling whisper in my ear, it's never 'just' anything.

Suddenly the vistas (if not the heavens) opened up. Lawns spread wide. Houses were graciously set back from the road, placed an equally discreet distance apart, each with its own amazing architectural story to tell. Shade trees and shrubs adorned and sheltered. I drove on. Way too soon, I came to the end of the road and what appeared to be the end of story. Turns out that was only the first chapter. The Riverton Yacht Club straddles a small Victorian-era landing, the only man-made interruption to the breathtaking natural view. Wintertime, there were no boats moored, no people about. Patient and proud, the Delaware flowed by. Time collapsed. Suddenly, I was the deer at the water's edge. I was the Indian stalking the deer. I was the Quaker settler, swapping goods for land. I was the transplanted railroad employee. Standing there, mind's eye a wide-angle lens, arms outstretched, reaching for the sky, I tried to take it all in, to be a part of the eternal beauty of it all. And for one brief moment, I was. I hadn't been looking for IT. I don't go around searching for IT. But sometimes IT just knocks me over the head and says, LOOK. HERE I AM.

Back on the road. Back to 'work'. Contemporary colonial-era river communities, both with handsome Quaker meeting houses, **Burlington** today is substantially larger and slightly more prosperous than sister city **Bristol**, lying only a Washington's stone throw across the Delaware. or a Maniac's hop skip and jump to twin city thrifting. Mill, the main street running through downtown Bristol has more shops than Saturday afternoon shoppers. They're all over at Caldor's, only a few blocks away, leaving us Maniac's with plenty of elbow room to park, shop and eat. Which of course leads us to...**Just Desserts Ice Cream Shoppe** down the street from Finders Keepers in Bristol, for the best lime (or orange) rickey, ever (according to Marvin and Morgan). Me? I prefer black and white ice cream sodas, heavy on the chocolate syrup, please and thank you.

Take Church Road, which runs from Palmyra right through **Cinnaminson**, which in turn appears to be nothing more than a mercantile crossroads and series of parking lots, cut in two by busy, busy, busy Rte. 130 and the usual discombobulation of traffic islands and concrete highway divides and jug handles. It left me ga ga. So did the scene in the parking lot outside the Acme. I'd stopped to pick up something for dinner. When I came back out I found my van sandwiched between two completely different cars than when I had gone inside. On one side of me sat a turquoise & white RV with a mural of Indians painted on the side. On the other? A red Mercury Cougar with an enormous French poodle sitting in the driver's seat, wearing a rhinestone collar. That about sums it up.

Moorestown is a place where I could live out my old age. For one thing it's built on a human scale, with a walk-about, Hi! How are Ya? town center. A banner stretching across Main Street announces the Citizen of the Year Award and Dinner. The good townspeople have sensibly placed the requisite hulking water tower way out on the edge of town so it won't spoil the picture-postcard perfect setting. Enormous shade trees spread their sheltering expanse over dappled green lawns, manicured one blade at a time. A huge, over-landscaped, white-columned brick bank, a private Friends school with tombstones protruding from the earth like so many evenly spaced cobbled stepping stones, ever so gently sweep away all notion of time. I'm beginning to understand just how important a role Quakers played in founding and settling our region. Another point in its favor? There's a supermarket I could drag on over to on foot. (Maybe even send Morgan over with the list. Hmmm. That has real possibilities.) I'm getting tired of being the family hunter-gatherer, van-schlepping all the time. One final inducement? There's a **great pizza joint** in town on Main Street. Crisp crust. Tangy tomato. Pillow-soft REAL mozzarella. Try it. You'll like it.

TOUR #14

14	Children's Home	Mt. Holly
6	Finders Keepers	Bristol (PA)
9	Flora's First Choice	Burlington
3	Furniture Resale Outlet	Riverton
1	The Happy Hanger	Palmyra
10	Moorestown Friends	Moorestown
12	Neat Repeats	Mt. Laurel
4	New to You	Willingboro
11	Nifty Thrifties	Moorestown
13	Resale Rack	Mt. Holly
8	Room to Grow ★	Burlington
5	Second Chance	Bristol (PA)
7	Wilhelmina Country Collections	Tullytown (PA)
2	Women's Association Thrift Shop	Riverton

*Note: This list has a shop's entire name. Names in review boxes may have been shortened a tad to fit. Numbers before each shop name correspond to their numbered location on each map. **Shops with a star sold Volume II. Volume III? ASK!**

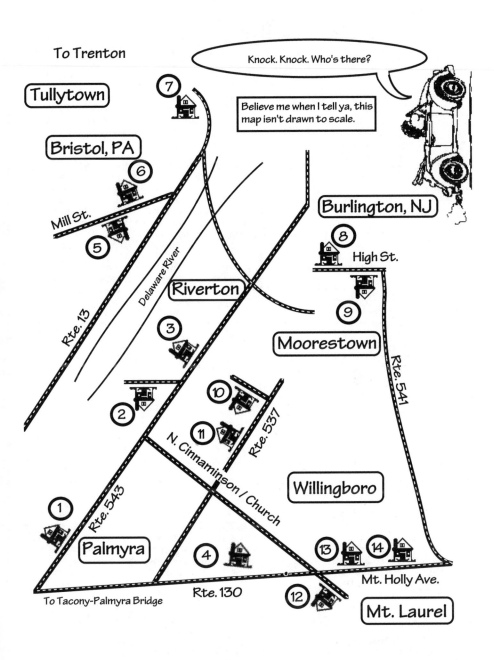

To Trenton

Knock. Knock. Who's there?

Tullytown

Bristol, PA

Believe me when I tell ya, this map isn't drawn to scale.

Mill St.

Burlington, NJ

High St.

Delaware River

Rte. 13

Riverton

Moorestown

Rte. 541

Rte. 537

N. Cinnaminson / Church

Willingboro

Rte. 543

Palmyra

Rte. 130

Mt. Holly Ave.

To Tacony-Palmyra Bridge

Mt. Laurel

TOUR #14 MAP Page 216

Children's Home	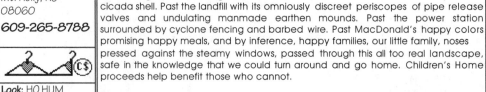
1725-B Hwy 38 Mt. Holly, NJ 08060 **609-265-8788**	Past the armored car fresh with its annually applied, heavy handed layer of camouflage paint, looking for all the world like an end of summer, nobody home, cicada shell. Past the landfill with its omniously discreet periscopes of pipe release valves and undulating manmade earthen mounds. Past the power station surrounded by cyclone fencing and barbed wire. Past MacDonald's happy colors promising happy meals, and by inference, happy families, our little family, noses pressed against the steamy windows, passed through this all too real landscape, safe in the knowledge that we could turn around and go home. Children's Home proceeds help benefit those who cannot.
Look: HO HUM **Goods:** DOWN & OUT–STATUS QUO **Prices:** LOW	Cutting a deal for a lower than low, watch the bottom line rent, Children's Home has chosen a prosperity free zone directly across from a prosperous shopping mall. Saturday, New Years Eve, the parking lot here is just as full as the mall. Young families mingle with retired people, tackling the racks and bins, looking to get lucky. Most looked like luck had taken a detour around their lives. So did the clothing. Lone wolf types prowled the **library size secondhand book selection,** reading, browsing, carting armloads. At 25¢ for individual paperbacks (10/$1.00) to 50¢ each for hardbacks (4/$1.00), so would I. But I never have the time to ready anymore, only write.
HOURS: Everyday 9-3:30, Sat 9-4	One little boy, brown eyes huge and appealing, lugged around a pair of roller skates half as big as he was. He really really wanted those skates. His mother hadn't yet given him a yes or no. Ophra's Random Act's of Kindness show fresh in my memory, I asked, "would you let me buy the skates for you? It would make me feel good." His eyes even bigger, he didn't say a word, but shook his head, yes. With his mother's permission, I handed over the $2.50. And yes, I did feel much better.
CLOSED: Holidays	**CONSIGNOR ALERT:** Donations only. Benefits Children's Home.

Finders Keepers	
401 Mill St. Bristol, PA 19007 **785-5678**	Losers weepers... Bristol is a small town holding on by its fingernails. The sign from the previous shop has been removed, leaving behind pock marks. Finders Keepers' facade looks like its been strafed. Wind-ravaged pennants are strung from pillar to post in a tattered attempt to attract the shopper's eye. I wish I had not looked. Inside, store length walls host built-in shelves displaying 'cheapo profundo' new bargain-basement household, low-end sidewalk vendor quality jewelry, sweatshirts and toys from Taiwan. His inventory of 10,000+ albums are what's "paying the rent these days."
Look: HO HUM **Goods:** DOWN & OUT – STATUS QUO **Prices:** LOW	Second-hand is limited to furniture. Most of it I would be embarrassed to put out in front of my home on trash day. Last year? There was one handsome pine dining room table from the 50's with lines etched into the wood, creating a box pattern. It was really nice at $45. There were no matching chairs, but maybe the next store over the horizon would have them, or as the shopkeeper suggests on the sign taped to the table top, it could be used as a drafting or conference table. This year? NaDa.
HOURS: Mon–Sat 10-5	**P.S.** Collect Antique radios and phonographs? Go to The Place on Pond St.
CLOSED: Holidays	**CONSIGNOR ALERT:** Buys outright only. Will come and appraise items.

Flora's First Choice

314 High St.
Burlington, N.J.
08016

609-386-9854

Look: HO HUM –
STATUS QUO

Goods: HO HUM–
STATUS QUO

Prices: LOW

HOURS: Mon, Tue,
Thu 10:30-5,
Fri 10:30-7, Sat 11-4

CLOSED: July &
August

A torn, dirty beige, bowling ball cover with its companion ball, color unknown, was jammed into the crevice between the metal door frame and the sloping concrete entranceway, propping open the front door to Flora's First Choice. Now that's what I'd call a use-what-you've-got-at-hand doorstop. It's also an eye-catching grand entrance. (3rd Edition? Bowling ball gone, replaced by a sensible shim. Rats!)

Burlington was midway through its annual street fair. The shop, at the epicenter of the day's activities, throbbed. Organized chaos reigned supreme, as did Flora. In regal secondhand splendor, she sat elbow-propped behind her workspace, eating lunch, issuing edicts, holding forth. Her steely eyes never missed a trick or a customer

Size-wise, children's picks up where Room To Grow, across the street, leaves off. **Racks were packed with inexpensive goodies.** Women's and men's garments lag slightly behind children's in quality, if not quantity. Although there was a fabulous charcoal gray men's overcoat, never worn, half cashmere, half wool, $85.00. A local couple delved among hangers, a free arm stretched over the top of the visor-height racks now and again, exchanging thumbs up, thumbs down. Excited by their discoveries, eyes flashing, they seemed inclined to choose "life over death."

Strewn hapazard around the room, under racks, behind racks, in unsorted boxes on the floor and in the large, almost inaccesible, double bay window are household items, books, shoes. Only God, Flora, and the insatiably curious know for certain what lurks beneath, behind, around and among. Roll up your sleeves and get busy.

CONSIGNOR ALERT: 50%-50% split. $3 annual fee. 60 days. Appointment preferred.

Furniture Resale Outlet

523 Howard St.
Riverton, NJ
08077

609-829-3300

Look: CLASS ACT

Goods: STATUS
QUO–TOP DRAWER

Prices: LOW–
MODERATE

HOURS: Mon–Sat
10-4, Thu 10-8

CLOSED: Holidays

"I never go into downtown Palmyra" said Harvey Katinsky, T. This became the Maniac's shopkeeper-quote-of-the-week. Riverton is all of 8 blocks away, a walking distance I would easily have doubled or tripled in one day's errands when we lived in Center City. And if Palmyra has a downtown in the way I understand the notion of downtown, I missed it. Just please, don't try to tell me Riverton has a downtown.

Probably because he's located in such a sleepy afterthought of a community, tucked away almost underneath the struts of the Tacony-Palmyra bridge, the owner here charges **relatively modest prices for family heirlooms**, less than he does for the secondhand 'new' stuff. Around here, "buying up" means ditching your six-piece solid, banded Deco mahogany bedroom set in the family lo these 70 years, for some compressed particle board in authentic wood laminate. Now it's on display here for $1,545, or about the same cost as its laminated counterpart at some cheesy but new furniture store. A walnut buffet fetched $350. A dark oak server/tea cart, $90. In the market for an electric wheelchair? It's yours for $800. A more contemporary, less significant eight-piece dining room set, ticketed at $1250.

The average-sized front room, which holds the better pieces, leads to a bottleneck passageway, which in turn opens up to reveal an enormous **warehouse in the rear** of the shop, **chock-full of the interesting and unusual in varying and altered states.**

CONSIGNOR ALERT: Buys outright. Delivery available.

The Happy Hanger 529 Cinnaminson Av. Palmyra, NJ 08065 **609-829-2121** **Look:** STATUS QUO **Goods:** STATUS QUO–TOP DRAWER **Prices:** LOW–HIGH **HOURS:** Mon–Fri 10-6, Sat 10-5 **CLOSED:** July	**LAST YEAR:** Seeing the boarded-up, abandoned house that shares the litter-strewn block with The Happy Hanger, we reluctantly got out of the car. Pulling open the rickety door, we walked inside to peeling paint, crowded racks and Tobi, the owner. Tobi's bright red hair and lips were as strong as her personality. She kept us there long enough to find out first impressions can be misleading. There was the neighborhood and the shop. Then there wasTobi and the merchandise . **THIS YEAR:** Tobi's up and moved to the condo in Florida, having sold her business to a young woman from New York who works in criminal justice. Her Aunt Sally, a Tobi regular, wanted to buy the shop. Sally's dream, backed by her niece's dough-re-mi is now reality. She acquires excellent one-of-a-kind garments from New York boutiques. She hopes to keep and nurture Tobi's customer list of high-profile shopaholics who seasonally closet weed languishing garments that no longer tickle their fancy. Dangling three figure original price tags, the gorgeous $30 (down from $45) Gillian navy crepe, three crossover spaghetti straps to a shoulder palazzo pants, and $89 (down from $99) Tom & Linda Platt pink sheath with shoulder hugging satin buttons and trim, prove once again, **that secondhand doesn't always mean pre-worn, no matter how many 'hands' it's passed through.** **LAST YEAR:** I told Tobi: sweep and paint the place, fix up the dressing room, get rid of 60% of the stuff and your store would rate 3 1/2 hangers. Palmyra: Sweep the sidewalks, find a tenant for the house next-door, and you'd go from a 2 1/2 to 3 hanger town. **THIS YEAR:** Sally, did just that. Here's your 3 1/2. Palmyra? Your turn. **CONSIGNOR ALERT:** 50-50% split. $2 annual fee. By appointment only.
Moorestown Friends  113 E. Main St. Moorestown, NJ 08057 **609-234-1567** **Look:** STATUS QUO **Goods:** HO HUM–CLASS ACT **Prices:** UP & DOWN **HOURS:** Tue–Sat 10-3 **CLOSED:** Saturdays in summer	First visit? A whole lineup of excellent small furniture skirted the parking lot. Second, third, and fourth visits? Some days inventory was better than others. Fifth visit? The fan I would have bought was sold; a small hutch was overpriced at $350. Furniture, when they have it, and **very good housewares**, which gratefully they never seem to run out of, are usually better than clothing. Although some days **women's is great!** A size-14 red corduroy with Christmassy cording and dropped waist, a Leslie Fay black two piece knit with white satin shawl-collar trimmed in pearls, each $20. A Limited black leather quilted bomber jacket with a busted zipper, again only $20. Go ahead, buy it. Even with tailoring fees it will still cost way less than brand-new. Tiny, the shop has more work/storage space than selling floor. Foor-to-ceiling, space-saving bins are what got me. I know, I know. You guys probably thought this was a great way to organize/display **(clean)** fold-up clothing dontions. Made me grumpy, sorting through all those beige Rubbermaid baskets. Made me think of all the **(dirty)** laundry waiting for me at home. T'was all so rumpled and unappealing, baskets hard to reach/balance. I know, I know, you fold, customers unfold. **P.S.** Sign is pale, low to the ground, easy to miss. **Miss the shop's driveway? Use the needlework store's drive. They share the same lot.** **P.P.S.** Relocating in Moorestown area before end of 1995. **CONSIGNOR ALERT:** Donations only.

Neat Repeats

Academy & Church Mt. Laurel, NJ 08054 **609-866-5680** **Look:** CLASS ACT **Goods:** STATUS QUO –CLASS ACT **Prices:** LOW–MODERATE **HOURS:** Tue– Fri 10-6, Thu 10-7, Sat 10-5	A friendly shopkeeper in nearby Moorestown turned me on to Neat Repeats. Last year the owner was commiserating with a regular that "it takes a lot of work to run a resale shop." That it does. Ann, **the very friendly owner of this roomy, clean, well-lit space in a fairly new, out-of-the-way suburban strip mall**, obligingly tried to steam out marks in an Anne Klein II red silk blouse for me. Marked down to $7.50 from $15 two months, it would have been a very good bargain indeed. Alas, alak, the boo-boos wouldn't come out. A second Anne Klein blouse, this time $7, tempted. Its hanger bumping neighbor, an originally less expensive label, was $12. Why? Other anomalies: Great selection of shoes, evening wear, and larger women sizes, but the all too prevalent swing from polyester flash to ho-hum woolens, crowding out an occasional quality label at fair prices, kept this store a good, solid three. One year later, as I silently undercover shopped with my ever-talkative husband, the owner was commiserating once again. This time with me! "Why," she wondered, "had the woman who had written the thrift shop book given her only three hangers, when the write-up had been four-hanger favorable?" After we left she must've put the pieces of Marvin's all too knowledgeable intervention together, as she called us up the very next day, New Year's, to ask what she could do to go from a three to a four. Taking the position that I cannot ethically review a shop and then turn around and consult to the owner (couldn't a review be considered a free mini-consultation?), I handed the phone over to Marvin, my loquatious sidekick, who just happens to be a real life business consultant. He advised. "Go ask your customers what would make them happier." Satisfied with the answer, she hung up to go do just that. Not every shopkeeper wants or needs to be a four. And not every customer wants to shop or can afford a four. And the resale world would be a boring place if everything were perfect, and perfectly the same.
CLOSED: Holidays	**CONSIGNOR ALERT:** 50%-50% split. 10 items/person in the store at any time. No fee. 60 days, 20%/30 days, 50%/60 days. By appointment only.

New to You

2363 Rt. 130N Willingboro, NJ 08046 **609-877-5575** **Look:** STATUS QUO **Goods:** HO HUM–STATUS QUO **Prices:** VERY LOW **HOURS:** Tue–Thu, Fri 10-5, Wed 1-5, Sat 11-5	Seven brand-new, blue work shirts all monogrammed with the name Mark, all priced at $2.50, lined up waiting for seven Marks to stumble into this find and snap them up, or seven men with a secondhand sense of humor. Other than these seven shirts for seven servicemen, the only other buy was the $4 pair of brand-new pink and white saddle shoes for Morgan. I didn't and probably never will, find anything here .I guess I have a different style of humor. Marvin sat outside and entered data in his Mac Powerbook–Duo laptop- new toy of choice. It's not a requirement in his maniac job description to come in, and he has shopped with me enough to know not to bother with this one. He could tell by the outside of this aging, set-aside mall with its long-abandoned, cracked concrete under the entranceway fish tank just what we were in for. It's small and cramped with worn Value City-type stuff. If you love Elvis, polyester and Velveeta cheese, this will fit your lifestyle profile. **The salesperson at the register was kind and helful.** Morgan wore the shoes every day. **Mark** , are you reading this? Are you out there?
CLOSED: Holidays	**CONSIGNOR ALERT:** 50%-50% split. No fee. 42 days. No appointment necesary.

Nifty Thrifties	
67 East Main St. Moorestown, NJ 08057 **609-235-6439** **Look:** CLASS ACT **Goods:** STATUS QUO–TOP DRAWER **Prices:** MODERATE-HIGH **HOURS:** Mon–Sat.10-4 **CLOSED:** Holidays	A nip and a tuck off Main Street, set back just far enough to miss if you, like me, are a stranger in town. It looked like just **another pretty house in a town full of pretty houses**, which, if you are in the upscale resale game, is just the look most of us are looking for. Another good sign: If a town as small as this has a Talbot, you can bet the town also has consignment clout. Trickle-down should be in effect, big time.

Another good sign: Coming in from the cold, I was revived by a blast of warm, scented air and a flash of color. I twirled around, taking it all in, anticipating the plunge. A magnificent swirl of white chiffon and satin three-piece cocktail suit (hand stitching on the inside!), $200. A Nicole Miller pink wool suit with intricate beadwork scattered all over the lapels, reduced (!) to $150. Small household items scattered around, all for sale, added their **winsome charm**. Mid-store, there's an **enormous selection of moderately priced everyday dresses, blouses, skirts, sweaters, play clothes, and coats.** The back room, done up in early afterthought, is devoted to larger sizes, end-of-season sale merchandise, and shoes up to size 11. Racks were crowded, some with one too many outdated garments. I'd like to see wire hangers given the ax. The shop and most of it's merchandise deserve better. There was a $5 bag sale rack. Everything on it could have been given to charity. But don't let these few negative opinions get you down; **this is an excellent shop.**

CONSIGNOR ALERT: 50%-50% split. $3 annual fee. 60 days. By appointment only. |
| **Resale Rack** |  |
| Rt. 38 Hainesport Shopping Center Mt. Holly, NJ 08060 **609-261-4421** **Look:** HO HUM–STATUS QUO **Goods:** HO HUM – STATUS QUO **Prices:** LOW **HOURS:** Mon–Sat 10-5 **CLOSED:** Holidays | We called from the road, lost, using the car phone two or three times to get our bearings. We were on the wrong side of Rte. 38, well within the speed limit, but going too fast to find the small white sign amidst all the other signs, the strip malls and the freestanding, one-of-a-kind buildings. Finally successful, I sauntered in alone. It had been Marvin's voice on the phone. I didn't want to be greeted by a wall of smiling concern and questions. In and out, that's my motto. I heard the owner and clerks conjecturing why he (Marvin) hadn't found them. "Was the sign that hard to read?" Answer: "Yes!" Owners often don't see what is staring them right in the face. The everyday familiar can become a lull-you-to-sleep steel trap. If I hadn't been on a mission, I wouldn't have bothered to turn around and around, making call after call, receiving poor directions, trying to find the place. As parents often forget they were children once, so shopkeepers forget to be customers. Forget how they can easily become lost in the flyby-jump-and-shout jumble of shops and signs.

Huge floor space and inventory. High racks, low racks, and anti-shoplifter mirrors taking it all in. Kids have a safe, secure cubby inside the front door and the double front windows. Customers can get lost in their thoughts and the selection. The only muffled sound is wire hangers scraping across plumber pipe racks. Much better for things like cribs and swing seats and car seats-- which only take up 10% of the floor-space-- than clothing. Racks of mostly played out play clothes, and seen-and-had their-design-day grown- up garments.

CONSIGNOR ALERT: Kids' under size 8 or anything valued under $15, buys outright. Otherwise under $20= 50%-50%, $20+ = **66% You -34% Shop.** $2 initial fee and 10¢/tag. |

Room to Grow	
311 High Street Burlington, NJ 08016 **609-387-9159**	Judy Kennedy was taking her grandson to Borders Bookstore one day to shop for a gift. In the back of her mind she was looking for a thrift shop guide her landlord had told her about. He'd seen it on television in the middle of Orien Reid's series on thrift shops. Orien held The Guide up to the camera and said, "BUY THIS BOOK."
	When Judy's grandson wandered away, momentarily lost in the bookstore, she left the gift and The Guide behind in her frantic haste to locate the missing toddler. Weeks passed. The Maniac traveling sideshow and van arrived in Burlington in the middle of the annual street fair and in the middle of Judy's plans to drop a note to the Maniac, asking to be included in the next edition. After doing my "maniac
Look: TOP DRAWER **Goods:** STATUS QUO–TOP DRAWER **Prices:** LOW	thing," I intentionally blew my cover, revealing my identity and purpose for shopping her store.
	If Judy had written the letter to me before we showed up, here's what she might have said:
HOURS: Tue–Sat 10-5, Fri 10-7	Dear Thrift Shop Maniac: My shop has tons and tons of new and used infant and toddler clothes and accessories, all of the highest quality. Inventory starts to thin out around size 7, ends after size 8. Rows of tiny bow ties, suspenders enough to hold up the pants of an army of little ones, bottles and bottle bags hanging from the walls like artwork. Cribs and color-coordinated crib bumpers, car seats and high chairs are scattered all around the room, filling in the spaces between the racks. There're two dressing rooms and a powder room so everyone can be comfortable. I think you'll like my shop. Sincerely yours, *Judy Kennedy*, Owner, Mother (but not Grandmother)
CLOSED: Holidays	**CONSIGNOR ALERT:** Buys outright. Consigns only expensive items. Ask.

Second Chance	
328 Mill St. Bristol, PA 19007 **785-4620**	Visually, the **handsome, custom-made interior** is reminiscent of a quaint, bygone era shop front, complete with dormered roof, shake shingles and colonial-style windows with well preserved cream-colored trim. This retail stage set was far better crafted and in much better, albeit dusty, condition than any of the skimpy furniture
	inventory lying in its forceful shadow. A couple, perhaps the owners, perhaps long-married, definitely not forthcoming, stayed behind the register area, he transfixed in the glare of the small-screen TV, she busy with woman's handiwork. Their attention never wavered. Mine did.
Look: STATUS QUO **Goods:** HO HUM – STATUS QUO **Prices:** LOW – MODERATE	There were one or two overpriced, not quite antique, older pieces in the window, leading me to believe something similar, perhaps even better, would be displayed inside. Not so. Inside were several older, cheaply constructed, room dividers and wall-to-wall storage areas and such, comingled with Scotch-(un)guarded, neanderthal, plaid, colonial sofas and such. Just as a truly ugly child loses whatever whimsy it had going for it with their passing into adolescence, there was no getting
HOURS: Mon–Fri 10-4, Sat 10-5	round it--these poorly designed pieces were growing older and uglier with every passing day. And unlike the plain child, they will never have the soul's inner beauty shining through.
CLOSED: Holidays	**CONSIGNOR ALERT:** Buys outright.

Wilhelmina Country Collections 369 Main St. Tullytown, PA 19007 **945-8606** 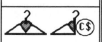 (P$) **Look:** CLASS ACT **Goods:** HO HUM – CLASS ACT **Prices:** LOW **HOURS:** Tue–Thu 11-7, Fri 11-9:30, Sat 9:30–3:30, Sun 1-5 **CLOSED:** Holidays	 Faded gold letters on the front door said 'Barber Shop.' Inside, a wall of mirrors framed in marble is all that's left of the shop's original history. Now, deep green and pink roses cascade all over the walls with stamped-tin crown molding. New York dealers and pickers should be coming here in droves. Her **prices are beyond fair.** Wilhelmina claims to have no professional training in art of any kind and yet, her **restless, creative being demonstrates that she has the hands and mind of a natural.** In the brief period between my visits, she's moved everything around, showing off each piece to its best advantage. Housed in the 1910 white-oak cupboard priced at $75 (could fetch up to$250) are generations' worth of small kitchen tools, pitchers, glassware. Above, sits a smaller oak cupboard from the same period and priced at $50, two-toned with the designer-correct amount of peeling green paint. An old suitcase--beaten, battered and brown--is brought back to life with a brand-new lining of draped chintz stapled to the inside, creating a small shrine to an assortment of secondhand finds. The shop is tiny. In warmer weather it spills out onto the generous swath of sidewalk, luring you inside. I'm hooked! **P.S.** The hours were just too long to fit here. Sometimes she's there on Monday, Tuesday and/or Wednesday. **Call first.** **CONSIGNOR ALERT:** Buys outright.
Women's Association Thrift Shop 520 Main St. Riverton, NJ 08077 **No Phone #**  (C$) **Look:** STATUS QUO **Goods:** HO HUM **Prices:** LOW **HOURS:** Thu 10-3 **CLOSED:** July & August	Julia Child's double volunteers here. She's a statuesque matron with the same deep, curiously quivering voice, her steady gaze flashing a bemused, merry twinkle. (I saw no sign of cooking sherry.) Myra and her sidekick hold forth **every Thursday, only on Thursdays.** These two stalwart ladies and the enormous handpainted black and gilt, turn of the century, Howard Parry real estate office, walk in safe over in the corner are the best to be found in this quaint shop. Located in a small river community founded long ago by families with names like Lippincott (U. of P. library) and Parry, it has atmospherics so thick you can feel them gathering round you like an old wool blanket over bare skin. **It's a wonderful place just to have a friendly chat** with whoever happens to be prowling along side you that day, solid citizen or spirit. Once we all joked about closing up shop and dashing off to do a little outlet shopping at Franklin Mills. They have been meaning to go, but didn't know the way. I promised to call Myra and tell her which exit off I-95 to use (Woodhaven). I like to keep my word. I'm old-fashioned, too. **CONSIGNOR ALERT:** Donations only. Benefits Women's Association of Calvary Presbyterian Church.

TOUR #15
CLOSING THE GAP: ANTIQUES TO TRASH PICKING IN ONE GENERATION

Mom used to run to **New Hope**. That's how the family came to describe it: She'd run there. Usually about once or twice a month. It was her hideaway, her get away from-it-all secret, her fix. Got so she knew every shop and every shopkeeper, even eating lunch with the locals, belly up to the bar (no, she wasn't drinking) at the old, pre-renovation **Logan Inn**, with the fireplace going strong and the gossip going even stronger. Could be I've extended Mom's flight path to include a wider circle of shops and towns. Yes indeedy, an argument could be made that I've just enlarged the radius of turf where her size 5 1/2 shoes (I'm a vitamin-induced baby-boomer size 9.) carried her. She'd take me with her once in a while; that's how I got to see her in action. We'd go from shop to shop, I'd look, she'd buy, we'd argue, then we'd take a break for lunch. It was my earliest maniac training experience.

Marvin used to spend whole summers away from the mean streets of Upper West Side Manhattan at Camp Olympia, a sports camp in nearby Buckingham. From the time he was 7 till he was 11, every summer meant weenie roasts and water skiing and swimming in the Delaware. Here he was close to Grandma Millie and Grandpa Larry, who spent their bucolic senior summers at a nearby farm resort, keeping in touch occasionally, but enjoying their time alone.

So it turns out that for us, New Hope is a sort of home away from home, even though we have such diverse memories, perspectives, and histories. It's one of the ties that bind. We've spent many a weekend here in the Logan Inn, room #5, and many a crisp fall afternoon browsing the fleas and doing the shops. Now Morgan, the next generation, comes with us for the occasional shopping expedition and celebratory birthday feast. It's in our blood now, you see.

It's also a place to avoid on Saturdays and Sundays in good weather, unless you bring your own parking space. We come weekends only when it's raining or cloudy and cold, or during the week to avoid the crowds. Being self-employed has its advantages. We love to nip into **Farley's**, the local book store, and wile away the time (even before they began selling our opus), then go back to our room and wile away even more time. **Havana** is another favorite place to recharge enough energy to wile away (time) again. At the upscale **Landing,** we willingly pay for the view and the desserts, and the rare birthday feast. Then there's Logan Inn's bar on a cold winter afternoon, huddling around the fire, sipping B&B, remembering summers past. Life is good. Walk across the wonderful old bridge spanning the Delaware River, a natural enough, man-made dividing line between Pennsylvania and New Jersey, to **Lambertville**. While having no known resale shops, poor dear, it is died and gone to antique heaven. There is **Phoenix Books**, a great secondhand book shop. **Full Moon** cafe on the main drag has a great brunch.

As the county seat, **Doylestown** is littered with tony law offices, and therefore innundated with places for the legal eagles to eat. It's a great place to spend the day, eat, walk around, eat, shop, eat. Avoid the obvious tourist trap. (Yuck!) Try one of the many small side street places. **Paganini** is great for lunch or dinner. In good weather you can sit outside and swat yellow jackets, swap secondhand war stories, and eat great and unusual pasta. **The Iron Skillet**, just around from Second Avenue's new location on West State Street, is less expensive, eminently hospitable, with a traditional breakfast-and lunch-only menu, and greenhouse sunlight streaming through any time of year. And no yellow jackets.

Down river, below Washington's crossing with it's landmark pine, planted in 1776, resplendent every December in 20th century Christmas lights, is **Yardley**. Discovered and settled back in the 1600's, it's news to us. We came upon it by accident when Marvin drove bravely into the unknown, the way I venture out to the supermarket every week. Jaw set tight, hands gripped on the steering wheel, he knew where he was going. (Ha!) Turns out he did. This man has more good things happen to him by accident than most people get to experience on purpose. (Should I laugh or cry?) (OK, I'm laughing.) Hard by the water's edge, here they use place names like Afton. The river damp, moss-encrusted place is so obviously genuine, you don't choke on the historic reference. (In very nearby **Peddler's Village**, you'd gag.) The most established-looking place to eat looks like somewhere my parents would have taken me when I was a child. It looks grown-up and expensive. Hungry? It could be a matter of shop, drop and run back upriver.

Well, enough of this. Gotta run. I haven't quite finished researching the Princeton area, and there's this really great shop I don't want to miss called....

TOUR #15

2	Consigning Women	Yardley
11	Consignment Galleries ★	New Britain
3	Encore	Yardley
12	Full Circle ★	New Britain
9	Grandma's	Doylestown
10	New & Nearly New Clothing	Doylestown
8	The Pinwheel	Doylestown
4	Raffael's	New Hope
5	Reruns ★	Lahaska
7	Second Avenue ★	Doylestown
6	Sondra's Second Look	Lahaska
13	Welcome House	Warminster
1	Worth Another Look	Yardley

*Note: This list has a shop's entire name. Names in review boxes may have been shortened a tad to fit. Numbers before each shop name correspond to their numbered location on each map. **Shops with a star sold Volume II. Volume III? ASK!**

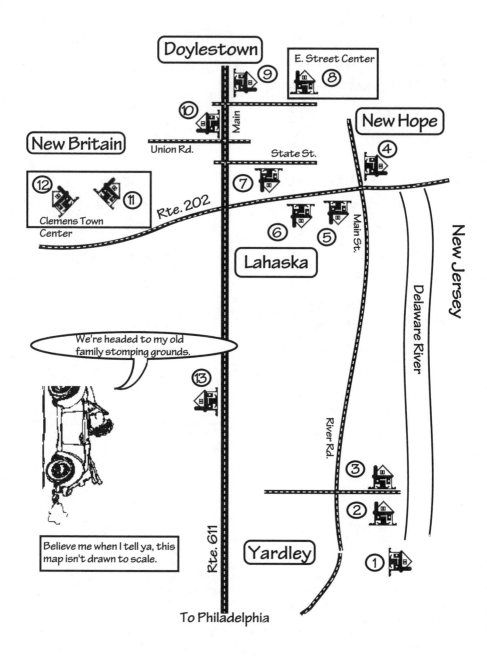

Consigning Women

85 Makefield Rd.
Yardley, PA 19067
428-1450

Look: CLASS ACT
Goods: STATUS
QUO – CLASS ACT
Prices: MODERATE

HOURS: Tue 10-7,
Wed–Sat 10-4:30

CLOSED: Holidays

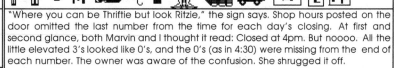

"Where you can be Thriftie but look Ritzie," the sign says. Shop hours posted on the door omitted the last number from the time for each day's closing. At first and second glance, both Marvin and I thought it read: Closed at 4pm. But noooo. All the little elevated 3's looked like 0's, and the 0's (as in 4:30) were missing from the end of each number. The owner was aware of the confusion. She shrugged it off.

While Marvin engaged the engagingly offbeat owner, I did my thing, wandering around deeper into the shop's (shall we say) romantically darkened, all-too-intimate rooms. Numerical oddities continued. This was the first time I'd been in a secondhand shop where all the prices ended in $.99. Curiously, later the same day, I came across a second shop using this pricing. In the smallest and darkest of the four rooms, I got to do some tippy-toe stretching exercises trying to reach the dress racks (I'm 5'6") **filled with some very accessibly priced, dynamite-looking stuff.**

Whenever we go to a new-to-us-shop like this one, we pull out The Guide and tell the shopkeeper about it, hoping to pique interest and lay a foundation for the review to come. Our undercover M.O.? We pose as enthusiastic consumers who discovered the book at a thrift or bookstore and are using it to further our passionate hobby. Curiously enough, the owner thought we meant to leave our extra copy of the $10 goodie with her for free, thereby relinquishing a friend's stocking-stuffer present (Ok, so we lied a little) to her. To that sign I'd add: "and act a trifle Ditzie."
P.S. Second Location at 55 E. Afton Ave. Yardley, PA 19067 **321-6180**.
CONSIGNER ALERT: 50%-50%. $6 annual fee. 60 days. No appointment. No limit.

Consignment Galleries

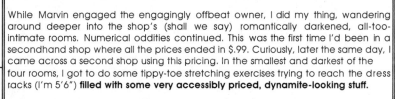

470 Clemens Town Ctr.
New Britain, PA
18901
348-5244

Look: CLASS ACT

Goods: STATUS
QUO –TOP DRAWER

Prices: HIGH

HOURS:
Mon–Fri 10-8,
Sat 10-5, Sun 12-5

CLOSED: Holidays

Howard is one of that rare breed, a true gentlemen: quiet, calm, professional, self-effacing and courteous. It's his merchandise that screams...

Contemporary, antique or reproduction, everything is consigned. Rather than referring to this as a secondhand shop, the more demuer term 'previously owned' best suits the likes of silver tea services and Baccarat brandy snifters. For $2,960, Howard will deliver the gargoyle- and brass-encrusted, solid oak Victorian double-decker buffet. Drop another $995 and you'd own the cherry dining room table. Just have to have the Depression-era kitchen cabinet in mint green and beige with the original black Bakelite pulls? Write a check for $395+ tax. $520 buys you a contemporary kitchen-corner set with a hinged-seat storage area. Drop $1700 bucks and - you could sleep in a four-piece bird's eye maple Victorian bedset tonight. (I would have loved to get it for Morgan, but I can't redecorate and write. It's one or the other.) Fading lace, handsewn quilts, prints, oils and watercolors and a large glass **display case chock full of estate quality jewelry and tiny treasures, all of it in immaculate condition.** There was even a Victorian wicker potty.

There are eleven Consignment Galleries in the USA, once part of a franchise that broke up over six years ago. Not only did Howard and his wife Joanne, partners in life and business, survive that trauma, they've doubled their floorspace by expanding into the vacated shop next door. Howard built the interior of the new addition by himself. He's good at that, too. (Some things, he'll tell you. Others...)
CONSIGNOR ALERT: 60% You-40% Shop. No fee. By appointment only. Delivery available for reasonable fee.

Encore Boutique	 $ ⬛ PF
94 S. Main St. #3 Yardley, PA 19067 **493-9130**	Marvin strode in ahead of me as I fussed in the rear parking lot with tape recorder and notebook in preparation for the first, unexpected undercover review of the day. The trials and tribulations of a critic. He walked in alone to what turned out to be a women's only secondhand shop, and just stood there by the register, waiting. Afterall, he knew why he was here. They weren't so sure. A cross dresser? A thief? When I caught up and came in, we all had a good laugh at the momentary confusion. He was too big to fit in any of the **incredibly gorgeous ball gowns**, anyway. He'll never have a stage career doing Judy Garland imitations. Although he's got those same draw-you-in sad, soft brown eyes...
Look: LEADING LADY **Goods:** TOUR DE FORCE **Prices:** MATINEE, BALCONY	I scurried around the swag-hung rooms with pink walls and cream-colored architectural details, details, details. God is in the details, I always say. And here they've got their details down. I roamed up and down the carpeted, gown-draped, shoe-lined stairwell and into the **wonderful oh-so-private working duds, bridal-and-cocktail-gown**-strewn, sunburst secondfloor with it's double mirror-hung, fit-for-a-diva dressing rooms. I tried on this and that while Marvin did his stand-up routine, taking the show on the road. He kept them laughing at the register as they deftly and
HOURS: Mon–Fri 10-5:30, Sat 10-4	good-naturedly processed him, an incoming consignor and several customers, all at once. And it was only 10:30am. What must the energy be like in this place by curtain call, after a Saturday 2pm matinee? Encore! Encore! The reviews are in. It's an entrepreneurial **tour de force**. A performance not to be missed.
CLOSED: Holidays	**CONSIGNOR ALERT:** 50%-50% split. $5 one time fee, 60 days. By appointment only. Thursday evening set aside for special consignors.

Full Circle	$ ⬛ L ☺ 🧸 PF
Rt. 202 @ Clemens Town Center New Britain, PA 18901 **340-0120**	Like the battered women and children they serve, Full Circle has gone through a period of radical transition. Open less than 2 years, the shop is gradually becoming cleaner and much better organized. **The racks and shelves are bursting with donations.** The drop-off, sorting, pricing, hanging-out and gossiping area behind the room-divider wall of grey metal display shelves, containing books and housewares is bursting with volunteers' tall tales of who did what to whom. Things are improving.
Look: BOTTOMFEEDER **Goods:** HO HUM– CLASS ACT **Prices:** LOW	Sandwiched between such traditional strip mall shops as Rite Aid and Hallmark Cards, this shop contradicts my time-honored policy of never bothering to look for a resale shop in a new mall. **Thrift has infiltrated the malls!** Even the mall's marquee has been called into play, announcing Full Circle's end-of-summer $5 bag sale in big bold black letters, right along busy Rte. 202 for all the world to see. Who would've thought! The third surprise is that this shopping center has *two* secondhand stores. But that's another story on another page.
HOURS: Mon–Sat 10-5	**P.S. Check out the Wig Room**. Inspired by the manager, who underwent chemotherapy three times, with the inevitable demoralizing hair loss, it is an intimate, private secondhand haven for cancer patients on a tight budget. New, the wigs ranged in cost from $60 to $1000; they all cost $10 here.
CLOSED: Holidays	**CONSIGNOR ALERT:** Donations only. Must drop off before 4pm. Call first.

Grandma's

No. End Rt. 611
Doylestown, PA
18901
348-5408

If you had 8 children who in turn made you a grandmother 22 times, you'd call it Grandma's Consignment Shop, too. Trouble is, Grandma and her consignors shopped low-end retailers exclusively, and stopped buying anything new except jeans, T's, and sweats back in the early 80s. It's small, it's cluttered, it's cramped. Sidewalk display 'featured' $8 (overpriced by $7.50 in my estimation) navy blue or brown polyester slacks, the fashion statement of choice for some little old ladies and men last seen boarding the gamblers' express bus to Atlantic City.

Look: HO HUM –
STATUS QUO

Goods: HO HUM –
STATUS QUO

Prices: CONFUSED

The best bet for your money was the circular rack of infant clothing, all within the $1 range and the seemingly endless supply of grown-up, infant and toddler "Baby's Gotta Have New Shoes." Back by the register off to your left, consistently overpriced evening and formal wear, seriously dated, non-vintage. Prices hovered around $50. Take off the zeros, and you've got it right. Marginally worthwhile: Rival crock pot, $10, and Kenmore electric frying pan, $15. Older, never used models sat in the window. A year later a Rival crock pot was still there. Same one? At 12:07pm, I couldn't get in to see. The shop was closed with no explanation, and Grandma was no where in sight. She had left her baby all alone.

HOURS:
Mon–Sat 11-7
Summer: Mon–Sat 11-6

CLOSED: Holidays

CONSIGNOR ALERT: 50%-50% split. $5/season. 10-item limit per week. 60 days. No appointment necessary but call first.

New & Nearly New Clothing

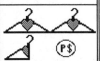

Main & Union Sts.
Doylestown, PA
18901
345-5050

Over the summer, the owner called and to ask me why her rating had been so low. It was a great relief, after dealing with a handful of really cranky shopkeepers in the same situation or far worse, to be able to discuss her review pleasantly. She listened. She didn't take it personally. She took it professionally. I told her confusion for me began before I even got inside, reading the shop sign. Driving by, I thought there were two shops at this location, because New and Nearly New Clothing is also Consignment Horizons. Those few words spoke volums. It told me, wife of a business consultant and therapist, that there was an identity crisis going on inside.

Look: STATUS QUO

Goods: HO HUM –
STATUS QUO

Prices: UP & DOWN

Overall, inventory was sparse, low-key and serviceable. **Housewares was the best** bet, although there just wasn't enough of it. Decorative pieces and wreaths, for instance, looked as if they had come from a neighborhood gift shop or the florist next-door. Kids' clothes had some worn knees. I saw Lands End and L.L. Bean type stuff, a few Ann Taylor and Talbot labels, leading me to believe I could find something here once in a rare while. At the other extreme were too many garments like the wraparound, whale and strawberry-embroidered golf skirts in hot pink or lime green. The space is pleasant enough. The woman working behind the counter that day was caring and professional. If they'd only get pickier about what they accept on consignment...Then the owner revealed she was an absentee owner. When she disclosed this information, I knew what needed changing, and so did she. I enjoyed talking with her, and wish her only the best, whatever her decision.

HOURS: Mon–Sat
10-5, Wed 10-6

CLOSED: Mondays
in July & August

CONSIGNOR ALERT: 50%-50% split. $2 fee. 42 weeks in store. 14 items. Wouldn't give consignment sheet: "they're expensive, they cost too much." This way, for sure.

The Pinwheel

505 East St. Ctr.
Doylestown, PA
18901
345-6111

Look: STATUS QUO
– CLASS ACT
Goods: STATUS
QUO–CLASS ACT
Prices: LOW–
MODERATE

HOURS: Mon–Fri
10-6, Sat 10-4:30

CLOSED: Last 2
weeks July & Jan

Ceiling fans whirred and clicked, marking time in rhythm to Barbra Streisand's unerring rendition of "I Wonder As I Wander," a favorite old English Christmas carol. (How did she know how far I had wandered already, and it was only 10:03am?) Down below on the shop floor, customers were swirling like fake snow on a movie set, falling all over the influx of holiday-circuit consignments, landing on fabulous bargains. At this hour most resale shops haven't even gotten around to opening the door. This one was already **doing business hand over fist**.

A Center City resale store could've easily commanded double the price for many of the the beautiful clothes. Hand-stenciled signs hung above every rack. This way you can tell at a glance that jeans have a rack to themselves by the front door, and Pinwheel Exclusives, the term they use for better goodies, have a nearby section to themselves. Housewares, diisplayed on shelves in the big front window, were inexplicably weak, although I did find a still-in-the-box shortbread mold for only $5.

When asked how they chose their unusual name, I was reminded that pinwheels, those eternally happy toys, go round and round, just like the clothes do here.

P.S. First-time visitor? This shop might be a teensy bit hard to find. Look for the Getty station on your right when driving North from Doylestown on Rte. 611, turn right.

CONSIGNOR ALERT: 50%-50% split, $5 semi-annual fee. 42 days, By appointment only. Be sure to pick up a copy of their consignment policy.

Raeffeal's

26 N. Main St.
New Hope, PA
18938
862-2181

Next Edition

Next Edition

HOURS: Mon–Thu
11-6, Fri & Sat 11-7,
Sun 11-6

CLOSED: Holidays

***Now* I can tell you.** As Evelyns, this was the place mentioned in the Diary of a Mad Maniac chapter where the woman friend? clerk? of the (former) owner was having a med-free day. Remember that one? I certainly do.

The new owner of newly named Raeffeal's called to let me know about the changeover. I said I would be only too happy to get the word out on the resale greapevine. Can't do more till next edition. (Next edition? I'm already thinking about next edition? God help me!)) Six months minimum, remember?

They are opening their doors on April 1, 1995. Good luck!

CONSIGNOR ALERT: Still scratching their heads over this one.

Reruns

5743 Rte. 202
Lahaska, PA 18931
794-7224

Look: TOP DRAWER

Goods: CLASS
ACT –TOP DRAWER

Prices: MODERATE

HOURS: Tue–Sat
10–5, Wed 12–7

CLOSED: Holidays

Newly nestled in among the oh-so-cute shops of Peddle'rs Village and Lahaska, with "Save It Pretty Mama" playing in the background on Channel 89.3, The Station with The Mood for any resale store worthy of its four hangers. **I knew I had a good one as soon as I walked in the door.** Not only does she have nice clothes, but she's got great chachas and accessories. Patti Gyuraki, the owner, also has created and nurtured an exquisite **bridal and evening wear salon.** All by itself, set off from the rest of the store with a floor-length mirror and all the requisite lace and frills and swags, is an entire room of first-class bridal gowns, mother-of-the-bride gowns, bridesmaids dresses, veils, shoes, whatever you need to get hitched and stay hitched.

In the **men's department** the groom can usually find a tuxedo or two among the **better quality** suits and sweaters. During a shoot for a news segment I did last fall, the producer from Channel 10 got hooked (he's already hitched) on resale, when he spied a very much needed tux for a wedding he HAD to attend. (No, silly, he was a guest, not a two-timing groom.)

CONSIGNOR ALERT: 50%–50% split. 60days. $5 semi-annual fee. By appointment.

Second Avenue

58 E. State St.
Doylestown, PA
18901
348-2775

Look: CLASS ACT

Goods: STATUS QUO
–TOP DRAWER

Prices: MODERATE

HOURS:
Mon–Fri 11–5,
Sat 10–4, Sun 12–4

CLOSED: Holidays

Last year my heart sank when I first entered the shop, only to discover that first impressions, however dramatic, can be wrong. What a relief! Then it happened again this year, only in reverse. This time my first impression was pure pleasure. A notice arrived in the mail announcing **they had moved** "uptown" upscale to THE shopper's block in downtown Doylestown. I walked in expecting to love it, only to discover I preferred the old shop's charm. Ouch!

Perhaps it's only a matter of time. When we moved into our home, nothing was first placed where it eventually wound up. I moved furniture and accent pieces around every few months, getting rid of those things that didn't work as I went, until it all came together. Right now it's too cluttered looking in this shop. The decorative, interior blue awning could become a unifying visual force. But right now, it sports old hats and bags, only adding to the visual overload. It would be a clever use of otherwise useless space if the shop didn't already look like an expensively over-accessorized woman. The woman (shop) should wear the clothes and jewelery (inventory), not the other way around. The just 'round the corner, just 'round the bend slow unfolding of the old shop, probably holding just as much stuff, kept the place from looking like it had all been tossed in a salad spinner.

You must know by now, I tilt higher ratings in favor of inventory quality, rather than shop design. I don't know why, but with the move quality seemed just a tad off, too. Reluctantly, I have to take away, rather than add to the ratings here. Maybe next year, after they've had a chance to look in the mirror and rethink the "outfit"...

 SHOPPER ALERT: Chachkas

CONSIGNOR ALERT: 50-50% split. $5/6mos. 60 days. 15 items/person/week. Consign Monday-Friday 11-4. No appointment necessary.

Sondra's Second Look	
Rte.202 Hollyberry Sq. Lahaska, PA 18931 **794-5579**	A hat wreath on the door. A private day care center inside. Last year, Mom, the owner, kept her cool as her three children sat on the floor cutting out colored paper strips, squabbling, wrestling, busy being kids. A crib was within arms reach of the register, convenient for naps and diaper changes. The scene warmed my heart,
	but the noise scrambled my brain. Then the youngest child pushed open the door and ran out with my Marvin, the toddler's older brother and Mom, the shopkeeper, in hot persuit. I know, I know, I'm always nudging for play areas. With a little rethinking, this could work. A buzz-you-in lock on the door, a fenced-off play area, so's the little buffalos can't roam, perhaps? This year the head count was down by two. Only the junior Olympic marathon runner remained. He was sacked out in the middle of the shop floor, curled up and cozy under a parrot green throw. Mom looked immeasurably calmer, too.
Look: STATUS–CLASS ACT	
Goods: STATUS – CLASS ACT	While he snoozed, I scooped up five pink satin boudoir pillows. Struck a deal for $3 each. Got a Le Creuset black au gratin for the unbelievably low price of $5! Left
Prices: MODERATE	behind a new orange cotton knit Outlander dress with the original tag of $79, now $28. There was also a beautiful off-white, wool petite Vittadini sweater for $12. A set of six, heavy-bottomed hand-blown beer glasses, also $12. Too bad the men's
HOURS: Tue–Sat 10-5	department was a bad joke. **If I lived around here, I'd be a regular**, while Marvin could pass the time in the **great little secondhand bookstore in the same small strip** mall. Bucks County Book Shop has graciously listed the other used book stores in the area on a map showing you how to find them. **SALE ALERT:** Semi-annual bag sale Sept. 5. $5 for a full grocery bag of stuff.
CLOSED. Holidays	**CONSIGNOR ALERT:** 50-50% split. $1 fee. 45 days. By appointment only.

Welcome House	
1248 Easton Rd. Warminster, PA 18976 **343-2079**	North of the Willow Grove Naval Air Station, or minutes south of Doylestown on Rt. 611, depending on which direction you are traveling. Set well back from the road and back in time. This is an old-time thrift store. No mistaking it for 'resale.' They even **negotiate prices** once in a while.
	Volunteers were unfailingly pleasant; most of the merchandise was unfailingly HO HUM. Walk in the front door and you practically trip over the housewares section, with the inevitable yogurt makers and jelly glasses overflowing the shelves. (What is it about yogurt makers? Every shop worth the name "thrift" seems to have three.) **Don't miss the basement** if you're a penny-pinching bargain hunter. That's where
Look: Upstairs: STATUS QUO	they put all the SALE stuff. It's mostly destined for mattress felt and cardboard, but I found an uncracked copy of Beard on Bread for 50¢ down here once. Do watch the
Basement: DOWN&OUT	steps, they're steep. The enormous parking lot is a real boon; this is a busy place.
Goods: HO HUM – STATUS QUO	**P.S.** Because ithe lot takes up so much of the front of the property and curbside is lined with trees and bushes, you might drive by and miss the store. It's set back
Prices: VERY LOW	really far. This has happened to me twice. Two bigger signs? Aimed at traffic?
HOURS: Mon–Sat 10-4	**SALE ALERT:** 50% off last two weeks of July, plus year-round basement sale.
CLOSED: Holidays	**CONSIGNOR ALERT:** Donations only. None accepted in July. Benefits the Pearl S. Buck Foundation.

Worth Another Look	

10 Penn Valley Dr. Yardley, PA 19067 **493-9544**	If you like decorating everything in brown, you'll feel right at home in this converted barn. People who surround themselves in brown are supposed to be conservative and earthy. I don't respond well to brown most of the time. I find it too noncommittal, too unimaginative. I'm into riveting black and white. Red red red. Royal blue. Strong purples. Dark or celadon green. Baby's-bottom pink. Maybe cream. Never brown.
	Except for cocoa on my moccaccino and Bassett's coffee ice cream and apple crisp. I like brown in my food, not on my walls and furniture, and rarely on my back. I know, I know. Now I've pissed off a lot of you brownies. And there are lots of you out there. Remember: to each her/his own. Now put down the axe, I've finished grinding mine. Let's go back to being friends, and finish this review.
Look: BROWN **Goods:** STATUS QUO **Prices:** STATUS QUO	All the while we shopped and hung out, the owner never once looked up from her enclosed, computerized, register control station. She never once smilled at a customer. She did do her best to maintain an efficiently even temperament in the face of an opening bell onslaught of incoming consignment appointments, outgoing consignment no-sells, and customers weaving through the shop and the transactions with a baby scooting around and emitting the occasional blood curd-
HOURS: Mon–Fri 10-6, Sat 10-5, Sun 11-4	ling scream. No mean feat. Marvin lucked out. He found one dynamite silk tie after another, one to give each of his male friends as presents. They ranged in price from $6 to $9. If that wasn't cheap enough, they were 25 or 50% off as well. **For $42.50 he bought seven ties, any one of which would have cost $50 to $65 at any swank men's shop.** This coup was an unusual stroke of good luck for this otherwise clean and well organized but brown, brown, brown shop. (Oops! It just slipped out.)
CLOSED: Holidays	**P.S.** Second shop located at 408 S. State St. Fenton Square, Newtown, PA **860-8810.** **CONSIGNOR ALERT:** 50%-50% split. $3.50 semi-annual fee subtracted from first check. 60 days. Consign Mon–Fri 10:30-4

TOUR #16
FROM LOW LYING CHICKEN COOPS TO THE HIGH WALLS OF ACADEMIA

Princeton is one of THE East Coast addresses. It reeks of charm. And money. And history. It's the ultimate picture-pretty, postcard, colonial era, high stakes, ivy league college town. Tightly clustered around the pinch-me-is-this-real, all too charming overload of the central core of shoppes, many of which are centuries old, once private, homes, are the old money families of town. In places like this there's always the moldy old money, and then the recently arrived (anything under 100 years).

Privet hedges held high, white-picket-fence-perfect downtown is itself surrounded by a high-density corridor of businesses willing to pay big-time salaries to attract and hold on to their upscale techno-wizard employees. Employees and their families who live in the surrounding walled, gated and mature tree-shrouded, vaguely, but solidly named "estates", who are ready, willing and sometimes able to pay big bucks for private schools, private tennis courts, private swimming pools, private golf links just a brief golf cart drive from private clubhouses in which to hold private parties. All this held near and dear and secure by private guards.

All this requires lots of fancy duds. And lots of fancy furnishings. All of which, sooner rather than later, Princetonians dropped dead while polishing, or inherited but can't stand, or got bored with, or never really liked in the first place, or bought too many of to ever get around to using, or can't be seen in twice, or...Enter the Maniacs, some of whom may be these same Princetonians, shopping undercover in volunteer disguise, or anticipating the social cold shoulder it could cause if word got out by bragging about it first. So clever. Why didn't I think of that? Doing Princeton? **Doodles** at 260 Nassau Street, practically rubbing shoulders with the Nearly New Shop, has amazingly good oriental takeout. Try the vegetarian dumplings and the scallion pancakes. Divine.

Flemington is an altogether different mindset. It is New Jersey's kinder, gentler answer to Pennsylvania's bus 'em in and bus 'em out boom town, Reading, a.k.a. the Outlet Capital of the Mid-Atlantic states. While there are crowds of crazed and glassy eyed, if-it's-cheap-I'll-buy-it-ready-to-draw-blood-if-you-get-in-the-way-of-my-bargain hunters, they are here in more manageable numbers. The sneakered, diagonally crossed and at-the-ready, pocketbook-swinging, credit card-waving, polyester-perfect, secure but not necessarily social crowd, is mixed in with calmer looking types who actually live in town and pay taxes. Residents who have a day in-day out investment in maintaining the small-town, high quality-of-life flavor that still exists, and is often bypassed by the free spending, just-one-more-bargain-starved shoppers swarming around the flyby Rte. 202 traffic circle.

The Maniac edge? Here we can double dip, doing a combination outlet crawl and secondhand shopping spree. And that's just what Nancy and Molly and Morgan and I did. We ended our day long spree with killer chocolate cake and cappuccino and juice at **The Market Roost**, 65 Main Street. They also have really yummie looking takeout. Flemington is so accustomed to being a tourist attraction they banded together and published a small guide to the shops, historic area and restaurants along with a map. They're readily available at 70 locations throughout town. Get one. They're chock full of info.

Surrounding Flemington and Princeton, two bustling, too-small-to-be-a-city but-too-big-to-be-town(s) in the fast disappearing farmland of Mercer, Middlesex and Hunterdon Counties, are any number of timelessly traditional small towns, each with its one and only thrift or resale shop. Towns with names like **Rosemont, Raritan, Hopewell, Skillman** and that full mouthful **Blawenburg**. A good map, a picnic lunch and lots of patience will turn up great memories and greater purchases if you're the type to take the day, take a chance and wander down two-lane roads set between ancient cornfields, haystack sentinels, and invading earth movers, busy scraping red earth raw to make room for the next development and the next. (Princeton's getting too crowded.) (The earth's getting too crowded.) (Recycle.)

Upriver from Lambertville in the small town of **Rosemont** you can have one of the best lunches ever. Just like B.A.T.S. in Bryn Athyn, my favorite new thrift shop, I almost don't want to tell you about this eatery. It's just that good. We're refugees of Mother's in New Hope. Refugees because the quality of life and food has slowly slipped and then passed away. We used to go to Mother's for Mother's Day, Father's Day, any day. We used to be willing to wait in long lines just to savor the food and the folks and the aura. Not anymore. It's OK now, kind of like acrylics and polyester are OK. It's a synthetic shadow of its former self. We mourned our loss, casting about for a new home away from home, a hang out.

Allah provides. While undercover shopping Sweet Repeats, housed in one of an attractively converted series of chicken coops (honest! ya gotta see it!), I asked another shopper, clearly a local, where we might eat. She and Sweet Repeats' delightful owner, who overheard our conversation, unanimously recommended **The Cafe** (Rtes. 519 & 604). So do I.

When Marvin and I walked in, something about it made me reminisce about Mother's. The menu was evocative. Assiduously anti-fashion diners, a curious crossbreed of Christmas tree farmers, probably conversant with Socrates in the original Greek, rubbed fork-raised elbows to dine alongside West Village escapees and weekday split-level, weekend wanna-be tourists playing let's pretend. Then we discovered our host Bill, was the former host at **Mother's**. Lunch was terrific, both times. We were happily reunited with good old just-like-mom energy.

TOUR #16

4	Consignment Collections	Flemington
9	Decorator's Consignment Gallery	Blawenburg
2	Fur Exchange	Flemington
5	Hand Me Downs	Hopewell
3	Hunterdon Exchange	Flemington
7	Joan's Attic	Princeton
6	Nearly New Shop	Princeton
8	Peanut Gallery	Blawenburg
10	Princeton Consignment Boutique	Skillman
1	Sweet Repeats	Rosemont

*Note: This list has a shop's entire name. Names in review boxes may have been shortened a tad to fit. Numbers before each shop name correspond to their numbered location on each map. **Shops with a star sold Volume II. Volume III? ASK!**

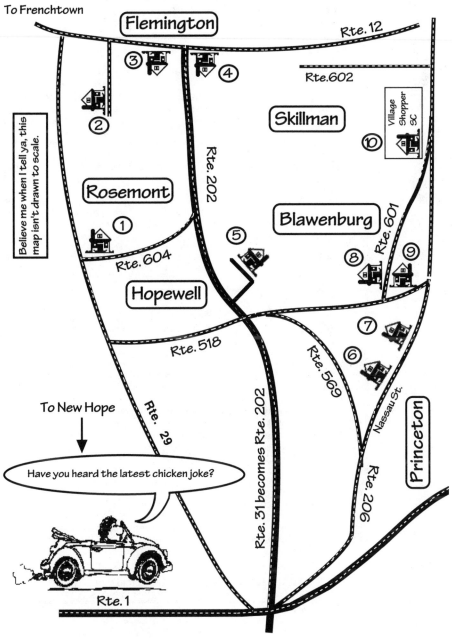

To Frenchtown

Flemington

Rte. 12

③

④

Rte.602

Skillman

Village Shopper SC

⑩

Believe me when I tell ya, this map isn't drawn to scale.

②

Rte. 202

Rosemont

Blawenburg

Rte. 601

①

⑤

⑧

⑨

Rte. 604

Hopewell

⑦

Rte. 518

⑥

Nassau St.

Rte. 569

Princeton

To New Hope

Have you heard the latest chicken joke?

Rte. 29

Rte. 31 becomes Rte. 202

Rte. 206

Rte. 1

TOUR #16 MAP Page 238

<table>
<tr><td>

Consignment Collections

</td><td>

</td></tr>
<tr><td>

171 Main St.
(Church &Main)
Flemington, NJ
08822
908-788-0103

Look: CLASS ACT

Goods: STATUS
QUO–TOP DRAWER

Prices: UP&DOWN

HOURS: Wed–Sat
10-5 Sun 12-4

CLOSED: Holidays

</td><td>

What drew Marvin deep into conversation was her **kind spirit** and the quick discovery (see Hand Me Downs) of their similarly shared backgrounds in the mental health field. She and Marvin happily and not so happily nattered on about alcoholism and changes in insurance, shortened hospital stays, treatment of choice, etc. While they yakked, I shopped.

Turns out, she and I had a lot of things in common, too, like the secondhand furniture she had selected to consign in her white-picket-fenced, well-maintained, large red brick house. The bureau with mirror-backed, hand-painted lavender roses, fit for an overpampered princess or retired member of the oldest profession. The carved plant stand (top messed up by careless previous owners), with twining, playful cherubs so real I wanted to pinch their little fat cheeks (both ends). And for ostentatious relief, the traditionally low to the ground, handsome, oriental black lacquer sofa. (What was that doing in Flemington, N.J.? It was certainly farther away from home than Marvin or I.) I could envision it in our new master and mistress bedroom suite (if we had one). Or the matching pair of cream-coloured, cane-backed, asymmetrical chairs for $250. I must have 'em for the living room, only there is no room left there, either. Marvin, we're moving. I need more room for all the **great furniture buys here.** (See what trouble I can get into when you talk too much!)

CONSIGNOR ALERT: 50%-50% under $100, **60%-40%/$100-$1000, 70% items over $1000.** No fee. 90 days. 10%/30 days. 20%/60 days. No appointment needed.

</td></tr>
</table>

<table>
<tr><td>

Decorators Consignment Gallery

</td><td>

</td></tr>
<tr><td>

Hwy. 518 & 601
Blawenburg, NJ
08504-0242
609-466-4400

Look: TOP DRAWER

Goods: CLASS
ACT–TOP DRAWER

Prices: HIGH–LOW
(see review)

HOURS:
Thu–Sun 12-6

CLOSED: August

</td><td>

The sign on her shop door read, "Kids must either have their hand held by a parent or be on a leash." No kidding. The woman who posted this sign is married to "the wrong Kidder of Kidder Peabody, the one from the poor side of the family." No kidding. Just ask her, she'll tell you. And she is also a self-described Ross Perot fan, deeply immersed in local and national politics. No kidding. Just ask her.

And she also has **one of the best shops around, anywhere.** No kidding. Just ask me. This is the first shop I've been in where the owner has taken the time to put a mini chart (is this where Ross got the idea for his TV charts?) on the back of each and every ticket, itemizing the percentage off markdown for each dated time interval. Nifty. Just check out the four dates on the back. The top date is the highest price, and only likely to snap the trap for the choicest items. (What am I saying, it's *all* choice!) Alongside each date is a price. That price descends, with each accompanying date as they march through one 4-week period after another. If you're local, and you 're willing to play chicken and stare down the oncoming shopping competition, you can use these dates to gage just how low you're willing to go and just how long you're willing to risk waiting to buy whatever has caught your fancy. And this shop caught mine. Third-party politics and **top-drawer secondhand** goods, coming and going.

CONSIGNOR ALERT: **60% You-40% Shop** if brought to shop, 50%-50% if picked up. 120 days, 10%/30 days. Appointment required for more than 20 items.

</td></tr>
</table>

Fur Exchange

41 Mine Street
Flemington, NJ
08822
908-782-3304

Look: TOP DRAWER

Goods: CLASS
ACT–TOP DRAWER

Prices: HIGH BUT
STILL FAIR

HOURS:
Every day 10-6

CLOSED: Holidays

We've all heard of Flemington, right? And then there's Flemington Furs. Well, this is where Flemington furs go when they're ready for a change of venue. Like when you turn in your Mercedes because its time to trade in and trade up, while the old gal still has some zing left. Well, I'd like to get a full length mink while I've still got some zing left under my hood. Here, you or I can do just that for half the original cost. After 17+ years, they know their pelts. **They've got racks and racks of furs in every size, shape, length, and color, all reconditioned and temptingly displayed, just like a regular fur salon.**

Four-hanger resale shops get the occasional good-to-great fur; few regularly have enough to warrant set-aside floor space. Here, seven days a week, walk into an entire boutique-quality shop full of the little critters. I know, I know. Put away the red spray paint. It's doubly too late for these guys. Go save the living. I'm of two minds about this stuff. I was raised to pour tea and wear mink, and wound up owning my own business and wearing "a good (never discuss one's personal politics) cloth coat." I love vegetarian and a fast-food hamburger has never once crossed these lips, but I still adore the occasional prime steak, medium rare, please. You'd think I was a Libra the way I keep arriving at these balanced opinions, but I'm a Virgo.

So anyway...are you listening, Marvin? The big 50 looms in the distance. Surprise me. Before I surprise you. I've already picked out a quietly glamourous, sensuously luxurious, shimmering, full-length, wraparound, mink for slightly under $2900. Ask them to sew 'The Maniac' into the lining. Pretty please.

CONSIGNOR ALERT: You trade in your old one and get credit toward another one.

Hand Me Downs

33 Railroad Place
Hopewell, NJ
08525
609-466-1606

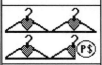

Look: CLASS ACT

Goods: STATUS
QUO – CLASS ACT

Prices: MODERATE

HOURS: Tue 10-2,
Wed–Sat 10-5,
Thu 10-7

CLOSED: Holidays

Driving around trying to find this shop, we were told to look for the train station, a gorgeous building just waiting for somebody to do something with it. Find it, and we'd find the shop. Eureka! We pulled over. A woman climbed into her car, ready to leave, just as we we arrived. Marvin, his usual outgoing self, approached and asked about the shop. She was the owner! She had a migraine and was on her way home. Having overheard her niece was still inside, I continued on. I hadn't been in the shop before, and had no idea what lay ahead. But after 14 years of marriage, I knew what was coming next, curbside. Marvin did what I call bumper and fender work (massage) for years, putting himself through life and school, using his magnificently intuitive hands to physically compliment all that he's learned about shrinking. (The results are in. The head and heart are connected.) Within minutes, she's told him her story, agreed to let him, a total stranger, work on her aching head, standing outside in the street. Whatta guy! The pain lessened, Marianne went home. Who was that masked stranger? Why, Dr. Maniac, of course.

As his trusty sidekick, having earned what I call my amateur black belt in New Age shrinking and wrapping, I had already noticed the fluorescent glare inside. This is a no–no. Right on cue, Marvin asked the niece behind the large desk to tell her aunt she should get full-spectrum fluorescent replacement bulbs to lessen the migraine frequency and intensity. I predict this **attractive, well-stocked shop** will continue to be one of central New Jersey's better secondhand kiddie shops, especially now that Marianne is feeling better. All it needs is a play area. Maybe she does, too.
P.S. A Girl Scout Authorized Equipment Agency and new christening outfits.
CONSIGNOR ALERT: 50%-50% split. $4 fee. 12 weeks. Clothes 90 days. Toys & equipment.30 item max. By appointment only.

Hunterdon Exchange	
155 Main Street Flemington, NJ 08822 **908-782-6229** 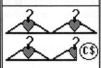	Jackets $1, skirts $1, dresses $1, golf balls 50¢! Oddball pricing with some great buys mixed in. Here of all places (and there were a lot places) after a 2 year search spanning two lost winters we finally found a pair of brand-new, secondhand ice skates for Marvin's earth grippers and grabbers (size 12 1/2EEE) for only $10. Now he can keep Morgan company on the ice as she whirls and twirls and leaps in her secondhand one-piece stretch suits and little frilly skirts and Susan Bristol sweaters. While he sat his gorgeous size 44L self down on the little bench in the far backroom trying on the skates to see if they fit, I prowled the shop, getting a feel for the place.
Look: STATUS QUO **Goods:** STATUS QUO–TOP DRAWER **Prices:** UP & DOWN	Rotating volunteers worked the rooms, hovered, prowled (for shoplifters?), did the books, handled customers, hesitating over facts like hours and consigning policies. **Lots and lots of charming housewares and curiosities,** like the Silvertone phonograph, sans needle, $65. **Crafts** displayed in the front room ran the price and quality gamut. I saw lots and lots of pillows, potholders and such. But then there was the 2-foot saw with the scene of a lighthouse and swirling surf, hand-painted on the blade. I'm not sure I get the drift (wood being the traditional material of choice). I do get that this shop is an idiosyncratic, timeless work of art (or piece of work?) Dare I haul out that old saw, "Saw is in the art of the potholder", or how about "I know art when I saw it"?
HOURS: Mon–Sat 10-4:30, Sun 1-4:30	
CLOSED: Holidays	**CONSIGNOR ALERT: 70% You-30% Shop.** $3 annual fee. Wednesdays for crafts, Thursdays, antiques. Donations accepted. Benefits Hunterdon Medical Center.

Joan's Attic	
Princeton Shp. Ctr. N. Harrison St. Princeton, NJ 08540 **609-252-1222** 	Isn't. An attic that is. It's situated at ground level in an older but wiser strip mall, and cozy-small enough to be dropped inside the real-life attic of one of Princeton's larger homes. Its ambience is well matched to its mission, and it's an emotionally perfect fit for its customers. All profits and donations benefit "familyborn, a consumer-oriented, in or out of hospital program...offer(ing) complete prenatal, birth, postpartum and gynecological services to women of all ages." Thoughtful signs in English and Spanish tell the shopper who is what, and what is where, and what's the deal.
Look: TOP DRAWER **Goods:** STATUS QUO–TOP DRAWER **Prices:** LOW–HIGH	From the gorgeous shopfront window filled with hand-painted and handcrafted furniture and clothing to the free-floating clouds hand-painted in frame-enclosed murals on the pastel-pretty walls to the **high quality clothing, accessories and toys,** it is a labor of love. **I loved this place, and it loved me right back.**
HOURS: Mon–Fri 10-4, Thu 10-8, Sat 10-5	**P.S.** Only breast pump rental in the area. Space provided for nursing mothers.
CLOSED: Christmas week	**CONSIGNOR ALERT:** 50%-50% split. $3 fee/visit. 25 items or less. 90 days. 25%/60 days. By appointment only. Benefits The Mildred Morgan Center for Birth & Women's Health.

Nearly New Shop

234 Nassau St.
Princeton, NJ
08540
609-924-5720

Look: STATUS QUO

Goods: HO HUM –
TOP DRAWER

Prices: LOW–HIGH

HOURS:
Mon–Sat 10-5

CLOSED: Holidays

More like Nearly Missed. Talk about **tucked away**. Don't blink or you'll miss it. Let me give you lots and lots of how-to-find-it type tips, 'cause the shop is worth the little bit of extra effort it might take you to find. The little walkway running alongside the mustard yellow trim and grey-stone Weldon Real Estate office leads straight to Princeton's time-honored charity family clothing shop. Go to the very rear, up the wide, wide red fire stairwell and into great bargains tucked in among the seriously serviceable. **I especially liked the evening wear section** right by the front door. Working the racks, I discovered a great heavy wool sweater for Marvin, a white brocade Jessica McClintock party dress ($15) for Morgan and a Jaeger grey wool and abalone-shell-buttoned sheath dress with huge hip pockets for me (only $24).

Too bad I had to leave them behind. I had run out of cash, and was running out of checks, and didn't even have enough to pay monthly bills. They don't take credit cards, and the weather was just too cold and miserable to wander around in the gathering gloom of late afternoon trying to find a MAC. Phooey! Next time I'll come loaded for bear.

P.S. No parking in the rear. You are doomed to circle Nassau & Chestnut Streets.

CONSIGNOR ALERT: 50%-50%. 36-days. $3 fee/25 items. By appointment. Extensive How-To sheet. Donations accepted. Benefits Princeton Day School Scholarship Fund.

Peanut Gallery

Hwy. #518 & #601
Blawenburg, NJ
08504
609-466-4500

Look: TOP DRAWER

Goods: STATUS
QUO–TOP DRAWER

Prices: MODERATE

HOURS:
Wed, Thu 11:30-
4:30, Fri, Sat 11-4

CLOSED:
Christmans week

It's brown and it's little and it's **irresistible**. You'll find you can't help coming back for more, as everything here costs peanuts.

CONSIGNOR ALERT: 50%-50% split. $1 annual fee. 90 days. Appointment preferred.

Princeton Consignment Boutique	
1378 (Rt. 206 So.) Village Shopper Skillman, NJ 08858 **609-924-2288**	Pushing hard against the driving rain and our flagging spirits, we wanted just one more stop, just one more shop. Intermittent morning showers had turned to an incessant twilight downpour. Wipers were useless. It was impossible to see. Making things worse (how could things get worse?), both sides of the street had large shopping centers. We went in one driveway and out another, searching. Fatigued, frustrated, Marvin pulled up to the curb and surrendered to the elements, resigned that this would be the one that got away. Turning to leave, we gasped in amazement. We were parked right in front of the shop.
Look: TOP DRAWER **Goods:** STATUS QUO–TOP DRAWER **Prices:** MODERATE	Waiting inside were three women as different looking as any three women could possibly be, but sharing an uncommonly blythe spirit. I felt as if I had stumbled out of the threatening forest of Snow White (the scene where the fleeing wicked witch falls to her death) only to land in the enchanted forest of Sleeping Beauty's three fairy godmothers. They fairly flew from one customer to another, from one rack to another, merrily laughing as they played off one another, waiting on dauntless fellow shoppers. **I was impressed by the racks of ballgowns** (the mice dress-sewing
HOURS: Tue-Sat 10-6, Thu 10-8	scene from Cinderella?), beautiful enough for any happy ending. Everyday wasn't as fanciful, but way better than the pre-fairy godmother Cinderella. In the midst of all this merriment, the unsuspecting owner started to tell US about OUR book. Without looking, she grabbed someone else's earlier, failed effort by mistake, waving it in her hand. Suppressing giggles, and without blowing our cover, we corrected the error of her ways. Brushing off fairy dust, we climbed back into our awaiting pumpkin. The day had a happy ending, afterall.
CLOSED: Holidays	**CONSIGNOR ALERT:** 50%-50% split. $2.50 fee. 60 days, 10%/21 day. By appointment.

Sweet Repeats	
Rtes. 519 & 604 Cane Farm Rosemont, NJ 08559 **609-397-9383** 	Driving around, semi-lost, like a bunch of headless chickens, spending another "working" Saturday on the road, we followed the Delaware River north, upriver from Lambertville, downriver from Frenchtown. We passed through New Hope, over the edge of Volume II's charted resale world, into the great unknown. Many moons ago, Sweet Repeats' owner sent me a pamphlet she compiled describing local shops. Intrigued, I made a mental note to track down her store. The town is nothing more than a crossroads, tiny enough to warrant chicken-crossing-the-road jokes, charming enough to warrant dual-income working stiffs like us, caught up in the daily struggle to (stylishly) survive, to give IT all up (well some of IT) and move here. What the well-crafted pink pamphlet failed to describe were her architectural circumstances: Forty traditionally low-slung chicken coops converted into a capitalistic enterprise zone. Don't be deterred, oh weak of heart (liver and gizzard).
Look: BLUE RIBBON **Goods:** GRADE A **Prices:** MEDIUM– EXTRA LARGE	I often fantasize moving to the country, until my conscious self butts in, forcing me to remember "there'd be no place to shop, Dorothy." The daydream becomes nightmare. But Sweet Repeats, like the crowing rooster that greets the rosy glow of dawn, is my happy wake up call. (Chicken jokes again!) Even a semi-city slicker like
HOURS: Wed–Sat 10-5	me could be very happy nested in among these converted coops. Here's the straight poop. **This is one of the nicest, friendliest women's-only secondhand shops, ever.** No feathers flew except in the packed-to-the-rafters "after 5:00 room" with prices so reasonable you won't spend all your egg money just to dress your size 4 (Cornish hen), or size 20 (full-breasted roaster) frame.
CLOSED: Holidays	**CONSIGNOR ALERT:** 50%-50% split. By appointment only.

TOUR #17
THE BIG PICTURE OVER THE LONG HAUL

The long ride to Allentown allowed me precious down time to look back over my life, look back over the last year, and remember. First notion to pop into my mind? A worrisome bit of cerebral cinder irritating my field of vision. Early subterranean grumblings from certain shopkeepers (who shall remain anonymous), had reverberated over the grapevine. It was always the same. Versions on a theme (and it wasn't by Paginini) they began with 'Just Who does She think She is?', followed by 'Just what are Her qualifications to be writing this book and criticizing Me?' They took it personally, you see. In their minds, the review wasn't about their store. It was about them. So, I titled a chapter head using their own rhetorical questioning in an attempt to bring background whispers to the forefront, making light of a serious issue. The gentle touch of humor can oftentimes diffuse a big knot of anger. It was called: Just Who Does She Think She Is, Anyway? Not one reader, by the way, has raised this question in all the thousands of letters and phone calls we've received.

Uncertain, inexperienced, and alone with this controversial new way of doing things, I sometimes asked myself The Big Ones. It's a responsibility, calling into question whether or not someone is doing a good job, and an even bigger one when you hold them up to public scrutiny. It was natural enough that they would want to turn the tables. When The Guide first came out almost no one, except for Marvin and Shopper Lady, understood what I was trying to do. Some got it ALL wrong. To this day I regularly get calls from owners seeking advertising space, asking how much it costs to get in The Guide. Patronizing me, others held it to be an "Oh, isn't that cute", here today gone tomorrow curiosity, hoping to water down The Guide's influence over their business. Or ignored it and me, hoping both would just go away. Many in the biz for decades, didn't and don't, understand their own power in the marketplace, or just how much they kept and keep themselves on the economic fringe. Or had any idea how they stacked up against the competition just down the street or (next door). Or how shopkeepers and customers alike wanted a handle on the basics.

We all had questions about hours, location, consignment policy. A few the-glass-is-half-empty types, private owners and volunteer managers alike, who by nature will never think there is enough to go around for them, got the idea immediately, and wouldn't let The Guide in their stores, even tried to squelch distribution. A very few the-glass-is-half-full types also understood immediately, and threw out the red carpet, offering to help.

So how does someone get to become the Thrift Shop Maniac? Where do they go for training? How do MY grades stack up? **Allentown holds part of the answer.**

I used to come here all the time in another life. I'd drive up the Pennsylvania Turnpike in my company subsidized blue Audi, the trunk filled with food and cooking equipment and pamphlets and brochures. I was headed to Hess's flagship store in downtown Allentown. Here comes the resume part. Do any of you out there remember getting freebie hot dogs thrust at you in department stores for a while there? I was partly responsible. I was the one who designed training programs for microwave oven demonstrators. It was part of my job description to teach them about the difference between ionizing and non-ionizing waves of energy, well enough to hold their own with doctors and x-ray technicians. (This from someone who had failed college Physics.) It was my job to teach them how to manage the ovens, cook the food, handle screaming kids and resistant parents, and sell, all at the same time. Kinda like that Helen Reddy song, "I Am Woman." (I had hired and trained the one guy to apply for the job. He bombed out.) I also regularly did personal appearances in department and appliance stores and occasional interviews on TV and radio, and performed a sort of on stage combination cooking lesson and stand up comedy act.

For a while I loved it. I was still around food. I had a great deal of independence. The ladies on my team were great! The job was just fringe enough. I was in a business made up mostly of women, but was only one of four with any rank above that of bookkeeper or steno or key punch operator working in a business dependent on our cheap labor. A business built by and for men, selling mostly to women. The company I worked for paid me almost no nevermind. My job was underwritten by the good ol' boy parent company back in the Midwest, a thriving, multi-national corporation. I cost the regional distributor where I worked very little. (The distributor has since, sadly but wisely, gone out of business under the parent company's always-get-rid-of-the-middleman-if-you-can theory and the distributor's Peter-Principal failure to respond to changes in the marketplace. Since I cost them little or no out of pocket money, that was another good reason to leave well enough alone if I was doing a good enough job. And I was. I bopped around the country side going from one hot dog town to one half baked back woods appliance store to another. I had a blast! But I also saw the writing on the wall. I and others like me, hired by my company and it's competitors, did our job educating the public to the joys of microwave cooking, too well. Eventually, we were phased out. I stopped coming to Allentown.

Keeping me on, the distributor assigned me a territory as an appliance salesman. I learned how to 'sell' myself and thereby enough refrigerators and air conditioners and dryers, etc. (white goods) to make my monthly 'numbers,' but I hated the life. As soon as you get within arm's length of your quota, they raise it on you. It was all top down, type-A, shell games. Unsuited, I lasted less than six months.

So here I was in Allentown once again. Same place, different raison d'être. Pulling maps and directions out of the ol' memory bank, it all started coming back. Driving down Seventh Street I could see that a lot had changed, a lot was the same. To this outsider, the area's topography and history, and therefore way of life, are unfamiliar enough that I was aware of being far away from home. A good feeling. One that affords perspective. The streets are just as clean, but they seem emptier. I remember many more pedestrians. Familiar landmarks still stand, but there are gaping holes where buildings have been torn down and not replaced. Hess's empire has been trimmed. The branch nearest home in Plymouth Meeting closed several years ago, but the downtown Allentown mother lode holds her head high. Cities all across our country, big and small, have been in retreat. So too, it could be argued, is our culture, our civilization. Here, the edges are frayed, the center is on hold and holding.

Resale has been one vibrant economic response to our country's financial malaise. Little Emmaus has taken up resale in a big way. We'd never been here before, but the long list of shop names on the database with **Emmaus, Emmaus, Emmaus** repeated over and over again gave me reason enough to want to come.

Arriving on the outskirts of Allentown, we made one of those map-free, unplanned, deeply intuitive guesses that have gotten us this far. We took a left hand turn onto Emmaus Avenue. It took us straight to Emmaus. Brilliant piece of deductive reasoning. Four benches, a flag pole with the American flag flying over a banner that proclaims, Tree City USA, and an enormous pine tree stand in the triangular, grassy plot of this angular, curiously shaped town center. Something as seemingly innocuous as planting shade trees can be a HOT TOPIC in a small town. It took a lot of insider power plays to raise the money, reactivate the dormant Shade Tree Commission (honest), and get the job done. Just ask **John Gold**, the self-styled local memory bank and all-around town booster, who jump-started the Commission and remains an active board member of the Chamber of Commerce since joining in 1962.

Sidewalks were crowded, the parking spots all taken. We got lucky again, and grabbed one just as somebody pulled out. I just sat there for a while and tried to take it 'all' in, something that can take seconds or a lifetime. Your choice. **Rodale, Rodale, Rodale** might as well be Emmaus' nickname. Corporate headquarters for this world-renowned publisher and promoter of all things organic and healthy are located at the eastern end and outbuildings are scattered all over town, with Fitness House serving meals to all the employees. **Richard's Market**, the Meridian Bank and next door, the old Gould Pharmacy, founded by Josiah Cole Gould, now in its 4th generation with John Gould Jr., its current proprietor/raconteur. The old pharmacy stands empty. They recently moved across the street to bigger digs. Over the old door way just under the roof the word *Deapodeke* (The Pharmacy) is printed in big black letters. Old German in origin, but transformed by the local Pennsylvania Dutch and Moravians. One very popular **diner (there are two, one going in, one going out of town)** serves up starch, starch and more starch, glistening with a sheen of grease. An ethnic culinary connection?

You must try **Lee Gribben's** takeout on 417 Chestnut St. in Emmaus. Their Pita Vegi made the clouds part and the rain stop. I thought I was back in Oregon as I feasted on sprouts and carrots and cucumber and Monterey Jack and sunflower seeds and a mustard-herb mayo dressing that dribbled down my chin as I sat outside in the car. If I had been feeling less politically correct that day, there was also ham, turkey, roast beef, BBQ chicken all available on a large assortment of breads. They have dreamy chocolate mini desserts, stylistically correct soda, soup, sandwiches and all sorts of all-American and international salads. A local potato chip, by a company named Good's, *was.*

The old-fashioned corner pet store was a great place for Marvin and Morgan and sidekick Nina to hang out while I did my Maniac thing. Mission completed, we finished the ride through town. Going further north and west, we traveled past a row-house corridor of so-clean-you-could-eat-off-'em streets and front steps, and the gnarled and pruned, plumber's pipe trellis, trained-to-within-an inch-of-its-life vine covered porches of a type and style found only hereabouts. Residential opened up and switched to commercial zoning. Look, Marvin! Pull over. There's another one. Look at those enormous brown jugs. What are they doing here? Why were they ever made? Where did they come from? We had arrived in Twin Jugs country.

TOUR #17

10	B&N	Emmaus
13	Community Thrift Store	Allentown
8	Elephant's Trunk	Emmaus
14	Good Shepherd	Allentown
15	Hidden Treasures	Hellertown
6	Men's Again	Allentown
7	Once Is Not Enuff	Emmaus
12	Pete's	Allentown
9	Positively Plus	Emmaus
1	Round Two	Coopersburg
4	Trinity Computers	Allentown
5	Twice As Nice - Children	Allentown
2	Twice As Nice - Women	Allentown
3	Twice As Nice - Treasures	Allentown
11	Twin Jugs	Emmaus

*Note: This list has a shop's entire name. Names in review boxes may have been shortened a tad to fit. Numbers before each shop name correspond to their numbered location on each map. **Shops with a star sold Volume II. Volume III? ASK!**

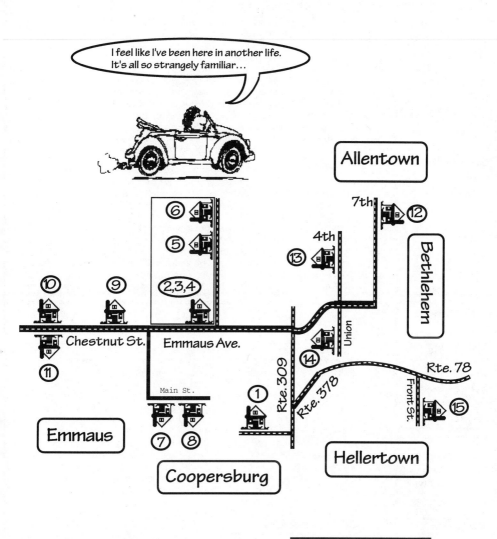

B & N	
4054 Chestnut St. Emmaus, PA 18049 **610-967-0329** **Look:** STATUS QUO **Goods:** HO HUM– TOP DRAWER **Prices:** MODERATE – HIGH **HOURS:** Mon–Thu 9-5:30, Fri, Sat 9-6, Sun 9-4 **CLOSED:** Holidays	It really wasn't a very pretty sight. An architectural underachiever, the building's misleading rough, grey concrete exterior provided shelter, only, for an **uncommonly practical treasure trove of earthly goods**. Once one of life's necessities, now a cast off, the couch potato, lay incumbent on one out of an ass-ortment of emminently forgettable sofas. Arms squeezing tight enough to mash, Morgan schlepped the half-baked $5 spud around with her on a whirlwind tour of the shop, clutched so tight it probably could've used the ($15) blood pressure kit. (She wouldn't pop for the potato with her allowance, so you can bet I wouldn't with mine.) Lined up, ready to use, were small appliances of every conceivable size, shape, price point and use, capable of toasting bread, brewing coffee, and popping corn (three in one?). Old fashioned clear, green and blue glass electrical insulators were massed and huddled, their value accorded by age and shade, their vibrant colors obscured in deep-as-they-were-wide shelves. Smack dab in the middle of this wall to wall linoleum gloom and doom, a Pioneer stereo system spread its glorious particle-board wings and sang out in heavenly, three (component) part harmony. Only $600, originally $1200. Cames with two 3.5' speakers all stacked like a heavy metal wedding cake. In the graveled parking lot was an Ivanhoe, portable, three burner gas range (catering equipment?) $100. Browning Pro-Competition bow and arrow set was marked $400, but he'd take $300. Fifteen years married to a brilliant, sensitive, retired hippie, active-do-gooder, and there he was, taking aim. Maybe he'd manage to scewer the couch potato, and put it out of its sainted misery (after Morgan released it from her grasp), by substituting the arrow for one of those baked potato nails. **CONSIGNOR ALERT:** Buys outright or **70% You-30% Store**. No fee. Open ended term.
Community Place	
144 N. 7th St. Allentown, PA 18102 **610-4342461**  **Look:** BOTTOMFEEDER **Goods:** DOWN & OUT–TOP DRAWER **Prices:** UP & DOWN **HOURS:** Tue–Fri 10-5, Sat 11-3 **CLOSED:** Holidays	The place is so depressing I didn't know where or how to begin. I almost walked out. Most clothes were dirty and drab except for a few never worn shirts from a Florida men's shop. Someone, worker ? customer? street person? scurried into the impromptu bunk bed of stacked sofas. Napping? The sight stopped me dead in my tracks. When I came to, I was standing in front of a long rectangular black enamel box, gently tapered at the top with feathery brush stroke flowers in faded glory, dead center. Frayed mover's heft belt, linked to the sides of the gizmo, drooped toward the floor. I stood in front of this contradiction of 1920's machinery disguised in a boudoir box. What in the world was it.? I lifted the lid. A ha! One of the earliest ever, museum quality, "all-you-have-to-do-ladies-is-just-stand-there-and-let-this-latest-miracle-invention-jiggle-off-the-pounds" exercizers. If the motor turned over, a collector would gladly kick in ten times the $40 price tag for this Tower of Boston slight of hand if not waist. A Nordic Trac will never look this good in seventy year Near a shelf of unpainted plaster casts from some hobby shop's oversupply, a solid brass, outdoor chandelier ($85) stood on end, precariously displayed in what might have been a high traffic area if the store had had any. **Bottomfeeder turned weight loss museum**, there was a gigantic, old fashioned Fairbanks Standard Scale, also black, also metal, trimmed in gold paint. Cast iron weights dangled from the sliding brass notched read-out arm extended across a wooden floor large enough to hold and weigh almost anything. Jenny? Jane? Richard? Next time you're in town doing a personal appearance, please donate a bucket and mop, some elbow grease, and volunteer some lessons in aerobic spring cleaning. **CONSIGNOR ALERT:** Buys outright now. Consignments soon. $10 local delivery fee

Elephant's Trunk

348 Main St.
Emmaus, PA 18049
610-967-6621

Look: CLASS ACT

Goods: STATUS QUO–TOP DRAWER

Prices: UP & DOWN

HOURS:
Mon – Sat 10-4

CLOSED: Holidays

I knew it. Looking in the sparse, precise window display, it had to be a charity resale run by Ladies of The Old School. Inventoy echoed the implied attitudes and values of the shop window's muted opening statement. "Stand up straight," instructed the wine glasses, placed just so. "Eat you oatmeal, it's getting cold," proclaimed the pristine white china. "Don't talk with your mouthfull", chided the crisply folded napkins. Joining forces with fellow customers in full winter dress parade, we marched around the outer circle created by display cases plunked in the middle, taking our morning constitutional.

Unexpectedly, I found myself entertaining the pleasurable possibility of buying at least one item per cubbyhole. Like the sweetly sentimental, a handpainted mug in celadon and pink with gold overlay, sporting a hefty $25 price tag, distinctively signed on the bottom by a long ago artist, Elizabeth Pitman Fleming. A set of fruit plates, priced $6 each, were propped up against the back of a book case shelf. Stashed behind? One of those backless, chiropractor- correct, sort of stools, sort of chairs, covered in brown furry plush, $10. Workmanship was worthy of the $35 price for a set of 8 etched, certified, limited edition mugs from Sweden. Design wasn't. Framed,homey homily embroidery "Friends are The Flowers in the Garden of Life", was on the money at $20, as were Italian, hand-painted, electrified candle holders, $60. **These staunchly self-sufficient ladies of a certain age still know what's what.**

CONSIGNOR ALERT: Benefits Planned Parenthood of North East Pennsylvania

Good Shepherd

1047 Union Blvd.
Allentown, PA
18103
610-437-4312

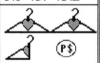

Look:
BOTTOMFEEDER

Goods: DOWN & OUT–STATUS QUO

Prices: LOW–MODERATE

HOURS:
Mon–Sat 9-5,
Thu 9-8

CLOSED: Holidays

The day had been a long one. We were thrifted out. Zooming out of town, looking for Rte. 309, heading for home, Marvin and I suddenly and unexpectedly yelled in unison: "There's another one!" The infamous Just One More Thrift Shop Syndrome, an insidious, chronic condition, kicked in. He got to wait outside in the car, reading his paper, managing Morgan and her friend Nina. I had to go in and do all the 'work'. I pushed back hangers to better inspect a toggled, hooded, red plaid stadium coat. At $48 it was the one good, albeit expensive item in the place. I gawked at the never worn requisite pink Mary Kay smock, $7.97, pulled from the crowded racks. I poked around the inevitable $1.97 sour cream glasses and florist vases, the soon-to-be-collectible purple Barney lunch box, lost in Maniac reverie..

Gradually it filtered through. Morgan had given up on staying in the car. She decided to join the hunt, bless her little mini Maniac heart. She appeared round the corner, lugging one of two enormous clear plastic bags filled to bursting with a menagerie of stuffed animals. I had seen them coming in, and prematurely rejoiced had remained behind. She blows off her fast money on a collection of the grubby little creatures, grown so large, there's no longer room for her in her bed. She's taken to sleeping in the (so far) doll free guest room double bed. One well-meaning customer (frustrated Grannie type?) without asking me, had given her 25¢ to make up the difference. Fatigue, and the prospect of four dozen mangy newcommers caused me to reach a state of maternal unreasonableness. I put my foot (and horns) down: We got into one of those Mother/Daughter things. "It's my house. No you can't." "It's my money. Yes, I can." Every shopper in the place turned to watch the ageless drama unfold. She reluctantly and vosciferously relinquished the controversial booty. The clerk graciously returned her money. I had won. Morgan stormed out the door. I had lost. I just knew I was going to have to pay, big time, all the way home. Such is life.

CONSIGNOR ALERT: Donations only. Benefits Good Shepherd Work Services.

Hidden Treasures

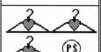

415 Front Street
Hellertown, PA
18055

610-838-0790

Look: TOP DRAWER

Goods: STATUS QUO

Prices: MODERATE

HOURS:
Mon-Sat 10-5

CLOSED: Holidays

Take one old side street garage in an old sitting around waiting for something, anything to happen little old town. **Apply** a generous coat of cream and rust colored paint to the exterior walls and three permanently pulled down, pull up entrance bays. **Hang** a hat wreath on the door. **Add** a lot of new country pine furniture with heart cut-outs and black steel hinges. **Scatter** giftty shoppe goods about like the stainless steel milk jug, a 50's jute box, a green go to market chicken crate, **Add** an equal measure of sturdy secondhand furniture, placed just so by a warm, outgoing personality. **Stir gently.**

There! Now you've got it. What, you say? What have you got? Why, the recipe for **a cutie pie of a shop,** that's what.

CONSIGNOR ALERT: 50%-50% split. No fee. 42 days. No appointment for small items.

Men's Again

2905 Emmaus Ave.
Allentown, PA
18103

610-797-6725

Look: CLASS ACT

Goods: STATUS QUO–CLASS ACT

Prices: LOW–MODERATE

HOURS: Mon-Wed & Sat 10-5, Thu & Fri 10-8, Sun 12-4

CLOSED: Holidays

Men have it rough, resale or retail. They just don't have as many shops, as many styles from which to choose. But here in Allentown, at least, where they have a secondhand shop all to themselves, the odds in their favor just got a little bit better. Whole families pass through this strip mall turned resale enterprise zone, spending the morning, doing all five stores. I inadvertently tracked the same family through women's, kids, and here to men's. A satisfied regular, he was trying on shoes, describing to his wife the other purchases he'd made here. Marvin and I scouted around, hoping he'd get lucky, too. Alas, the dice didn't roll in our favor. But I did see some **better than average duds.**

A Maniac First occurred here: a full-dress army uniform, braids and epaulets and all, size 42, $50. The pants, however, were a different shade of blue from the jacket. Is that regulation? A civilian-issue Polo, navy blue blazer, with the requisite snappy brass buttons, could have been purchased here for only $38. Silk ties ranged from $5 to $8, depending on design and condition. A Land's End oxford-cloth button-down shirt was $6. There was a classic London Fog, double-breasted raincoat, with lining and belt intact and in excellent condition, 34S, and also $50. We all know what that would have cost at nearby Hess's Department Store, the dominant retailer in the region. Nothing here that would knock 'em dead at the baccarat tables in Monte Carlo or wow 'em over lunch at Bicci's during the height of the Palm Beach season. Most regular guys, however, are Joe Better-Than-Average by day, and only Bond in their dreams. Who REALLY cares what the high rollers are up to except their tailors? 'No one would ever know' wardrobes Men's Again will wow 'em while you attend that marketing meeting at the conference center in King of Prussia, address the academic symposium in Princeton, or dine at the club.

CONSIGNOR ALERT: 50%-50% split. 10¢ tagging fee/item. 60 days. Reduced at their discretion. By appointment only.

Once Is Not Enuff

4th & Main Sts.
Emmaus, PA 18049
610-967-4383

Look: TOP DRAWER
Goods: STATUS QUO–TOP DRAWER
Prices: MODERATE
HOURS: Mon–Wed & Sat 10-5, Thu & Fri 10-5, Sun 12-4

CLOSED: Holidays

A customer actually sucked wind coming in this place. Entering just one step behind, I heard the sound and couldn't begin to imagine what had caused such an involuntary, unladylike noise to emerge from the depths of such a well-dressed, well mannered woman (entering, she held the door for me and smiled), only to do exactly the same thing myself. We were **overcome with admiration** for the immediate, hit you in the face splendor of it all. Wow. Escada in Emmaus. Who woulda thunk!

Jo stood at the register wearing a rhinestone pin that spelled her name, barely stopping to catch her breath. Positioned under a glamorous chandelier, she rang up sale after sale. Customers lined-up around the jewelery display case, spending the time aimably, waiting their turn. At a second, jewelery bedecked work station over in the corner, Nancy, the owner and yet another employee, fielded phone calls, answered customers' questions. The place was jumpin'. Roaming the racks I felt like a kid turned loose in a candy store with a her week's allowance jingling in her pocket. I didn't know what to grab first. I wound up buying a pair of on sale ($42) ankle height black cowboy boots for Zydeco dancing (Thank you, Virginia) and a winter white, Anne Klein, 3/4 length jacket ($48) to wear over some of my sleevless evening dresses.(Marvin shouldn't have stayed in the car.) Both items had been on my shopper lady wish list. Chauvanistically, I never dreamed they would turn up way out here in "the boonies". The Escada was a never worn, rust colored shearling jacket with matching earmuffs, no less, marked down to $425 from God only knows what ($2500?). **I could live happily ever after in Emmaus.** Coulda fooled me.

CONSIGNOR ALERT: 50%-50% split. No fee. 60 days. By appointment: Mon–Sat 10:30-3:30. 25 items/30 minute appointment. Hangers only.

Pete's

231 N. Seventh St.
Allentown, PA 18102
610-433-4481

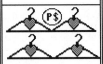

Look: CLASS ACT
Goods: STATUS QUO–TOP DRAWER
Prices: ?
HOURS: Fri, Sat & Sun 10-5

CLOSED: Holidays

Seventh Avenue, New York City and Seventh Street, Allentown share a common name and purpose. There the similarity ends. Saturday afternoons in Manhattan are bust out city. Allentown, same time, different venue, you could roll a bowling ball down this main shopping drag, hitting no one and nothing. It's all but desserted.I didn't expect much from the abbreviated name on the window, and the shopper free enterprise zone. Fake out smarty pants! Extensive inventory in the block long shop ranged from **safe secondhand to the wierd and wonderful. My kinda place.** I'd barely gotten a fix on the place, when Pete popped down the steps from the secondfloor bench, table and chair showroom. He immediately assumed a deep and abiding interest on my part in the oversized, gently curving veneered German bookcase, circa 1927, simply because I was stopped in front of it, slackjawed. He was right. How did this simply elegant, bigger than life import make it to America intact? He demonstrated the pull apart pin process. "The whole thing can be strapped on top of a station wagon. Got a station wagon?" he enterprisingly enquired. A similar, but less masterfully crafted wardrobe from the same era was $450. A Janssen piano like the one I'd pounded with bravado as a child, $1100.

What else caught my eye? An early radio in it's own wooden cabinet. Five piece, off white, demurely scaled, blissfully bastardized, Made in America (1930's?) French provincial living room set, canning in tact, $800. Four brass poles spanning the ceiling supported a showroom's worth of light fixtures from every age, for every mood. 18 pieces of boudoire bakalite, $95. Detroit Star enameled gas range. Wrought iron trellise and ivy covered arch way ($75). **Mind-boggling!**

CONSIGNOR ALERT: They buy everything outright.

Positively Plus	
427 Chestnut St. Emmaus, PA 18049 **610-966-4025**	Cute enough, the name doesn't quite 'do' it. Hard to tell at first, drive-by glance what's going on here. The ole grey matter registered the name, but really responded to the word reasale in smaller letters on the window. A well-trained creature of conditioned reflex, I automatically pulled over and parked. Inside, name recognition kicked in after bumping into a two piece Elizabeth. Oh, it's for larger women! Although sizes start at 14, and I wear anything from 6 (unusual, but it's happened) to 12 (more like it), up to a 14 (ouch) depending on the manufacturer, the cut and just how many times something's been laundered, there was little in the 'lower' registers to tempt. **Inventory began to get serious around 18, though there wasn't depth or breadth in any size until the 20's.**
Look: STATUS QUO **Goods:** STATUS QUO **Prices:** MODERATE **HOURS:** Wed-Sun 10:30-3:30 **CLOSED:** Holidays	Slim pickins can be explained by a confluence of dates on the secondhand calendar, and retail reality. **1)** October saw their grand opening. Full figure consignors haven't heard about this place on the good-news-doesn't-always-travel-fast grapevine, or if they have, they have yet to make their mental U Turns. Habit still takes them down that old, familiar resale rut to a shop that only makes a passing nod in their direction with all of two feet of rack space in 16 and up. **2)** It was February. Inventory is skimpy most places. **3)** Women's larger sizes are still the orphan of retail, although adoption papers are in the works. Manufacturers and retailers are taking that first sip of wake up and smell the coffee; beautiful, big as real life models are regularly appearing in catalogues if not runways. Spring's a commin'. A change of seasons and the corresponding growth spurt of consignments should give this friendly newcommer the gentle nudge it needs. Get out the word, ladies. **The nearest shop in your size is over an hour away in Jenkintown. The only other one I know? Way south in Collingswood., NJ.** **CONSIGNOR ALERT:** 50%-50%. $5 yearly fee. 90 days. 20%/30 days. 40%/60days. By appointment only. 25 items/appointment. No reconsignments.

Round Two	
Fairmont Village SC Rte. 309 Coopersburg, PA 18036 **610-282-3612**	Christmastime, shops usually cut back or end winter consignments. Racks thin out, shelves are bare. Puxsatawney Phil's necessarily unpredictable thumbs-up or down to spring, coincides with the traditionally certain melting trickle of warm weather consignments, heralding the great March and April thaw. Phil and I were confused. The consignment/donations calendar said spring, the two-stores-wide, densely packed inventory predicted six more weeks of winter. Perplexed, I began my rack attack, hoping to lay claim to mountains of booty.
	I considered buying the Eddie Bauer cream colored flannel shirt with pink and white floral embroidery on the collar, $8, with an additional 20% off. Morgan nixed it. The one and only outfit I personally considered was an overpriced Carol Little two-piece for $60. Even presale, $45 would have been more like. The black-and-white Macy's Evan Picone houndstooth was the best men's had to offer. At $25 minus that 20%, it was **a real bargain**, but it was one size too small for Marvin's 44L he-man frame. An assortment of colorful, never worn, $12 NBA basketball shirts were sure to find a gym locker soon, just not ours. We like to keep the money for the 'home' team. **Tons of toys**, all out of reach. Curiously for a family store, none placed for immediate gratifi-cation. Signs ironically proclaimed: "Toys Are Not To Be Played With." **P.S. 24-hour return policy.**
Look: CLASS ACT **Goods:** STATUS QUO **Prices:** MODERATE **HOURS:** Mon-Fri 10-8, Sat 10-4, Sun 12-4 **CLOSED:** Holidays	**CONSIGNOR ALERT:** 50%-50% if you don't reclaim unsold items. 40% You-60% Store if you do. Expensive items 50%-50%. 42 days. 50 items/appointment.

Trinity Computers	
2915 W. Emmaus Ave. Allentown, PA 18103 **610-791-4889**	Go through women's. Down the stairs to the basement. Pry yourself free of all the inviting secondhand books. Pass through furniture and housewares. Head toward the sunlight passing through the glass doorway. Trinity is in the corner office. That's the hard way. Or come around the side of the building alongside the parking lot, past the frilly lingere and down the outside set of steps. That's the easy way. Either way, you're there (or here).
	According to Marvin, "it's mostly new computer equipment and special configured systems which they build from scratch. They had some used items for sale which were fairly recent models."
Look: CLASS ACT **Goods:** HO HUM **Prices:** ASK	
HOURS: Mon-Wed 10-5, Thu, Fri 10-8, Sat 10-4	**P.S.** They offer a **30-60 day warranty** depending on the item's age and condition.
CLOSED: 1 week in Summer.	**CONSIGNOR ALERT:** They take trade ins and then sell them as used components.

Twice As Nice-Women	
2915 Emmaus Ave. Allentown, PA 18103 **610-797-6722** 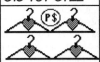	It was the end of January, the end of the winter season. It was our first foray into Allentown and Bethlehem, virgin territory lying far to the north of the known Maniac world. Excitement mounted. What shops would we discover? What treasures would we unearth? What would the natives be like? Wandering around with nothing more than car phone and outdated data bank, no map, no guide, no clue. It was also our first dumb-luck stop of the day. **Coming here, we felt like the first explorers to accidentally stumble upon the mythic City of Gold.**
Look: TOP DRAWER **Goods:** STATUS QUO-TOP DRAWER **Prices:** MODERATE	It's an entire 'pueblo' (read **strip mall**) **of interconnecting, jointly owned, but separately managed shops, full to overflowing.** Housed in individual buildings that achieve a common bond of shared esthetic standards (under shared roofs), with women's predictably outshining the others. Remember just how many more women's first-sale shops exist out there in the big world of retail, and you, too, could forecast this historic turn of events. Two sunny rooms flanked either end of the shop, interconnected by the jewelry and selling/consigning area. Vaulting two-story ceilings, skylights and gently circling ceiling fans showed off to great advantage the
HOURS: Mon–Wed & Sat 10-5, Thu & Fri 10-8, Sun 12-4	sisterhood of uppercrust and wannabe labels. Last year's unworn J. Crew with 30's-style buttons tiptoeing up the front of a bias-cut, ankle length, dainty, flower strewn dress, $40. It's original price tags still attached, bumped up against the label likes of Neiman Marcus and Anne Klein. Bridal gowns, ranging in price and quality from $20 to $400, were stored democratically in identical plastic zippered protective shields.
	I envision frequent return shopping expeditions, shipping back bundles of booty to home base. **P.S.** The natives were friendly.
CLOSED: Holidays	**CONSIGNOR ALERT:** 50%-50% split. 10¢ tagging fee/item. 60 days. Reduced at their discretion. By appointment only.

Twice As Nice-Children	
2905 Emmaus Ave. Allentown, PA 18103 **610-797-6763** **Look:** CLASS ACT **Goods:** HO HUM– CLASS ACT **Prices:** LOW – MODERATE **HOURS:** Mon–Wed. & Sat 10-5, Thu & Fri 10-8, Sun 12-4 **CLOSED:** Holidays	Busy as a playground on a Saturday afternoon in spring. Parents milling about, a couple with their heads together weighing the wear and tear left in a pair of boy's trousers. Children over in the play corner, happily and intently drawing, sharing toys, playing store. Grownups gathered around the registered doing the real thing. No playing around with the fact that Twice As Nice had more of Morgan's sizes 12 through 14 than most stores have for their entire inventory. **Indeed the inventory in infants through preteen was really extensive.** So were the number of shoppers. Lots and lots of play and school clothes make this the sort of place I'd think of more for everyday, like popping my daily Flintstones' chewable vitamins (I give Marvin all the purple ones. He likes them. I don't.) But for that rare, once-in-a-while special occasion outfit you might have to think twice, look thrice. Looks like local families think of it once a week, every week, as many knew each other and the busy clerks by name. **CONSIGNOR ALERT:** 50%-50% split. 10¢ tagging fee/item. 60 days. Reduced at their discretion. By appointment only.

Twice As Nice	
Treasures & Books in the basement underneath Women's **Look:** STATUS QUO **Goods:** STATUS QUO **Prices:** MODERATE **HOURS:** Same as womens except closed on Sunday. **CLOSED:** Holidays	There was method to my madness (as usual). I had mulled over The Situation for quite some time. Lumping them together in one review, I would have had to award something like three or three and a half hangers to this mall size enterprise. Understandably, customers and shopkeepers alike would have cried foul, because of the all-too-obvious unfair discrepancies this would have created. So I decided to review each shop separately. Practically speaking, I reasoned, they are each under separate managers, with their own business cards, but with a shared consignment policy and hours. Inventory reflects each manager's aptitude for the 'sport.' My game plan? Let each one stand or fall on its own merits. Cracks in Twice As Nice's team strategy only appeared when we got to the basement (the owner's dugout), and even then only after scouting the secondhand book department, a **cozy, well organized hideaway with a well worn seat or two** for inveterate bookworms and bored husbands. Inexplicably, furniture and collectibles didn't meet rigorous standards applied to the other shops. No staff member appeared. The few customers who wandered down here were forced to skate around the snowdrift of work papers scattered across the glass surfaces in order to discover a pin here, a necklace there, lying under the avalanche. Second-string housewares, china, and collectibles beat out furniture, hands down. Furniture was a no-win. Better it had been a no-show. They're in a huddle over this one. **CONSIGNOR ALERT:** Buys outright.

Twin Jugs

4033 Chestnut St.
Emmaus, PA 18049

610-967-4010

Look: STATUS QUO

Goods: STATUS QUO–CLASS ACT

Prices: MODERATE

HOURS: Tue–Sat 10-5:30

CLOSED: Holidays

Stupendous, irridescent brown jugs, placed at either side of the entrance, overshadow the shop. They've seen proprietors come, and they've seen 'em go. Risky to move, too functional-looking to grace a garden, and with no pickle factory in sight, here they stay. How they got here is lost in the mists. The shopkeeper, a recent Long Island transplant, gracefully accepted the inevitability of it all, when she incorporated them into the name of her shop. After all, locals had been calling her place Two Jugs and other variations on the theme before she'd even gotten around to thinking of a name. Delayed as long as she could, finally the workman just had to know what name to put on the new blue-and-white-stripped awning. Hoping to avoid some, if not all, of the inevitable snickers, she chose twin over two.

A happy confluence of eras, prices and esthetic identities. Cranberry-colored old-fashioned lemonade set, nine pieces, $295. You could get a modern, watered-down version at Caldors for around $24, but the lemonade just wouldn't taste as good. A complete set of Balzac, leather bound, $65. An incongruous bulldog astride the lid of a delicate face-powder dish. Starving Artist quality rendering of enormous orange flowers, a noncompetitive $39, displayed on the wall amidst sweetly old-fashioned prints and watercolors above a handsome maple hutch, $225. "Mother's A Person" poem (bet you didn't know that!), accompanying photograph predating the 1965 copyright date by at least 30 years, clipped from the newspaper and framed, not far from a cobalt blue fruit dish, $125.

Marvin chatted with the equally outgoing owner. He discovered five shopowners from Allentown had used The Guide to 'do' Glenside, enjoying a busman's holiday. Little did she suspect, as they pleasantly passed the time, she was in the midst of having her (solid wood) tables favorably turned on her, as I undercover shopped her **charming, idiosyncratic country refuge**.

CONSIGNOR ALERT: 50%-50% split. No fee. 90 days. Drop in. She makes housecalls.

TOUR #18
ON A CLEAR DAY, YOU CAN SEE MONTGOMERYVILLE

Around here, the few kids who dare to wear chains and leather and colors, have pink cheeks. Try as they might, evoking all the capital A for A•t•t•i•t•u•d•e Dude their all too young lives could muster, they couldn't quite pull off The Look. I saw two such wannabes, the only pedestrians in sight, one wide striding in black lace-up boots, too big for his britches, the other, younger and shorter, but matched in intensity of purposelessness, trying to keep pace with his friend. They were set in profile against a great swath of all too 'real' Americana.

New new new **Souderton** sits atop a crossroads of competing strip malls that straddle two traffic-intensive intersections. I drove through one half-road, half-parking lot zoning nightmare and into another, trying to retrace steps laid down on my first visit when Marvin was driving and I was laptopping away. Got some wonderful directions from a woman I knew at a glance must be a local, and with her kind help found old, original Soudertown, a few sleepy blocks down the road. Around here, some voices tease an outsider's ear with the almost decipherable, but ultimately unfamiliar Old German. The eerily quiet streets of staunchly cozy houses conceal from view yet another, older warren of parking lots and apartment buildings. Not much going on. At least not much visible to the casual drive-through Maniac. Probably those two boys could produce a better read on the place, with their all-too-eager, time-honored adolescent rebellion in full flower.

Driving home, a good days 'work' done, the relentlessly high energy of Souderton's residents, out for another day's shopping, coursed and swirled behind me, reduced by ever-narrowing rearview hindsight into a bumper-car unamusement park. Old Glory waved on high, gigantic Christmas candles with foot-high electronic wicks flickered, orange and purple pennants were flapping, red banners waving in the economic crosscurrents. MacDonald's and Burger King, with a Boston Chicken well on its way, are the only culinary (non)events in town. They anchored the intersection and kept it from flying away in a shopper-induced frenzy. (I know, it's probably un-American of me, but I don't do fast-food burgers. Chicken, maybe, but not burgers.)

The golf ball and tee-shaped water tower, a monument to American engineering know-how, loomed behind me over the exit ramp leading into and out of town. The radio station was changing over to a new host. Kate Smith, daily dusted off for the event, was singing "God Bless America," her voice resonating with all the glory and theatrical gusto she could summon. She soared to the inevitable climax, poised and paced with a great precision drawn from a lifetime of practice. Through the winter-bare trees covering the sloping hillsides stretching downward toward the valley, I could clearly see forever. Or at least to **Montgomeryville**. Other small towns, each with a flag flying, each with a distinctively shaped water tower: mushroom, basketballs on stilts, hour glass, all standing proud in the late afternoon sunshine. A flock of starlings, balanced on a wire over the highway, shared the view. Tears welled in my eyes. My heart was full. God I love it. I feel so privileged to be doing what I'm doing, writing and shopping and getting paid to do it. Only in America.

My only prior acquaintance with **Telford** was the sign over the Godshall's family meat stand at the Farmer's Market in Chestnut Hill. Home base? Telford, PA. With my home base almost an hour away, Telford, PA. might as well have been Brigadoon, PA. for all I knew of the area. We all have a task and maintenance circle to our lives, a comfort zone within which we travel to go to work, do chores, play. Until beginning this little adventure of mine, **Fresh Fields** and **Atlantic Books** (Yes, they do carry The Guide) in Montgomeryville were the furthest points north on Rte. 309 that I regularly traveled, the edge of my everyday world. The two very worthwhile shops in town with their overload of inventory and atmospherics, do nothing to dispel this slightly surreal quality. And finding **Kim Nguyen** (what's a Vietnamese restaurant doing in these parts?) at Reliance & South Third, only added to the growing mystique. I actually ate in the **Towne Restaurant**, recommended by Opy at the Telford Exchange. Starving, I asked for a fast, clean place, where a woman alone would feel comfortable. She was right on the money. I arrived three minutes before the 2pm closing. With nary a grumble they served up my bowl of steaming chili, raw onions and melting cheese, even though I could plainly see through the pass through they were in the middle of breaking down. (Lord how I remember doing that. Scrub the burners, polish the stainless steel, mop the floor.) Without so much as a mutter, they even buttered my bread! Thank you, Emma & Ron.

Quakertown is a name I grew up with, one that became almost as familiar as my own. To the daughter of a four-generation dynasty of undertakers, Quakertown and Boyertown Casket Company trucks rumbling into the funeral home driveway and rustling bills of lading scattered upon my father's desk were ordinary, everyday sights and sounds to me, a touchstone happily unavailable to most. Because of this childhood memory snippit, I imagined I knew the place. Driving up Rte. 309, closing in on contemporary, real life Quakertown, I couldn't swivel my head left and right fast enough trying to take it all in. Preliminary sights and sounds included the all too usual roadside commercial contrapuntal crash-and-bang zoning stretching from "sea to shining sea", and steadily replacing the "amber waves of grain." Brick's Trucks, Campers and Country Structures' gazebos and storage sheds, the inevitable Psychic Reader across from the inevitable Adult World Video Store, car dealerships with banners flying, Hess's department store, the Farm & Family Center, and a Seafood Shanty Restaurant and Yacht Club (100 miles inland). My family used to take me here when it was called Trainer's. All this going on in the very Heart of Bucks County (according to the banners). There gonna get clogged arteries. A thousand years from now, if some enterprising anthropologist were to dig up this mishmash (assuming it got buried all at once in the first place--Pompeii revisited), she'd have a field day (and a lifelong career) discerning the inner meaning of it all.

So what is the meaning of it all? When was the last time we REALLY looked at what we've wrought? At what we visually and functionally take for granted every day of our lives? This is the aftershock, the fallout we're all reverberating from the invention of the automobile. Don't get me wrong, I'm not advocating a return to the horse and buggy era. I looove my van and my freedom. But don't you think we've got to rethink this one? If we don't aren't we headed down the garden path to the great downswing inevitably and inexorably experienced by every civilization before us? Each preceding group of people sowed the seeds of their success and self destruction. Plague, floods, famine, war, arid dunes where once there was a fertile valley. Like it on not, we've got pollution and drugs and guns in the street. And yes I do believe there is a straight line connecting this and what I see on every roadside, every day, everywhere I go.

The absolute best bet for me, the place I would gladly take any newly arrived immigrant or visitor to 'get' the intermediate step between turn of the century small town life and the suburban sprawl closing this century is the venerable, viable **Quakertown Farmer's Market**. I looove it. Pierogies, pretzels, great French fries; a stand-up, big-as-life John Wayne cutout; secondhand tires sold by men wearing clothing the same color as their merchandise; vacuum cleaner repair; diffuse, dewey-eyed, pastel portraits of Indian maidens; crisp local potato chips; computer generated poems personalized with your name; pinball machines; dogfood bowls shaped like bones with two implanted stainless steel bowls; oversized, overstuffed, Scotchguarded furniture; a barber shop; a beauty parlor; sweatshirts with penguins, Koala, and coyotes in unnatural gold and glitter; several meat stands; a fish market and two groceries (and a bathroom) all under one roof. No farmers. (As you head north on Rte. 309, it's over to your right on Front Street on the edge of town. It's open Friday & Saturday 10-10, Sunday 10-6).

To find Quakertown's town center, almost a mile off 309, turn right at Seafood Shanty and follow the dazzling assortment of dolphin, snowman, cupid, sun and moon, skier, and angel (with a sword?) banners affixed to every other front porch (don't worry, banners and wind stockings will start appearing in secondhand stores soon) along with the American flag, and the inevitable wreaths ranging from Christmas leftovers to a straw heart wrapped in red ribbon (it was mid February). Looking for donations, the community has strung a gigantic SOS, Save our Station, poster over the Victorian-era train station while it's undergoing repairs. We ate at **Patrick's** on West Broad Street. It's a large white stucco building with shamrock green trim. Stick to the Irish food.

P.S. Saw my first (new) wind stocking for sale in a resale shop in Pottstown on Thursday, March 2. It was a pink and black pig with a big grin on its snout! Told ya.

TOUR #18

6	A Touch Of Class	Souderton
1,2,3,& 4	Care & Share	Souderton
5	Carpenter's What Not	Quakertown
9	Goodwill	Quakertown
8	Koffel's Curiosity Shop	Telford
10	Pack's Twice Around	Telford
7	Telford Exchange	Telford

*Note: This list has a shop's entire name. Names in review boxes may have been shortened a tad to fit. Numbers before each shop name correspond to their numbered location on each map. **Shops with a star sold Volume II. Volume III? ASK!**

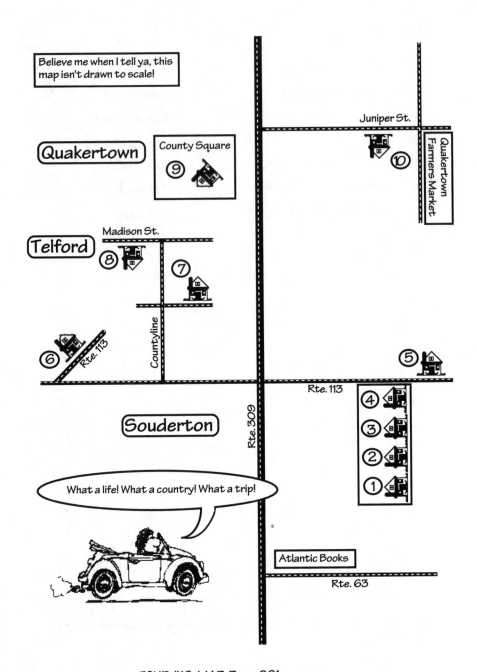

Believe me when I tell ya, this map isn't drawn to scale!

Quakertown

County Square
⑨

Juniper St.

⑩

Quakertown Farmers Market

Madison St.

Telford
⑧

⑦

Countyline

Rte. 113

⑥

⑤

Rte. 113

④

③

Souderton

Rte. 309

②

①

What a life! What a country! What a trip!

Atlantic Books

Rte. 63

TOUR #18 MAP Page 261

A Touch of Class	
110 Main Street Souderton, PA 18964 **721-0880** 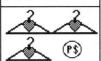	Bobby pins are back. They've been rediscovered by the X, Y and/or Z Generation, who're sporting them, three to a finger wave, with all the vanity of grandmothers' tortoise-shell-combed tresses. Those hair-pulling, mini banes of my childhood existence come to mind because of the way the clothes here are hung. Remember how a brand-new package of ordinary, everyday bobby pins were all lined up like good little soldiers, rigidly standing at attention across their cardboard terrain, ready to do battle against your fingers' adolescent agility and your wayward hair? In this tiny shop, in this quiet little town, the good owner must have some long, lonely end-of-season days on her hands.
Look: STATUS QUO **Goods:** HO HUM– STATUS QUO **Prices:** LOW	Mother's Wear navy-and-white-dot maternity dress at $20 was the best of a brief maternity section. Casual Corner pants, black with white dots and stretch waist, $6.50, robins egg blue and white dot one piece short set, $10.50 (lots of dots). Polyester purple suit with a single, dramatic gold button, $18. A silk Cimarron olive-green short-sleeve, wrap-top straight-skirt dress for $20. A slightly bedraggled size-14 Carol Little blue-and-white-striped denim blazer. These were the top women's labels and looks in the place. Children's was scanty both visits. For Souderton,
HOURS: Tue–Sat 10-4 Fri 10-8	where litter wouldn't dare linger and each clean white front porches face off with everybody else's clean white front porch, cleanliness must be next to godliness. But some of those old-time Saturday night bathers weren't just getting ready for Sunday morning go-to-church. Some of them also wanted a hot night on the town.
CLOSED: Holidays and July	**P.S.** Closes a couple of weeks during Christmas, reopens with January sale. **CONSIGNOR ALERT:** 50%-50% split. No fee. 90 days. Drop and run. Wednesday-Saturday. By appointment on Tuesdays.

Care & Share	
3496 Bethlehem Pk. Souderton, PA. 18964 **723-0315** 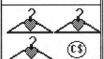	O.K. everybody. I want you to close your eyes. Go on. Close them. Now look inside your mind's eye and imagine hangers, thousands of them. Each one lovingly adorned with hand crocheted yarn covers in brilliant neon colors, bumping up against each other on clothing racks in an hallucinogenic rainbow. OK. Got it? Well, what you've just imagined is the backdrop to the opening scene of a four act play going on every day here in Souderton. Mennonite ladies, probably every single Mennonite lady in Pennsylvania, has lovingly crafted these hanger covers so the clothing won't slip off, so it will stay neat and tidy and off the floor, just like home.
Look: CLASS ACT **Goods:** HO HUM – CLASS ACT **Prices:** LOW	**Fours shops in a brand new strip mall**, three resale and one new nifty gift shoppe. I saw: Old sheet music and dress patterns from the 20's and 30's. An original Maytag galvanized steel electric washer with ringer attachment, no repairman in sight. The very same unused wax candle Christmas carolers from the 50's that we used to have at home. Virginal white majorette boots with tassels intact. Hooded pink-satin jacket, " Margaret" in Korean and English symmetrically emblazoned on either side of gaudy red, yellow and blue embroidered flowers. Scores of hangered women's stockings hanging womanless from a rack, like so many fish filets drying in the fluorescent sun. You can shop this place straight, like a real-life department store, or play the angels/angles, pretending it's a retro-neo-wonderland. Whatever.
HOURS: Mon–Thu & Sat 10-5, Fri 10-8:30	Whichever. **I had a ball**. You'll give and get a lot of big smiles coming and going. **P.S.** Operated by the same folks that bring us Crossroads in Norristown.
CLOSED: Holidays	**CONSIGNOR ALERT:** Donations only. Benefits Mennonite Central Committee and their worldwide relief organization.

<table>
<tr><td colspan="2">

Carpenter's What Not

</td></tr>
<tr><td>

1208 Rte. 309
Quakertown, PA
18960
257-6810

Look: DOWN & OUT
Goods:
DOWN & OUT
Prices: UNMARKED

HOURS: Wed, Thu,
Fri 12-5, Sat 11-4

CLOSED: Holidays

</td><td>

More not, than what.

A beautiful antique lamp, it's once decorative, faded gold shade and fringe now torn, stood in the middle of the wreckage. I can picture the scene. It stood there in all its glory, lording it over the grand piano, giving out its light across countless pages of sheet music, as family members sang their favorite tunes together and were warmed in it's glowing circle. Now the music is gone. The lamp sits forlorn in the corner, offered up along with the memories, all for a price. Everything else was dirty and decrepit. Someone had turned out the light.

When we called to check out our facts, they picked up the phone, said "Hello" a couple of times and hung up. Phone and shop can both use some attention. Trying to find them? Go up Old Bethlehem Pike, cross Rte. 563, they're near the diner.

CONSIGNOR ALERT: Buys outright. Will work things out.

</td></tr>
</table>

<table>
<tr><td colspan="2">

Goodwill

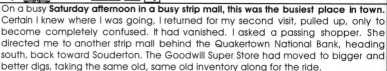

</td></tr>
<tr><td>

Country Square
Shopping Center
240 West End Blvd.
Quakertown, PA
18951
536-2442

Look: CLASS ACT
BOTTOMFEEDER

Goods: DOWN &
OUT–STATUS QUO

Prices: LOW

HOURS: Mon–Thu &
Sat 9:30-6,

Fri 9:30-9,

Sun 12-5

CLOSED: Holidays

</td><td>

On a busy **Saturday afternoon in a busy strip mall, this was the busiest place in town.** Certain I knew where I was going, I returned for my second visit, pulled up, only to become completely confused. It had vanished. I asked a passing shopper. She directed me to another strip mall behind the Quakertown National Bank, heading south, back toward Souderton. The Goodwill Super Store had moved to bigger and better digs, taking the same old, same old inventory along for the ride.

Blue and white 'company' banners dangled everywhere from the supermarket-size, white suspended ceiling. Good price. Good value. Good selection. Some Goodwills, just like the real estate values of some neighborhoods, are better than others. Maybe they should have named themselves Greatwill. Then the banners could have screamed Great price. Great value. Great selection...and the inventory could have been expected to live up to that promise.

Cruising housewares, I saw a pink, blue and white rabbit piñata, a small hideous souvenir vase from Florida covered with shells that would have better been left on the beach, an artistic rendering of Mt. Rushmore commemorating the Bicentennial and made of an assortment of minerals that would have better been left in the earth, a circular beige plastic microwave oven muffin/cupcake dish, a red gorilla candle. Abercrombie & Fitch, 100% oxford cloth men's shirt with blue and white stripes was the one piece of clothing in the whole huge place I would have considered buying. It was the right price, but the wrong size.

A gaggle of unattended kids were busy occupying themselves as best they could over in a corner. (No play area. Wise up, Goodwill.) One little four-year old-boy had self-sufficiently strapped on a pair of roller skates and hesitantly set off on a store-wide adventure. Left behind and stranded, an older but not wiser child ineffectually yelled out, "They don't fit ya," to the back of his long-gone new friend as he glided away across the smooth surface of the shiny linoleum floor.

CONSIGNOR ALERT: Donations only.

</td></tr>
</table>

Koffel's Curiosity Shop

26 Madison Ave.
Telford, PA 18969
723-9365

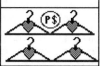

Look: TIMELESS
Goods: HO HUM–
TOP DRAWER
Prices: LOW–HIGH

HOURS:
Tue–Sat 11-6. Call
ahead.

CLOSED: Holidays

The sign outside the front door says, "We sell anything". They're not kidding. Stainless steel sterilizing drum and lid, skis, ski boots, ski poles, kerosene and electric heaters, window fans, a hideous $5000, overwrought, overpriced, hand-carved, gargoyle encrusted chest, plain Jane original, world revolutionizing wooden ice box, farm tools, woodworking tools, who-knows-what-tools, heavy aluminum restaurant stock pot and professional heft cutting board, sweet faced dolls, bicycles, electronic artifacts, porcelain-on-steel coal stove, 40's bamboo furniture set, unpainted plaster hobby figurines waiting for the brush wielding senior, worn-thin exercise bicycles, forgettable and collectible crystal and china, aluminum window shades, musical instruments and tapes, guns and war momentos, a drop dead gorgeous $295 vanity, it's matching dresser $250, and six drawer highboy $295. A lyrically beautiful 20's twin bed set and nightstand with sadly peeling paint, intricate machine carved trim and handpainted bouquets, intact. A Fairbanks scale $150. A child's striped sling-back beach chair from the 40's and a 3'-high electric bull horn. Whew! **Whoever. Whatever. Whenever. Beats discount department stores hands down any day for pricing, assortment and the sheer slack-jawed, wide-eyed, head scratching wonderment of it all.** Look for the low-to-the-ground bright yellow sign parked at the corner of Madison and Main. Winter? Wear your scarf and mittens inside. Unheated, it's so cold you can see your breath. But the owner's office with it's black-and-white memories plastered all over the wall is full of the warmth of a long life well lived. And then some.

CONSIGNOR ALERT: Buys outright. Closes up to go on regular shopping expeditions.

Pack's Twice Around

312 Juniper St.
Quakertown, PA
18951
536-8887

Look: STATUS QUO
Goods: HO HUM –
STATUS QUO
Prices: LOW

HOURS:
Mon & Sat 10-2,
Tue, Wed & Thu
10-5, Fri.10-6

CLOSED: Holidays

Morgan and Marvin and I tooled around Quakertown until we finally found this family-run store tucked away on a side street in the middle of a residential neighborhood. Morgan scoped out the place, finally selecting a green-and-purple striped dress with black turtleneck and cuffs made of sweatshirt fabric. We liked its warmth and shape and softness, agreeing that the sequins on the floral appliqué work on the bodice had to go. Snip snip snip went the scissors. Amped down, it no longer had that too-much-too-soon look so prevalent in little girls' (and big girls') clothing. Often, all a bargain garment needs to update and uplift it's sagging spirits is a nip and a tuck, a new set of buttons, a change in hem length. Presto chango.

Mother Nature had effected her own annual wardrobe change by the time I got a-round to my second Quakertown expedition. November's brilliant fall colors of ye-llow and orange and red had been replaced by February's blanket of white. Icey stalagmites were forming under the steady drip of a leaking front door roof. I stepped around the pointed mound and went inside. Trolling the racks alone, I ducked behind racks, surreptitiously talking notes into my tape recorder. Here's what I found: $3.75 heart-shaped front door zither,$7.75. Stephano denim vest with hearts and lace overlay, $4.75. YOU Babes brightly colored top and a $6.75 separate pale blue dress with pink flowers and lace collar, same label. The best in men's was a $6.75, 42R tan London Fog jacket, Gap khaki shirt, $4.75, royal blue Gap T, $2.75 and two LaCoste cotton pique polos, navy or red, never worn, $4.50. Women's had a two-piece LIZ marked down 50% from $8.75, and a Clifford & Willis banana-colored, wrapped-neck, cotton top, and a Gap snap front, brilliant green floral sweatshirt fabric jacket, $4.50 each. They're waiting for spring. Or you. Whichever comes first.

CONSIGNOR ALERT: 50%-50% split. $3/season fee. 90 days. Drop & run 1st-15th of mo.

Telford Exchange	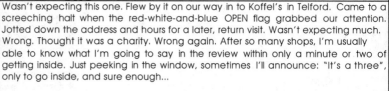
527B S. Main St. Telford, PA 18969 **723-9870** **Look:** STATUS QUO **Goods:** STATUS QUO–TOP DRAWER **Prices:** LOW– MODERATE **HOURS:** Wed & Thu 11-5, Fri 11-6, Sat 10-4 **CLOSED:** Holidays	Wasn't expecting this one. Flew by it on our way in to Koffel's in Telford. Came to a screeching halt when the red-white-and-blue OPEN flag grabbed our attention. Jotted down the address and hours for a later, return visit. Wasn't expecting much. Wrong. Thought it was a charity. Wrong again. After so many shops, I'm usually able to know what I'm going to say in the review within only a minute or two of getting inside. Just peeking in the window, sometimes I'll announce: "It's a three", only to go inside, and sure enough...

Wrong again. Outside in the driveway, I had predicted a 2 1/2, maybe 3, mumbling something about "fumes from the on-premises, dry cleaning establishment sharing the building, must have gotten to them." Furniture placed outside on display was overpriced particle board. (Safe to say, no one would steal it.)

Once inside, however, I wasn't so smug. It's **loaded with great goodies**, collected by sisters Opy and Des, who share unusual first names and have a familial in-law connection to the place stretching back 60 years. Indeed, most of the original wallpaper is still hanging. The first floor is beginning to look like a charming version of one of those houses where the people never go out anymore. Slowly they accumulate themselves into living in only one room. In this case, Opy and Des sit at their shared desk surrounded by wending corridors of other people's floor-to-ceiling, time-stacked treasures.

Meander through the house, bump into your own memories, recollection jogging collectibles and pictures and antique boxes and **tender, quirky treasures**, up the narrow stairs into the darkened former bedrooms now crowded with clothes. Some a design surprise, some traditional quality. There is even one room set aside for evening wear and bridal wear, so small the racks block out the light as if they were curtains. Bring your imagination and a flashlight. But come. **CONSIGNOR ALERT: Collectibles: 70%You-30%Shop.** Clothing: 50%-50%. 90 days. 50%/90 days. Call first. "Don't drop off anything or we'll keep it." |

TOUR #19
OVER HILL AND (LANS) DALE WE"LL SKIP(PACK) AND AMBLE(R)

Skippack was a part of my life as far back as my earliest childhood memories. Marguerite de Angeli's exquisitely crafted, beautifully illustrated storybooks brought historic Skippack (and Germantown and Olde City Philadelphia and other colonial towns) to life. Skippack School was as real to me as my own. I still have my well-worn copies of Miss de Angeli's classics and add to my small collection as I find others in secondhand book and thrift shops. Now, I read them to Morgan, at bedtime. I was almost as reluctant a shopper as my father on family shopping trips to Skippack. It's a ladies-who-lunch kind of place. Climbing trees and snarfing peanut butter and jelly, sitting cross-legged on the great slate, sun-warmed slabs at McMichael Park's war memorial with best buddy Nancy was more like it. (Even then we were hand-printing our own neighborhood newspaper, charging family and neighbors a dime.)

These days, Skippack's quaintly demure, cohesively colonial facades hide the rumblings of change from the eyes of the casual (and not so casual) shopper. 'If it was good enough for us it's good enough for you' hasn't been quite good enough lately. Upstart newcomer shopkeepers (they'll do it every time) are casting about for their own newfangled ways to market and publicize the area and give it an economic goose. All grown up now, I see that the time I spent here undercover shopping was just my cup of tea. I highly recommend a full-time tea and sometime coffee shop called **A Special Occasion,** 4049 Skippack Pike. And **Mal's Diner** is my kind of place. In unison, molars relaxed, forks poised in the air midway to intended destinations, when I walk in. They sized up the stranger in their midst, then went back to eating with the silent precision of the Marine Drill Team. Kids' 'Why I love Mal's' drawings were hung all over one wall. Hungry hunters chowed down, describing the one that got away. Three-piece suits swapped their next moves on the corporate chessboard.

☞ Maniac Hot Tip: Looking for how to transformational thrift ideas? Regular retail **Roses and Ivy** is inspirational! Ask for Granny or Rose or Gail, the owner. Get out your glue guns and get going. Tell them I sent you.

Lansdale has a reputation for being something of a Rip Van Winkle. It's a sleepy town, surrounded by bright eyed and bushy tailed communities like Blue Bell. Despite the rousing Cavalcade of Bands and the jump start the town gets every year from the wildly popular antique car show, Lansdale has kept to its own slower pace. Newcomer shopkeepers may be ready to shake things up just a bit. Just ask Marie at **Fajitas Mexican** (214 North Broad). That's where I went for a lunch break one day. Got a beans, beans, musical beans-and-cheese burrito, opinions on the side, an exuberant earful to go. There's also the culinarily mysterious, **Indo-Pakistani food market** across the street, called **City of Joy.** Or try **Luigi's,** next to the gorgeous Victorian era train station, building and rails plunked like an enormous sandcastle obstacle course running right through the middle of town. Locals frequent **Marie's** coffee shop on West Main for breakfast. Just outside of town on Welsh Road, inexplicably lost in strip-mall obscurity (Montgomery Commons), is the amazingly good and inexpensive standout **Ristorante Toscano**. For very local color, drop in at **North Penn Senior Center** and check out the afghans and pot holders and crochet-covered hangers. They also sell chocolate by the box. Dying for a **hand-dipped ice cream cone or loose chocolates**? There's a shop on Main near Care Bears for that, too. Do the town. And if Marie and people like her have their way, maybe next edition or so, they'll have finished snoozing.

Equally historic **Gwynedd**, lacking a town center to ground it in commercial space and time, is a bucolic, residential pass-through on your way to somewhere else. My recommendation? Stop for the three quaint thrift and resale shops on Rte. 202, midway between Lansdale and Skippack, plan to eat before or after. The traditional landmark establishment is way too leisurely and way too expensive for our purposes.

Ambler is short and sweet. The town's two main maniac attractions, newcommer Breslin's and oldtimmer Prima Donna, lure me here, but so far I've never lingered long enough afterwards to eat in town. Suggestion? Ask Katie at Breslin's were she likes to go. She'll be glad to tell you. (Tell her I said so. Then tell me what she says.)

Montgomeryville Mart is going through enormous make-or-break changes. I saw several secondhand furniture stores trying to make a go of it, including the relocated Horsham Supply from last year's edition. These, combined with Magical Mystery Music, if you're a musician, could make for a worthwhile shopping visit. **Food stands** inside sell quickie sit-down or take-out. The **oriental buffet** and **sausage** places are good and inexpensive. There's also a **produce** stand, all things **coffee and tea** stand and **bakery** inside, so you can shop for dinner. I hope all of this is still factual by the time the Guide gets into your hands. I didn't write up any of the secondhand furniture shops inside because everything is so unsettled here right now. Maybe next edition. **Fresh Fields** is just a brief jaunt up Rte. 309. You MUST shop here if you haven't already. Had I been designing cutting edge markets instead of cutting-edge guides, this is exactly what I would have wanted to see developed. (Also great for take-out.) **Atlantic Book Warehouse,** just up on Rte. 309 stocks and sells The Guide, hand over fist, at a tight-fisted discount. They keep it sitting up by the register. Thanks, Brian.

TOUR #19

6	Belfry Bargains	Gwynedd
4	Breslin's Consignment Corner ★	Ambler
10	Done Overs Thrift Shop	Lansdale
11	Encore Boutique	Lansdale
7	Gwynedd Women's & Children's Exchange	North Wales
5	Magical Mystery Music	Montgomeryville
8	Priceless Treasures	North Wales
3	Prima Donna	Ambler
2	Repeat Boutique	Skippack
9	Salvation Army	Lansdale
1	Second Seitz	Skippack
14	Sweet Repeats	Lansdale
13	Wear Bear's Closet	Lansdale
12	West Main Consignment	Lansdale

*Note: This list has a shop's entire name. Names in review boxes may have been shortened a tad to fit. Numbers before each shop name correspond to their numbered location on each map. **Shops with a star sold Volume II.** Volume III? Ask!

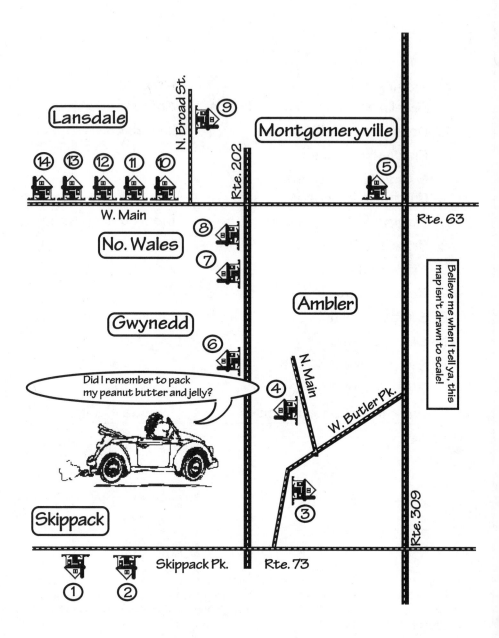

Belfry Bargains

Rte. 202
Gwynedd, PA
19436

699-3441

Look: STATUS QUO

Goods: STATUS QUO–TOP DRAWER

Prices: LOW

HOURS: Mon–Fri 10-1, Sat 10-4

CLOSED: Mid-June thru mid-Sept

Locals warned me to be careful. "You could get rear-ended trying to find and then make the gravel-churning turn into the shop's driveway, located on 202, just south of the William Penn Inn." Belfry Bargains, dedicated to the memory of some long gone, but not forgotten minister, housed in a white-clapboard and green-shuttered house, hard by the church's stone-and-moss encrusted bell tower, is aptly named.

Abuzz with activity in preparation for the opening of the Christmas shop, but dark and gloomy in parts of the downstairs, it has its share of aging, sometimes confused, but **always cordial volunteers,** who run the predictible gamut. They range from 'Ask Mary, she knows,' as they sit Buddha-like by the register "doing their time" types to the briskly efficient, see-all, know-all, do-all types who do double duty for their more sedentary sisters. What the locals didn't tell me were what **great buys** you could find here, especially in the small but choice housewares and women's evening wear sections. **Women's everyday and men's,** especially **suits, weren't bad either,** with men's posted prices ranging from 50¢ for belts to $12 for suits with Boyds labels. I saw a Nippon Executive Wear-label dress in grey wool with black velvet trim, and a Jones black velvet cocktail dress with wide satin sash, both $35. Inexplicably, children's clothing up to size 12, located on the top level, most inconveniently for already overburdened moms, was the weakest.

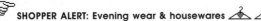

SHOPPER ALERT: Evening wear & housewares

CONSIGNOR ALERT: 60% You-40% Shop. $5 fee. Mon, Wed, first Sat 10-noon. By appointment. Donations accepted. Benefits Neighborhood Outreach program.

Breslin's Consignment Corner

16 N. Main St.
Ambler, PA 19002

628-3974

Look: CLASS ACT–TOP DRAWER

Goods: STATUS QUO–TOP DRAWER

Prices: LOW–MODERATE

HOURS: Tue–Thu & Sat 10-4, Fri 10-5

CLOSED: First 3 weeks in August

After growing up in the business by her mother's side, Katie Breslin has opened her own thrift shop with all the panache and confidence of a 20-year veteran. This addition to Ambler's downtown shopping area is already crowded enough and successful enough to be experiencing growing pains. **It's charming, it's cozy,** with sun streaming through the lace-hung picture window. Color-coordinated clothing racks and homy displays of merchandise show she learned her lessons well.

On my first visit here, there was a $400 hand-painted music cabinet and an old copper washtub with lid and handles for $125, the kind often reinvented for parties as a wine cooler. The music cabinet has now been incorporated into permanent display, the tub is long gone. There are loads of designer labels and stylishly current fashions for the whole family. **Men's is definitely worth a look-see.** Marvin did really well here last visit.

Katie's family tradition of **low-key, unruffled friendliness and good service** continues. She carries on mom's invention, **drop-and-run consignment,** which is just that: drop your things and run. They'll do the rest. Ask for details.

CONSIGNOR ALERT: 50%-50% split. No fee. Tuesday-Friday. 20%/4 weeks.

Done Overs Thrift Shop	

133 E. Main St. Lansdale, PA 19446 **368-4564**	Simple syrup sweet, a Christian radio station DJ droned on in the background. After "Praise The Lord," "Sinners Repent" and "Send in Your Money," everything else was redundant. "Make A Great Noise Unto The Lord" is so often reduced to a sanctimoniously flat and unctuous ooze of a "sound." I like my messages and messengers to have a little more grit and gumption. "Seek and Ye Shall Find" may be a good one to dust off right about now.
	What the good people here are seeking is money toward a youth outreach program dedicated to rescuing "unchurched teenage street kids" (their words) and run by Youth Quest Evangelistic Association of Lansdale.
Look: STATUS QUO **Goods:** HO HUM–STATUS QUO **Prices:** LOW	Like-minded thrifters, even those with low esthetic horizons and lower bank balances, must do a lot of seeking here. Furniture doubles as display, but even so, stuff spews haphazardly onto the floor. Tread gently, or the crunch you hear may be your next purchase. I love time spent rummaging, when the time is richly rewarding and the visuals are great. Unfortunately, this was not a matter of "Going To My Greater Reward." Time was, places like this survived and prospered
HOURS: Mon & Thu 11-4:30, Wed 11-3 Fri 11-5:30, Sat 10:30-4:30	on good intentions. During these days of gentrified resale, it's getting too competitive for anything less than entrepreneurial evangelical fervor. "Here Endeth the First Lesson."
CLOSED: Holidays	**CONSIGNOR ALERT:** Donations only. Benefits Youth Quest. Will pick up furniture only.

Encore Boutique	

55 E. Main St. Lansdale, PA 19446 **362-9194**	Shop signs say, "Open at 10," but the shopkeepers arrives and turns up the lights at 10:20 or 10:40. Yoga exercises ran late, the mood wasn't right, the kid was home sick. Opening gun here? 10:01am the owner was gizmo-injecting price tags onto a new consignment. She must be a morning person like me. But the entire time I was there, she never looked up, never said hello. Neither did I. My reason? Not wanting to blow my cover. A radio talk show host offered up yet another ratings-induced, nonstory on Princess Di, jumping on her poor anorectic bones (and everything else plaguing the poor dear), like every other talk show host around this poor, tired, world of ours. Let me tell you about shopaholic. You gotta be a little nuts, thrifting 2 days out of 2 and already racking up #3, this far away from home, this early on a weekday
Look: STATUS QUO **Goods:** HO HUM–STATUS QUO **Prices:** LOW	morning, this early in the week. Rows of mirror-shiny Mary Janes were all lined up, ready to taunt the first nun to fly through the door. Garment labels like Blair, Ship 'n' Shore, and Gimbels, almost put me to sleep like an oft-repeated bedtime story. High end stuff? A lone Vittadini sweater, a YOU Babes navy and white, girl's romper. $6.95 was the most frequently
HOURS: Tue–Fri 10-5, Sat 10-4	recurring price on the size 3 to 18 tags. If working hard was what mattered most, this would-be-Cinderella-story owner would be in glass slippers by now. Alas, most shoes were Taiwanese plastic. Where's the wake-up call from the Palace?
CLOSED: Holidays	**CONSIGNOR ALERT:** 40% You–60% Shop. No fee. By appointment only.

Gwynnedd Exchange

     $:) P𝖿

536 DeKalb Pike
North Wales, PA
19454
699-6810

 (P$)

Look: CLASS ACT

Goods: STATUS QUO–CLASS ACT

Prices: LOW – MODERATE

A garden-variety secondhand shop, located near Rhoads Garden on a still bucolic stretch of Rte. 202, studded with barns, carriage houses, and colonial-era stone farm houses, rapidly being crowded out by new development and the ensuing mad rush, rush hour traffic. Although more an every day daisy than an exotic hothouse bloom, the Gwynedd Women's and Children's Exchange is the sweetest smelling secondhand shop I've ever been in. The source? Renuzit has this really great new line of air fresheners out called Botanicals...Yeah, I asked. Just had to know how they got it to smell so great in here. (I usually hate fake smells, and rarely wear perfume.)

The fresh scent was a subtle indicator of the care that goes into giving this perennial shop its **cozy appeal**. The woman behind the counter gave off her own inner glow. In my book (pun intended), the children's section had a slight edge over the mostly conservative women's department. Got Morgan a Gap turtleneck, Jet Set purple stretch pants and white hand-painted shirt for next Christmas, all for $7. I happened upon their January clearance. Left behind the Jessica McClintock brocade, even though it was only $20. Green just isn't Morgan's color. Except for two pair of unworn Stuart Weitzman black granny boots, originally tagged $100 here and reeduced to $85 when they didn't sell, most things were **inexpensive, in good condition,** but not prize-winning garden club entries. I yearned to possess Stu's grannies, but they were half a size too small, pinching my tootsies, and in my opinion, overpriced by $20. That pinched, too.

P.S. Come spring, a maternity department .

HOURS:
Tue–Sat 10-4

 **SHOPPER ALERT:** Children's

CLOSED: Last 2 weeks in July.

CONSIGNOR ALERT: 50%-50% split. $5 fee. 90 days. 50%/60 days. Appointment preferred.

Magical Mystery Music

   CC P𝖿

Mongomeryville
Mart Rt.63
Montgomeryville,PA
18936
542-8847

(P$)

Look: STATUS QUO
Goods: STATUS QUO–CLASS ACT
Prices: MODERATE – VERY LOW

HOURS: Fri, Sat 11-9:30, Sun 11-5 and by appt.

CLOSED: Holidays

Morgan and I prowled the Mart for the better part of an afternoon, doing our girl thing. We had a grand old time shopping and hanging out, even though the place is going through a painfully obvious upheaval. Many stalls had changed hands in the last year and many were empty. Many were filled with what must be the fast-turnover crowd, shopkeepers big on drive and low on concept, cash and experience.

Wandering around, we found this place. It had a small constant flow of musicians. While I've never played anything but the piano, and that marginally, I know enough to see that **many of the electric and acoustic guitars were as beautiful as sculpture.**

Marvin was a former bass player in a blues band in his high school days. Morgan and I enticed him back here when he returned to pick us up. Once we got him inside, he got quiet. His body let go. I could see him relax. He handled the guitars reverently, selecting them for their worth as instruments as much as their ability to evoke memories. He traveled far and wide in just a very short time, and returned to us a happier hunk. Moral? Hold on to the melody if not the instrument.

P.S. Per Marvin: "It's not Sam Ash Music in New York, so you won't find B.B. King's Lucille, but there was a good old Gretsch full body and a Fender bass circa 1969."

Priceless Treasures	
536 DeKalb Pike North Wales, PA 19454 **699-0445** **Look:** CLASS ACT **Goods:** STATUS QUO–TOP DRAWER **Prices:** LOW **HOURS:** Wed-Sat 11-4 **CLOSED:** Holidays	Wowie zowie. It's a secondhand **nifty gifty shoppe**. Athough she could take the concept even further. How about gift boxes and custom wrapping and fancy shop name tags and gift cards and wrapping paper and dried floral ararngements and (unused) paper party supplies, and retail shop overrun candles, and and and. My imagination runs wild. It often does. Maybe all this would cost the owner, and therefore the customer, too much. Maybe it's just the ticket. **Right now the shop is almost everything a secondhand hostess and gift giver could possibly want in one stop shopping.** (Gwynedd Exchange is around the corner in the same building. You could get your hostess outfit there.) Anyway, she's really on to something. There are many chachka-only shops and such, but this one captures the feel of a genuine gift shop. Mirrors, exceptionally unusual and unusually inexpensive, linens, jewelry, handbags, china and crystal, area rugs, cookware, placemats, clocks, lamps and paintings, the usual familiar assortment, all secondhand. **Charmingly on target but off the beaten track.** How about better signage outside, and maybe something at busy Rte. 63 and 202 as well? A little gloomy inside, but it was gloomy outside, too, that day. How about slightly higher wattage and a spot or two? Cozy, but with rock music and vacuuming booming and whooshing through the ceiling from the apartment above. How about taped waterfalls and lovebirds calling and quasi-oriental bell chimes and soaring violins? (There I go again.) Or maybe just a quieter, dirtier upstairs tenant. That would be a lot cheaper, and a lot less trouble. **CONSIGNOR ALERT:** 50%-50% split. No fee. Also buys outright. By appointment.

Prima Donna	
6 W. Butler Ave. Ambler, PA 19002 **646-0189** 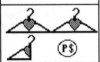 **Look:** STATUS QUO **Goods:** HO-HUM–CLASS ACT **Prices:** LOW–MODERATE **HOURS:** Mon-Sat 10-4. Closed Tue **CLOSED:** July and August	Every generation has made use of thrift shops. Our grandmothers and mothers shopped this way. Our generation is simply rediscovering a resource that's always been there. *This* 24-year-old resource is run by a discreetly dressed, but outspoken thrift-shop veteran. Prima Donna is as much about what it doesn't have as what it does have. No computers, let alone plastic tagging gizmos, it's all safety-pinned price tags put on by hand. No background music or wall-to-wall carpets. What this store does have are floors worn by years of neighborhood foot traffic. Obscured by the well-organized racks, I couldn't help but overhear strongly voiced opinions about the Ambler political scene, leading me to imagine a quarter of a century's worth of neighborhood gossip and lore. **This is one-stop, old-time thrift shopping.** There's **something for almost everybody**: kids' clothes, a small but unexciting collection of chachkas, a **substantial assortment of men's** clothing from solid-citizen Brooks Brothers to upscale up-and-coming Alexander Julian. As is usually the case, there's a disproportionately larger amount of women's clothing. The front window sported three recent, high-style outfits. The shop itself had more utilitarian, slightly dated garments. Ambler is not a high-profile, high-fashion kind of place. Consignments reflect the neighborhood. **CONSIGNOR ALERT:** 50%-50% split. No fee. By appointment. First-time 10-item limit.

Repeat Boutique

4072 Skippack Pike
Skippack, PA 19474
610-584-8887

Look: STATUS QUO

Goods:
STATUS QUO

Prices: LOW

HOURS: Wed & Thu
& Sun 12-5, Fri 10-7,
Sat 10-5

CLOSED: Holidays

The clerk was talkative at just the right moments, and left me alone to shop when I indicated that was what I needed. Left to my devices, I discovered a Toby Lerner, white lace ankle-length skirt with the original $360 price tag attached, priced here at $80, and re-reduced to $40 for their 50% off orange-and-blue dot sale. Unfortunately, what "repeats and repeats in my ear (is) don't you stay little fool, you know you can't win," an old song title that stuck in my mind and wouldn't shake loose.

40% Me-60% the Shop? Naaa. Now for a shopper, it might initially seem to make no never mind. But for the consignor surely, eventually for the shop and ultimately the shopper, it does make a difference, sometimes a BIG difference. Do the math. It's simple. Ten percent more on a consignment worth thousands, can make a significant difference to the bottom line, and therefore where consignors will park their Jags and BMWs. This shop, with its shortsighted 40% policy, has attracted the low end of the consignment spectrum. Not even a cheap, but adorable, little Neon pulled in the drive. Of all the privately owned shops I've reviewed, only a few others have this lopsided split. (Maybe they have their financial reasons. What could they be? Steep rent?) The vast majority, whether expensive or inexpensive, are 50-50%. Charities, who usually charger lower prices, can range up to 60% or even 75% to the consignor. Shopkeeper, do yourself and us a favor. Change this one, please. Then I'll change my tune. Maybe by next year, your lot will be full of new, mid-range cars.

CONSIGNOR ALERT: 50%-50% split. No fee. 90 days. By appointment only.

Salvation Army

1601 No. Broad St.
Lansdale, PA
19446
362-9468

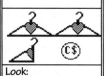

Look:
BOTTOMFEEDER

Goods: DOWN &
OUT–CLASS ACT

Prices: IRRATIC

HOURS:
Mon–Sat 9-5

CLOSED: Holidays

I had heard there was a Salvation Army around here somewhere. Traffic is fierce. Narrow in-and-out drives come up fast. The rear lot was inaccessible. Workers unloading a delivery truck and a semi-permanent tractor trailer, used as additional impromptu space to process donations, took up all the spaces. This is the smallest Salvation Army shop, ever. Swooping in at first light, the thrift locusts descended, picked the newly stocked shelves clean, and flew on to the next massing. Devastation was total. It should have gotten evening news coverage. An elderly woman with a walker careened into one of the narrowly placed display shelves, accidentally snaring and breaking some otherwise forgettable piece of bric-a-brac. Staff quickly swept it up without comment.

Makeshift work space in a rear corner of the selling floor is used to process incoming bags and bundles. Some interior or set designer might make good use of two old wooden tool boxes I saw displayed, reduced to $25 and $35. Unused quilts in original, see-through plastic, commanded the unSalvation-Army-like price of $75 and $100. A Maniac First: Fredricks of Hollywood label on some innocuous enough looking undies. But what I bought was a white Portuguese bud vase for $3 (that's more like it), the kind that has five finger size openings, each just big enough to hold a single stem. Sorry, Marvin. I left the Christopher Haynes red wool cardigan behind, even though it was a great buy at $4. Marvin doesn't really like red. It would have sat in his closet. Two well-heeled types were working the racks finding lots of stuff, while an out-of-state mom, killing time between visits with her grown-up daughter, had to "get out of the place, fast." It gave her the creeps. To each her own.

CONSIGNOR ALERT: Donations only.

Second Seitz

4084 Skippack Pk.
Skippack, PA 19474
610-584-8117

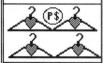

Look: TOP DRAWER

Goods: STATUS QUO–TOP DRAWER

Prices: LOW!

HOURS: Tue 1-7, Thu 1-7, Fri 1-8, Sat & Sun 12-5

CLOSED: Holidays

Well worth the trip, but hard to find in the intricate jumble of Skippack Village's densely packed shops. **Nothing would ever have prepared me for this one, and nothing will ever be quite the same.** Not me. Not my wardrobe. Not after coming here. Pattienne, the owner, is a redhead possessing a colossal personality, packed into a 5'2" frame. As a former Breck Shampoo child model (during their two pastel color years) and now a 5-year contract model for L'Oréal, she sports a minimum of three, never-before-known-to-occur-in-nature shades of long, Scarlett O'Hara curls bobbed over one ear, the crown curls one scissor-snip away from a crew. (Mine is chin length straight, with a wash and dry cut.) Her 2" wine-colored nails were gold laced. (Mine are keyboard short, the unvarnished truth.)

Commuting to New York once a week for a dye, a do and a shoot, then running around town picking up goodies for her shop, she probably blends right in. She doesn't blend in in Skippack. They've come to accept, appreciate, and even imitate her by now. After being in her presence for a half hour, I can understand why. So here I am, wanting something quietly elegant for an upcoming charity fashion show. That's like Katharine Hepburn asking Mae West to dress her. Or Hillary Clinton calling up Madonna for a wardrobe consult. Coincidentally, we both wore Joan Vass outfits, but not so's you'd notice. That's how different the same designer looked on us (but common ground after all?). While I've been ranting on about how unusual she looked, perhaps you've begun wondering when I'm going to get to the point: What about the shop? I've been describing it all along. **Pattienne, vibrant, fun, frilly, glamorous, sensational glitz and glitter *is* the shop.** I might just acquire a new look, a new me. Then again...on her it looks natural.
P.S. Ask about personal shopping services.

CONSIGNOR ALERT: Buys outright. Consign Tuesdays or by appointment only.

Sweet Repeats

425 W. Main St.
Lansdale, PA 19446
855-3700

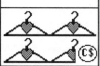

Look: CLASS ACT

Goods: HO HUM – CLASS ACT

Prices: LOW

HOURS:
Mon–Fri 10-6
Sat 10-4

CLOSED: Holidays

I looooved this place. Dripping in style, it reeks of atmosphere. It's a whimsical playground. Some places I've entered, marched through like soldiers on parade, reached the rear of the shop, turned and marched right back out the front door in two minutes, flat. **This place grabbed me, two steps in, and wouldn't let go,** holding my interest for 40 minutes. Both times. Artists, fashion designers, set designers, funky fashion plates, students of life, theatrical and magical types, con artists, collectors, and wannabes of every size, shape and description. All you amnesiacs who just woke up and need to gently make up for lost time. Wistful for the good ol' days? Don't much like being in this century? Fashion history, like every peel of the historic onion, repeats itself every decade or three. What's old is new, what's new is stored in someone's trunk, somewhere. And here it's all happening, all over the place, all over again.

I come to pull it around me like a security blanket, a talisman, protecting me against the onslaught of relentlessly unimaginative masses of thrift, resale and secondhand shops waiting for me out there. Poking around in this place, appreciating the caprice that composes and compiles the color-coordinated still lifes and outfits pulled together from a fertile mind and a cross section of decades and owners, may or may not be what you want surrounding you at home or on your person. But it certainly is good to carry around the home-sweet memory of it all.

NEW LOCATION ALERT: New store opens 3/6/95 on Butler Pike in Ambler **540-5858.**

CONSIGNOR ALERT: Donations only. Benefits The Lamb Foundation of Lansdale.

Wear Bear's Closet

319 W. Main St.
Lansdale, PA
19446
362-6757

Look: STATUS QUO
Goods: STATUS QUO
Prices: MODERATE

HOURS: Tue-Sat 10-5

CLOSED: Holidays

Micki Miller was energetic enough to mail me a copy of her flyer announcing the April 1st shop opening, and clever enough to lure me in and land me by thoughtfully taking the time to list four other, noncompeting, nearby shops, their addresses and phone numbers and directions to the area. Of course I came.

Coming and going, I discovered her outside, leaning against the shop, pulling hard on a cigarette. She's a smoker, who thoughtfully and sensibly smokes outside. Toy after out-of-reach toy lined the upper shelves around the ceiling edges, some old, some new, some used, some not, a great replacement for those saccharine duck-bunny borders in so many kiddie secondhand shops (and kids' bedrooms). Micki, bring a few repeats and rejects down to ankle-biter level, please.

Few party clothes, more **equipment, mostly play and school stuff. The front room is visually fun** with clothing up to size 14, but really anything larger than an 8 is to be found in quantities only on the jeans rack. The back room "Maternity Den" (bears, remember) is early afterthought. A lot of floor and wall space is going to waste back there. Maybe this is where she might set aside space for a Smoke-Free-the-Bear-Cub "Play Den."

CONSIGNOR ALERT: Clothing: 60%You-40%Shop. 50%-50% toys & equipment. $2 fee. 90 days. By appointment only.

West Main Consignment

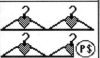

305 W. Main St.
Lansdale, PA
19446
855-8533

Look: CLASS ACT
Goods: STATUS QUO–CLASS ACT
Prices: MODERATE

HOURS: Mon–Fri 10-5
Sat 10-4

CLOSED: Holidays

Tuesday evening I taught a Thrift Shop Mania class at North Penn High School Fall Adult Ed Program. Here it was Thursday morning. I was finishing up my second round of undercover shopping field trips for this area, the first completed in May. Back then I overheard the shop was changing hands. An employee of ten years was to buy out the current owner. This tidbit was a contributing factor in waiting so long. I wanted to see if any significant changes would take place in what was a **very well run, above average resale shop**, once the transition was made.

"Doing" the men's department, I struck up a conversation with a fellow thrifter. She asked me (of all people) if I knew where the other "good" shops were. She lived in Allentown, but worked in this area, and wasn't familiar with Lansdale. As we got deeper and deeper into the particulars I spilled the beans. I told her about The Guide. She couldn't wait to go to the nearest bookstore, but she didn't know how to get to that, either. So I sold her one of my last remaining copies, right out of the back of the van. I swore her to secrecy. We went back to shopping our separate ways.

As she and I bellied up to the counter to make our purchases (I got Morgan a purple teddy-bear-fuzz Patagonia jacket for $15.), the new owner, an old pro, without recognizing me, began to tell my fellow maniac about The Guide and my class, and the fact that I would be doing tours soon. My but word does travel fast in a small town. I braced myself, wondering where the conversation would go. The only tense moment came when the new owner registered a low level peeve. "We've ONLY been here ten years" and "she still hadn't gotten around to reviewing us".

To all customer appearances, and customer appearances are all that count, nothing has changed but the owners. **The transition was seamless.** 'Allentown' told me she plans to return. She had done her own 'undercover' review. Don't we all?

CONSIGNOR ALERT: 50%-50%. $2 fee. By appointment. 25 items or less. On hangers.

TOUR #20
CAN WE EAT OUR PIE AND HAVE IT TOO?

So here I am riding up Rte. 422, high wide and handsome, right before the exit to Limerick, when an old-fashioned alternative makes a modern-day splash against a bold blue background. Two windmills face into the air currents, silently and safely producing electricity. The backward-glancing, forward-looking company that has erected them to supply their own electrical needs has also had the silouette of windmills painted across the cornflower-blue field of a squat, rounded supply tank. The next nearest windmill is 20 miles away on a small working farm up Rte. 29, headed into the hills along the Perkiomen Creek.

A long stretch of highway, a slight rise in the road, and Limerick's nuclear power plant twin towers slowly come into view. They are inescapable. No matter where you look, there they are, from every perspective, from almost every front window or back door. **And before the Mayor and Chamber of Commerce of every town around here start breathing down my neck, know that we are all affected.** Not just Pottstown or Royersford or Phoenixville. Driving around, I tried to imagine what it would be like to be a resident and live with THE VIEW, taking it for granted as I went about my everyday life, as a mother, a lifelong East Coast resident, and an avowed pennypinching recycling activist. Driving into the otherwise innocuous, every-day charm of small-town Pottstown was worrisome.

So, here we are: **Pottstown. Zipf's** is a BIG candy shop on High Street. The name Smith appears on store fronts with explainable regularity. **Mrs. Smith's** pie factory anchors the base of town, cranking out apple, lemon meringue, and cherry confections, day in and day out for so long their original metal pie plates are fast becoming collectible. I've see them commanding as much as $6 as far away as Norristown. I bought one even before coming here. I like the holes. They help make a crisp crust. I make a mean apple pie. My lemon meringue is dynamite. Just ask me. And then there's the fresh banana with apricot glaze, whipped cream, and layer of dark chocolate over the crust. There I go again. So anyway... I ate lunch at the **Brookside Family Restaurant.** I waited forty minutes for: dry pork chops, metalic tasting applesauce (too old?), instant mashed potatoes, a friendly waitress, and a clean bathroom. Better luck at **V.I.P. Family Restaurant** on High Street, sandwiched (tuna on toasted white with lettuce, mayo on the side) between the train station and the gorgeous ELK's Victorian mansion clubhouse.

Phoenixville is waiting. Waiting to rise from the cold ashes of the darkened steel mills that used to burn as bright as Vulcan's forge. Phoenix Bridge. Phoenix Steel. Not just words. Names. Names that built this town and others like it. Names that gave men good honest work. Names that fed families and kept them warm. Names that are fading from memory. Fading, but not gone. The walls of **Buff's** restaurant are lined with yellowed newspaper clippings. Old men, eating lunch around the spotless counter, remember. The mighty arched bridges ringing the town and connecting it to the outside world, remember. Rusting yard rails and crumbling coal bins remember. The gigantic Victorian, intricate brick train station, slate roof open to the sky, as if equally gigantic moths landed and nibbled, remembers. They're still here, still able to tell their stories. All we have to do is listen.

A brash, brightly colored mural attempts to recapture the town's glory days. It's primary colors and in-your-face energy are far more vibrant than anything doing on the streets below. More socialist than democratic, the bulky, heroic style is reminiscent of DPW projects of the 30's, updated for the 90's. The story it tells is far too big and bold for the cramped space. Driving by, all I remember is looking up at this neck-craning flyby swirl of love's labor lost. (Matthew, our resident caretaker and about-to-graduate Temple art student, spent part of last year's summer vacation perched high up on scaffolding, as he helped whitewash the wall in preparation for the mural. All he remembers is looking down...). **Joseph's**, a posh, white table cloth restaurant situated in the **Hotel Washington** with its intricate second story, wrought iron, faux porch so prevalent hereabouts, has a cheap, come-on luncheon menu with sandwiches and such. It's probably a local hang-out for the middle management and up types who work for Eastman Kodak and Smith Kline and live in the new tract homes springing up like April grass all around the outskirts of town.

Here and in nearby **Royersford** residents use their porches. Each railed and spindled domain is filled with aluminum glides, folding chairs, wood-slat swinging benches and old wooden rockers. Memories hang in the air. Memories of a life that's vanished. Each house, each porch, each factory stack, each barge lock, each railroad tie has its version. They know all too well that the Industrial Revolution is over. The age of international mass communications and home offices is upon us.

These small towns never knew what hit them. They are only just beginning to figure out what to do post steel. Letters to the Editor in the local newspaper debate the best way to educate the next generation. While the debate rages, kids lack the equipment and training that will position us as a nation to compete internationally, once again. If the parents don't know from computer, how can we expect them to understand why their kids MUST. The issue always seems to be having to choose one way or the other. Republican or Democrat. Feelings or facts. Right or wrong. I don't get it. Both sides, all sides have part of the answer. This having to choose either the left OR right side of the brain stuff doesn't cut it. It's old kill-the-dinosaur-or-be-killed thinking. Let's build bridges to both sides, just like before. Just like the Phoenix Bridge company. The answer is lying right around us in the ruins. It always is.

Rte. 422 is the main high-speed drag connecting all the towns hereabouts. Rte. 29 bisects it, running East to West, leading to **Collegeville** on the right and **Phoenixville** to the left. Right before this momentous choice point, **Oak's Flea Market** rises up out of the winter-flattened fields. Might be worth a look-see. And whatever is that magnificent mini-mutant White House? Take the Oaks's Exit and let me know.

Another town, another flea, this time the **Power House**, a long low brick structure across the Perkiomen Creek from the **Collegeville Inn**. My parents used to bring us here for one of their famous smorgasbord overloads of green jello and all things carbo. (I knew better even then.) The place must have had hardening of the economic arteries. It's closed. Just across the street, **Speck's Broasted Chicken** is doing a booming business, and looks like THE Maniac place for lunch. Down Rte. 29, there's a narrow, two-lane arched stone bridge, connecting the town to the rest of the world. It stradles the creek right behind the **Perkiomen Bridge Hotel**. Their glassed-in porch overlooking the water might be a good spot to eat, too. Built in 1799 to horse and buggy body specs, but still very much in use, the bridge, funded by a $20,000 lottery, is one of the oldest of its kind in the State. If it gets backed up, so does everything else. The first time I was here, young men from Penn State were taking advantage of Saturday noon rush-hour buildup to solicit tin-can-clanking coin donations for children's cancer research. Darting in and out of traffic, their rhythm matched the synchronized traffic lights as they went from red to green and back again.

P.S. Don't try to buy computer equipment secondhand at a bottomfeeder. By the time the equipment filters down, it's usually already three or four generations behind. The exception to this rule of thumb (and there's always an exception, isn't there?), is to go to a store that specializes in secondhand computer equipment. Even then...the new stuff is getting so cheap, relative to what it cost just a few years ago, you may still want new, new, new. We have passed on the ensuing generations of computers Marvin has lugged home, giving them first to me, then to Morgan. Every time he trades up, we trade up (or is it down?). If you have to choose, choose a home computer over a TV. Choose a home computer over a second car, over a vacation. But choose. Get off your butt, read up on it, prowl the stores, take a class. Four year olds will play with one while grownups tremble in fear and dread. I know. I've been there. Marvin had almost given up hope. But now we are a three-Apple-a-day MacFamily. Morgan's been on-line since she was 3. She just got her own 'office' space set up in her room this week. CD ROM is next. (Marvin, tell me again. Why do we need a CD-ROM?)

TOUR #20

8	Amy's Attic	Pottstown
10	Carol's Outgrown Shop	Pottstown
2	Collegeville Consignments	Collegeville
11	Evergreen	Pottstown
3	Musagi	Phoenixville
1	Next To New Shop	Collegeville
5	Phoenixville Hospital Thrift	Phoenixville
4	Scioli's	Phoenixville
6	Second Chance Shop	Royersford
7	Select Furniture	Pottstown
9	Wendy's Collectibles	Pottstown

*Note: This list has a shop's entire name. Names in review boxes may have been shortened a tad to fit. Numbers before each shop name correspond to their numbered location on each map. **Shops with a star sold Volume II. Volume III? ASK!**

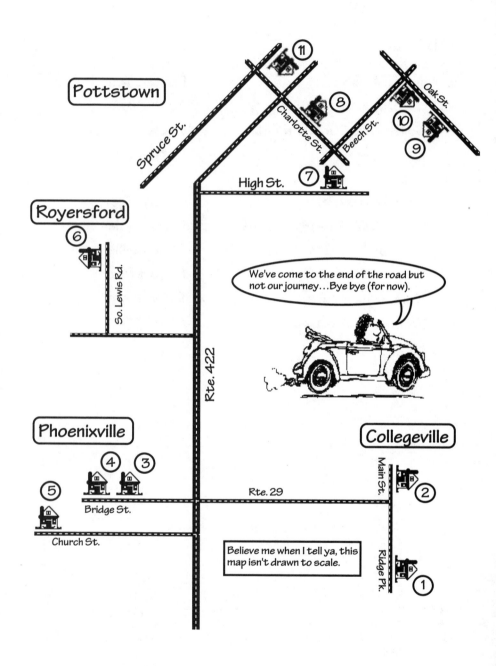

TOUR #20 MAP Page 281

Amy's Attic

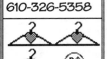

Beech & Charlotte Sts.
Pottstown, PA
19464
610-326-5358

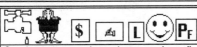

(P$)

Look: STATUS QUO
Goods: STATUS QUO
Prices: UP & DOWN

HOURS:
Mon–Sat 10-5

CLOSED: Holidays

Another first floor 'attic,' capable of holding two or three houses' worth of attics, big enough to require two salespeople to manage. Amy wasn't in. Even so, workers gossiped and worked and worked and gossiped. Customers trickled in. I wandered around unrecognized and unassisted. **Regulars were greeted by name** and joined in the ongoing gabfest. Signs over by the register noted ongoing sales by ticket color & date: Jan. 16-Feb. 1, 20% off, Jan.1–15, 30% off, etc., up to 75% off. I saw items stamped September, when they were first consigned. Items dated August – December 1 were $1. **There was a freewheeling, wide-ranging assortment.**

One of those clipout-food-coupon-section-quality, send-away-for-sets of hand-painted plates, this time an animal theme, was displayed in the here, there, and everywhere china and housewares section. A grizzly bear, a red wolf and a pair of snow leopards, mother and cub, were harmlessly posed in vivid color for the dangerously high price of $40 each. Portable potty seats, only $5. Catalog-new furniture was available on order. A set of American Sweetheart Rose china was originally marked $175, firm. That price was Xed out, black crayoned down to $100. (And still overpriced by half.) An exercycle was reduced to $50. Nearby lay a copy of Your First Ferret in paperback. Clothing ranged from a skinny-minny, never-worn, Cotton Express show-your-stuff sheath, original price tag of $54 still attached, on sale here for $18, to a large selection of graying bras, men's underpants, T's and sweats. They contrasted sharply with the whiter than white, unworn, pretty as a picture, communion dresses protected under drycleaner sheets of clear plastic.

CONSIGNOR ALERT: 50%-50% split. $2 annual fee. 60 days. 20%/30 days, 50%/45 days. Drop and run.

Carol's Outgrown Shop

402 N. Charlotte St.
Pottstown, PA 19464
610-323-8320

(P$)

Look: CLASS ACT
Goods: HO HUM– CLASS ACT
Prices: LOW

HOURS: Mon, Tue & Thu 11-5, Fri & Sat 10-5

CLOSED: 2nd week in July & 3rd week in August

$ L P

Carol may soon outgrow her own shop. **It grabs you at the display shelves as soon as you enter, and won't put you down or let you go until you hit the rear wall** of floor-to-ceiling shoes, linens and jeans. Each and every rack required a push and a shove just to get a peek at the oversupply of color-grouped blouses, shirts, slacks, skirts, dresses, suits and sweaters. Ropes of necklaces, bracelets and baubles hung from the wall in a **ravishingly colorful display** of cheap thrills. A rack of crisp whites for those of you whose jobs require the 'Look, not a speck of dirt here, there or anywhere' mystique. (I used to wear whites. The dreck on some of those kitchen floors would make my wooden clogs curl up.) Even the air was 'full.' Rock n' roll music filled the store till Carol and I were alone. At least now the air waves were qui

I clumped around in a pair of black waterproof Sporto boots, one size too large, considering them and the inventory which ranged from **the mundane:** LIZ straight denim skirt in excellent condition for $10, ditto the banana-colored Gloria Vanderbilt jeans. A flannel-lined, khaki bush jacket with lots of snapped and flapped pockets, $19.95. **To the miraculous:** I'd NEVER seen a wet suit in a family thrift store. (Once or twice in a bottomfeeder.) But here it was: size 10, turquoise and black, $20. Anybody out there interested in taking a dive? A 1995 Physician's Desk Reference (PDR to those in the biz) was only $25. I'd never seen one of those--current--before, either. Is there a doctor in the house? Most professional tomes seen whilst thrifting are 7to 8 years old, and virtually useless, although the fair market price takes an upswing when they are REALLY old because of their curiosity value. Speaking of up, watch your step, coming and going, it's a doozie.
P.S. Signs EVERYWHERE say **"Closed Wednesday."**
CONSIGNOR ALERT: 50%-50% split. No fee. 60 days. No appointment needed.

Collegeville Consignments	
323 Main St. Collegeville, PA 19426 **610-489-8150** **Look:** STATUS QUO **Goods:** HO HUM– CLASS ACT **Prices:** LOW – MODERATE **HOURS:** Mon & Tue 10-5, Wed & Fri 10- 6, Thu 10-8, Sat 10-4 **CLOSED:** Holidays	Main Street isn't much. It doesn't look like you're really supposed to park along here, it's so narrow. Perched, nevertheless, on the northern edge of the all-too-brief town center of what could have been called Ursinusville is Collegeville Consignments. The owner was getting ready for a well deserved end-of-winter vacation. Signs posted over the register area said not to come by again until she reopened February 27. So that's when I timed my second visit for this tour. That way I could get 'em all in one fell swoop. Furniture was limited to small, easy-to-carry pieces like the big, welcoming, take-your-ease, wooden rocker. A $50 black jean two-piece outfit with mirrored geometric disks surrounded by hot-colored embroidery looked like a mall-crawler matador outfit. A pretty Vittadini blue-and-green cotton summer dress with drop waist and big pockets was $18. A pink Eve Stillman nightgown only $10. **Men's was good to great.** I spotted a custom made English tweed jacket, size 46, with woven leather buttons, pockets attached on the bias like a hunting jacket, hand-done topstitching 'holding it' all together. Housewares held wacky, suitably wooden-headed $6.50 figures holding signs like "I have PMS and a loaded gun. Any questions?" Others, shaped like sheep, quipped: "Ewe ain't fat. Ewe is fluffy." All very handmade by Becky. Imperial cowboy boots, new, were marked down to $85, near an 'instructional' Hopalong Cassidy video. New Leanin' Tree greeting cards. Gourmet coffee will be sold starting April 15! **CONSIGNOR ALERT:** 50%-50% split. $6 fee. 90 days. 20%/30 days, 50%/60 days. By appointment only.

Evergreen	
810 Spruce Street Pottstown, PA 19464 **610-970-9925** **Look:** TOP DRAWER **Goods:** STATUS QUO–TOP DRAWER **Prices:** LOW–HIGH **HOURS:** Mon–Fri 9:30-6, Sat 9:30-5 Call for summer evening hours **CLOSED:** Holidays	Right from the beginning, they had me here. Back in elementary school I really thought I was hot stuff when I learned the difference between deciduous and coniferous. Nancy will tell you I never did learn how to spell either word, though. (She can.) Eventually I learned how the world is organized; there's a pattern to everything if only we know how and where to look. Just like here. They've got their organizational patterns **down to a science.** The large brick building has a parking lot all to itself. **The place is new and sunny and clean. The front windows were filled with stuff that peaked my curiosity.** That usually gets me hooked, too. The very first thing I saw was a bamboo-and-rattan chair just like the ones we sold at Bloomies during my horrendous 6- or 7-month stint as a furniture salesperson. I knew, long ago and far away, that chair had been $295. In the here and now it was $49, only needing a coiled length or two of rattan to restore it to pristine, showroom glory. That would cost you about $5 and 15 minutes. A deal. The $295 oak chopping block kitchen set with four ladderback, roped-seat chairs was great. So too the identical LIZ blouses, one denim, the other beige polyester, both with tiny box pleats gathered and stitched down the front, $8.50 each. The Van Sciver mahogany and brass hat rack for $100 would be a terrific organizational opening statement to any business office. Ya never know...I loooved Bette Midler's song. **And now I looove this shop.** I heard somewhere once that "cynics are only disappointed romantics." Come. You won't be disappointed. I promise. **CONSIGNOR ALERT:** Furniture & baby equipment **60-65% You, 30-35% Shop.** Clothing 50%-50% split. No fee. 60 days (clothes). By appointment only.

Musagi	$ ☺ P_F P_$
217 Bridge St. Phoenixville, PA 19460 **610-983-3993** (C$)	Old, floor boards squeaked with every step toward the front bay. Slanted stacks of clothes were piled precariously, wire hangers askew, bundles and bags were thrown to the floor in a generous overflow of as-yet-unprocessed donations. One topless, see-through plastic bin held change purses, a Smurf, a penny, costume jewelry, lace trim, seam binding, more change purses, a pink-and-white stuffed football. I know because I accidentally toppled it with my elbow. It was placed atop the counter, atop another plastic box holding…"Hello," called out the voice behind the counter, behind the boxes. Startled, I knocked over the box. Oops.
Look: HO HUM - STATUS QUO **Goods:** HO HUM– STATUS QUO **Prices:** LOW (when marked)	Installed behind this walled encampment of other people's giveaways was Alexandrina Malungu, Executive Director, psychologist and, for the moment, lone volunteer. A refugee from Rwanda, she too had searched for a new home, one far away from the madness of her homeland. One step ahead of the donations surrounding her, she had succeeded, only to find herself surrounded by the growing madness in our country. She appraised the situation, rolled up her sleeves, and dug in. She's here to help. Musagi Personal Care Home provides "Loving Care, Support,
HOURS: Mon–Fri 10-5, Sat 10-2	Guidance, Companionship, Medical, Psychiatric and Dental Services…" to older adults who "cannot cope with life or its problems without help". Making a go of it, but short of money, short of staff, this **absolutely delightful, wise and witty woman** could use some of our help. Hello… **P.S.** Be sure to read the poem, "On This Day" hanging over the register.
CLOSED: Holidays	**CONSIGNOR ALERT:** Donations only. Benefits Musagi Personal Care Home, Ltd.

Next To New Shop	☺ ☂ ⚘ 🛒 $ 🖼 🧸 P_F
3761 Ridge Pike Collegeville, PA 19426 **610-489-2477** (P$)	I've come to think not a few shopowners will rue their choice of name once they get a gander at The Guide. What may have sounded innovative only seems redundant when you get a peek at the long list of names using Second Hand Something Or Other, New, Next to New, Nearly New and Almost New. So here I am again, parked outside another Next to New. What makes it so new and different? or or bigger and better? or special? if not the name?
Look: STATUS QUO **Goods:** HO HUM – CLASS ACT **Prices:** LOW	Well for one thing it shares a parking lot and property with Dewayne's auto repair shop next-door. Now, that's different. In good weather, outside on the concrete skirt, they display the usual lineup assortment of carriages, car seats and big plastic toys. **The first floor is a colorful overload**, overflowing with toys on top of every rack (but only a few available in the play area). **Infants' and toddlers' clothing was equa-lly extensive.** I scrambled past the large set aside office and sorting area and up the narrow stairs to the second floor of what was once somebody's home. That's not unusual. The rooms upstairs, four former bedrooms, were very small and
HOURS: Tue & Wed Fri & Sat 10-4, Thu 10-8	except for the last one, too dark. But they were clean and well organized. So far, more usual than not. Up here, where the larger kids' stuff is hung, there were several outfits I considered buying for Morgan. A $20 black velvet dress with jewels and gold bursts (but she hasn't worn last year's party dress, yet), a red-plaid two-piece short set for $10 (but she hates red), a soft flannel nightgown (but she has a drawer full) and a Land's End down jacket (she's run out of hook space). Enough is enough, I decided. Now that's different for me.
CLOSED: Holidays and 1 week in summer.	**P.S.** One-week return for credit with receipt and tags in-tact. 👉 **SHOPPER ALERT:** Little Kids clothes & toys 👕 👕 👕 👕 **CONSIGNOR ALERT:** 50%-50% split. $1/20 items. 90 days. 25%/30, 50%/60days. By appointment only.

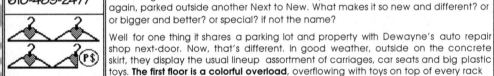

Phoenixville Hospital Thrift	 $ L ☺ P_F
227 Church Street Phoenixville, PA 19453 **610-983-1491** 	It was noonish. I was hungry. This was to be my last stop before the internal 'lunch whistle' went off full blast. I was wondering mostly about where I would eat, and only a little about the shop. It wasn't exactly an attention grabber, and my stomach kept making its own demands. The two dears at the front desk, backs to the shop's front window and door, were idly passing the time, preoccupied by appraising the possible worth of a practically worthless piece of purple pottery. One hesitantly observed that because it had a stamp of some kind on the bottom it was probably worth more. Worth more than what? I found myself asking myself as I roamed the lovingly preserved, museum-quality panorama entitled "Hospital Volunteer Thrift Shop, circa 1954."
Look: STATUS QUO **Goods:** HO HUM - STATUS QUO **Prices:** LOW	The other woman, being a more agreeable sort than I, agreed with her seated sidekick that "that was probably so." Then they launched into a detailed recipe swap. "Take some potatoes, some sausage, a package (or was it a can) of soup, stir it all together, and bake till done." Did I get it right? Normally this down home pot boiler wouldn't have sent me anywhere but to the seltzer bottle, but the description of the local sausage did make it sound tasty, and I was very hungry...so I did the only thing I could under the circumstances. I left to go eat lunch.
HOURS: Tue–Fri 10-4 Sat 10-1 Donations: Mon 7-11:30	**P.S.** There was one significant item worth reporting: a $10 white mohair Cotton Express sweater, large enough to be a dress, hanging on a nail on the squared-off column by the front door. Remember: No matter how I go on about these places, **you can almost always find SOMETHING.** Even if it's only a new recipe.
CLOSED: July and August	**CONSIGNOR ALERT:** Donations only. Benefits Phoenixville Hospital.

Scioli's	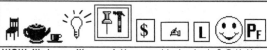 $ L ☺ P_F
235 Bridge St. Phoenixville, PA 19460 **610-935-0118** 	**WOW. It's huge. It's great.** You want just a taste? O.K. Here goes. A pair of red, white and blue, 12'-high wooden soldiers. A 15' bar and mirrored back in solid, take-apart mahogany. An 80- or 90-year old watercolor of a miniature bark canoe, strewn with faded pansies. (I sould go back and get that.) 1950's hefty, wide-body bikes. Same-era Magnavox TVs, slatted-pine futon frame, steamer trunks, aluminum porch swing, outdated globes, Chippendale chair frames, stripped, almost stripped, going to be stripped... Enough already. Take the elevator. Take a hike. Go see for yourself. The owner's friendly and likes to talk. He'll tell you the rest.
Look: STATUS QUO **Goods:** STATUS QUO–TOP DRAWER **Prices:** MODERATE	**P.S.** It's also hard to find. It's a shop within a shop. Faz's Fashions are sold on the first floor, with a few pieces of furniture on display scattered here and there. The main furniture showrooms are in the enormous basement and two top floors, connected by an eight-person freight elevator. **I loooved the dangling, bloody plastic foot.** Nice touch.
HOURS: Mon–Sat 9-5:30, Call first.	
CLOSED: Holidays	**CONSIGNOR ALERT:** Buys outright. Willing to consign. Ask.

Second Chance Shop

61 S. Lewis Rd.
Royersford, PA
19468

610-948-2957

Look: CLASS ACT

Goods: STATUS QUO-CLASS ACT

Prices: LOW

HOURS: Tue, Wed & Fri 9:30-5, Thu 9:30-7, Sat 9:30-4

CLOSED: 3rd week in July.

Attention, moms and dads. Boogie up (or down) Rte. 422. Get off at the Royersford exit. It's only a hop, skip and jump up (or down) the road. Look for the Catholic church on one corner, TOM'S in big letters on the roof across the street. Walnut & South Lewis with Domino's Pizza on the corner is what you want. That's where the bargains are. The owner is **kid-caring**, and she likes grown-ups, too. She smiled and greeted everyone, knowing most by name and stage of childbearing. "Oh, I see you've had your second." or "So how are the other four?"

There's a large rack of good everyday maternity, sharing the narrow, no-more-than-two-people-at-a-time back room with chair swings, carriages, car seats. On a wet, cold February afternoon, the **racks were full to bursting** with good, every-day infants' to toddlers' through size 12 to 14. I saw Esprit, Heartstrings, Amy Byer and Gap in the racks, Little Tykes and Casco on the shelves. Aisles were crowded with moms, beginner models asleep in carriers, experimental models crawling and creeping across the clean new carpet, up and running prototypes quietly crayoning over in the corner. Lots of life. That so many were out and about in such dreary weather attested to the favorable reviews local customers are already giving this place.

I couldn't bear the stress of staying for long, afraid I might get preggers just hanging around. But I'll be back. Marvin just learned he's going to be a grandfather. His 25-year-old beauty, Erica, called with the good news just this week. I guess that means that I'm going to be a.....Oh No! No! Not that. Anything but that. I'm far too young. Aren't I? But if Marvin is four years younger than I am...Let's do the math. That must mean...Morgan will be an Aunt. And that makes me a Grandmaniac!
P.S. They have a public bathroom.

CONSIGNOR ALERT: 50%-50% split. No fee. 120 days. Appointment needed to consign clothing; none needed for toys or equipment.

Wendy's Collectables

310 Oak Street
Pottstown, PA
19464

610-326-1435

Look: HO HUM

Goods: HO HUM-STATUS QUO

Prices: UP & DOWN

HOURS: Mon–Fri 11-6, Sat 12-6. Sunday by appointment only.

CLOSED: Holidays

I was dumbstruck at the disparity between the shop inventory and the owner's magnificently designed, but illegible business card. The card is all ruffles and old-fashioned flourishes, resplendent in very expensive full color. There's a New Age-Space Age picture melding dreamy, passive maidens holding a picture-within-a-picture of men hard at work, making and creating God only knows what in some sort of neoclassical setting. Ya gotta see it. That's the disparity. The similarity between card vision and shop reality is the cramped overflow of tiny writing attempting to amass too much information in too small a space. (Remind you of anything else?) In other words, you can't read the blankety-blank phone number.

This stylistic impasse echoes the cramped **overflow of a relatively large inventory housed in equally small quarters.** She's lent her lighthearted, storybook name to a place that sells the gritty basics of real life. A Kero heater, $50. Black lacquer enter-tainment center, $200. Magic Chef four burner gas mini-range, $150. Twin mattress and box spring set, $100. Blue and white office chair, $10, microwave cart, $30. Metal file cabinet, $25. General Electric, side-by-side refrigerator (a bowl of charcoal wisely placed inside to eliminate the olfactory memory of someone elses' leftovers), $250. Kitchen set of brown, brown, brown vinyl and aluminum, $75. Scotchguarded brown, brown, brown plaid sofa, $125. Everything you'd need to set up function without form housekeeping.

CONSIGNOR ALERT: Buys outright.

Select Furniture	
433 High St. Pottstown, PA 19464 **610-323-3819**	John pointed his long bony, arthritic finger in my face. His dirty blond fading to white hair (as in color) was combed back behind his ears. Curls grazed the collar of his even dirtier (as in dirt) navy quilt jacket. The furnace had quit only hours before. He was cold. He'd had a beer for lunch and worried if I could smell it on his breath. It must have helped to warm him up. Chin slanted down and to the side, he looked at me from under his bushy eyebrows and began to tell me stories about his family life, his children, about what was wrong with the world today, about religion, about the nuclear power plant in Limerick. His eyes were watery with age, cold slate blue like the ocean right before a storm. His heart was big, his mind roamed freely. He spoke lucidly and with fervor like the prophets of the Old Testament. His furnace was stoked.
Look: HO HUM **Goods:** HO HUM–STATUS QUO **PRICES:** UNMARKED	
HOURS: Mon – Sat 9-5	I spent 20 minutes listening and 3 minutes talking. It was one of the most interesting lectures (sermons?) I've ever heard while thrifting. Especially because he sees most things the way I do, and because he still cares so fiercely. I guess it sounds silly, but **I came to love this man in the short time I was with him.** Now don't get all excited, he's a happily married, 70's grandfather. And I'm not even a grandmother, yet. (Erica, take your time.) What got him started on this wide-ranging riff? My Q & A about a dozen or so old, leather-bound Bibles, some handwritten in pen and ink in Latin, carelessly tossed on a shelf. Seems they had sold a Guttenberg from the stack only last week for $1,000 (?) If so it was way too cheap. Other than the recently vacuumed-to-within-an-inch-of-its-life purple shag rug, with each and every 'hair' standing on end, and the incongrous outdoor plastic furniture with umbrella open to keep the fluorescent glare down, and the enormous wide-mouthed plastic bas-relief Christmas carolers circa 1954, John was the most interesting objet d'art d'place. Stop in when you're in the mood for a little uplift, a little downdraft.
CLOSED: Holidays	**CONSIGNOR ALERT:** Buys outright.

EPILOGUE: THE END (OF THE GUIDE) IS AT HAND

Did any of you ever hear of a guy named Tesla? A contemporary of Edison, he was our modern-day Prometheus. Some people thought he was a genius. Others thought he was seriously nuts. He used to go up into the mountains near his home in the middle of violent thunderstorms and do electrical experiments. According to rumors circulated by fellow scientists and a few townspeople, he was trying to find a way to supply the world with free electricity. Some believe he found the way. Then the story gets as dark and stormy as some of those nights, when he went out alone, climbing higher and higher toward the source of all that unchained energy. Competition, government, big business, money, the human craving for power and, of course, greed, stepped in and took over. Today, Edison is the one we read about in history books. But some think Edison was the plaything of the dark side. (Heresy, I know. Sorry, but many think it's true.) Tesla had dared to reach for the gods. He was destroyed in the process by men. But he's been going through something of a reclamation lately. Enough time has gone by, enough of the main players are dead now, that there are books being written about him and a recent biography on the tube.

Here's a riddle for you. See if you can figure out the answer.

Two chimneys stand silent
taking turns spewing smoke,
while workers inside, feet up
take a toke. Headless robots
outside, cross the countryside
stride, over brook, stream and
boulder while joined at the
shoulder by miles of high wire,
that song birds avoid preferring
a high flyer to swoon or expire.
Right in our midst, our fate they
conspire, as they light up our homes
(and then melt down to Chinar?)

> The answer to this riddle is a Limerick.

We're burying our heads if we think we're any safer in Center City or Reading or Princeton than Limerick or Three Mile Island if a well placed employee or three at one of these sights doesn't get a good night's sleep, or takes one pull too many. I was in Greece only weeks after Chernobyl.

Greece, mind you. Where they had to take their shoes off before coming inside and couldn't eat the local produce for weeks and months afterward because of the fallout from the Russian disaster. People had rashes, headaches. Calves were born deformed. Their own government didn't warn the Greeks of the cloud of hot droplets that rained down over them on Easter weekend. The weekend any Greek with 2 square feet of earth to his name was out in the countryside, roasting lamb with garlic and rosemary, celebrating the holiday...outdoors. Our own government has a long and inglorious history of covering up man-made disasters like atomic testing in the Pacific, the Nevada desert and Washington state, and the ensuing high rates of cancer among islanders, soldiers and dairy farmers lying downwind.

As Maniacs, we're all trying to save a buck. Can you imagine what it would be like if that wild-eyed dreamer and fellow maniac Tesla had had his way? We'd all be getting FREE energy. (PECO's gonna love that one.) Then there's the issue of recycling. Just where do you suppose all that hot junk goes when they're 'done' with it. It's not exactly like recycling old clothing. Clothing gets worn, resold, worn, resold, worn out. It either gets thrown out and eventually goes back to the earth, or gets shown in a museum somewhere, or keeps on giving used as rags, rag paper, mattress stuffing, rug pads...harmless enough (except maybe for the bleach and dyes going into our water supply. But the more we recycle, the less harm done.). No such luck with all the leftovers back at the power plant. They get stored deep in the mountains, waiting.

Waiting for what? An earthquake? Or some poor fool a thousand years from now who unknowingly reopens Pandora's Box? Or the usual, inescapable assortment every civilization produces: pirate captains of industry wanting to make a fast buck, disgruntled activists turned terrorists, garden variety con artists, and general all-around adventurers. Think Egypt and tomb robbers. Think how long it took to translate the Rosetta stone. Think BIG MESS. And what about the question of increased rates of cancer in those living near transmitters? The final straw for me came listening to a radio talk show. The scientist being interviewed described, and I quote: "The entire East Coast is a cancer corridor." Cheery thought.

Most days we take so much for granted, until we stop to add it all up: Automobile pollution, coughing smokers lighting up while pregnant, steroid- enhanced fast-food hamburgers, slash and burn in our life-support system known as the rain forest, the shrinking ozone layer, the guys with their finger on the button, herbicides seeping deep into underground streams, terrorism, racism, overpopulation, famine, right-to-lifers killing, child abuse, eating disorders, AIDS, diminishing effectiveness of antibiotics, songbirds dying off, guns in our schools, lead poisoning, drug addiction, Serbia, Rwanda, Somalia, homelessness, depleted schools of fish off New England, Chernobyl, earthquakes up and down the Pacific coastline, Chechnya, Camden, Chester (C's are problematic.).

Wilhelm Reich, M.D. psychiatrist/psychoanalyst and founder of the American College of Orgonomy, was another infamous, wise madman, now long dead. He was prosecuted by our government back in the late 1940's and 50's, the glory days of paranoid political witch-hunts. In one of his many newly rediscovered books, popular enough to be reprinted again and again, he described the emotional plague which has seeped into modern life. The plague of anger and hate and denial born of our lost connection to our bodies and our feelings. His was the last public book burning in America brought to us by the U.S. Food and Drug Administration. He was sent to prison for the crime of ignoring an FDA ban on the transporting of the Orgone Energy Accumulator (a device he invented and used for treating a variety of illnesses) across state lines. By refusing to recant and play along with the prevailing national mood, he died imprisoned and in disgrace. Adherents recreate his experiments with energy, looking for The Source.

Tesla, Reich. They had a lot in common. They stepped outside the common bounds of accepted thought and discussion. They were ahead of their time. They dared to be different. They lost. But they won. Now they are being vindicated. If Shirley MacLaine can sell millions of copies of books, writing in everyday language about the same wild and woolly stuff and not get burned at the stake...If Oprah can keep millions of viewers tuned in, listening and learning about hyperbaric chambers one day, incest and alcoholism and weight loss the next, and we follow along, learning with her the value of expressing our feelings in this life, and exploring with guests who've had near-death experiences about what it might be like in the next...there's hope for this sad, tired world of ours yet.

I know I've probably lost some of you right around here. There she goes of the deep end again, some of you must be thinking. What does any of this have to do with thrift shopping? Let me try to pull this all together for myself and you. I know it's all pieces in the same puzzle, but I haven't put it into words before, even for myself. Here goes.

Every one of us counts, from the meanest life to the most exalted. Every secondhand shop counts in just the same way. If you choose to look, you can always find something good in the most wretched soul, just as you can always find something good in the most impoverished thrift shop in the most derelict neighborhood. Driving around researching Volume III, I found more than I was looking for and less than I had hoped. I found more than enough material for this next edition. But I also found all the extremes our region, our country and our world have to offer. People were friendly, others indifferent, a rare few downright hostile. Some communities sparkled with all the brilliance of Camelot, others were drab and depressed. Some shops could be mistaken for a Parisian boutique on the Champs Elysées or Fifth Avenue in New York. Others? I wonder how they manage or why they bother to open. But whether we see them as being on the way up, or peaked and on the way down, or already at bottom doesn't ultimately matter. We are all part of the same planet, all members of the same universe. We will all rise and fall together.

From long ago, but never far away, is a vivid memory from when I was only 13, living at the effect of a four-generations-long cycle of anger and helplessness and despair. I promised myself at the end of one of those all too terrible, all too ordinary days that "This will end with me." The room lit up. I was surrounded by energy. I had felt terribly alone. I wasn't anymore. Something very important happened in that moment. The power of it is still reverberating throughout my life. At the time, I thought it was only about me. Lonely, scared, a child, I thought I was promising myself and my children, if I had any, that I would make a better life for me and mine than the one I was experiencing then. Slowly but surely over the years, I have kept that promise to myself. These days I've come to understand that the vow made so long ago wasn't only about me or for me. I must still keep that promise to Morgan and Erica and their children. So must we all to all our children. We can begin to keep our promises by not being scared off from daring to follow our dreams. Marvin likes to say "Do what scares you the most." He urged and supported me. He encouraged me to do something I had never done before, something no one had ever thought to do before. He helped me publish the Guide. I urge you to follow your dreams and to make a difference.

Those small statured, timelessly wise ancient Yanumami Indians living in glorious isolation, deep in the jungle high up under the clouds in South America warned us what was coming, right before they rolled up the stone, forever preventing access to their paradise in the mountains. "Are you listening, Little Brother?" they asked.

P.S. I think Tesla and Reich just needed better marketing sense.